Roasted Pepper and Artichoke Spread
page 239

Barbecued Black Beans with Sweet Potatoes
page 213

Chicken
Casablanca
page 92

Banana Loaf
page 259

Fix-It and Forget-It®

Diabetic Cookbook

REVISED & UPDATED

FIX-IT and FORGET-IT®

Diabetic Cookbook

REVISED & UPDATED

550 Slow Cooker Favorites—to include everyone!

Phyllis Pellman Good with  American Diabetes Association®

Good Books®

Intercourse, PA 17534
800/762-7171
www.GoodBooks.com

Fix-It and Forget-It Diabetic Cookbook, Revised and Updated is based on
Fix-It and Forget-It Diabetic Cookbook, published by Good Books, 2005.

Cover illustration and illustrations throughout the book by Cheryl Benner
Design by Cliff Snyder

FIX-IT AND FORGET-IT® DIABETIC COOKBOOK: REVISED AND UPDATED
Copyright © 2013 by Good Books, Intercourse, PA 17534

International Standard Book Number: 978-1-56148-778-3 (paperback edition)
International Standard Book Number: 978-1-56148-779-0 (comb-bound paperback edition)
International Standard Book Number: 978-1-56148-780-6 (hardcover gift edition)
Library of Congress Catalog Card Number: 2012952532

The information in this book has been developed with care and accuracy and is presented in good faith.
However, no warranty is given nor are results guaranteed. Neither the author nor the publisher has control
over the materials or procedures used, and neither has any liability for any loss or damage related to
the use of information contained in the book. Should any corrections be needed, they will be posted at
www.GoodBooks.com. If a correction is not posted, please contact custserv@GoodBooks.com.

Publisher's Cataloging-in-Publication Data
Good, Phyllis Pellman.
    Fix-it and forget-it diabetic cookbook, revised and updated : 550 slow cooker favorites
-- to include everyone! / Phyllis Pellman Good, American Diabetes Association.
    p. cm.
    ISBN 978-1-56148-778-3 (pbk.)
    ISBN 978-1-56148-779-0 (plastic comb)
    ISBN 978-1-56148-780-6 (hardcover)
    Includes index.

1. Diabetes --Diet therapy --Recipes. 2. Electric cooking, Slow. I. Fix-it and forget-it
diabetic cookbook, revised and updated : five hundred and fifty slow cooker favorites --
to include everyone! II. American Diabetes Association. III. Title.

RC662 .G66 2013
641.5/6314 --dc23   2012952532

Table of Contents

Suggested Healthy Serving Sizes for People with Diabetes

These serving sizes are here to help you determine simple, healthy portion sizes in general. These serving sizes are not intended to be used for all of the recipes in this cookbook.

Appetizer dips: 1-2 Tbsp.

Beans and legumes, cooked: ½ cup

Beverages: 1 cup

Desserts: ½ cup, ⅛ pie

Fruit: ½ cup

Frozen desserts: ½ cup

Grains and pasta side dishes: ½ cup

Main-dish sauces (for pasta, etc.): ½ cup

Meat, poultry and seafood, cooked: 3-4 ounces, about the size of a deck of cards

One-dish meals (meat, poultry, seafood, meatless), cooked: 1-1½ cups

Salad dressings, barbecue sauce: 2 Tbsp.

Salads: ½ cup fruit, grain, or bean salads; 1½ to 2 cups lettuce salads

Sauces: 2 Tbsp.

Soup: ¾-1 cup (as a side dish or appetizer); 1-1½ cups (as a main dish)

Vegetables, cooked: ½ cup

Welcome to Fix-It and Forget-It Diabetic Cookbook, Revised and Updated

The recipes in this collection are for everyone! No more isolating persons with diabetes at mealtime. In fact, these delicious recipes offer both great taste and nutritional value—and easy preparation—the *Fix-It and Forget-It* trademark.

The American Diabetes Association joined us in this *Cookbook*, using their know-how to adapt the recipes and analyze them so they fit into nutritional meal plans. Each recipe is accompanied by Exchange Lists/Food Choices and its Basic Nutritional Values. Persons with diabetes need this information so they can manage their calories and their carb, fat, and sodium counts.

Managing Diabetes Day-to-Day

Absolutely do not miss the "Week of Menus and Meal Plans" on pages 13-20. This is gold for anyone trying to eat a specific number of calories each day. (For each day of the week, there's a menu with 1300 calories and another with 1800 calories, depending on your size and nutritional needs.)

You'll get ideas for how to put a meal together so that everyone eating can enjoy the food, while sticking to healthy nutritional goals.

When eating, you'll want to flip often to page 6, "Learning Portion Control," until you've learned to recognize appropriate food amounts at a glance.

Phyllis Pellman Good

How We Calculated the Recipes' Nutritional Analyses

The nutritional analysis for each recipe includes all ingredients except those labeled "optional," those listed as "to taste," or those calling for a "dash."

If an ingredient is listed with a second choice, the first choice was used in the analysis.

If a range is given for the amount of an ingredient, the first number was used.

Foods listed as "serve with" at the end of a recipe, or accompanying foods listed without an amount, were not included in the recipe's analysis.

In recipes calling for cooked rice, pasta, or other grains, the analysis is based on the starch being prepared without added salt or fat, unless indicated otherwise in the recipe.

The analyses were done assuming that meats were trimmed of all visible fat, and that skin was removed from poultry, before being placed in the slow cooker.

Relax and Enjoy These Recipes!

Mealtimes should be refreshing. Now you can relax and enjoy these recipes because you know the content of what you're preparing and how that will affect a meal plan.

These easy-to-prepare recipes take so little time and attention, they'll help you stick to your food goals.

Diabetes need not keep us from all gathering around the table together, eating tasty, wholesome food.

After all, a diet that's healthy for persons with diabetes is healthy for everyone. And everyone can eat and enjoy it when you use recipes from *Fix-It and Forget-It Diabetic Cookbook, Revised and Updated: 550 Slow Cooker Favorites— to include Everyone!*

Phyllis Pellman Good

Tips for Healthier, Happier Eating

How to Plan Healthy Meals

Healthy meal planning is an important part of diabetes care. If you have diabetes, you should have a meal plan specifying what, when, and how much you should eat. Work with a registered dietitian to create a meal plan that is right for you. A typical meal plan covers your meals and snacks and includes a variety of foods. Here are some popular meal-planning tools:

1. **An exchange list** is a list of foods that are grouped together because they share similar carbohydrate, protein, and fat content. Any food on an exchange list may be substituted for any other food on the same list. A meal plan that uses exchange lists will tell you the number of exchanges (or food choices) you can eat at each meal or snack. You then choose the foods that add up to those exchanges.

2. **Carbohydrate counting** is useful because carbohydrates are the main nutrient in food that affects blood glucose. When you count carbohydrates, you simply count up the carbohydrates in the foods you eat, which helps you manage your blood glucose levels. To find the carbohydrate content of a food, check the Nutrition Facts label on foods or ask your dietitian for help. Carbohydrate counting is especially helpful for people with diabetes who take insulin to help manage their blood glucose.

3. **The Create Your Plate method** helps people with diabetes put together meals with evenly distributed carbohydrate content and correct portion sizes. This is one of the easiest meal-planning options because it does not require any special tools—all you need is a plate. Fill half of

your plate with nonstarchy vegetables, such as spinach, carrots, cabbage, green beans, or broccoli. Fill one-quarter of the plate with starchy foods, such as rice, pasta, beans, or peas. Fill the final quarter of your plate with meat or a meat substitute, such as cheese with less than 3 grams of fat per ounce, cottage cheese, or egg substitute. For a balanced meal, add a serving of low-fat or nonfat milk and a serving of fruit.

No matter which tool you use to plan your meals, having a meal plan in place can help you manage your blood glucose levels, improve your cholesterol levels, and maintain a healthy blood pressure and a healthy weight. When you're able to do that, you're helping to control—or avoid—diabetes.

Learning Portion Control

Portion control is an important part of healthier eating. Weighing and measuring your foods helps you familiarize yourself with reasonable portions and can make a difference of several hundred calories each day. You want to frequently weigh and measure your foods when you begin following a healthy eating plan. The more you practice weighing and measuring, the easier it will become to accurately estimate portion sizes.

You'll want to have certain portion-control tools on hand when you're weighing and measuring your foods. Remember, the teaspoons and tablespoons in your silverware set won't give you exact measurements. Here's what goes into your portion-control toolbox:

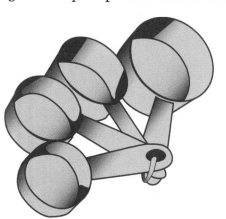

- Measuring spoons for ½ teaspoon, 1 teaspoon, ½ tablespoon, and 1 tablespoon
- A see-through 1-cup measuring cup with markings at ¼, ⅓, ½, ⅔, and ¾ cup
- Measuring cups for dry ingredients, including ¼, ⅓, ½, and 1 cup.

You may already have most of these in your kitchen. Keep them on your counter—you are more likely to use these tools if you can see them. Get an inexpensive

food scale ($5–15) for foods that are measured in ounces, such as fresh produce, baked goods, meats, and cheese.

When you're weighing meat, poultry, and seafood, keep in mind that you will need more than 3 ounces of raw meat to produce a 3-ounce portion of cooked meat. For example, it takes 4 ounces of raw, boneless meat— or 5 ounces of raw meat with the bone—to produce 3 cooked ounces. About 4½ ounces of raw chicken (with the bone and skin) yields 3 ounces cooked. Remember to remove the skin from the chicken before eating it.

There are other easy ways to control your portions at home in addition to weighing and measuring:

- Eat on smaller plates and bowls so that small portions look normal, not skimpy.
- Use a measuring cup to serve food to easily determine how much you're serving and eating.
- Measure your drinking glasses and bowls, so you know how much you're drinking or eating when you fill them.
- Avoid serving your meals family-style because leaving large serving dishes on the table can lead to second helpings and overeating.
- Keep portion sizes in mind while shopping. When you buy meat, fish, or poultry, purchase only what you need for your meal.

When you're away from home, your eyes and hands become your portion-control tools. You can use your hand to estimate teaspoons, tablespoons, ounces, and cups. The tip of your thumb is about 1 teaspoon; your whole thumb equals roughly 1 tablespoon. Two fingers lengthwise are about an ounce, and

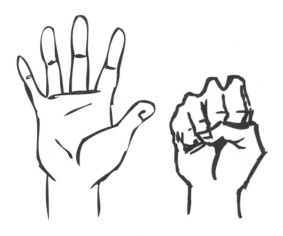

3 ounces is about the size of a palm. You can use your fist to measure in cups. A tight fist is about half a cup, whereas a loose fist or cupped hand is closer to a cup.

These guidelines are true for most women's hands, but some men's hands are much larger.

The palm of a man's hand is often the equivalent of about 5 ounces. Check the size of your hand in relation to various portions.

Remember that the more you weigh and measure your foods at home, the easier it will be to estimate portions on the road.

Controlling your portions when you eat at a restaurant can be difficult. Try to stay away from menu items with portion descriptors that are large, such as "giant," "supreme," "extra-large," "double," "triple," "king-size," and "super." Don't fall for deals in which the "value" is to serve you more food so that you can save money. Avoid all-you-can-eat restaurants and buffets.

You can split, share, or mix and match menu items to get what you want to eat in the correct portions. If you know that the portions you'll be served will be too large, ask for a take-home container when you place your order and put half of your food away before you start eating.

Gradually, as you become better at portion control, you can weigh and measure your foods less frequently. If you feel like you are correctly estimating your portions, just weigh and measure once a week, or even once a month, to check that your portions are still accurate. A good habit to get into is to "calibrate" your portion control memory at least once a month, so you don't start overestimating your portion sizes. Always weigh and measure new foods and foods that you tend to overestimate.

Frequently Asked Questions about Diabetes and Food

1. *Do people with diabetes have to eat a special diet?*

   No, they should eat the same foods that are healthy for everyone – whole grains, vegetables, fruit, and small portions of lean meat. Like everyone else, people with diabetes should eat breakfast, lunch, and dinner and not put off eating until dinnertime. By then, you are ravenous and will eat too much. This sends blood sugar levels soaring in people with diabetes, and doesn't allow them to feel hungry for breakfast the next morning.

2. *Can people with diabetes eat sugar?*

   Yes, they can. Sugar is just another carbohydrate to the body. All carbohydrates, whether they come from dessert, breads, or carrots, raise blood sugar. An equal serving of brownie and of baked potato raise your blood sugar the same amount. If you know that a rise in blood sugar is coming, it is wise to focus on the size of the serving.

   The question of "how much sugar is too much?" has to be answered by each one of us. No one who wants to be healthy eats a lot of sugar.

3. *What natural substances are good sugar substitutes? Are artificial sweeteners safe for people with diabetes?*

   Honey, agave nectar, maple syrup, brown sugar, and white sugar all contain about the same amount of calories and have a similar effect on your blood glucose levels. All of these sweeteners are a source of carbohydrates and *will* raise blood glucose quickly.

   If you have diabetes, you can use these sweeteners sparingly if you work them into your meal plan. Be aware of portion sizes and the carbohydrate content of each sweetener:
   - 1 tablespoon honey = about 64 calories, 17 grams of carbohydrate
   - 1 tablespoon brown sugar = about 52 calories, 13 grams of carbohydrate
   - 1 tablespoon white sugar = about 48 calories, 13 grams of carbohydrate
   - 1 tablespoon agave nectar = about 45 calories, 12 grams of carbohydrate

- 1 tablespoon maple syrup = about 52 calories, 13 grams of carbohydrate
- 1 packet of artificial sweetener = about 4 calories, <1 gram of carbohydrate

Artificial sweeteners are a low-calorie, low-carb option. Because they are chemically modified to be sweeter than regular sugar, only a small amount is needed to sweeten foods and drinks. There are several different artificial sweeteners available under various brand names: stevia, aspartame, acesulfame-K, saccharin, or sucralose. These are safe for people with diabetes when used in moderate amounts.

4. *How many grams of carbohydrates should someone with diabetes eat per day? How many at each meal?*

This is a very common question. About 45–60 grams of carbohydrates per meal is a good *starting point* when you are carb-counting. If you follow that recommendation, you will be eating a total of 135–180 grams of carbohydrates per day. However, some people may need more, and some may need less. Talk with your health care team to create an individualized meal plan to help you meet your health goals.

5. *What types of fruit can I eat? Is canned or fresh fruit better for people with diabetes?*

You can eat any type of fruit if you work it into your meal plan. Fruits are loaded with vitamins, minerals, and fiber. Fresh, canned, or frozen fruit without added sugars are all good options. You get a similar amount of nutrients from each. When you buy canned fruit, be sure the fruit has been canned in water or juice—not in syrup.

Fruit is nutritious, but it is not a "free food." The following portions have about 15 grams of carbohydrates:

- 1 small piece of whole fruit such as a small apple, small orange, or kiwifruit
- ½ cup of frozen or canned fruit
- ¾–1 cup of fresh berries or melon
- ⅓–½ cup 100% no-sugar-added fruit juice
- 2 tablespoons of dried fruit

6. *Besides meat, what can I eat to make sure I get enough protein?*

There are many protein sources. Proteins that are low in saturated and trans fats are the best options. Choose lean sources of protein like these:

- Eggs, egg whites, and egg substitutes
- Vegetarian proteins: beans, soy products, veggie burgers, nuts, and seeds
- Low-fat or nonfat dairy products
- Fish and shellfish
- Poultry without the skin
- Cheeses with 3 grams of fat or less per ounce
- When you do eat meat, choose lean cuts

People with diabetes can follow a vegetarian or vegan diet. Plant-based diets that include some animal products like eggs and milk can be a healthy option. However, animal products are not necessary. A mix of soy products, vegetables, fruits, beans, and whole grains provides plenty of protein and nutrients.

7. *Why should I eat whole grains instead of refined grains?*

Even a food made with 100% whole-wheat flour will raise your blood glucose levels. All grains—whole or not—affect blood glucose because they contain carbohydrates. However, you shouldn't completely avoid starchy foods. People with diabetes need some carbohydrates in their diet.

Whole grains are a healthy starch option because they contain fiber, vitamins, and minerals. Choose whole-wheat or whole-grain foods over those made with refined grains, but watch your portion sizes.

8. *Can people with diabetes eat potatoes and sweet potatoes?*

Yes! Starchy vegetables are healthy sources of carbohydrates. They also provide you with important nutrients like potassium, fiber, and vitamin C. You can include them in your meal plan as part of a balanced meal. Just pay attention to portion sizes and avoid unhealthy toppings. If you are carb counting, remember that there are about 15 grams of carbohydrates in:

- ½ cup of mashed potatoes
- ½ cup of boiled potatoes
- ¼ of a large baked potato with the skin

9. *Without salt and fat, food tastes bland. What can I do?*

When you are preparing healthy foods, try to limit added fats and extra salt. Look for recipes that use herbs (fresh or dried) and spices for flavor instead. There are many spice blends available in the baking aisle at the grocery store—choose salt-free blends. Other healthy ways to flavor your foods include:

- Squeezing lemon or lime juice on vegetables, fish, rice, or pasta
- Using onion and garlic to flavor dishes
- Baking meats with sugar-free barbecue sauce or any low-fat marinade
- Adding low-fat, low-calorie condiments, such as mustard, salsa, balsamic vinegar, or hot sauce

10. *Are gluten-free products okay for people with diabetes to eat?*

About 1% of the total population has celiac disease, which is an allergy to gluten—a protein found in wheat, rye, and barley. About 10% of people with type 1 diabetes also have celiac disease. People with celiac disease or gluten intolerance should follow a gluten-free diet.

However, unless you have one of these conditions, following a gluten-free diet is unnecessary and can make meal planning more difficult. Gluten-free products may contain more grams of carbohydrates per serving than regular products. For example, gluten-free bread can have twice as many grams of carbohydrates as whole-wheat bread. You can use gluten-free products and recipes, but just be sure to check the carbohydrate content and calories.

A Week of Meals and Menus
(with nutritional totals for each day!)

DAY 1 (1,300 Calories)

BREAKFAST
1 slice seven-grain toast
1 serving Pumpkin Butter (see page 244)
Fruit salad, made with
- ½ cup fresh blueberries
- ½ cup fresh raspberries
- ¼ small banana

Egg-substitute omelet, made with
- 2 tsp canola oil (for cooking egg substitute)
- ½ cup egg substitute
- ¼ cup canned mushrooms
- ½ cup fresh spinach

LUNCH
1 serving Southwest Chicken and White Bean Soup
  (see page 161)
Salad, made with
- 1 cup mixed salad greens
- ¼ small apple, cut into chunks
- 25 seedless raisins
- 4 honey-roasted walnut halves

Mix together for dressing:
- ½ tsp curry powder
- 2 packets Splenda
- 2 Tbsp fat-free Italian salad dressing

DINNER
1 serving Turkey Meat Loaf and Potatoes
  (see page 100)
1 cup steamed broccoli spears
½ cup cherry tomatoes

SNACK
4 oz nonfat skim yogurt (look for about 64 calories)

Nutrient Totals

Calories: 1299
Protein: 91.6 g
Carbohydrate: 150.4 g
Dietary Fiber: 27.4 g
Total Sugars: 58.1 g
Total Fat: 42.8 g
Saturated Fat: 7.056 g
Monounsaturated Fat: 15.5 g
Polyunsaturated Fat: 17.1 g
Cholesterol: 194.5 mg
Sodium: 2195 mg

DAY 2 (1,300 Calories)

BREAKFAST
1 serving Oatmeal Morning (see page 254)
8 oz skim milk with Vitamin A
6 oz black coffee (use a no-calorie sweetener
  instead of sugar)

LUNCH
Turkey bacon, lettuce, and tomato sandwich, made
  with
- 2 slices medium-thickness cooked turkey bacon
- 1 medium tomato, sliced
- 4 red lettuce leaves
- 1 Tbsp light mayo
- 2 slices whole-wheat toast

Carrot salad, made with
- ½ cup grated carrots
- 13 raisins
- 2 tsp canola oil
- 2 Tbsp cider vinegar
- 2 Tbsp lemon juice
- ¼ tsp pepper, red or cayenne
- 1 sprig chopped cilantro
- 4 dry-roasted peanuts, chopped, without salt

DINNER (you may use a no-salt spice blend of your choice
  as seasoning, e.g., Mrs. Dash)
3 oz salmon, Atlantic, wild, baked
1 small baked potato, no salt
1 cup frozen broccoli spears, steamed
1 small whole-wheat dinner roll
2 Tbsp light margarine spread

SNACK
1 medium pear

Nutrient Totals

Calories: 1292
Protein: 64 g
Carbohydrate: 159 g
Dietary Fiber: 25.1 g
Total Sugars: 53.5 g
Total Fat: 50.8 g
Saturated Fat: 7.409 g
Monounsaturated Fat: 17.4 g
Polyunsaturated Fat: 22.2 g
Cholesterol: 89.8 mg
Sodium: 1626 mg

DAY 3 (1,300 Calories)

BREAKFAST
½ whole-wheat bagel
1 serving of Pumpkin Butter (see page 244) (leftover)
1 oz fat-free cream cheese
½ cup 1" melon balls (cantaloupe or honeydew)
4 oz nonfat fruit yogurt, sweetened with low-calorie
  sweetener
6 roasted almonds, without salt
Omelet, made with
  • 1 tsp canola oil
  • ½ cup egg substitute
  • 1 oz cheddar or colby cheese, low sodium,
    low fat

LUNCH
1 serving Easy Hamburger Vegetable Soup
  (see page 142)
Salad, made with
  • 1 cup shredded or chopped Bibb or Boston lettuce
  • ½ small tomato
  • ¼ cup chopped celery
  • ½ cup cucumber slices
Salad dressing, made with
  • 4 tsp olive oil
  • 3 Tbsp balsamic vinegar
1 slice toasted rye bread

DINNER
1 cup succotash (corn & lima beans), frozen,
  added to ½ cup chopped fresh tomato
3 oz trout, baked or broiled
1 small lemon wedge (for juice on fish)
1 slice seven-grain bread
1 Tbsp light margarine

SNACK
1 Clementine orange
10 pistachios (unsalted)

Nutrient Totals

Calories: 1292
Protein: 64 g
Carbohydrate: 159 g
Dietary Fiber: 25.1 g
Total Sugars: 53.5 g
Total Fat: 50.8 g
Saturated Fat: 7.409 g
Monounsaturated Fat: 17.4 g
Polyunsaturated Fat: 22.2 g
Cholesterol: 89.8 mg
Sodium: 1626 mg

DAY 4 (1,300 Calories)

BREAKFAST
1 whole-wheat round waffle (4 inch diameter)
¾ cup blueberries
1 Tbsp sugar-free syrup
1 Tbsp light margarine
10 dry-roasted pecans (½ ounce), no salt
4 oz nonfat fruit yogurt, sweetened with low-cal
  sweetener
½ cup egg substitute (scrambled)

LUNCH
Tuna salad plate, made with
  • 3-oz can tuna in water, drained
  • 2 Tbsp light mayonnaise
  • 1 Tbsp pickle relish
  • 1 medium celery stalk (8 inches), chopped
Vegetables, on the plate
  • 5 lettuce leaves (to line plate)
  • ¼ cup broccoli florets
  • 3 green bell pepper rings
  • 1 small tomato, cut in quarters
  • 1 cucumber, sliced
Coleslaw, made with
  • ½ cup chopped green cabbage
  • ¼ cup grated carrots
  • 1 Tbsp light mayonnaise
  • 2 Tbsp cider vinegar
3 crispbread crackers, wheat or rye, extra crispy

DINNER
1 serving Herbed Lamb Stew (see page 120)
6 asparagus spears, steamed
¼ cup sweet and sour red cabbage

SNACK
1 small peach
6 cashews, roasted, without salt

Nutrient Totals

Calories: 1297
Protein: 84.5 g
Carbohydrate: 159.2 g
Dietary Fiber: 26.5 g
Total Sugars: 28.8 g
Total Fat: 34.3 g
Saturated Fat: 8.364 g
Monounsaturated Fat: 18.5 g
Polyunsaturated Fat: 12.2 g
Cholesterol: 151.7 mg
Sodium: 1541 mg

DAY 5 (1,300 Calories)

BREAKFAST
1 cup low-fat cottage cheese
Cinnamon toast, made with
- ½ whole-wheat English muffin
- 1 Tbsp light margarine
- 1 packet Splenda
- ¼ tsp ground cinnamon

Fruit salad, made with
- ½ small banana
- 1 cup blackberries

LUNCH
1 serving Smothered Lentils (see page 74)
1 thin slice toasted corn-rye bread
1 Tbsp light margarine
Tomato-mozzarella salad, made with
- ½ oz part-skim mozzarella cheese, cut into small pieces
- ½ small tomato, sliced
- 1 Tbsp balsamic vinegar
- 1 tsp olive oil

DINNER
3 oz boneless, skinless chicken breast, roasted
Roasted vegetables (preheat oven to 450°F, coat
  with oil and chopped garlic, and roast for 30
  minutes or until done, stirring every 10 minutes)
- 1 Tbsp olive oil
- 1 garlic clove, chopped
- 1 beet
- 2 small mushrooms
- ¼ cup cubed eggplant
- 5 string beans
- ½ small red potato with skin

Fruit salad, made with
- 10 small watermelon balls
- ½ cup blueberries

SNACK
2 cups air-popped popcorn
1 Tbsp light margarine

Nutrient Totals

Calories: 1317
Protein: 94.7 g
Carbohydrate: 155.2 g
Dietary Fiber: 37.9 g
Total Sugars: 52.4 g
Total Fat: 36.8 g
Saturated Fat: 8.29 g
Monounsaturated Fat: 20.1 g
Polyunsaturated Fat: 6.505 g
Cholesterol: 102.4 mg
Sodium: 1230 mg

DAY 6 (1,300 Calories)

BREAKFAST
Breakfast parfait, made with (in layers)
- ¾ cup Honey Almond Flax Kashi Go Lean Crunch cereal
- 1 apricot, sliced
- 6 oz nonfat fruit yogurt, sweetened with low-cal sweetener
- 15 hazelnuts, chopped

LUNCH
Rice and bean burrito, made with
- 1 small whole-wheat flour tortilla
- ¼ cup cooked black beans
- ¼ cup cooked brown rice
- ¼ cup shredded romaine lettuce
- ¼ cup chopped tomatoes
- ½ ounce reduced-fat Mexican cheese blend
- 1 ounce guacamole

Salad, made with
- 1 cup chopped lettuce
- ½ cup sliced cucumber
- 4 cherry tomatoes

Dressing, made with
- 2 tsp olive oil
- 2 Tbsp red wine vinegar

DINNER
1 serving Moist Poultry Dressing (see page 214)
3 oz cooked boneless, skinless roasted turkey, dark meat
1 cup cooked cauliflower
½ cup cooked broccoli
1 whole-wheat dinner roll
1 Tbsp light margarine

SNACK
1 cup red cherries
4 roasted almonds

Nutrient Totals

Calories: 1305
Protein: 68.3 g
Carbohydrate: 149.6 g
Dietary Fiber: 28.2 g
Total Sugars: 29.6 g
Total Fat: 47.4 g
Saturated Fat: 9.362 g
Monounsaturated Fat: 28.4 g
Polyunsaturated Fat: 11 g
Cholesterol: 113.1 mg
Sodium: 1544 mg

DAY 7 (1,300 Calories)

BREAKFAST

Weekend Crepes (mix the batter the evening before, cover, and refrigerate)
Batter, made with
- 1 oz almond milk
- 1 oz water
- 1¾ tsp canola oil
- 0–2 small packets Splenda (depending on desired sweetness)
- ½ tsp vanilla extract
- ¼ cup all-purpose flour
- ⅛ tsp salt

In the morning, grease a small pan with ¼ tsp canola oil. Heat until hot. Pour batter into pan until it covers the bottom. Cook on one side and flip over. Do not burn.

Filling, made with
- ½ cup low-fat cottage cheese
- 3 walnuts, chopped
- 1 cup blackberries

LUNCH

1 small whole-wheat dinner roll
Chicken salad, made with
- ¼ cup broiled chicken breast, skin removed
- ¼ cup chopped celery
- 1 Tbsp chopped onion
- 1 garlic clove, chopped
- 1 Tbsp light mayonnaise
Strawberry salad, made with
- 1 cup chopped Boston lettuce
- 1 cup strawberries
- 9 cashews
Dressing, blend together
- ¼ cup strawberries
- 1 tsp canola oil
- 2 Tbsp cider vinegar
- 1–2 packets Splenda (depending on desired sweetness)
1 plum

DINNER

1 serving Very Special Spinach (see page 189)
4 oz buffalo patty, cooked in 2 tsp peanut oil
1 small baked potato
Peas and mushroom stir-fry, made with
- ½ cup snow peas
- ¼ cup Portobello mushrooms
- 1 tsp olive oil

SNACK

10 Honeydew melon balls

Nutrient Totals

Calories: 1302
Protein: 90 g
Carbohydrate: 153.3 g
Dietary Fiber: 27.3 g
Total Sugars: 49.5 g
Total Fat: 58.1 g
Saturated Fat: 9.203 g
Monounsaturated Fat: 25.8 g
Polyunsaturated Fat: 18.8 g
Cholesterol: 191.1 mg
Sodium: 1220 mg

Oils are good for your heart. The solid fats—butter, margarine, shortening, and lard—are bad for your heart.

DAY 1 (1,800 Calories)

BREAKFAST
1½ slices seven-grain toast
2 servings Pumpkin Butter (see page 244)
Fruit salad, made with
- ½ cup fresh blueberries
- ½ cup fresh raspberries
- ¼ banana

Egg-substitute omelet, made with
- 2 Tbsp canola oil (for cooking egg substitute)
- ½ cup egg substitute
- ¼ cup canned mushrooms
- ½ cup fresh spinach

LUNCH
1 serving Southwest Chicken and White Bean
    Soup (see page 161)
Salad, made with
- 1 cup mixed salad greens
- 1 small apple, cut into chunks
- 25 seedless raisins
- 8 honey-roasted walnut halves

Mix together for dressing:
- ½ tsp curry powder
- 2 packets Splenda
- 2 Tbsp fat-free Italian salad dressing

DINNER
1 serving Turkey Meat Loaf and Potatoes
    (see page 100)
1 cup steamed broccoli spears
½ cup cherry tomatoes

SNACK
4 oz nonfat skim yogurt (look for about 64 calories)
1 oz dry-roasted pistachios

Nutrient Totals

Calories: 1822
Protein: 101.4 g
Carbohydrate: 186.8 g
Dietary Fiber: 33.4 g
Total Sugars: 79.2 g
Total Fat: 83.5 g
Saturated Fat: 10.9 g
Monounsaturated Fat: 35.7 g
Polyunsaturated Fat: 32.3 g
Cholesterol: 194.5 mg
Sodium: 2256 mg

DAY 2 (1,800 Calories)

BREAKFAST
1 serving Oatmeal Morning (see page 254)
8 oz skim milk with Vitamin A
6 oz black coffee (use a no-calorie sweetener
    instead of sugar)
1 small orange

LUNCH
Turkey bacon, lettuce, and tomato sandwich,
    made with
- 2 slices medium-thickness cooked turkey bacon
- 1 medium tomato, sliced
- 4 red lettuce leaves
- 1 Tbsp light mayo
- 2 slices whole-wheat toast

Carrot salad, made with
- ½ cup grated carrots
- 13 raisins
- 2 tsp canola oil
- 2 Tbsp cider vinegar
- 2 Tbsp lemon juice
- ¼ tsp pepper, red or cayenne
- 1 sprig chopped cilantro
- 4 dry-roasted peanuts, chopped, without salt

½ cup 98% fat-free chocolate ice cream

DINNER
3 oz salmon, Atlantic, wild, baked
1 small baked potato, no salt
1 cup frozen broccoli spears, steamed
1 small whole-wheat dinner roll
2 Tbsp light margarine spread
2 Tbsp reduced-fat sour cream

SNACK
1 medium pear
14 walnut halves

Nutrient Totals

Calories: 1817
Protein: 94.9 g
Carbohydrate: 196.7 g
Dietary Fiber: 33.3 g
Total Sugars: 79 g
Total Fat: 81.5 g
Saturated Fat: 13.5 g
Monounsaturated Fat: 22.2 g
Polyunsaturated Fat: 38.3 g
Cholesterol: 170.4 mg
Sodium: 1744 mg

DAY 3 (1,800 Calories)

BREAKFAST
1 whole-wheat bagel
1 serving of Pumpkin Butter (see page 244) (leftover)
1 oz fat-free cream cheese
½ cup 1" melon balls (cantaloupe or honeydew)
4 oz nonfat fruit yogurt, sweetened with
  low-calorie sweetener
10 roasted almonds, without salt
Omelet, made with
  • 1 Tbsp canola oil
  • ½ cup egg substitute
  • 1 oz cheddar or colby cheese, low sodium, low fat

LUNCH
1 serving Easy Hamburger Vegetable Soup
  (see page 142)
Salad, made with
  • 1 cup shredded or chopped Bibb or Boston
    lettuce
  • 1 small tomato
  • ¼ cup chopped celery
  • ½ cup cucumber slices
Salad dressing, made with
  • 3 Tbsp olive oil
  • 4 Tbsp balsamic vinegar
  • 1 slice toasted rye bread
1 gold kiwifruit

DINNER
1 cup succotash (corn & lima beans), frozen,
  added to ½ cup chopped fresh tomato
3 oz trout, baked or broiled
1 small lemon wedge (for juice on the trout)
1 slice 7-grain bread
1 Tbsp light margarine without saturated fat

SNACK
1 Clementine orange
19 pistachios (unsalted)

Nutrient Totals

Calories: 1795
Protein: 88.4 g
Carbohydrate: 181 g
Dietary Fiber: 30.7 g
Total Sugars: 49.5 g
Total Fat: 86.9 g
Saturated Fat: 14 g
Monounsaturated Fat: 51.7 g
Polyunsaturated Fat: 16.2 g
Cholesterol: 94.5 mg
Sodium: 2143 mg

DAY 4 (1,800 Calories)

BREAKFAST
1 whole-wheat round waffle (4 inch diameter)
1 cup blueberries
1 Tbsp sugar-free syrup
2 Tbsp light margarine
20 dry-roasted pecans, no salt
6 oz nonfat fruit yogurt, sweetened with
  low-calorie sweetener
½ cup egg substitute (omelet), with sautéed
  • ½ cup kale
  • ½ small tomato, chopped
  • 1 Tbsp chopped onion

LUNCH
Tuna salad plate, made with
  • 5-oz can tuna in water, drained
  • 2 Tbsp light mayonnaise
  • 1 Tbsp pickle relish
  • 1 medium celery stalk (8 inches), chopped
2 oz low-sodium, low-fat Colby cheese
Vegetables, on the plate
  • 5 lettuce leaves (to line plate)
  • ¼ cup broccoli florets
  • 3 green bell pepper rings
  • 1 small tomato, cut in quarters
  • 1 cucumber, sliced
  • 1 Tbsp hummus (for dipping)
Coleslaw, made with
  • ½ cup chopped green cabbage
  • ¼ cup grated carrots
  • 1 Tbsp light mayonnaise
  • 2 Tbsp cider vinegar
3 crispbread crackers, wheat or rye, extra crispy
½ cup diced pineapple
¼ cup raspberries

DINNER
1 serving Herbed Lamb Stew (see page 120)
8 medium asparagus spears, steamed
¼ cup sweet and sour red cabbage
1 Tbsp light margarine

SNACK
1 small peach
9 cashews, roasted, without salt

Nutrient Totals

Calories: 1788, Protein: 120.4 g, Carbohydrate: 197.5 g,
Dietary Fiber: 37 g, Total Sugars: 41.6 g, Total Fat: 57.7 g,
Saturated Fat: 13.1 g, Monounsaturated Fat: 29.6 g,
Polyunsaturated Fat: 17.5 g, Cholesterol: 181 mg
Sodium: 1844 mg

DAY 5 (1,800 Calories)

BREAKFAST
1½ cups low-fat cottage cheese
Cinnamon toast, made with
- 1 whole-wheat English muffin
- 2 Tbsp light margarine
- 1 packet Splenda
- ¼ tsp ground cinnamon

Fruit salad, made with
- ½ small banana
- 1 cup blackberries

LUNCH
1 serving Smothered Lentils (see page 74)
2 thin slices toasted corn-rye bread
1 Tbsp light margarine
Tomato-mozzarella salad, made with
- 1½ oz part-skim mozzarella cheese, cut into small pieces
- 1 small tomato, sliced
- 1 Tbsp balsamic vinegar
- 2 tsp olive oil

DINNER
3 oz boneless, skinless chicken breast, roasted
Roasted vegetables (preheat oven to 450°F, coat with oil and chopped garlic, and roast for 30 minutes or until done, stirring every 10 minutes)
- 1 Tbsp olive oil
- 1 garlic clove, chopped
- 1 beet
- 2 small mushrooms
- ½ cup cubed eggplant
- 5 string beans
- ½ small red potato with skin

Fruit salad, made with
- 10 small watermelon balls
- ½ cup blueberries

SNACK
3 cups air-popped popcorn
2 Tbsp light margarine
7 dry-roasted almonds, without salt

Nutrient Totals

Calories: 1817, Protein: 94.9 g, Carbohydrate: 196.7 g, Dietary Fiber: 33.3 g, Total Sugars: 79 g, Total Fat: 81.5 g, Saturated Fat: 13.5 g, Monounsaturated Fat: 22.2 g, Polyunsaturated Fat: 38.3 g, Cholesterol: 170.4 mg Sodium: 1744 mg

DAY 6 (1,800 Calories)

BREAKFAST
Breakfast parfait, made with (in layers)
- ¾ cup Honey Almond Flax Kashi Go Lean Crunch cereal
- 1 apricot, sliced
- 8 medium strawberries
- 6 oz nonfat fruit yogurt, sweetened with low-calorie sweetener
- 15 hazelnuts, chopped

LUNCH
Rice and bean burritos, made with
- 2 small whole-wheat tortillas
- ⅓ cup cooked black beans
- ¼ cup cooked brown rice
- ½ cup shredded romaine lettuce
- ¼ cup chopped tomatoes
- 1 ounce reduced-fat Mexican cheese blend
- 2 ounces guacamole

Salad, made with
- 1 cup chopped lettuce
- ½ cup sliced cucumber
- 4 cherry tomatoes

Dressing, made with
- 1 Tbsp olive oil
- 2 Tbsp red wine vinegar

DINNER
1 serving Moist Poultry Dressing (see page 214)
5 oz cooked boneless, skinless roasted turkey, dark meat
1 cup cooked cauliflower
½ cup cooked broccoli
2 whole-wheat dinner rolls
1 Tbsp light margarine

SNACK
1¼ cups red cherries
9 roasted almonds

Nutrient Totals

Calories: 1794
Protein: 96.8 g
Carbohydrate: 198 g
Dietary Fiber: 35.7 g
Total Sugars: 36.7 g
Total Fat: 69.1 g
Saturated Fat: 14.5 g
Monounsaturated Fat: 39 g
Polyunsaturated Fat: 15.3 g
Cholesterol: 169.2 mg
Sodium: 2164 mg

DAY 7 (1,800 Calories)

BREAKFAST
Weekend Crepes (mix the batter the evening
   before, cover, and refrigerate)
Batter, made with
  - 1 oz almond milk
  - 1 oz water
  - 1¾ tsp canola oil
  - 0–2 small packets Splenda (depending on
    desired sweetness)
  - ½ tsp vanilla extract
  - ¼ cup all-purpose flour
  - ⅛ tsp salt

*In the morning, grease a small pan with ¼ tsp
canola oil. Heat until hot. Pour batter into pan until
it covers the bottom. Cook on one side and flip
over. Do not burn.*

Filling, made with
  - ½ cup low-fat cottage cheese
  - 6 walnuts, chopped
  - 1 cup blackberries
  - 1 small banana, sliced

LUNCH
2 small whole-wheat dinner rolls
Chicken salad, made with
  - ¼ cup broiled chicken breast, skin removed
  - ¼ cup chopped celery
  - 1 Tbsp chopped onion
  - 1 garlic clove, chopped
  - 2 Tbsp light mayonnaise
Strawberry salad, made with
  - 1½ cups chopped Boston lettuce
  - 1 cup strawberries
  - 13 cashews
Dressing, blend together
  - ¼ cup strawberries
  - 2 tsp canola oil
  - 2 Tbsp cider vinegar
  - 1–2 packets Splenda (depending on desired
    sweetness)
1 plum

DINNER
1 serving Very Special Spinach (see page 189)
4 oz buffalo patty, cooked in 2 tsp peanut oil
1 small baked potato
Peas and mushroom stir-fry, made with
  - 1 cup snow peas
  - ¼ cup Portobello mushrooms
  - 1 Tbsp olive oil

SNACK
10 honeydew melon balls
5 cantaloupe melon balls
8 dry-roasted peanuts without salt

Nutrient Totals

Calories: 1817
Protein: 94.9 g
Carbohydrate: 196.7 g
Dietary Fiber: 33.3 g
Total Sugars: 79 g
Total Fat: 81.5 g
Saturated Fat: 13.5 g
Monounsaturated Fat: 22.2 g
Polyunsaturated Fat: 38.3 g
Cholesterol: 170.4 mg
Sodium: 1744 mg

*Exercise helps your body use insulin more
efficiently, so it lowers your blood sugars more
than normal — that's why insulin doses can usually
be decreased before and after exercise.*

Beef Main Dishes

Beef Stew

Wanda S. Curtin, Bradenton, FL
Paula King, Harrisonburg, VA
Miriam Nolt, New Holland, PA
Jean Shaner, York, PA
Mary W. Stauffer, Ephrata, PA
Alma Z. Weaver, Ephrata, PA

Makes 6 servings

Prep. Time: 35 minutes
Cooking Time: 4-12 hours
Ideal slow-cooker size: 4-qt.

2 lbs. beef chuck, cubed,
   trimmed of fat
1 tsp. Worcestershire sauce
¼-½ cup flour
¾ tsp. salt
½ tsp. pepper
1 tsp. paprika
1½ cups beef broth
half garlic clove, minced
1 bay leaf
4 medium carrots, sliced
2 medium onions, chopped
1 rib celery, sliced
3 medium potatoes, diced,
   unpeeled

1. Place meat in slow cooker.
2. Combine flour, salt, pepper, and paprika. Stir into meat until coated thoroughly.
3. Add remaining ingredients. Mix well.
4. Cover. Cook on low 10-12 hours, or high 4-6 hours. Stir before serving.

Exchange List Values
- Starch 1.5
- Vegetable 2.0
- Carbohydrate 2.0

Basic Nutritional Values
- Calories 278
  (Calories from Fat 55)
- Total Fat 6 gm
  (Saturated Fat 1.9 gm,
  Polyunsat Fat 0.5 gm,
  Monounsat Fat 2.8 gm)
- Cholesterol 75 mg
- Sodium 598 mg
- Total Carb 28 gm
- Dietary Fiber 4 gm
- Sugars 7 gm
- Protein 28 gm

You can cut back on the number of calories you get each day and still eat your favorite foods — just reduce how much of them you eat. Control your portion sizes to control your weight!

Beef Stew with Shiitake Mushrooms

Kathy Hertzler
Lancaster, PA

Makes 6 servings

Prep. Time: 30 minutes
Cooking Time: 8-9 hours
Ideal slow cooker size: 4- or 5-qt.

12 new potatoes, cut into quarters
½ cup chopped onions
8-oz. pkg. baby carrots
3.4-oz. pkg. fresh shiitake mushrooms, sliced, *or* 2 cups regular white mushrooms, sliced
16-oz. can whole tomatoes
14½-oz. can beef broth
½ cup flour
1 Tbsp. Worcestershire sauce
1 tsp. sugar
1 tsp. dried marjoram
¼ tsp. pepper
1 lb. beef stewing meat, cubed, trimmed of fat

1. Combine all ingredients except beef in slow cooker. Add beef.
2. Cover. Cook on low 8-9 hours. Stir well before serving.

Exchange List Values
- Starch 2.0
- Meat, lean 1.0
- Vegetable 2.0

Basic Nutritional Values
- Calories 254
- Cholesterol 38 mg
- (Calories from Fat 29)
- Sodium 534 mg
- Total Fat 3 gm
- Total Carb 39 gm
- (Saturated Fat 0.9 gm, Polyunsat Fat 0.4 gm, Monounsat Fat 1.4 gm)
- Dietary Fiber 5 gm
- Sugars 8 gm
- Protein 18 gm

Bavarian Beef

Naomi E. Fast
Hesston, KS

Makes 8 servings

Prep. Time: 35 minutes
Cooking Time: 6-7 hours
Ideal slow cooker size: 4- or 5-qt.

3-lb. boneless beef chuck roast, trimmed of fat
1 Tbsp. canola oil
3 cups sliced carrots
3 cups sliced onions
2 large kosher dill pickles, chopped
1 cup sliced celery
½ cup dry red wine *or* beef broth
⅓ cup German-style mustard
2 tsp. coarsely ground black pepper
2 bay leaves
¼ tsp. ground cloves
1 cup water
⅓ cup flour

1. Brown roast on both sides in oil in skillet. Transfer to slow cooker.
2. Add remaining ingredients.
3. Cover. Cook on low 6-7 hours.
4. Remove meat and vegetables to large platter. Cover to keep warm.
5. Mix flour with 1 cup of broth until smooth. Return to cooker. Turn on high and stir, cooking until broth is smooth and thickened.
6. Serve over noodles or spaetzle.

Exchange List Values
- Starch 0.5
- Meat, lean 3.0
- Vegetable 2.0

Basic Nutritional Values
- Calories 251
- Cholesterol 73 mg
- (Calories from Fat 76)
- Sodium 525 mg
- Total Fat 8 gm
- Total Carb 17 gm
- (Saturated Fat 2.4 gm, Polyunsat Fat 0.9 gm, Monounsat Fat 3.8 gm)
- Dietary Fiber 4 gm
- Sugars 7 gm
- Protein 26 gm

Dawn's Mushroom Beef Stew

Dawn Day
Westminster, CA

Makes 10 servings

Prep. Time: 35 minutes
Cooking Time: 6-8½ hours
Ideal slow cooker size: 4- or 5-qt.

1 lb. sirloin, cubed,
   trimmed of fat
2 Tbsp. flour
1 Tbsp. canola oil
1 large onion, chopped
2 garlic cloves, minced
½ lb. button mushrooms,
   sliced
2 ribs celery, sliced
3 large carrots, sliced
3-4 large potatoes, cubed
2 tsp. seasoning salt
14½-oz. can beef stock,
   or 2 bouillon cubes
   dissolved in 1⅔ cups
   water
½-1 cup good red wine

1. Dredge sirloin in flour and brown in skillet. Reserve drippings. Place meat in slow cooker.
2. Sauté onion, garlic, and mushrooms in drippings just until soft. Add to meat.
3. Add all remaining ingredients.
4. Cover. Cook on low 6 hours. Test to see if vegetables are tender. If not, continue cooking on low for another 1-1½ hours.
5. Serve with crusty bread.

Exchange List Values
- Starch 1.5
- Vegetable 2.0
- Meat, lean 1.0
- Fat 0.5

Basic Nutritional Values
- Calories 247
  (Calories from Fat 49)
- Total Fat 5 gm
  (Saturated Fat 1.1 gm,
  Polyunsat Fat 1.0 gm,
  Monounsat Fat 2.8 gm)
- Cholesterol 38 mg
- Sodium 572 mg
- Total Carb 33 gm
- Dietary Fiber 5 gm
- Sugars 7 gm
- Protein 17 gm

Beef Burgundy and Bacon

Joyce Kaut
Rochester, NY

Makes 6 servings

Prep. Time: 25 minutes
Cooking Time: 6-8¼ hours
Ideal slow cooker size: 3- or 4-qt.

1 slice bacon, cut in
   squares
2 lbs. sirloin tip *or* round
   steak, cubed, trimmed
   of fat
1 tsp. canola oil
¼ cup flour
⅛ tsp. salt
½ tsp. seasoning salt
¼ tsp. dried marjoram
¼ tsp. dried thyme
¼ tsp. pepper
1 garlic clove, minced
1 beef bouillon cube,
   crushed
1 cup burgundy wine
¼ lb. fresh mushrooms,
   sliced
2 Tbsp. cornstarch
2 Tbsp. cold water

1. Cook bacon in skillet until browned. Remove bacon.
2. Coat beef with flour and brown on all sides in canola oil.
3. Combine steak, bacon drippings, bacon, seasonings, garlic, bouillon, and wine in slow cooker.
4. Cover. Cook on low 6-8 hours.
5. Add mushrooms.
6. Dissolve cornstarch in water. Add to slow cooker.
7. Cover. Cook on high 15 minutes.
8. Serve over noodles.

Exchange List Values
- Starch 0.5
- Meat, lean 3.0

Basic Nutritional Values
- Calories 202
  (Calories from Fat 63)
- Total Fat 7 gm
  (Saturated Fat 2.0 gm,
  Polyunsat Fat 0.6 gm,
  Monounsat Fat 3.5 gm)
- Cholesterol 76 mg
- Sodium 389 mg
- Total Carb 8 gm
- Dietary Fiber 0 gm
- Sugars 1 gm
- Protein 25 gm

Try to keep your daily sodium intake as low as possible (below 2,300 milligrams) by choosing ingredients that are reduced in sodium or have no added salt.

Tempting Beef Stew

Patricia Howard
Albuquerque, NM

Makes 10 servings

Prep. Time: 20 minutes
Cooking Time: 10-12 hours
Ideal slow cooker size: 4- or 5-qt.

2 lbs. beef stewing meat,
   trimmed of fat
3 carrots, sliced thin
1-lb. pkg. frozen green peas
   with onions
1-lb. pkg. frozen green
   beans
16-oz. can whole *or* stewed
   tomatoes
½ cup beef broth
½ cup white wine
¼ cup brown sugar
4 Tbsp. tapioca
½ cup bread crumbs
1½ tsp. salt
1 bay leaf
pepper to taste

1. Combine all ingredients
in slow cooker.
2. Cover. Cook on low
10-12 hours.
3. Serve over noodles, rice,
couscous, or biscuits.

Exchange List Values
- Starch 1.0
- Meat, lean 1.0
- Vegetable 2.0

Basic Nutritional Values
- Calories 203
  (Calories from Fat 36)
- Total Fat 4 gm
  (Saturated Fat 1.1 gm,
  Polyunsat Fat 0.4 gm,
  Monounsat Fat 1.8 gm)
- Cholesterol 45 mg
- Sodium 588 mg
- Total Carb 24 gm
- Dietary Fiber 4 gm
- Sugars 12 gm
- Protein 18 gm

Variation:
In place of the tapioca,
thicken stew with ¼ cup
flour dissolved in ⅓-½ cup
water. Mix in and turn cooker
to high. Cover and cook for
15-20 minutes.

Tip:
Prepare this Tempting
Beef Stew before your guests
arrive. Give yourself time to
relax instead of panicking in
a last-minute rush.

Hungarian Barley Stew

Naomi E. Fast
Hesston, KS

Makes 8 servings

Prep. Time: 25 minutes
Cooking Time: 5 hours
Ideal slow cooker size: 4-qt.

2 Tbsp. canola oil
1½ lbs. beef cubes,
   trimmed of fat
2 large onions, diced
1 medium-sized green
   pepper, chopped
28-oz. can whole tomatoes
½ cup ketchup
⅔ cup dry small pearl
   barley
½ tsp. salt
½ tsp. pepper
1 Tbsp. paprika
10-oz. pkg. frozen baby
   lima beans
3 cups water
1 cup fat-free sour cream

1. Brown beef cubes in oil
in skillet. Add onions and
green peppers. Sauté. Pour
into slow cooker.
2. Add remaining ingredi-
ents except sour cream.
3. Cover. Cook on high 5
hours.
4. Stir in sour cream before
serving.

Exchange List Values
- Starch 1.5
- Meat, lean 2.0
- Vegetable 2.0

Basic Nutritional Values
- Calories 286
  (Calories from Fat 67)
- Total Fat 7 gm
  (Saturated Fat 1.3 gm,
  Polyunsat Fat 1.5 gm,
  Monounsat Fat 3.6 gm)
- Cholesterol 44 mg
- Sodium 558 mg
- Total Carb 36 gm
- Dietary Fiber 6 gm
- Sugars 11 gm
- Protein 20 gm

Wash-Day Stew

Naomi E. Fast
Hesston, KS

Makes 14 servings

Prep. Time: 20 minutes
Cooking Time: 6-7 hours
Ideal slow cooker size: 4- or 5-qt.

1½-2 lbs. lean lamb *or* beef, cubed, trimmed of fat
2 15-oz. cans garbanzo beans, drained
2 15-oz. cans white beans, drained
2 medium onions, peeled and quartered
1 qt. water
½ tsp. salt
1 tomato, peeled and quartered
1 tsp. turmeric
3 Tbsp. fresh lemon juice
8-10 pita bread pockets

1. Combine ingredients in slow cooker.
2. Cover. Cook on high 6-7 hours.
3. Lift stew from cooker with a strainer spoon and stuff in pita bread pockets.

Exchange List Values
- Starch 3.0
- Meat, lean 1.0

Basic Nutritional Values
- Calories 287
  (Calories from Fat 38)
- Total Fat 4 gm
  (Saturated Fat 1.1 gm,
  Polyunsat Fat 0.9 gm,
  Monounsat Fat 1.3 gm)
- Cholesterol 31 mg
- Sodium 440 mg
- Total Carb 42 gm
- Dietary Fiber 7 gm
- Sugars 5 gm
- Protein 20 gm

Note:

I learned to prepare this nutritious meal from a student from Iran, who was attending graduate school at the University of Nebraska. Fatimeh explained to me that her family prepared this dish every wash day. Very early in the morning, they made a fire in a large rock-lined pit outside. Then they placed a large covered kettle, filled with the above ingredients, over the coals to cook slowly all day. At the end of a day of doing laundry, the food was ready with a minimum of preparation. Of course, they started with dry beans and dry garbanzos, presoaked the night before. They served this Wash-Day Stew spooned into pita bread and ate it with their hands.

1-2-3-4 Casserole

Betty K. Drescher
Quakertown, PA

Makes 8 servings

Prep. Time: 20 minutes
Cooking Time: 7-9 hours
Ideal slow cooker size: 4-qt.

1 lb. 90%-lean ground beef
2 onions, sliced
3 carrots, thinly sliced
4 potatoes, thinly sliced, unpeeled
½ tsp. salt
⅛ tsp. pepper
1 cup cold water
½ tsp. cream of tartar
10¾-oz. can 98% fat-free, reduced sodium cream of mushroom soup
¼ cup fat-free milk
½ tsp. salt
⅛ tsp. pepper

1. Layer in greased slow cooker: ground beef, onions, carrots, ½ tsp. salt, and ⅛ tsp. pepper.
2. Dissolve cream of tartar in water in bowl. Toss sliced potatoes with water. Drain.
3. Combine soup and milk. Toss with potatoes. Add remaining salt and pepper. Arrange potatoes in slow cooker.
4. Cover. Cook on low 7-9 hours.

Exchange List Values
- Starch 1.5
- Vegetable 1.0
- Meat, lean 1.0
- Fat 0.5

Basic Nutritional Values
- Calories 216
  (Calories from Fat 59)
- Total Fat 7 gm
  (Saturated Fat 2.6 gm,
  Polyunsat Fat 0.5 gm,
  Monounsat Fat 2.6 gm)
- Cholesterol 37 mg
- Sodium 503 mg
- Total Carb 24 gm
- Dietary Fiber 3 gm
- Sugars 6 gm
- Protein 15 gm

Variations:
1. Substitute sour cream for the milk.
2. Top potatoes with ½ cup shredded cheese.

Audrey's Beef Stew

Audrey Romonosky
Austin, TX

Makes 6 servings

Prep. Time: 35 minutes
Cooking Time: 8 hours
Ideal slow cooker size: 4-qt.

3 medium carrots, sliced
3 medium potatoes, cubed, unpeeled
2 lbs. beef chuck, cubed, trimmed of fat
2 cups water
2 beef bouillon cubes
1 tsp. Worcestershire sauce
½ tsp. garlic powder
1 bay leaf
¼ tsp. salt
½ tsp. pepper
1 tsp. paprika
3 onions, chopped
1 rib celery, sliced
¼ cup flour
⅓ cup cold water.

1. Combine all ingredients except flour and ⅓ cup cold water in slow cooker. Mix well.
2. Cover. Cook on low 8 hours.
3. Dissolve flour in ⅓ cup water. Stir into meat mixture. Cook on high until thickened, about 10 minutes.

Exchange List Values
- Starch 1.5
- Meat, lean 2.0
- Vegetable 2.0

Basic Nutritional Values
- Calories 287
  (Calories from Fat 54)
- Total Fat 6 gm
  (Saturated Fat 1.8 gm,
  Polyunsat Fat 0.5 gm,
  Monounsat Fat 2.8 gm)
- Cholesterol 75 mg
- Sodium 501 mg
- Total Carb 30 gm
- Dietary Fiber 5 gm
- Sugars 9 gm
- Protein 28 gm

Herbed Beef Stew

Carol Findling
Princeton, IL

Makes 8 servings

Prep. Time: 35 minutes
Cooking Time: 4-12 hours
Ideal slow cooker size: 4-qt.

1 lb. beef round, cubed, trimmed of fat
4 Tbsp. seasoned flour*
1½ cups beef broth
1 tsp. Worcestershire sauce
1 garlic clove
1 bay leaf
4 medium carrots, sliced
3 medium potatoes, cubed, unpeeled
2 medium onions, diced
1 rounded tsp. fresh thyme, *or* ½ tsp. dried thyme
1 rounded tsp. chopped fresh basil, *or* ½ tsp. dried basil
1 Tbsp. fresh parsley, *or* 1 tsp. dried parsley
1 rounded tsp. fresh marjoram, *or* 1 tsp. dried marjoram

1. Put meat in slow cooker. Add seasoned flour. Toss with meat. Stir in remaining ingredients. Mix well.

2. Cover. Cook on high 4-6 hours, or low 10-12 hours.

Exchange List Values
- Starch 1.5
- Vegetable 2.0
- Meat, lean 1.0

Basic Nutritional Values
- Calories 220
  (Calories from Fat 33)
- Total Fat 4 gm
  (Saturated Fat 1.2 gm,
  Polyunsat Fat 0.3 gm,
  Monounsat Fat 1.5 gm)
- Cholesterol 43 mg
- Sodium 445 mg
- Total Carb 28 gm
- Dietary Fiber 4 gm
- Sugars 7 gm
- Protein 18 gm

*Seasoned Flour
1 cup flour
1 tsp. salt
1 tsp. paprika
¼ tsp. pepper

Pot Roast

Carole Whaling
New Tripoli, PA

Makes 8 servings

Prep. Time: 30 minutes
Cooking Time: 10-12 hours
Ideal slow cooker size: 4-qt.

4 medium potatoes, cubed
4 medium carrots, sliced
1 medium onion, sliced
3-4 lb. rump roast, *or* pot roast, bone removed, and cut into serving size pieces, trimmed of fat
1 tsp. salt
½ tsp. pepper
1 bouillon cube
½ cup boiling water

1. Put vegetables and meat in slow cooker. Stir in salt and pepper.

2. Dissolve bouillon cube in water, then pour over other ingredients.

3. Cover. Cook on low 10-12 hours.

Exchange List Values
- Starch 1.0
- Meat, lean 3.0
- Vegetable 1.0

Basic Nutritional Values
- Calories 246
  (Calories from Fat 56)
- Total Fat 6 gm
  (Saturated Fat 2.2 gm,
  Polyunsat Fat 0.3 gm,
  Monounsat Fat 2.5 gm)
- Cholesterol 73 mg
- Sodium 485 mg
- Total Carb 20 gm
- Dietary Fiber 3 gm
- Sugars 4 gm
- Protein 27 gm

Zesty Swiss Steak

Marilyn Mowry
Irving, TX

Makes 6 servings

Prep. Time: 35 minutes
cooking Time: 3-10 hours
Ideal slow cooker size: 4-qt.

3-4 Tbsp. flour
½ tsp. salt
¼ tsp. pepper
1½ tsp. dry mustard
1½-2 lbs. round steak, trimmed of fat
1 Tbsp. canola oil
1 cup sliced onions
1 lb. carrots, sliced
14½-oz. can whole tomatoes

1 Tbsp. brown sugar
1½ Tbsp. Worcestershire sauce

1. Combine flour, salt, pepper, and dry mustard.

2. Cut steak in serving pieces. Dredge in flour mixture. Brown on both sides in oil in saucepan. Place in slow cooker.

3. Add onions and carrots.

4. Combine tomatoes, brown sugar, and Worcestershire sauce. Pour into slow cooker.

5. Cover. Cook on low 8-10 hours, or high 3-5 hours.

Exchange List Values
- Vegetable 3.0
- Meat, lean 3.0

Basic Nutritional Values
- Calories 236
  (Calories from Fat 71)
- Total Fat 8 gm
  (Saturated Fat 1.9 gm,
  Polyunsat Fat 1.0 gm,
  Monounsat Fat 3.6 gm)
- Cholesterol 64 mg
- Sodium 426 mg
- Total Carb 18 gm
- Dietary Fiber 3 gm
- Sugars 9 gm
- Protein 23 gm

Hearty Beef Stew

Charlotte Shaffer
East Earl, PA

Makes 5 servings

Prep. Time: 30 minutes
Cooking Time: 5-6 hours
Ideal slow cooker size: 4-qt.

2 lbs. stewing beef, cubed, trimmed of fat
5 medium carrots, sliced
1 large onion, cut in chunks
3 ribs celery, sliced
22-oz. can stewed tomatoes
½ tsp. ground cloves
2 bay leaves
¼ tsp. salt
¼-½ tsp. pepper

1. Combine all ingredients in slow cooker.

2. Cover. Cook on high 5-6 hours.

Exchange List Values
- Vegetable 4.0
- Meat, lean 3.0

Basic Nutritional Values
- Calories 270
  (Calories from Fat 66)
- Total Fat 7 gm
  (Saturated Fat 2.2 gm,
  Polyunsat Fat 0.5 gm,
  Monounsat Fat 3.4 gm)
- Cholesterol 90 mg
- Sodium 575 mg
- Total Carb 21 gm
- Dietary Fiber 5 gm
- Sugars 10 gm
- Protein 31 gm

Variations:

1. Substitute 1 whole clove for ½ tsp. ground cloves. Remove before serving.

2. Use venison instead of beef.

3. Cut back the salt and use 1 tsp. soy sauce.

When you buy meat, fish, and poultry, buying only enough for your meals will reduce overeating.

Judy's Beef Stew

Judy Koczo
Plano, IL

Makes 6 servings

Prep. Time: 35 minutes
Cooking Time: 5-12 hours
Ideal slow cooker size: 4-qt.

2 lbs. stewing meat, cubed, trimmed of fat
5 medium carrots, sliced
1 medium onion, diced
3 ribs celery, diced
5 medium potatoes, cubed
28 oz. can tomatoes
⅓-½ cup quick-cooking tapioca
½ tsp. salt
½ tsp. pepper

1. Combine all ingredients in slow cooker.
2. Cover. Cook on low 10-12 hours, or high 5-6 hours.

Exchange List Values
• Starch 2.0   • Meat, lean 2.0
• Vegetable 3.0

Basic Nutritional Values
• Calories 357   • Cholesterol 75 mg
  (Calories from Fat 55) • Sodium 518 mg
• Total Fat 6 gm   • Total Carb 47 gm
  (Saturated Fat 1.8 gm, • Dietary Fiber 7 gm
  Polyunsat Fat 0.6 gm, • Sugars 10 gm
  Monounsat Fat 2.8 gm) • Protein 29 gm

Variation:
   Add 1 whole clove and 2 bay leaves to stew before cooking.

Slow-Cooker Stew

Trudy Kutter
Corfu, NY

Makes 8 servings

Prep. Time: 35 minutes
Cooking Time: 8-10 hours
Ideal slow cooker size: 4-qt.

2 lbs. boneless beef, cubed, trimmed of fat
4-6 celery ribs, sliced
6-8 medium carrots, sliced
6 medium potatoes, cubed, unpeeled
2 medium onions, sliced
28-oz. can tomatoes
¼ cup minute tapioca
1 tsp. salt
¼ tsp. pepper
½ tsp. dried basil *or* oregano
1 garlic clove, minced

1. Combine all ingredients in slow cooker.
2. Cover. Cook on low 8-10 hours.

Exchange List Values
• Starch 2.0   • Meat, lean 1.0
• Vegetable 3.0

Basic Nutritional Values
• Calories 299   • Cholesterol 56 mg
  (Calories from Fat 42) • Sodium 549 mg
• Total Fat 5 gm   • Total Carb 42 gm
  (Saturated Fat 1.4 gm, • Dietary Fiber 7 gm
  Polyunsat Fat 0.5 gm, • Sugars 11 gm
  Monounsat Fat 2.1 gm) • Protein 23 gm

Italian Stew

Ann Gouinlock
Alexander, NY

Makes 6 servings

Prep. Time: 30 minutes
Cooking Time: 8-10 hours
Ideal slow cooker size: 4-qt.

1½ lbs. beef cubes
2-3 carrots, cut in 1-inch chunks
3-4 ribs celery, cut in ¾-1-inch pieces
1-1½ cups coarsely chopped onions
14½-oz. can stewed, *or* diced tomatoes
⅓ cup minute tapioca
1½ tsp. salt
¼ tsp. pepper
¼ tsp. Worcestershire sauce
½ tsp. Italian seasoning

1. Combine all ingredients in slow cooker.
2. Cover. Cook on low 8-10 hours.

Exchange List Values
• Starch 0.5   • Meat, lean 2.0
• Vegetable 2.0

Basic Nutritional Values
• Calories 188   • Cholesterol 56 mg
  (Calories from Fat 41) • Sodium 508 mg
• Total Fat 5 gm   • Total Carb 18 gm
  (Saturated Fat 1.4 gm, • Dietary Fiber 3 gm
  Polyunsat Fat 0.3 gm, • Sugars 6 gm
  Monounsat Fat 2.1 gm) • Protein 19 gm

Venison or Beef Stew

Frances B. Musser
Newmanstown, PA

Makes 6 servings

Prep. Time: 35 minutes
Cooking Time: 8-9 hours
Ideal slow cooker size: 4-qt.

1½ lbs. venison *or* beef cubes
2 Tbsp. canola oil
1 medium onion, chopped
4 medium carrots, peeled and cut into 1-inch pieces
1 rib celery, cut into 1-inch pieces
4 medium potatoes, peeled and quartered
12-oz. can whole tomatoes, undrained
10½-oz. can beef broth
1 Tbsp. Worcestershire sauce
1 Tbsp. parsley flakes
1 bay leaf
¼ tsp. salt
¼ tsp. pepper
2 Tbsp. quick-cooking tapioca

1. Brown meat cubes in skillet in oil over medium heat. Transfer to slow cooker.
2. Add remaining ingredients. Mix well.
3. Cover. Cook on low 8-9 hours.

Exchange List Values
- Starch 1.5
- Vegetable 2.0
- Meat, very lean 3.0
- Fat 1.0

Basic Nutritional Values
- Calories 313
  (Calories from Fat 70)
- Total Fat 8 gm
  (Saturated Fat 1.5 gm,
  Polyunsat Fat 2.1 gm,
  Monounsat Fat 3.5 gm)
- Cholesterol 102 mg
- Sodium 552 mg
- Total Carb 29 gm
- Dietary Fiber 4 gm
- Sugars 7 gm
- Protein 31 gm

Variations:
1. Substitute 1½ tsp. garlic salt and 1 tsp. salt for 2½ tsp. salt.
2. For added color and flavor, add 1 cup frozen peas 5 minutes before end of cooking time.

Venison Swiss Steak

Dede Peterson
Rapid City, SD

Makes 6 servings

Prep. Time: 25 minutes
Cooking Time: 7½-8½ hours
Ideal slow cooker size: 4-qt.

2 lbs. round venison steak
¼ cup flour
2 tsp. salt
½ tsp. pepper
1 Tbsp. canola oil
2 medium onions, sliced
2 ribs celery, diced
1 cup diced carrots
2 cups fresh, *or* stewed, tomatoes
1 Tbsp. Worcestershire sauce

1. Combine flour, salt, and pepper. Dredge steak in flour mixture. Brown in oil in skillet. Place in slow cooker.
2. Add remaining ingredients.
3. Cover. Cook on low 7½-8½ hours.

Exchange List Values
- Starch 0.5
- Vegetable 2.0
- Meat, very lean 4.0
- Fat 1.0

Basic Nutritional Values
- Calories 277
  (Calories from Fat 59)
- Total Fat 7 gm
  (Saturated Fat 1.7 gm,
  Polyunsat Fat 1.6 gm,
  Monounsat Fat 2.5 gm)
- Cholesterol 135 mg
- Sodium 527 mg
- Total Carb 14 gm
- Dietary Fiber 3 gm
- Sugars 6 gm
- Protein 39 gm

Swiss Steak

Wanda S. Curtin
Bradenton, FL

Jeanne Hertzog
Bethlehem, PA

Makes 6 servings

Prep. Time: 25 minutes
Cooking Time: 3-10 hours
Ideal slow cooker size: 4-qt.

1½ lbs. round steak, about
    ¾" thick, trimmed of fat
2-4 tsp. flour
½-1 tsp. salt
¼ tsp. pepper
1 medium onion, sliced
1 medium carrot, chopped
1 rib celery, chopped
14½-oz. can diced
    tomatoes, *or* 15 oz. can
    tomato sauce

1. Cut steak into serving
pieces.
2. Combine flour, salt,
and pepper. Dredge meat in
seasoned flour.
3. Place onions in bottom
of slow cooker. Add meat. Top
with carrots and celery and
cover with tomatoes.
4. Cover. Cook on low 8-10
hours, or high 3-5 hours.
5. Serve over noodles or
rice.

Exchange List Values
• Vegetable 2.0   • Meat, lean 2.0

Basic Nutritional Values
• Calories 172   • Cholesterol 64 mg
  (Calories from Fat 48) • Sodium 381 mg
• Total Fat 5 gm   • Total Carb 8 gm
  (Saturated Fat 1.7 gm,   • Dietary Fiber 2 gm
  Polyunsat Fat 0.3 gm,   • Sugars 4 gm
  Monounsat Fat 2.2 gm) • Protein 22 gm

Margaret's Swiss Steak

Margaret Rich
North Newton, KS

Makes 6 servings

Prep. Time: 25 minutes
Cooking Time: 9 hours 15
    minutes
Ideal slow cooker size: 4-qt.

1 cup chopped onions
½ cup chopped celery
2 lb. ½-inch thick round
    steak, trimmed of fat
¼ cup flour
3 Tbsp. oil
1 tsp. salt
¼ tsp. pepper
16-oz. can diced tomatoes
¼ cup flour
½ cup water

1. Place onions and celery
in bottom of slow cooker.
2. Cut steak in serving-size
pieces. Dredge in ¼ cup flour.
Brown on both sides in oil
in saucepan. Place in slow
cooker.
3. Sprinkle with salt and
pepper. Pour on tomatoes.
4. Cover. Cook on low 9
hours. Remove meat from
cooker and keep warm.
5. Turn heat to high. Blend
together ¼ cup flour and
water. Stir into sauce in slow
cooker. Cover and cook 15
minutes. Serve with steak.

Exchange List Values
• Starch 0.5   • Meat, lean 4.0
• Vegetable 1.0   • Fat 0.5

Basic Nutritional Values
• Calories 305   • Cholesterol 85 mg
  (Calories from Fat 124) • Sodium 592 mg
• Total Fat 14 gm   • Total Carb 14 gm
  (Saturated Fat 2.8 gm,   • Dietary Fiber 2 gm
  Polyunsat Fat 2.4 gm,   • Sugars 4 gm
  Monounsat Fat 7.0 gm) • Protein 30 gm

Nadine & Hazel's Swiss Steak

Nadine Martinitz
Salina, KS

Hazel L. Propst
Oxford, PA

Makes 8 servings

Prep. Time: 30 minutes
Cooking Time: 6-8 hours
Ideal slow cooker size: 4-qt.

3 lb. round steak, trimmed
    of fat
⅓ cup flour
1 tsp. salt
½ tsp. pepper
3 Tbsp. canola oil
1 large onion, sliced
1 large pepper, sliced
14½-oz. can stewed
    tomatoes, *or* 3-4 fresh
    tomatoes, chopped
water

1. Sprinkle meat with flour,
salt, and pepper. Pound both
sides. Cut into 6 or 8 pieces.
Brown meat in canola oil over
medium heat on top of stove,
about 15 minutes. Transfer to
slow cooker.
2. Brown onion and pep-
per. Add tomatoes and bring

30

to boil. Pour over steak. Add water to completely cover steak.

3. Cover. Cook on low 6-8 hours.

Exchange List Values
- Vegetable 2.0
- Fat 0.5
- Meat, lean 4.0

Basic Nutritional Values
- Calories 296
- Cholesterol 96 mg
- (Calories from Fat 116)
- Sodium 547 mg
- Total Fat 13 gm
- Total Carb 11 gm
- (Saturated Fat 2.9 gm,
- Dietary Fiber 1 gm
- Polyunsat Fat 1.9 gm,
- Sugars 4 gm
- Monounsat Fat 6.4 gm)
- Protein 33 gm

Variation:

To add some flavor, stir in your favorite dried herbs when beginning to cook the steak, or add fresh herbs in the last hour of cooking.

Beef, Tomatoes, & Noodles

Janice Martins
Fairbank, IA

Makes 8 servings

Prep. Time: 20 minutes
Cooking Time: 6-8 hours
Ideal slow cooker size: 4-qt.

1½ lbs. stewing beef, cubed, trimmed of fat
¼ cup flour
2 cups stewed tomatoes (if you like tomato chunks), *or* 2 cups crushed tomatoes (if you prefer a smoother gravy)
1 tsp. salt
¼-½ tsp. pepper
1 medium onion, chopped
water
12-oz. bag noodles

1. Combine meat and flour until cubes are coated. Place in slow cooker.

2. Add tomatoes, salt, pepper, and onion. Add water to cover.

3. Cover. Simmer on low 6-8 hours.

4. Serve over cooked noodles.

Exchange List Values
- Starch 2.0
- Meat, lean 2.0
- Vegetable 1.0

Basic Nutritional Values
- Calories 286
- Cholesterol 83 mg
- (Calories from Fat 46)
- Sodium 490 mg
- Total Fat 5 gm
- Total Carb 39 gm
- (Saturated Fat 1.8 gm,
- Dietary Fiber 2 gm
- Polyunsat Fat 0.7 gm,
- Sugars 4 gm
- Monounsat Fat 2.1 gm)
- Protein 20 gm

Big Beef Stew

Margaret H. Moffitt
Bartlett, TN

Makes 8 servings

Prep. Time: 25 minutes
Cooking Time: 9 hours
Ideal slow cooker size: 4- or 5-qt.

---

3 lb. beef roast, cubed, trimmed of fat
1 large onion, sliced
1 tsp. dried parsley flakes
1 medium green pepper, sliced
3 ribs celery, sliced
4 medium carrots, sliced
28-oz. can tomatoes with juice, undrained
1 garlic clove, minced
2 cups water

1. Combine all ingredients.

2. Cover. Cook on high 1 hour. Reduce heat to low and cook 8 hours.

3. Serve on rice or noodles.

Exchange List Values
- Vegetable 3.0
- Meat, lean 3.0

Basic Nutritional Values
- Calories 224
- Cholesterol 85 mg
- (Calories from Fat 61)
- Sodium 248 mg
- Total Fat 7 gm
- Total Carb 12 gm
- (Saturated Fat 2.1 gm,
- Dietary Fiber 3 gm
- Polyunsat Fat 0.4 gm,
- Sugars 7 gm
- Monounsat Fat 3.1 gm)
- Protein 28 gm

Note:

For additional pep, add ¾ tsp. black pepper.

Spanish Round Steak

Shari Jensen
Fountain, CO

Makes 6 servings

Prep. Time: 25 minutes
Cooking Time: 8 hours
Ideal slow cooker size: 4-qt.

1 small onion, sliced
1 rib celery, chopped
1 medium green bell
  pepper, sliced in rings
2 lbs. round steak,
  trimmed of fat
2 Tbsp. chopped fresh
  parsley, *or* 2 tsp. dried
  parsley
1 Tbsp. Worcestershire
  sauce
1 Tbsp. dry mustard
1 Tbsp. chili powder
2 cups canned tomatoes
2 tsp. dry minced garlic
½ tsp. salt
¼ tsp. pepper

1. Put half of onion, green
pepper, and celery in slow
cooker.
2. Cut steak into serving-
size pieces. Place steak pieces
in slow cooker.
3. Put remaining onion,
green pepper, and celery over
steak.
4. Combine remaining
ingredients. Pour over meat.
5. Cover. Cook on low 8
hours.
6. Serve over noodles or
rice.

Exchange List Values
- Vegetable 2.0
- Meat, lean 3.0

Basic Nutritional Values
- Calories 222
  (Calories from Fat 67)
- Total Fat 7 gm
  (Saturated Fat 2.3 gm,
  Polyunsat Fat 0.5 gm,
  Monounsat Fat 3.0 gm)
- Cholesterol 85 mg
- Sodium 414 mg
- Total Carb 8 gm
- Dietary Fiber 2 gm
- Sugars 5 gm
- Protein 30 gm

Slow-Cooked Pepper Steak

Carolyn Baer
Conrath, WI
Ann Driscoll
Albuquerque, NM

Makes 8 servings

Prep. Time: 25 minutes
Cooking Time: 6-7 hours
Ideal slow cooker size: 4-qt.

1½-2 lbs. beef round steak,
  cut in 3" × 1" strips,
  trimmed of fat
2 Tbsp. canola oil
¼ cup soy sauce
1 garlic clove, minced
1 cup chopped onion
1 tsp. sugar
¼ tsp. pepper
¼ tsp. ground ginger
2 large green peppers, cut
  in strips
4 medium tomatoes cut
  in eighths, *or* 16 oz. can
  diced tomatoes

½ cup cold water
1 Tbsp. cornstarch

1. Brown beef in oil in
saucepan. Transfer to slow
cooker.
2. Combine soy sauce,
garlic, onions, sugar, salt,
pepper, and ginger. Pour over
meat.
3. Cover. Cook on low 5-6
hours.
4. Add green peppers and
tomatoes. Cook 1 hour longer.
5. Combine water and
cornstarch to make paste. Stir
into slow cooker. Cook on
high until thickened, about 10
minutes.
6. Serve over rice or
noodles.

Exchange List Values
- Vegetable 2.0
- Meat, lean 2.0

Basic Nutritional Values
- Calories 174
  (Calories from Fat 68)
- Total Fat 8 gm
  (Saturated Fat 1.5 gm,
  Polyunsat Fat 1.3 gm,
  Monounsat Fat 3.7 gm)
- Cholesterol 48 mg
- Sodium 546 mg
- Total Carb 10 gm
- Dietary Fiber 2 gm
- Sugars 6 gm
- Protein 17 gm

Invite a friend or family member to do any 10 of the tips in this book with you. It's easier when you have company!

Asian Pepper Steak

Donna Lantgen
Rapid City, SD

Makes 6 servings

Prep. Time: 20 minutes
Cooking Time: 6-8 hours
Ideal slow cooker size: 4-qt.

1 lb. round steak, sliced thin, trimmed of fat
3 Tbsp. light soy sauce
½ tsp. ground ginger
1 garlic clove, minced
1 medium green pepper, thinly sliced
4-oz. can mushrooms, drained, *or* 1 cup sliced fresh mushrooms
1 medium onion, thinly sliced
½ tsp. crushed red pepper

1. Combine all ingredients in slow cooker.
2. Cover. Cook on low 6-8 hours.
3. Serve as steak sandwiches topped with provolone cheese, or over rice.

Exchange List Values
- Vegetable 1.0   • Meat, lean 2.0

Basic Nutritional Values
- Calories 122
  (Calories from Fat 32)
- Total Fat 4 gm
  (Saturated Fat 1.2 gm,
  Polyunsat Fat 0.2 gm,
  Monounsat Fat 1.5 gm)
- Cholesterol 43 mg
- Sodium 368 mg
- Total Carb 6 gm
- Dietary Fiber 2 gm
- Sugars 3 gm
- Protein 16 gm

Powerhouse Beef Roast with Tomatoes, Onions, and Peppers

Donna Treloar
Gaston, IN

Makes 6 servings

Prep. Time: 20 minutes
Cooking Time: 8-10 hours
Ideal slow cooker size: 4- or 5-qt.

3 lb. boneless chuck roast, trimmed of fat
1 garlic clove, minced
1 Tbsp. canola oil
2-3 medium onions, sliced
2-3 sweet green and red peppers, sliced
16-oz. jar salsa
2 14½-oz. cans Mexican-style stewed tomatoes

1. Brown roast and garlic in oil in skillet. Place in slow cooker.
2. Add onions and peppers.
3. Combine salsa and tomatoes and pour over ingredients in slow cooker.
4. Cover. Cook on low 8-10 hours.
5. Slice meat to serve.

Exchange List Values
- Vegetable 4.0   • Meat, lean 4.0

Basic Nutritional Values
- Calories 327
  (Calories from Fat 97)
- Total Fat 11 gm
  (Saturated Fat 3.1 gm,
  Polyunsat Fat 1.3 gm,
  Monounsat Fat 4.7 gm)
- Cholesterol 106 mg
- Sodium 565 mg
- Total Carb 19 gm
- Dietary Fiber 5 gm
- Sugars 12 gm
- Protein 38 gm

Variation:
Make Beef Burritos with the leftovers. Shred the beef and heat with remaining peppers, onions, and ½ cup of the broth. Add 1 Tbsp. chili powder, 2 tsp. cumin, and salt to taste. Heat thoroughly. Fill warm flour tortillas with mixture and serve with sour cream, salsa, and guacamole.

Steak San Morco

Susan Tjon
Austin, TX

Makes 6 servings

Prep. Time: 15 minutes
Cooking Time: 6-10 hours
Ideal slow cooker size: 4-qt.

2 lbs. stewing meat, cubed, trimmed of fat
1 envelope sodium-free dry onion soup mix (see recipe on page 261)
29-oz. can peeled, *or* crushed, tomatoes
1 tsp. dried oregano
garlic powder to taste
2 Tbsp. canola oil
2 Tbsp. wine vinegar

1. Layer meat evenly in bottom of slow cooker.
2. Combine soup mix, tomatoes, spices, oil, and vinegar in bowl. Blend with spoon. Pour over meat.
3. Cover. Cook on high 6 hours, or low 8-10 hours.

Exchange List Values
• Carbohydrate 0.5   • Meat, lean 3.0
• Vegetable 1.0

Basic Nutritional Values
• Calories 237   • Cholesterol 75 mg
  (Calories from Fat 94)   • Sodium 252 mg
• Total Fat 10 gm   • Total Carb 10 gm
  (Saturated Fat 2.1 gm,   • Dietary Fiber 2 gm
  Polyunsat 1.7 gm,   • Sugars 5 gm
  Monounsat Fat 5.5 gm)   • Protein 25 gm

Pat's Meat Stew

Pat Bishop
Bedminster, PA

Makes 5 servings

Prep. Time: 25 minutes
Cooking Time: 4-10 hours
Ideal slow cooker size: 4-qt.

1-2 lbs. beef roast, cubed, trimmed of fat
1 tsp. salt
¼ tsp. pepper
2 cups water
2 small carrots, sliced
2 small onions, sliced
4-6 small potatoes, unpeeled, chunked
¼ cup quick-cooking tapioca
1 bay leaf
10-oz. pkg. frozen peas, *or* mixed vegetables

1. Brown beef in saucepan. Place in slow cooker.
2. Sprinkle with salt and pepper. Add remaining ingredients except frozen vegetables. Mix well.
3. Cover. Cook on low 8-10 hours, or on high 4-5 hours. Add vegetables during last 1-2 hours of cooking.

Exchange List Values
• Starch 2.0   • Meat, lean 1.0
• Vegetable 1.0

Basic Nutritional Values
• Calories 257   • Cholesterol 45 mg
  (Calories from Fat 33)   • Sodium 567 mg
• Total Fat 4 gm   • Total Carb 36 gm
  (Saturated Fat 1.1 gm,   • Dietary Fiber 6 gm
  Polyunsat 0.3 gm,   • Sugars 7 gm
  Monounsat Fat 1.7 gm)   • Protein 20 gm

Ernestine's Beef Stew

Ernestine Schrepfer
Trenton, MO

Makes 6 servings

Prep. Time: 20 minutes
Cooking Time: 7-8 hours
Ideal slow cooker size: 4-qt.

1½ lbs. stewing meat, cubed, trimmed of fat
2¼ cups no-added-salt tomato juice
10½-oz. can consomme
1 cup chopped celery
2 cups sliced carrots
4 Tbsp. quick-cooking tapioca
1 medium onion, chopped
¼ tsp. salt
¼ tsp. pepper

1. Combine all ingredients in slow cooker.
2. Cover. Cook on low 7-8 hours. (Do not peek.)

Exchange List Values
• Starch 0.5   • Meat, lean 2.0
• Vegetable 2.0

Basic Nutritional Values
• Calories 193   • Cholesterol 57 mg
  (Calories from Fat 40)   • Sodium 519 mg
• Total Fat 4 gm   • Total Carb 17 gm
  (Saturated Fat 1.4 gm,   • Dietary Fiber 3 gm
  Polyunsat Fat 0.3 gm,   • Sugars 7 gm
  Monounsat Fat 2.1 gm)   • Protein 21 gm

Becky's Beef Stew

Becky Harder
Monument, CO

Makes 8 servings

Prep. Time: 30 minutes
Cooking Time: 6-8 hours
Ideal slow cooker size: 4- or 5-qt.

1½ lbs. beef stewing meat,
  cubed, trimmed of fat
2 10-oz. pkgs. frozen
  vegetables—carrots,
  corn, peas
4 large potatoes, unpeeled,
  cubed
1 bay leaf
1 medium onion, chopped
15-oz. can stewed tomatoes
  of your choice—Italian,
  Mexican, *or* regular
8-oz. can tomato sauce
2 Tbsp. Worcestershire
  sauce
1 tsp. salt
¼ tsp. pepper

1. Put meat on bottom of slow
cooker. Layer frozen vegetables
and potatoes over meat.
2. Mix remaining ingredients
together in large bowl and pour
over other ingredients.
3. Cover. Cook on low 6-8
hours.

Exchange List Values
• Starch 2.0   • Meat, lean 1.0
• Vegetable 2.0

Basic Nutritional Values
• Calories 259   • Cholesterol 42 mg
(Calories from Fat 31) • Sodium 506 mg
• Total Fat 3 gm   • Total Carb 39 gm
(Saturated Fat 1.0 gm, • Dietary Fiber 6 gm
Polyunsat Fat 0.4 gm,   • Sugars 9 gm
Monounsat Fat 1.6 gm) • Protein 19 gm

Santa Fe Stew

Jeanne Allen
Rye, CO

Makes 6 servings

Prep. Time: 25 minutes
Cooking Time: 4½-6½ hours
Ideal slow cooker size: 4-qt.

2 lbs. sirloin, *or* stewing
  meat, cubed, trimmed
  of fat
2 Tbsp. canola oil
1 large onion, diced
2 garlic cloves, minced
1½ cups water
1 Tbsp. dried parsley
  flakes
1 beef bouillon cube
1 tsp. ground cumin
¼ tsp. salt
3 medium carrots, sliced
1 lb. frozen green beans
1 lb. frozen corn
4-oz. can diced green chilies

1. Brown meat, onion, and
garlic in oil in saucepan until
meat is no longer pink. Place
in slow cooker.
2. Stir in remaining
ingredients.
3. Cover. Cook on high 30
minutes. Reduce heat to low
and cook 4-6 hours.

Exchange List Values
• Starch 1.0   • Meat, lean 3.0
• Vegetable 3.0

Basic Nutritional Values
• Calories 322   • Cholesterol 75 mg
(Calories from Fat 99) • Sodium 554 mg
• Total Fat 11 gm   • Total Carb 30 gm
(Saturated Fat 2.2 gm, • Dietary Fiber 7 gm
Polyunsat Fat 2.0 gm,   • Sugars 10 gm
Monounsat Fat 5.6 gm) • Protein 28 gm

Gone-All-Day Casserole

Beatrice Orgish
Richardson, TX

Makes 8 servings

Prep. Time: 35 minutes
Cooking Time: 6-8 hours
Ideal slow cooker size: 4- or 5-qt.

1 cup uncooked wild rice,
  rinsed and drained
1 cup chopped celery
1 cup chopped carrots
2 4-oz. cans mushrooms,
  stems and pieces,
  drained
1 large onion, chopped
1 clove garlic, minced
½ cup slivered almonds
1 beef bouillon cube
1¼ tsp. seasoned salt
2 lbs. boneless round
  steak, cut into 1-inch
  cubes, trimmed of fat
3 cups water

1. Place ingredients in
order listed in slow cooker.
2. Cover. Cook on low 6-8
hours or until rice is tender.
Stir before serving.

Exchange List Values
• Starch 1.0   • Meat, lean 3.0
• Vegetable 1.0

Basic Nutritional Values
• Calories 264   • Cholesterol 56 mg
(Calories from Fat 77) • Sodium 615 mg
• Total Fat 9 gm   • Total Carb 23 gm
(Saturated Fat 1.7 gm, • Dietary Fiber 4 gm
Polyunsat Fat 1.3 gm,   • Sugars 4 gm
Monounsat Fat 4.5 gm) • Protein 24 gm

Full-Flavored Beef Stew

Stacy Petersheim
Mechanicsburg, PA

Makes 6 servings

Prep. Time: 30 minutes
Cooking Time: 8 hours
Ideal slow cooker size: 4-qt.

2 lb. beef roast, cubed, trimmed of fat
2 cups sliced carrots
2 cups diced potatoes, unpeeled
1 medium onion, sliced
1½ cups frozen *or* fresh peas
2 tsp. quick-cooking tapioca
½ tsp. salt
½ tsp. pepper
8-oz. can tomato sauce
1 cup water
1 Tbsp. brown sugar

1. Combine beef and vegetables in slow cooker. Sprinkle with tapioca, salt, and pepper.
2. Combine tomato sauce and water. Pour over ingredients in slow cooker. Sprinkle with brown sugar.
3. Cover. Cook on low 8 hours.

Exchange List Values
- Starch 1.0
- Meat, lean 3.0
- Vegetable 2.0

Basic Nutritional Values
- Calories 271
  (Calories from Fat 54)
- Total Fat 6 gm
  (Saturated Fat 1.9 gm, Polyunsat Fat 0.4 gm, Monounsat Fat 2.8 gm)
- Cholesterol 75 mg
- Sodium 539 mg
- Total Carb 26 gm
- Dietary Fiber 5 gm
- Sugars 11 gm
- Protein 28 gm

Variation:
Add peas one hour before cooking time ends to keep their color and flavor.

Lazy Day Stew

Ruth Ann Gingrich
New Holland, PA

Makes 8 servings

Prep. Time: 30 minutes
Cooking Time: 8 hours
Ideal slow cooker size: 4-qt.

2 lbs. stewing beef, cubed, trimmed of fat
2 cups diced carrots
2 cups diced potatoes, unpeeled
2 medium onions, chopped
1 cup chopped celery
10-oz. pkg. lima beans
2 tsp. quick-cooking tapioca
1 tsp. salt
½ tsp. pepper
8-oz. can tomato sauce
1 cup water
1 Tbsp. brown sugar

1. Place beef in bottom of slow cooker. Add vegetables.
2. Sprinkle tapioca, salt, and pepper over ingredients.
3. Mix together tomato sauce and water. Pour over top.
4. Sprinkle brown sugar over all.
5. Cover. Cook on low 8 hours.

Exchange List Values
- Starch 1.0
- Meat, lean 2.0
- Vegetable 2.0

Basic Nutritional Values
- Calories 229
  (Calories from Fat 41)
- Total Fat 5 gm
  (Saturated Fat 1.4 gm, Polyunsat Fat 0.4 gm, Monounsat Fat 2.1 gm)
- Cholesterol 56 mg
- Sodium 558 mg
- Total Carb 25 gm
- Dietary Fiber 5 gm
- Sugars 8 gm
- Protein 22 gm

Variation:
Instead of lima beans, use 1½ cups green beans.
Rose M. Hoffman
Schuylkill Haven, PA

Beef with Mushrooms

Doris Perkins
Mashpee, MA

Makes 6 servings

Prep. Time: 20 minutes
Cooking Time: 5 hours
Ideal slow cooker size: 4-qt.

1½ lbs. stewing beef,
  cubed, trimmed of fat
4-oz. can mushroom
  pieces, drained (save
  liquid)
half a garlic clove, minced
¾ cup sliced onions
3 Tbsp. canola oil
1 beef bouillon cube
1 cup hot water
8-oz. can tomato sauce
2 tsp. sugar
2 tsp. Worcestershire sauce
1 tsp. dried basil
1 tsp. dried oregano
½ tsp. salt
⅛ tsp. pepper

1. Brown meat, mushrooms, garlic, and onions in shortening in skillet.
2. Dissolve bouillon cube in hot water. Add to meat mixture.
3. Stir in mushroom liquid and rest of ingredients. Mix well. Pour into slow cooker.
4. Cover. Cook on high 3 hours, or until meat is tender.
5. Serve over cooked noodles, spaghetti, or rice.

Exchange List Values
- Vegetable 2.0
- Meat, lean 2.0
- Fat 1.0

Basic Nutritional Values
- Calories 210
  (Calories from Fat 101)
- Total Fat 11 gm
  (Saturated Fat 1.8 gm,
  Polyunsat Fat 2.3 gm,
  Monounsat Fat 6.1 gm)
- Cholesterol 56 mg
- Sodium 385 mg
- Total Carb 8 gm
- Dietary Fiber 2 gm
- Sugars 5 gm
- Protein 19 gm

Beef Pot Roast

Alexa Slonin
Harrisonburg, VA

Makes 10 servings

Prep. Time: 30 minutes
Cooking Time: 10-12 hours
Ideal slow cooker size: 4- or 5-qt.

2 medium potatoes, cubed,
  or 2 medium sweet
  potatoes, cubed
8 small carrots, cut in
  small chunks
2 small onions, cut in
  wedges
2 ribs celery, chopped
2½-3 lb. beef chuck, *or* pot
  roast, trimmed of fat
2 Tbsp. canola oil
¾ cup water, dry wine, *or*
  tomato juice
1 Tbsp. Worcestershire
  sauce
1 tsp. instant beef bouillon
  granules
1 tsp. dried basil

1. Place vegetables in bottom of slow cooker.
2. Brown roast in oil in skillet. Place on top of vegetables.
3. Combine water, Worcestershire sauce, bouillon, and basil. Pour over meat and vegetables.
4. Cover. Cook on low 10-12 hours.

Exchange List Values
- Starch 0.5
- Vegetable 2.0
- Meat, lean 2.0
- Fat 0.5

Basic Nutritional Values
- Calories 233
  (Calories from Fat 78)
- Total Fat 9 gm
  (Saturated Fat 2.1 gm,
  Polyunsat Fat 1.3 gm,
  Monounsat Fat 4.1 gm)
- Cholesterol 61 mg
- Sodium 231 mg
- Total Carb 16 gm
- Dietary Fiber 3 gm
- Sugars 5 gm
- Protein 22 gm

Wear a medical alert bracelet or necklace that says "diabetes"—not to call attention to your condition, but to tell medical personnel to check your sugar level if an emergency happened.

Easy Pot Roast and Veggies

Tina Houk
Clinton, MO
Arlene Wines
Newton, KS

Makes 6 servings

Prep. Time: 20 minutes
Cooking Time: 6-8 hours
Ideal slow cooker size: 4- or 5-qt.

3-4 lb. chuck roast,
   trimmed of fat
4 medium potatoes, cubed,
   unpeeled
4 medium carrots, sliced,
   or 1 lb. baby carrots
2 celery ribs, sliced thin
1 envelope dry onion soup
   mix
3 cups water

1. Put roast, potatoes,
carrots, and celery in slow
cooker.
2. Add onion soup mix and
water.
3. Cover. Cook on low 6-8
hours.

Exchange List Values
- Starch 1.5
- Vegetable 1.0
- Meat, lean 3.0

Basic Nutritional Values
- Calories 325
  (Calories from Fat 76)
- Total Fat 8 gm
  (Saturated Fat 2.9 gm,
  Polyunsat Fat 0.5 gm,
  Monounsat Fat 3.6 gm)
- Cholesterol 98 mg
- Sodium 560 mg
- Total Carb 26 gm
- Dietary Fiber 4 gm
- Sugars 6 gm
- Protein 35 gm

Variations:
1. To add flavor to the
broth, stir 1 tsp. kitchen
bouquet, ½ tsp. salt, ½ tsp.
black pepper, and ½ tsp.
garlic powder into water
before pouring over meat and
vegetables.
Bonita Ensenberger
Albuquerque, NM

2. Before putting roast in
cooker, sprinkle it with the
dry soup mix, patting it on so
it adheres.
Betty Lahman
Elkton, VA

Simple Pot Roast

Janet L. Roggie
Linville, NY

Makes 8 servings

Prep. Time: 10 minutes
Cooking Time: 10-12 hours
Ideal slow cooker size: 4-qt.

3 potatoes, thinly sliced
2 large carrots, thinly sliced
1 onion, thinly sliced
1 tsp. salt
½ tsp. pepper
3-4 lb. pot roast, trimmed
   of fat
½ cup water

1. Put vegetables in bottom
of slow cooker. Stir in salt
and pepper. Add roast. Pour
in water.
2. Cover. Cook on low
10-12 hours.

Exchange List Values
- Starch 1.0
- Vegetable 1.0
- Meat, lean 3.0

Basic Nutritional Values
- Calories 219
  (Calories from Fat 55)
- Total Fat 6 gm
  (Saturated Fat 2.2 gm,
  Polyunsat Fat 0.3 gm,
  Monounsat Fat 2.5 gm)
- Cholesterol 73 mg
- Sodium 361 mg
- Total Carb 14 gm
- Dietary Fiber 2 gm
- Sugars 3 gm
- Protein 26 gm

Variations:
1. Add ½ tsp. dried dill,
a bay leaf, and ½ tsp. dried
rosemary for more flavor.
2. Brown roast on all sides
in saucepan in 2 Tbsp. oil
before placing in cooker.
Debbie Zeida
Mashpee, MA

Rump Roast and Vegetables

Kimberlee Greenawalt
Harrisonburg, VA

Makes 8 servings

Prep. Time: 20 minutes
Cooking Time: 5-12 hours
Ideal slow cooker size: 4- or 5-qt.

1½ lbs. small potatoes (about 10), *or* medium potatoes (about 4), halved, unpeeled
2 medium carrots, cubed
1 small onion, sliced
10-oz. pkg. frozen lima beans
1 bay leaf
2 Tbsp. quick-cooking tapioca
2-2½ lb. boneless beef round rump, round tip, *or* pot roast, trimmed of fat
2 Tbsp. canola oil
10¾-oz. can condensed vegetable beef soup
¼ cup water
¼ tsp. pepper

1. Place potatoes, carrots, and onions in slow cooker. Add frozen beans and bay leaf. Sprinkle with tapioca.
2. Brown roast on all sides in oil in skillet. Place over vegetables in slow cooker.
3. Combine soup, water, and pepper. Pour over roast.
4. Cover. Cook on low 10-12 hours, or high 5-6 hours.
5. Discard bay leaf before serving.

Exchange List Values
- Starch 2.0
- Vegetable 1.0
- Meat, lean 2.0

Basic Nutritional Values
- Calories 288
  (Calories from Fat 71)
- Total Fat 8 gm
  (Saturated Fat 1.9 gm,
  Polyunsat Fat 1.3 gm,
  Monounsat Fat 3.7 gm)
- Cholesterol 50 mg
- Sodium 349 mg
- Total Carb 32 gm
- Dietary Fiber 6 gm
- Sugars 5 gm
- Protein 22 gm

Hearty New England Dinner

Joette Droz
Kalona, IA

Makes 8 servings

Prep. Time: 40 minutes
Cooking Time: 8-10 hours
Ideal slow cooker size: 4- or 5-qt.

2 medium carrots, sliced
1 medium onion, sliced
1 celery rib, sliced
3 lb. boneless chuck roast, trimmed of fat
¼ tsp. pepper
1 envelope dry onion soup mix
2 cups water
1 Tbsp. vinegar
1 bay leaf
half a small head of cabbage, cut in wedges
2 Tbsp. melted margarine, *or* butter
2 Tbsp. flour
1 Tbsp. dried minced onion
2 Tbsp. prepared horseradish
½ tsp. salt

1. Place carrots, onion, and celery in slow cooker. Place roast on top. Sprinkle with pepper. Add soup mix, water, vinegar, and bay leaf.
2. Cover. Cook on low 7-9 hours. Remove beef and keep warm. Just before serving, cut into pieces or thin slices.
3. Discard bay leaf. Add cabbage to juice in slow cooker.
4. Cover. Cook on high 1 hour, or until cabbage is tender.
5. Melt margarine in saucepan. Stir in flour and onion.
6. Add 1½ cups liquid from slow cooker. Stir in horseradish and ½ tsp. salt. Bring to boil.
7. Cook over low heat until thick and smooth, about 2 minutes. Return to cooker and blend with remaining sauce in cooker.
8. When blended, serve over or alongside meat and vegetables.

Exchange List Values
- Vegetable 2.0
- Meat, lean 3.0
- Fat 0.5

Basic Nutritional Values
- Calories 234
  (Calories from Fat 85)
- Total Fat 9 gm
  (Saturated Fat 2.7 gm,
  Polyunsat Fat 1.3 gm,
  Monounsat Fat 4.0 gm)
- Cholesterol 74 mg
- Sodium 607 mg
- Total Carb 11 gm
- Dietary Fiber 3 gm
- Sugars 6 gm
- Protein 26 gm

Easy Beef Stew

Connie Johnson
Loudon, NH

Makes 6 servings

Prep. Time: 35 minutes
Cooking Time: 6-8 hours
Ideal slow cooker size: 4- or 5-qt.

1 lb. stewing beef
1 cup cubed turnip
2 medium potatoes, cubed,
  unpeeled
1 large onion, sliced
1 garlic clove, minced
2 large carrots, sliced
½ cup green beans, cut up
½ cup peas
1 bay leaf
½ tsp. dried thyme
1 tsp. chopped parsley
2 Tbsp. tomato paste
2 Tbsp. celery leaves
¼ tsp. salt
¼ tsp. pepper
1 qt., *or* 2 14½-oz. cans,
  lower-sodium beef broth

1. Place meat, vegetables,
and seasonings in slow
cooker. Pour broth over all.
2. Cover. Cook on low 6-8
hours.

Exchange List Values
• Starch 1.0   • Meat, lean 1.0
• Vegetable 2.0

Basic Nutritional Values
• Calories 175   • Cholesterol 38 mg
 (Calories from Fat 29) • Sodium 466 mg
• Total Fat 3 gm   • Total Carb 21 gm
 (Saturated Fat 0.9 gm, • Dietary Fiber 5 gm
 Polyunsat Fat 0.3 gm, • Sugars 6 gm
 Monounsat Fat 1.4 gm) • Protein 16 gm

Pot Roast with Gravy and Vegetables

Irene Klaeger
Inverness, FL

Jan Pembleton
Arlington, TX

Makes 6 servings

Prep. Time: 30 minutes
Cooking Time: 4-10 hours
Ideal slow cooker size: 4-qt.

3-4 lb. bottom round,
  rump, *or* arm roast,
  trimmed of fat
¼ tsp. salt
2-3 tsp. pepper
2 Tbsp. flour
¼ cup cold water
1 tsp. Kitchen Bouquet,
  or gravy browning
  seasoning sauce
1 garlic clove, minced
2 medium onions, cut in
  wedges
4 medium potatoes, cubed,
  unpeeled
2 carrots, quartered
1 green bell pepper, sliced

1. Place roast in slow
cooker. Sprinkle with salt and
pepper.
2. Make paste of flour and
cold water. Stir in Kitchen
Bouquet and spread over
roast.
3. Add garlic, onions,
potatoes, carrots, and green
pepper.
4. Cover. Cook on low 8-10
hours, or high 4-5 hours.
5. Taste and adjust seasonings before serving.

Exchange List Values
• Starch 1.5   • Meat, lean 3.0
• Vegetable 2.0

Basic Nutritional Values
• Calories 336   • Cholesterol 98 mg
 (Calories from Fat 75) • Sodium 577 mg
• Total Fat 8 gm   • Total Carb 28 gm
 (Saturated Fat 2.9 gm, • Dietary Fiber 4 gm
 Polyunsat Fat 0.5 gm, • Sugars 7 gm
 Monounsat Fat 3.4 gm) • Protein 36 gm

"Smothered" Steak

Susan Yoder Graber
Eureka, IL

Makes 6 servings

Prep. Time: 20 minutes
Cooking Time: 8 hours
Ideal slow cooker size: 4-qt.

1½-lb. chuck, *or* round,
  steak, cut into strips,
  trimmed of fat
⅓ cup flour
¼ tsp. pepper
1 large onion, sliced
1 green pepper, sliced
14½-oz. can stewed
  tomatoes
4-oz. can mushrooms,
  drained
2 Tbsp. soy sauce
10-oz. pkg. frozen French-
  style green beans

1. Layer steak in bottom
of slow cooker. Sprinkle with
flour, salt, and pepper. Stir
well to coat steak.
2. Add remaining ingredi-
ents. Mix together gently.
3. Cover. Cook on low 8
hours.
4. Serve over rice.

Variations:

1. Use 8-oz. can tomato sauce instead of stewed tomatoes.

2. Substitute 1 Tbsp. Worcestershire sauce in place of soy sauce.

Mary E. Martin
Goshen, IN

Exchange List Values
- Vegetable 4.0   • Meat, lean 2.0

Basic Nutritional Values
- Calories 222   • Cholesterol 64 mg
  (Calories from Fat 50) • Sodium 613 mg
- Total Fat 6 gm   • Total Carb 19 gm
  (Saturated Fat 1.7 gm, • Dietary Fiber 4 gm
  Polyunsat Fat 0.4 gm,   • Sugars 7 gm
  Monounsat Fat 2.3 gm)   • Protein 25 gm

Veal and Peppers

Irma H. Schoen
Windsor, CT

Makes 4 servings

Prep. Time: 15 minutes
Cooking Time: 4-7 hours
Ideal slow cooker size: 4-qt.

1½ lbs. boneless veal, cubed
3 green bell peppers, quartered
2 onions, thinly sliced
½ lb. fresh mushrooms, sliced
1 tsp. salt
½ tsp. dried basil
2 cloves garlic, minced
28-oz. can tomatoes

1. Combine all ingredients in slow cooker.
2. Cover. Cook on low 7 hours, or on high 4 hours.
3. Serve over rice or noodles.

Variation:

Use boneless, skinless chicken breast instead of veal.

Exchange List Values
- Vegetable 3.0   • Fat 0.5
- Meat, very lean 3.0

Basic Nutritional Values
- Calories 194   • Cholesterol 95 mg
  (Calories from Fat 31) • Sodium 555 mg
- Total Fat 3 gm   • Total Carb 16 gm
  (Saturated Fat 0.9 gm, • Dietary Fiber 4 gm
  Polyunsat Fat 0.5 gm,   • Sugars 9 gm
  Monounsat Fat 1.0 gm)   • Protein 26 gm

Beef and Beans

Robin Schrock
Millersburg, OH

Makes 8 servings

Prep. Time: 20 minutes
Cooking Time: 6-9 hours
Ideal slow cooker size: 4-qt.

1 Tbsp. prepared mustard
1 Tbsp. chili powder
½ tsp. salt
¼ tsp. pepper
1½-lb. boneless round steak, cut into thin slices, trimmed of fat
2 14½-oz. cans diced tomatoes, undrained
1 medium onion, chopped
1 beef bouillon cube, crushed
16-oz. can kidney beans, rinsed and drained

1. Combine mustard, chili powder, salt, and pepper. Add beef slices and toss to coat. Place meat in slow cooker.
2. Add tomatoes, onion, and bouillon.
3. Cover. Cook on low 6-8 hours.
4. Stir in beans. Cook 30 minutes longer.
5. Serve over rice.

Exchange List Values
- Starch 0.5   • Meat, lean 2.0
- Vegetable 1.0

Basic Nutritional Values
- Calories 182   • Cholesterol 48 mg
  (Calories from Fat 40) • Sodium 582 mg
- Total Fat 4 gm   • Total Carb 16 gm
  (Saturated Fat 1.3 gm, • Dietary Fiber 4 gm
  Polyunsat Fat 0.4 gm,   • Sugars 6 gm
  Monounsat Fat 1.8 gm)   • Protein 21 gm

Three-Bean Burrito Bake

Darla Sathre
Baxter, MN

Makes 8 servings

Prep. Time: 20 minutes
Cooking Time: 8-10 hours
Ideal slow cooker size: 4-qt.

1 Tbsp. canola oil
1 onion, chopped
1 green bell pepper,
    chopped
2 garlic cloves, minced
16-oz. can pinto beans,
    drained
16-oz. can kidney beans,
    drained
15-oz. can black beans,
    drained
4-oz. can sliced black
    olives, drained
4-oz. can green chilies
2 15-oz. cans no-added-salt
    diced tomatoes
1 tsp. chili powder
1 tsp. ground cumin
6 6" flour tortillas
1 cup shredded Co-Jack
    cheese
sour cream

1. Sauté onions, green peppers, and garlic in large skillet in oil.
2. Add beans, olives, chilies, tomatoes, chili powder, and cumin.
3. In greased slow cooker, layer ¾ cup vegetables, a tortilla, ⅓ cup cheese. Repeat layers until all those ingredients are used, ending with sauce.

4. Cover. Cook on low 8-10 hours.
5. Serve with dollops of sour cream on individual servings.

Exchange List Values
- Starch 2.5
- Meat, lean 1.0
- Vegetable 2.0
- Fat 1.0

Basic Nutritional Values
- Calories 346
  (Calories from Fat 99)
- Total Fat 11 gm
  (Saturated Fat 3.3 gm,
  Polyunsat Fat 1.5 gm,
  Monounsat Fat 4.8 gm)
- Cholesterol 15 mg
- Sodium 573 mg
- Total Carb 48 gm
- Dietary Fiber 12 gm
- Sugars 8 gm
- Protein 16 gm

Beef Stew Bourguignonne

Jo Haberkamp
Fairbank, IA

Makes 6 servings

Prep. Time: 25 minutes
Cooking Time: 10-12 hours
Ideal slow cooker size: 4-qt.

2 lbs. stewing beef, cut in
    1-inch cubes, trimmed
    of fat
2 Tbsp. canola oil
10¾-oz. can condensed
    golden cream of
    mushroom soup
1 tsp. Worcestershire sauce
⅓ cup dry red wine
½ tsp. dried oregano
¼ tsp. salt
½ tsp. pepper
½ cup chopped onions
½ cup chopped carrots
4-oz. can mushroom
    pieces, drained

½ cup cold water
¼ cup flour

1. Brown meat in oil in saucepan. Transfer to slow cooker.
2. Mix together soup, Worcestershire sauce, wine, oregano, salt and pepper, onions, carrots, and mushrooms. Pour over meat.
3. Cover. Cook on low 10-12 hours.
4. Combine water and flour. Stir into beef mixture. Turn cooker to high.
5. Cook and stir until thickened and bubbly.
6. Serve over noodles.

Exchange List Values
- Carbohydrate 1.0
- Fat 0.5
- Meat, lean 3.0

Basic Nutritional Values
- Calories 266
  (Calories from Fat 106)
- Total Fat 12 gm
  (Saturated Fat 2.5 gm,
  Polyunsat Fat 2.5 gm,
  Monounsat Fat 5.7 gm)
- Cholesterol 77 mg
- Sodium 585 mg
- Total Carb 12 gm
- Dietary Fiber 2 gm
- Sugars 2 gm
- Protein 26 gm

Three-Pepper Steak

Renee Hankins
Narvon, PA

Makes 10 servings

Prep. Time: 15 minutes
Cooking Time: 5-8 hours
Ideal slow cooker size: 4- or 5-qt.

3 bell peppers—one red, one orange, and one yellow pepper (or any combination of colors), cut into ¼"-thick slices
2 garlic cloves, sliced
1 large onion, sliced
1 tsp. ground cumin
½ tsp. dried oregano
1 bay leaf
3-lb. beef flank steak, cut in ¼-½"-thick slices across the grain
salt to taste
14½-oz. can diced tomatoes in juice
jalapeño chilies, sliced, *optional*

1. Place sliced peppers, garlic, onion, cumin, oregano, and bay leaf in slow cooker. Stir gently to mix.
2. Put steak slices on top of vegetable mixture. Season with salt.
3. Spoon tomatoes with juice over top. Sprinkle with jalapeño pepper slices if you wish. Do not stir.
4. Cover. Cook on low 5-8 hours, depending on your slow cooker. Check after 5 hours to see if meat is tender.

If not, continue cooking until tender but not dry.

Tip:
We love this served over noodles, rice, or torn tortillas.

Exchange List Values
• Vegetable 1.0   • Lean Meat 4.0

Basic Nutritional Values
• Calories 220 (Calories from Fat 70)   • Cholesterol 85 mg
• Sodium 135 mg
• Total Fat 8 gm (Saturated Fat 3.0 gm, Polyunsat Fat 0 gm Monounsat Fat 2.5 gm)   • Total Carb 7 gm
• Dietary Fiber 1 gm
• Sugars 3 gm
• Protein 30 gm

Succulent Steak

Betty B. Dennison
Grove City, PA

Makes 4 servings

Prep. Time: 20 minutes
Cooking Time: 9-10 hours
Ideal slow cooker size: 4-qt.

1½-lb. round steak, cut ½-¾-inch thick, trimmed of fat
¼ cup flour
½ tsp. salt
¼ tsp. pepper
¼ tsp. paprika
2 medium onions, sliced
4-oz. can sliced mushrooms, drained
½ cup beef broth

2 tsp. Worcestershire sauce
2 Tbsp. flour
3 Tbsp. water

1. Mix together ¼ cup flour, salt, pepper, and paprika.
2. Cut steak into 5-6 pieces. Dredge steak pieces in seasoned flour until lightly coated.
3. Layer half of onions, half of steak, and half of mushrooms into cooker. Repeat.
4. Combine beef broth and Worcestershire sauce. Pour over mixture in slow cooker.
5. Cover. Cook on low 8-10 hours.
6. Remove steak to serving platter and keep warm. Mix together 2 Tbsp. flour and water. Stir into drippings and cook on high until thickened, about 10 minutes. Pour over steak and serve.

Exchange List Values
• Starch 0.5   • Meat, lean 4.0
• Vegetable 2.0

Basic Nutritional Values
• Calories 295 (Calories from Fat 73)   • Cholesterol 96 mg
• Sodium 601 mg
• Total Fat 8 gm (Saturated Fat 2.6 gm, Polyunsat Fat 0.5 gm, Monounsat Fat 3.4 gm)   • Total Carb 18 gm
• Dietary Fiber 3 gm
• Sugars 6 gm
• Protein 36 gm

You can reduce the amount of salt — or even eliminate it — in many recipes without changing the dish's taste.

Steak Stroganoff

Marie Morucci
Glen Lyon, PA

Makes 6 servings

Prep. Time: 15 minutes
Cooking Time: 3-7 hours
Ideal slow cooker size: 4-qt.

2 Tbsp. flour
½ tsp. garlic powder
½ tsp. pepper
¼ tsp. paprika
1¾-lb. boneless beef round
  steak, trimmed of fat
10¾-oz. can reduced-
  sodium, 98% fat-free
  cream of mushroom
  soup
½ cup water
1 envelope sodium-free
  dried onion soup mix
  (see recipe on page 261)
9-oz. jar sliced mushrooms,
  drained
½ cup fat-free sour cream
1 Tbsp. minced fresh
  parsley

1. Combine flour, garlic
powder, pepper, and paprika
in slow cooker.
2. Cut meat into
1½×½-inch strips. Place in
flour mixture and toss until
meat is well coated.
3. Add mushroom soup,
water, and soup mix. Stir
until well blended.
4. Cover. Cook on high
3-3½ hours, or low 6-7 hours.
5. Stir in mushrooms, sour
cream, and parsley. Cover
and cook on high 10-15
minutes, or until heated
through.

Exchange List Values
• Carbohydrate 1.0 • Meat, lean 3.0

Basic Nutritional Values
• Calories 256   • Cholesterol 77 mg
  (Calories from Fat 66) • Sodium 390 mg
• Total Fat 7 gm   • Total Carb 17 gm
  (Saturated Fat 2.4 gm, • Dietary Fiber 2 gm
  Polyunsat Fat 0.5 gm, • Sugars 5 gm
  Monounsat Fat 2.8 gm) • Protein 29 gm

Garlic Beef Stroganoff

Sharon Miller
Holmesville, OH

Makes 6 servings

Prep. Time: 20 minutes
Cooking Time: 7-8 hours
Ideal slow cooker size: 4- or 5-qt.

2 tsp. sodium-free beef
  bouillon powder
2 4½-oz. jars sliced
  mushrooms, drained
  with juice reserved
1 cup mushroom juice,
  with boiling water added
  to make a full cup
10¾-oz. can 98% fat-free,
  lower-sodium cream of
  mushroom soup
1 large onion, chopped
3 garlic cloves, minced
1 Tbsp. Worcestershire
  sauce
1½ lbs. boneless round
  steak, cut into thin
  strips, trimmed of fat
2 Tbsp. canola oil
6-oz. fat-free cream cheese,
  cubed and softened

1. Dissolve bouillon in
mushroom juice and water in

slow cooker.
2. Add soup, mushrooms,
onion, garlic, and Worcestershire sauce.
3. Sauté beef in oil in skillet. Transfer to slow cooker
and stir into sauce.
4. Cover. Cook on low 7-8
hours. Turn off heat.
5. Stir in cream cheese
until smooth.
6. Serve over noodles.

Exchange List Values
• Carbohydrate 0.5 • Meat, lean 2.0
• Vegetable 1.0   • Fat 0.5

Basic Nutritional Values
• Calories 202   • Cholesterol 51 mg
  (Calories from Fat 73) • Sodium 474 mg
• Total Fat 8 gm   • Total Carb 10 gm
  (Saturated Fat 1.8 gm, • Dietary Fiber 2 gm
  Polyunsat Fat 1.4 gm, • Sugars 4 gm
  Monounsat Fat 3.9 gm) • Protein 21 gm

Machaca Beef

Jeanne Allen
Rye, CO

Makes 12 servings

Prep. Time: 15 minutes
Cooking Time: 10-12 hours
Ideal slow cooker size: 4-qt.

1½-lb. beef roast
1 large onion, sliced
4-oz. can chopped green
  chilies
2 beef bouillon cubes
1½ tsp. dry mustard
½ tsp. garlic powder
1 tsp. seasoning salt
½ tsp. pepper
1 cup salsa

1. Combine all ingredients
except salsa in slow cooker.
Add just enough water to cover.

2. Cover cooker and cook
on low 10-12 hours, or until
beef is tender. Drain and
reserve liquid.

3. Shred beef using two
forks to pull it apart.

4. Combine beef, salsa, and
enough of the reserved liquid
to make desired consistency.

5. Use this filling for burritos, chalupas, quesadillas,
or tacos.

Exchange List Values
• Meat, lean 1.0

Basic Nutritional Values
• Calories 69
(Calories from Fat 20)
• Total Fat 2 gm
(Saturated Fat 0.7 gm,
Polyunsat Fat 0.1 gm,
Monounsat Fat 0.9 gm)
• Cholesterol 24 mg
• Sodium 392 mg
• Total Carb 3 gm
• Dietary Fiber 1 gm
• Sugars 2 gm
• Protein 9 gm

Apple and Onion Beef Pot Roast

Betty K. Drescher
Quakertown, PA

Makes 8 servings

Prep. Time: 25 minutes
Cooking Time: 5-6 hours
Ideal slow cooker size: 4-qt.

3-lb. boneless beef roast,
  cut in half, trimmed
  of fat
2 Tbsp. canola oil
1 cup water
1 tsp. seasoning salt
½ tsp. soy sauce
½ tsp. Worcestershire
  sauce
¼ tsp. garlic powder
1 large tart apple,
  quartered
1 large onion, sliced
2 Tbsp. cornstarch
2 Tbsp. water

1. Brown roast on all sides
in oil in skillet. Transfer to
slow cooker.

2. Add water to skillet to
loosen browned bits. Pour
over roast.

3. Sprinkle with seasoning
salt, soy sauce, Worces-
tershire sauce, and garlic
powder.

4. Top with apple and
onion.

5. Cover. Cook on low 5-6
hours.

6. Remove roast and
onion. Discard apple. Let
stand 15 minutes.

7. To make gravy, pour
juices from roast into
saucepan and simmer until
reduced to 2 cups.

8. Combine cornstarch
and water until smooth in
small bowl. Stir into beef
broth.

9. Bring to boil. Cook
and stir for 2 minutes until
thickened.

10. Slice pot roast and
serve with gravy.

Exchange List Values
• Carbohydrate 0.5   • Meat, lean 3.0

Basic Nutritional Values
• Calories 208
(Calories from Fat 85)
• Total Fat 9 gm
(Saturated Fat 2.4 gm,
Polyunsat Fat 1.3 gm,
Monounsat Fat 4.6 gm)
• Cholesterol 73 mg
• Sodium 265 mg
• Total Carb 5 gm
• Dietary Fiber 1 gm
• Sugars 2 gm
• Protein 24 gm

All-Day Roast

Moreen Weaver
Bath, NY

Makes 10 servings

Prep. Time: 20 minutes
Cooking Time: 7-9 hours
Ideal slow-cooker size: 6 qt.

3 carrots, cut in 1" chunks
4 medium potatoes, cut in
   1" chunks
1 lb. frozen *or* fresh green
   beans
1 large onion, cut in wedges
1½ cups water
3-lb. beef roast, visible fat
   removed
2 cloves garlic, minced
salt to taste
pepper to taste
10¾-oz. can cream of
   mushroom soup
2 Tbsp. Worcestershire
   sauce
1 recipe Onion Soup Mix,
   Salt-Free (see recipe on
   page 261)

1. Place vegetables and
water into slow cooker.
2. Place beef roast on
top of vegetables.
3. Sprinkle
garlic over meat,
followed by salt
and pepper to
taste.
3. Spoon
cream of
mushroom soup
over seasoned
meat.
4. Gently pour
Worcestershire sauce
over soup.

5. Sprinkle with dry onion
soup mix.
6. Cover. Cook on high 5-6
hours.
7. Reset temperature to
low. Continue cooking 2-3
more hours, or until vegetables and meat are fork-tender
but not dry or mushy.

Exchange List Values
- Starch 1.0
- Vegetable 2.0
- Lean Meat 3.0
- Fat 0.5

Basic Nutritional Values
- Calories 290 (Calories from Fat 70)
- Total Fat 8 gm (Saturated Fat 3.0 gm, Polyunsat Fat 1.0 gm, Monounsat Fat 3.0 gm)
- Cholesterol 75 mg
- Sodium 340 mg
- Total Carb 26 gm
- Dietary Fiber 4 gm
- Sugars 5 gm
- Protein 29 gm

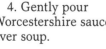

Roast

Tracey Yohn
Harrisburg, PA

Makes 6 servings

Prep. Time: 15 minutes
Cooking Time: 5-12 hours
Ideal slow cooker size: 4-qt.

2 lb. shoulder roast,
   trimmed of fat
1 tsp. pepper
1 tsp. garlic salt
1 small onion, sliced in
   rings
1 cup boiling water
1 beef bouillon cube

1. Place roast in slow
cooker. Sprinkle with pepper,
and garlic salt. Place onion
rings on top.
2. Dissolve bouillon cube
in water. Pour over roast.
3. Cover. Cook on low
10-12 hours, or on high 5-6
hours.

Exchange List Values
- Meat, lean 3.0

Basic Nutritional Values
- Calories 148 (Calories from Fat 49)
- Total Fat 5 gm (Saturated Fat 1.9 gm, Polyunsat Fat 0.2 gm, Monounsat Fat 2.3 gm)
- Cholesterol 65 mg
- Sodium 407 mg
- Total Carb 2 gm
- Dietary Fiber 0 gm
- Sugars 1 gm
- Protein 22 gm

Savory Sweet Roast

Martha Ann Auker
Landisburg, PA

Makes 8 servings

Prep. Time: 20 minutes
Cooking Time: 12-16 hours
Ideal slow cooker size: 4-qt.

3-lb. blade, *or* chuck, roast, trimmed of fat
2 Tbsp. canola oil
1 onion, chopped
10¾-oz. can reduced-sodium, 99% fat-free cream of mushroom soup
½ cup water
¼ cup sugar
¼ cup vinegar
¾ tsp. salt
1 tsp. prepared mustard
1 tsp. Worcestershire sauce

1. Brown meat in oil on both sides in saucepan. Put in slow cooker.
2. Blend together remaining ingredients. Pour over meat.
3. Cover. Cook on low 12-16 hours.

Exchange List Values
• Carbohydrate 1.0 • Meat, lean 3.0

Basic Nutritional Values
• Calories 241
(Calories from Fat 92)
• Total Fat 10 gm
(Saturated Fat 2.7 gm,
Polyunsat Fat 1.4 gm,
Monounsat Fat 4.7 gm)
• Cholesterol 74 mg
• Sodium 424 mg
• Total Carb 11 gm
• Dietary Fiber 0 gm
• Sugars 8 gm
• Protein 25 gm

Dilled Pot Roast

C.J. Slagle
Roann, IN

Makes 6 servings

Prep. Time: 15 minutes
Cooking Time: 7-9 hours
Ideal slow cooker size: 4-qt.

3-lb. beef pot roast, trimmed of fat
¾ tsp. salt
¼ tsp. pepper
2 tsp. dried dillweed, *divided*
¾ cup water, *divided*
1 Tbsp. vinegar
3 Tbsp. flour
1 cup fat-free sour cream

1. Sprinkle both sides of meat with salt, pepper, and 1 tsp. dill. Place in slow cooker. Add ¼ cup water and vinegar.
2. Cover. Cook on low 7-9 hours, or until tender. Remove meat from pot. Turn to high.
3. Dissolve flour in ½ cup water. Stir into meat drippings. Stir in additional 1 tsp. dill. Cook on high 5 minutes. Stir in sour cream. Cook on high another 5 minutes.
4. Slice meat and serve with sour cream sauce over top.

Exchange List Values
• Carbohydrate 0.5 • Meat, lean 4.0

Basic Nutritional Values
• Calories 260
(Calories from Fat 73)
• Total Fat 8 gm
(Saturated Fat 2.9 gm,
Polyunsat Fat 0.3 gm,
Monounsat Fat 3.4 gm)
• Cholesterol 101 mg
• Sodium 403 mg
• Total Carb 10 gm
• Dietary Fiber 0 gm
• Sugars 3 gm
• Protein 34 gm

In addition to your regular doctor, have someone—a certified diabetes educator, nurse practitioner, or nurse case manager—whom you can contact on short notice to discuss problems or questions that come up, such as unexplained high blood sugars or sudden illness.

Beef Roast with Mushroom Barley

Sue Hamilton
Minooka, IL

Makes 6 servings

Prep. Time: 10 minutes
Cooking Time: 6-8 hours
Ideal slow-cooker size: 6 qt.

1 cup pearl barley (not quick-cook)
½ cup onion, diced
6½-oz. can mushrooms, undrained
1 tsp. minced garlic
1 tsp. Italian seasoning
¼ tsp. black pepper
2-lb. beef chuck roast, visible fat removed
1¾ cups beef broth

1. Put barley, onion, mushrooms with liquid, and garlic in slow cooker.
2. Sprinkle seasoning and pepper over top.
3. Add roast. Pour broth over all.
4. Cover. Cook 6-8 hours on low, or until meat is fork-tender and barley is also tender.

Tip:
Serve this with mashed potatoes. They'll benefit from the delicious broth in this dish.

Exchange List Values
• Starch 2.0   • Lean Meat 3.0

Basic Nutritional Values
• Calories 275   • Cholesterol 65 mg
  (Calories from Fat 45)   • Sodium 395 mg
• Total Fat 5 gm   • Total Carb 29 gm
  (Saturated Fat 2.0 gm,   • Dietary Fiber 6 gm
  Polyunsat Fat 0 gm   • Sugars 1 gm
  Monounsat Fat 2.0 gm)   • Protein 26 gm

Hungarian Goulash

Audrey Romonosky
Austin, TX

Makes 6 servings

Prep. Time: 20 minutes
Cooking Time: 8¼ hours
Ideal slow cooker size: 4-qt.

2 lbs. beef chuck, cubed, trimmed of fat
1 medium onion, sliced
½ tsp. garlic powder
½ cup ketchup
2 Tbsp. Worcestershire sauce
1 Tbsp. brown sugar
¼ tsp. salt
2 tsp. paprika
½ tsp. dry mustard
1 cup cold water
¼ cup flour
½ cup water

1. Place meat in slow cooker. Add onion.
2. Combine garlic powder, ketchup, Worcestershire sauce, brown sugar, salt, paprika, mustard, and 1 cup water. Pour over meat.
3. Cover. Cook on low 8 hours.
4. Dissolve flour in ½ cup water. Stir into meat mixture.

Cook on high until thickened, about 10 minutes.
5. Serve over noodles.

Exchange List Values
• Carbohydrate 1.0   • Meat, lean 2.0

Basic Nutritional Values
• Calories 207   • Cholesterol 65 mg
  (Calories from Fat 52)   • Sodium 444 mg
• Total Fat 6 gm   • Total Carb 15 gm
  (Saturated Fat 2.0 gm,   • Dietary Fiber 1 gm
  Polyunsat Fat 0.3 gm,   • Sugars 7 gm
  Monounsat Fat 2.3 gm)   • Protein 23 gm

Beef Burgundy

Jacqueline Stefl
East Bethany, NY

Makes 6 servings

Prep. Time: 20 minutes
Cooking Time: 8-10 hours
Ideal slow cooker size: 4-qt.

5 medium onions, thinly
    sliced
2 lbs. stewing meat, cubed,
    trimmed of fat
1½ Tbsp. flour
½ lb. fresh mushrooms,
    sliced
1 tsp. salt
¼ tsp. dried marjoram
¼ tsp. dried thyme
⅛ tsp. pepper
¾ cup beef broth
1½ cups burgundy wine

1. Place onions in slow
cooker.
2. Dredge meat in flour.
Put in slow cooker.
3. Add mushrooms, salt,
marjoram, thyme, and
pepper.
4. Pour in broth and wine.
5. Cover. Cook 8-10 hours
on low.
6. Serve over cooked
noodles.

Exchange List Values
• Vegetable 3.0   • Meat, lean 3.0

Basic Nutritional Values
• Calories 219   • Cholesterol 75 mg
(Calories from Fat 54)   • Sodium 576 mg
• Total Fat 6 gm   • Total Carb 14 gm
(Saturated Fat 1.9 gm,   • Dietary Fiber 2 gm
Polyunsat Fat 0.4 gm,   • Sugars 5 gm
Monounsat Fat 2.8 gm)   • Protein 26 gm

Chinese Pot Roast

Marsha Sabus
Fallbrook, CA

Makes 6 servings

Prep. Time: 20 minutes
Cooking Time: 8-10 hours
Ideal slow cooker size: 4-qt.

3-lb. boneless beef pot
    roast, trimmed of fat
2 Tbsp. flour
1 Tbsp. canola oil
2 large onions, chopped
¼ cup light soy sauce
¼ cup water
½ tsp. ground ginger

1. Dip roast in flour and
brown on both sides in oil
in saucepan. Place in slow
cooker.
2. Top with onions.
3. Combine soy sauce,
water, and ginger. Pour over
meat.
4. Cover. Cook on high 10
minutes. Reduce heat to low
and cook 8-10 hours.
5. Slice and serve with rice.

Exchange List Values
• Carbohydrate 0.5   • Meat, lean 4.0

Basic Nutritional Values
• Calories 272   • Cholesterol 98 mg
(Calories from Fat 94)   • Sodium 446 mg
• Total Fat 10 gm   • Total Carb 9 gm
(Saturated Fat 3.1 gm,   • Dietary Fiber 1 gm
Polyunsat Fat 1.1 gm,   • Sugars 4 gm
Monounsat Fat 4.7 gm)   • Protein 34 gm

Wine Tender Roast

Rose Hankins
Stevensville, MD

Makes 10 servings

Prep. Time: 15 minutes
Cooking Time: 8-10 hours
Ideal slow cooker size: 4- or 5-qt.

2½-lb. chuck roast
1 cup thinly sliced onion
½ cup chopped apple,
    peeled *or* unpeeled
3 cloves garlic, chopped
1 cup red wine
salt and pepper

1. Put roast in slow cooker.
Layer onions, apples, and
garlic on top of roast.
2. Carefully pour wine
over roast without disturbing
its toppings.
3. Sprinkle with salt and
pepper.
4. Cover. Cook on low 8-10
hours, or until meat is tender
but not dry.

Exchange List Values
• Lean Meat 4.0

Basic Nutritional Values
• Calories 160   • Cholesterol 75 mg
(Calories from Fat 45)   • Sodium 85 mg
• Total Fat 5 gm   • Total Carb 2 gm
(Saturated Fat 2.0 gm,   • Dietary Fiber 0 gm
Polyunsat Fat 0 gm   • Sugars 1 gm
Monounsat Fat 2.0 gm)   • Protein 25 gm

Chuck Wagon Beef

Charlotte Bull
Cassville, MO

Makes 10 servings

Prep. Time: 20 minutes
Cooking Time: 8-10 hours
Ideal slow cooker size: 4-qt.

4-lb. boneless chuck roast,
   trimmed of fat
1 tsp. garlic salt
¼ tsp. black pepper
2 Tbsp. canola oil
6 garlic cloves, minced
1 large onion, sliced
1 cup water
1 bouillon cube
2 tsp. instant coffee
1 bay leaf, *or* 1 Tbsp.
   mixed Italian herbs
3 Tbsp. cold water
2 Tbsp. cornstarch

1. Sprinkle roast with garlic
salt and pepper. Brown on all
sides in oil in saucepan. Place
in slow cooker.

2. Sauté garlic and onion in
meat drippings in saucepan.

3. Add water, bouillon
cube, and coffee. Cook over
low heat for several minutes,
stirring until drippings
loosen. Pour over meat in
cooker.

4. Add bay leaf or herbs.

5. Cover. Cook on low 8-10
hours, or until very tender.
Remove bay leaf and discard.
Remove meat to serving
platter and keep warm.

6. Mix water and corn-
starch together until paste
forms. Stir into hot liquid and
onions in cooker.

7. Cover. Cook 10 minutes
on high or until thickened.

8. Slice meat and serve
with gravy over top or on the
side.

Exchange List Values
- Vegetable 1.0
- Meat, lean 3.0

Basic Nutritional Values
- Calories 211
  (Calories from Fat 83)
- Total Fat 9 gm
  (Saturated Fat 2.5 gm,
  Polyunsat Fat 1.1 gm,
  Monounsat Fat 4.3 gm)
- Cholesterol 78 mg
- Sodium 271 mg
- Total Carb 4 gm
- Dietary Fiber 1 gm
- Sugars 2 gm
- Protein 26 gm

French Dip Roast

Patti Boston
Newark, OH

Makes 8 servings

Prep. Time: 15 minutes
Cooking Time: 5-12 hours
Ideal slow cooker size: 4-qt.

1 large onion, sliced
3-lb. beef bottom roast,
   trimmed of fat
½ cup dry white wine, *or*
   water
½ of 1-oz. pkg. dry au jus
   gravy mix
2 cups lower sodium 100%
   fat-free beef broth

1. Place onion in slow
cooker. Add roast.

2. Combine wine and
gravy mix. Pour over roast.

3. Add enough broth to
cover roast.

4. Cover. Cook on high 5-6
hours, or low 10-12 hours.

5. Remove meat from
liquid. Let stand 5 minutes
before slicing thinly across
grain.

Exchange List Values
- Meat, lean 3.0

Basic Nutritional Values
- Calories 177
  (Calories from Fat 55)
- Total Fat 6 gm
  (Saturated Fat 2.2 gm,
  Polyunsat Fat 0.3 gm,
  Monounsat Fat 2.5 gm)
- Cholesterol 74 mg
- Sodium 376 mg
- Total Carb 3 gm
- Dietary Fiber 1 gm
- Sugars 2 gm
- Protein 25 gm

If you prefer creamy salad dressing, try diluting it with a little vinegar or lemon juice. You'll eat fewer calories, but still have a brightly flavored salad.

Dripped Beef

Mitzi McGlynchey
Downingtown, PA

Makes 8 servings

Prep. Time: 10 minutes
Cooking Time: 6-7 hours
Ideal slow cooker size: 4-qt.

3 lb. chuck roast, trimmed of fat
½ tsp. salt
1 tsp. seasoned salt
1 tsp. white pepper
1 Tbsp. rosemary
1 Tbsp. dried oregano
1 Tbsp. garlic powder
1 cup water

1. Combine all ingredients in slow cooker.
2. Cover. Cook on low 6-7 hours.
3. Shred meat using two forks. Strain liquid and return liquid and meat to slow cooker. Serve meat and au jus over mashed potatoes, noodles, or rice.

Exchange List Values
• Meat, lean 3.0

Basic Nutritional Values
• Calories 165   • Cholesterol 73 mg
(Calories from Fat 56)   • Sodium 384 mg
• Total Fat 6 gm   • Total Carb 2 gm
(Saturated Fat 2.2 gm,   • Dietary Fiber 1 gm
Polyunsat Fat 0.3 gm,   • Sugars 0 gm
Monounsat Fat 2.5 gm)   • Protein 24 gm

Old World Sauerbraten

C.J. Slagle
Roann, IN
Angeline Lang
Greeley, CO

Makes 8 servings

Marinating Time: 24-36 hours
Prep. Time: 15 minutes
Cooking Time: 6-8 hours
Ideal slow cooker size: 4-qt.

3½-lb. beef rump roast, trimmed of fat
1 cup water
1 cup vinegar
1 lemon, sliced
10 whole cloves
1 large onion, sliced
4 bay leaves
6 whole peppercorns
1 Tbsp. salt
2 Tbsp. sugar
12 gingersnaps, crumbled

1. Place meat in deep ceramic or glass bowl.
2. Combine water, vinegar, lemon, cloves, onion, bay leaves, peppercorns, salt, and sugar. Pour over meat. Cover and refrigerate 24-36 hours. Turn meat several times during marinating.
3. Place beef in slow cooker. Pour 1 cup marinade over meat.
4. Cover. Cook on low 6-8 hours. Remove meat.
5. Strain meat juices and return to pot. Turn to high. Stir in gingersnaps. Cover and cook on high 10-14 minutes. Slice meat. Pour finished sauce over meat.

Exchange List Values
• Carbohydrate 0.5   • Meat, lean 4.0

Basic Nutritional Values
• Calories 235   • Cholesterol 86 mg
(Calories from Fat 73)   • Sodium 416 mg
• Total Fat 8 gm   • Total Carb 10 gm
(Saturated Fat 2.6 gm,   • Dietary Fiber 0 gm
Polyunsat Fat 0.4 gm,   • Sugars 4 gm
Monounsat Fat 3.5 gm)   • Protein 29 gm

Sour Beef

Rosanne Hankins
Stevensville, MD

Makes 8 servings

Prep. Time: 10 minutes
Cooking Time: 8-10 hours
Ideal slow cooker size: 4-qt.

3 lb. pot roast, trimmed of fat
⅓ cup cider vinegar
1 large onion, sliced
3 bay leaves
½ tsp. salt
¼ tsp. ground cloves
¼ tsp. garlic powder

1. Place roast in slow cooker. Add remaining ingredients.
2. Cover. Cook on low 8-10 hours.

Exchange List Values
• Meat, lean 3.0

Basic Nutritional Values
• Calories 169   • Cholesterol 73 mg
(Calories from Fat 55)   • Sodium 194 mg
• Total Fat 6 gm   • Total Carb 3 gm
(Saturated Fat 2.2 gm,   • Dietary Fiber 1 gm
Polyunsat Fat 0.3 gm,   • Sugars 2 gm
Monounsat Fat 2.5 gm)   • Protein 24 gm

Chili and Cheese on Rice

Dale and Shari Mast
Harrisonburg, VA

Makes 6 servings

Prep. Time: 15 minutes
Cooking Time: 4 hours
Ideal slow cooker size: 4-qt.

1 lb. extra-lean ground beef
1 medium onion, diced
1 tsp. dried basil
1 tsp. dried oregano
16-oz. can light red kidney beans
15½-oz. can chili beans
1½ cups stewed tomatoes, drained
2 cups cooked rice
6 Tbsp. fat-free grated cheddar cheese

1. Brown ground beef and onion in skillet. Drain. Season with basil and oregano.
2. Combine all ingredients except rice and cheese in slow cooker.
3. Cover. Cook on low 4 hours.
4. Serve over cooked rice. Top with cheese.

Exchange List Values
- Starch 2.5
- Meat, lean 2.0
- Vegetable 2.0
- Fat 0.5

Basic Nutritional Values
- Calories 371
- Cholesterol 49 mg
- (Calories from Fat 78)
- Sodium 745 mg
- Total Fat 9 gm
- Total Carb 46 gm
- (Saturated Fat 3.2 gm,
- Dietary Fiber 9 gm
- Polyunsat Fat 0.6 gm,
- Sugars 7 gm
- Monounsat Fat 3.6 gm)
- Protein 26 gm

Spanish Rice

Loretta Krahn
Mt. Lake, MN

Makes 8 servings

Prep. Time: 20 minutes
Cooking Time: 6-10 hours
Ideal slow cooker size: 4- or 5-qt.

1¾ lbs. 90%-lean ground beef, browned
2 medium onions, chopped
2 medium green peppers, chopped
28-oz. can tomatoes
8-oz. can tomato sauce
1½ cups water
2½ tsp. chili powder
½ tsp. salt
2 tsp. Worcestershire sauce
1½ cups rice, uncooked

1. Combine all ingredients in slow cooker.
2. Cover. Cook on low 8-10 hours, or high 6 hours.

Exchange List Values
- Starch 2.0
- Meat, lean 2.0
- Vegetable 2.0
- Fat 0.5

Basic Nutritional Values
- Calories 335
- Cholesterol 60 mg
- (Calories from Fat 79)
- Sodium 550 mg
- Total Fat 9 gm
- Total Carb 40 gm
- (Saturated Fat 3.3 gm,
- Dietary Fiber 3 gm
- Polyunsat Fat 0.6 gm,
- Sugars 8 gm
- Monounsat Fat 3.7 gm)
- Protein 24 gm

Green Chili Stew

Jeanne Allen
Rye, CO

Makes 8 servings

Prep. Time: 25 minutes
Cooking Time: 4-6 hours
Ideal slow cooker size: 4-qt.

2 Tbsp. oil
2 garlic cloves, minced
1 large onion, diced
1 lb. extra-lean ground sirloin
⅓ lb. ground pork
3 cups reduced-sodium chicken broth
2 cups water
2 4-oz. cans diced green chilies
4 large potatoes, diced
10-oz. pkg. frozen corn
1 tsp. black pepper
1 tsp. crushed dried oregano
½ tsp. ground cumin
½ tsp. salt

1. Brown onion, garlic, sirloin, and pork in oil in skillet. Cook until meat is no longer pink. Drain.
2. Combine all ingredients in slow cooker.
3. Cover. Cook on low 4-6 hours, or until potatoes are soft.

Exchange List Values
- Starch 2.0
- Meat, lean 2.0
- Vegetable 1.0
- Fat 0.5

Basic Nutritional Values

- Calories 309
  (Calories from Fat 99)
- Total Fat 11 gm
  (Saturated Fat 3.1 gm,
  Polyunsat Fat 1.6 gm,
  Monounsat Fat 5.3 gm)
- Cholesterol 47 mg
- Sodium 529 mg
- Total Carb 33 gm
- Dietary Fiber 5 gm
- Sugars 5 gm
- Protein 20 gm

Note:
Excellent served with warm tortillas or corn bread.

Beef and Lentils

Esther Porter
Minneapolis, MN

Makes 12 servings

Prep. Time: 30 minutes
Cooking Time: 6-8 hours
Ideal slow cooker size: 4- or 5-qt.

1 medium onion
3 whole cloves
5 cups water
1 lb. dry lentils
1 tsp. salt
1 bay leaf
1 lb. (or less) ground beef,
browned and drained
½ cup ketchup
¼ cup molasses
2 Tbsp. brown sugar
1 tsp. dry mustard
¼ tsp. Worcestershire sauce
1 medium onion, finely
chopped

1. Stick cloves into whole onion. Set aside.
2. In large saucepan, combine water, lentils, salt, bay leaf, and whole onion with cloves. Simmer 30 minutes.
3. Meanwhile, combine all remaining ingredients in slow cooker. Stir in simmered ingredients from saucepan. Add additional water if mixture seems dry.
4. Cover. Cook on low 6 hours and check to see if the lentils are tender. If not, cook an additional hour and check again. Repeat if needed.

Exchange List Values

- Starch 1.5
- Carbohydrate 0.5
- Vegetable 1.0
- Meat, lean 1.0

Basic Nutritional Values

- Calories 230
  (Calories from Fat 39)
- Total Fat 4 gm
  (Saturated Fat 1.5 gm,
  Polyunsat Fat 0.3 gm,
  Monounsat Fat 1.7 gm)
- Cholesterol 22 mg
- Sodium 342 mg
- Total Carb 32 gm
- Dietary Fiber 9 gm
- Sugars 11 gm
- Protein 17 gm

Note:
Freezes well.

Variation:
Top with sour cream and/or salsa when serving.

Cowboy Casserole

Lori Berezovsky
Salina, KS

Makes 6 servings

Prep. Time: 25 minutes
Cooking Time: 5-6 hours
Ideal slow cooker size: 4-qt.

1 medium onion, chopped
1¼ lbs. 90%-lean ground beef, browned, drained, and patted dry
6 medium potatoes, sliced, unpeeled
1 clove garlic, minced
16-oz. can kidney beans
15-oz. can diced tomatoes mixed with 2 Tbsp. flour, or 10¾-oz. can tomato soup
¼ tsp. salt
¼ tsp. pepper

1. Layer onions, ground beef, potatoes, garlic, and beans in slow cooker.
2. Spread tomatoes or soup over all. Sprinkle with salt and pepper.
3. Cover. Cook on low 5-6 hours, or until potatoes are tender.

Exchange List Values

- Starch 2.5
- Vegetable 2.0
- Meat, lean 2.0

Basic Nutritional Values

- Calories 373
  (Calories from Fat 73)
- Total Fat 8 gm
  (Saturated Fat 3.2 gm,
  Polyunsat Fat 0.6 gm,
  Monounsat Fat 3.4 gm)
- Cholesterol 57 mg
- Sodium 567 mg
- Total Carb 48 gm
- Dietary Fiber 7 gm
- Sugars 8 gm
- Protein 27 gm

Try to use healthy oils instead of solid fats when cooking: scramble an egg in olive oil instead of margarine.

Meal-in-One-Casserole

Elizabeth Yoder
Millersburg, OH
Marcella Stalter
Flanagan, IL

Makes 8 servings

Prep. Time: 20 minutes
Cooking Time: 3 hours
Ideal slow cooker size: 4-qt.

1 lb. ground beef
1 medium onion, chopped
1 medium green pepper, chopped
15¼-oz. can whole kernel corn, drained
4-oz. can mushrooms, drained
¼ tsp. pepper
11-oz. jar salsa
5 cups uncooked medium egg noodles
28-oz. can no-added-salt diced tomatoes, undrained
1 cup shredded fat-free cheddar cheese

1. Cook beef and onion in saucepan over medium heat until meat is no longer pink. Drain. Transfer to slow cooker.

2. Top with green pepper, corn, and mushrooms. Sprinkle with pepper. Pour salsa over mushrooms.

3. Cover and cook on low 3 hours.

4. Cook noodles according to package in separate pan.

5. Drain and add to slow cooker after mixture in cooker has cooked for 3 hours. Top with tomatoes. Sprinkle with cheese.

Exchange List Values
- Starch 1.5
- Meat, lean 2.0
- Vegetable 2.0

Basic Nutritional Values
- Calories 282
  (Calories from Fat 67)
- Total Fat 7 gm
  (Saturated Fat 2.7 gm,
  Polyunsat Fat 0.8 gm,
  Monounsat Fat 2.9 gm)
- Cholesterol 58 mg
- Sodium 393 mg
- Total Carb 34 gm
- Dietary Fiber 4 gm
- Sugars 8 gm
- Protein 21 gm

Mary Ellen's Barbecued Meatballs

Mary Ellen Wilcox
Scatia, NY

*Makes about 60 small meatballs
(10 servings)*

Prep. Time: 40 minutes
Cooking Time: 5 hours
Ideal slow cooker size: 4-qt.

Meatballs:
¾ lb. ground beef
¾ cup bread crumbs
1½ Tbsp. minced onion
½ tsp. horseradish
3 drops Tabasco sauce
2 eggs, beaten
¼ tsp. salt
½ tsp. pepper
1 Tbsp. canola oil

Sauce:
¾ cup ketchup
½ cup water
¼ cup cider vinegar
2 Tbsp. brown sugar
1 Tbsp. minced onion
2 tsp. horseradish
1 tsp. dry mustard
3 drops Tabasco
dash pepper

1. Combine all meatball ingredients except canola oil. Shape into ¾-inch balls. Brown in oil in skillet. Place in slow cooker.

2. Combine all sauce ingredients. Pour over meatballs.

3. Cover. Cook on low 5 hours.

Exchange List Values
- Starch 0.5
- Carbohydrate 0.5
- Meat, lean 1.0
- Fat 0.5

Basic Nutritional Values
- Calories 148
  (Calories from Fat 57)
- Total Fat 6 gm
  (Saturated Fat 1.8 gm,
  Polyunsat Fat 0.8 gm,
  Monounsat Fat 2.8 gm)
- Cholesterol 63 mg
- Sodium 378 mg
- Total Carb 14 gm
- Dietary Fiber 1 gm
- Sugars 6 gm
- Protein 9 gm

Make exercise fun — do something silly today.

Cranberry Meatballs

Char Hagner
Montague, MI

Makes 30 servings, 2 meatballs per serving

Prep. Time: 30 minutes
Baking Time: 30 minutes
Cooking Time: 2 hours
Ideal slow cooker size: 2-qt.

Meatballs
2 lbs. 90%-lean ground beef
⅓ cup parsley flakes
2 Tbsp. soy sauce
½ tsp. garlic powder
2 Tbsp. minced onion
1 cup cornflake crumbs
2 eggs
½ cup ketchup

Sauce
14-oz. can jellied cranberry sauce
12-oz. bottle chili sauce
2 Tbsp. brown sugar
1 Tbsp. lemon juice

1. In a large mixing bowl, combine meatball ingredients until well mixed.
2. Form into 50-60 meatballs and put in lightly greased 9×13 baking pan.
3. Bake at 350° for about 30 minutes, or until meatballs are cooked through. (Cut one open to test.)
4. While meatballs are baking, combine sauce ingredients in saucepan. Heat over low heat until cranberry sauce and brown sugar melt.

Stir frequently.
5. Place baked meatballs in slow cooker. Pour sauce over meatballs, making sure that all are covered in sauce if you've layered them into the cooker.
6. Cover. Cook on low 2 hours, or until sauce is bubbly.
7. Turn slow cooker to Warm and serve with toothpicks.

Exchange List Values
- Carbohydrate 1.0 • Lean Meat 1.0

Basic Nutritional Values
- Calories 105 • Cholesterol 30 mg
  (Calories from Fat 25) • Sodium 310 mg
- Total Fat 3 gm • Total Carb 12 gm
  (Saturated Fat 1.0 gm, • Dietary Fiber 1 gm
  Polyunsat Fat 0 gm • Sugars 7 gm
  Monounsat Fat 1.0 gm) • Protein 7 gm

Swedish Meatballs

Zona Mae Bontrager
Kokomo, IN

Makes 12 servings

Prep. Time: 40 minutes
Cooking Time: 4½-5¼ hours
Ideal slow cooker size: 4-qt.

¾ lb. ground beef
½ lb. ground pork
½ cup minced onions
¾ cup fine dry bread crumbs
1 Tbsp. minced parsley
1 tsp. salt
⅛ tsp. pepper
½ tsp. garlic powder
1 Tbsp. Worcestershire sauce

1 egg
½ cup fat-free milk
2 Tbsp. canola oil

Gravy:
¼ cup flour
¼ tsp. salt
¼ tsp. garlic powder
⅛ tsp. pepper
1 tsp. paprika
2 cups boiling water
¾ cup fat-free sour cream

1. Combine meats, onions, bread crumbs, parsley, salt, pepper, garlic powder, Worcestershire sauce, egg, and milk.
2. Shape into balls the size of a walnut. Brown in oil in skillet. Reserve drippings, and place meatballs in slow cooker.
3. Cover. Cook on high 10-15 minutes.
4. Stir flour, salt, garlic powder, pepper, and paprika into hot drippings in skillet. Stir in water and sour cream. Pour over meatballs.
5. Cover. Reduce heat to low. Cook 4-5 hours.
6. Serve over rice or noodles.

Exchange List Values
- Starch 1.0 • Fat 1.0
- Meat, lean 1.0

Basic Nutritional Values
- Calories 168 • Cholesterol 48 mg
  (Calories from Fat 78) • Sodium 368 mg
- Total Fat 9 gm • Total Carb 11 gm
  (Saturated Fat 2.5 gm, • Dietary Fiber 0 gm
  Polyunsat Fat 1.2 gm, • Sugars 2 gm
  Monounsat Fat 4.1 gm) • Protein 11 gm

Sweet and Sour Meatballs

Elaine Unruh
Minneapolis, MN

Makes 8 main-dish servings, or 20 appetizer servings

Prep. Time: 45 minutes
Cooking Time: 6 hours
Ideal slow cooker size: 4-qt.

Meatballs:
2 lbs. ground beef
1¼ cups bread crumbs
¼ tsp. salt
1 tsp. pepper
2-3 Tbsp. Worcestershire
  sauce
1 egg
½ tsp. garlic salt
¼ cup finely chopped
  onions

Sauce:
20-oz. can pineapple
  chunks, juice reserved
½ cup chopped green
  peppers
3 Tbsp. cornstarch
¼ cup cold water
1 cups ketchup
2 Tbsp. Worcestershire
  sauce
¼ tsp. salt
¼ tsp. pepper
¼ tsp. garlic salt

1. Combine all meatball ingredients. Shape into 60 meatballs. Brown in skillet, rolling so all sides are browned. Place meatballs in slow cooker.

2. Pour juice from pineapples into skillet. Stir into drippings.

3. Combine cornstarch and cold water. Add to skillet and stir until thickened.

4. Stir in ketchup and Worcestershire sauce. Season with salt, pepper, and garlic salt. Add green peppers and pineapples. Pour over meatballs.

5. Cover. Cook on low 6 hours.

Exchange List Values
- Carbohydrate 1.0   • Fat 0.5
- Meat, lean 1.0

Basic Nutritional Values
- Calories 150   • Cholesterol 37 mg
  (Calories from Fat 48) • Sodium 430 mg
- Total Fat 5 gm   • Total Carb 16 gm
  (Saturated Fat 1.9 gm, • Dietary Fiber 1 gm
  Polyunsat Fat 0.3 gm,   • Sugars 7 gm
  Monounsat Fat 2.2 gm)   • Protein 10 gm

Suit-Yourself Veggies with Beef

Carol Eberly
Harrisonburg, VA

Makes 6 servings

Prep. Time: 25 minutes
Cooking Time: 6-8 hours
Ideal slow-cooker size: 4-5 qt.

3 cups grated raw carrots
2½ cups onions, sliced thin
6 cups grated raw potatoes
1 lb. 90%-lean ground
  beef, browned and
  drained
salt to taste
pepper to taste
1 Tbsp. Worcestershire
  sauce
10¾-oz. can cream of
  mushroom soup

1. Grate and slice vegetables either in the amounts above, or to suit tastes of those you're serving and size of your slow cooker.

2. Place layer of grated carrots in bottom.

3. Lay onion slices on top of carrots. Season with salt and pepper.

4. Place potatoes on top of onions.

5. Put ground beef on top of vegetables.

6. Combine soup and Worcestershire sauce in a small bowl.

7. Spoon soup mixture over all.

8. Cover. Cook 6-8 hours on low, or until vegetables are as tender as you like them.

Exchange List Values
- Starch 1.5   • Lean Meat 2.0
- Vegetable 2.0   • Fat 1.0

Basic Nutritional Values
- Calories 300   • Cholesterol 45 mg
  (Calories from Fat 80) • Sodium 535 mg
- Total Fat 9 gm   • Total Carb 34 gm
  (Saturated Fat 3.5 gm, • Dietary Fiber 5 gm
  Polyunsat Fat 1.5 gm,   • Sugars 7 gm
  Monounsat Fat 3.0 gm)   • Protein 19 gm

Swedish Cabbage Rolls

Jean Butzer
Batavia, NY
Pam Hochstedler
Kalona, IA

Makes 6 servings, 2 cabbage rolls per serving

Prep. Time: 35 minutes
Cooking Time: 7-9 hours
Ideal slow cooker size: 4- or 5-qt.

12 large cabbage leaves
1 egg, beaten
¼ cup fat-free milk
¼ cup finely chopped
  onions
¾ tsp. salt
¼ tsp. pepper
1 lb. ground beef, browned
  and drained
1 cup cooked rice
8-oz. can tomato sauce
1 Tbsp. brown sugar
1 Tbsp. lemon Juice
1 tsp. Worcestershire sauce

1. Immerse cabbage leaves in boiling water for about 3 minutes or until limp. Drain.
2. Combine egg, milk, onions, salt, pepper, beef, and rice. Place about ¼ cup meat mixture in center of each leaf. Fold in sides and roll ends over meat. Place in slow cooker.
3. Combine tomato sauce, brown sugar, lemon juice, and Worcestershire sauce. Pour over cabbage rolls.
4. Cover. Cook on low 7-9 hours.

Exchange List Values
- Starch 0.5
- Vegetable 2.0
- Meat, lean 2.0
- Fat 0.5

Basic Nutritional Values
- Calories 219
  (Calories from Fat 79)
- Total Fat 9 gm
  (Saturated Fat 3.4 gm,
  Polyunsat Fat 0.5 gm,
  Monounsat Fat 3.7 gm)
- Cholesterol 80 mg
- Sodium 603 mg
- Total Carb 18 gm
- Dietary Fiber 2 gm
- Sugars 7 gm
- Protein 17 gm

Stuffed Cabbage

Barbara Nolan
Pleasant Valley, NY

Makes 6 servings

Prep. Time: 35 minutes
Cooking Time: 6-8 hours
Ideal slow cooker size: 4- or 5-qt.

4 cups water
12 large cabbage leaves
1 lb. ground beef, lamb, *or*
  turkey
½ cup cooked rice
½ tsp. salt
⅛ tsp. pepper
¼ tsp. dried thyme
¼ tsp. nutmeg
¼ tsp. cinnamon
6-oz. can tomato paste
¾ cup water

1. Boil 4 cups water in deep kettle. Remove kettle from heat. Soak cabbage leaves in hot water 5 minutes, or just until softened. Remove. Drain. Cool.
2. Combine ground beef, rice, salt, pepper, thyme, nutmeg, and cinnamon. Place 2 Tbsp. of mixture on each leaf.
3. Roll up firmly. Stack stuffed leaves in slow cooker.
4. Combine tomato paste and ¾ cup water until smooth. Pour over cabbage rolls.
5. Cover. Cook on low 6-8 hours.

Exchange List Values
- Vegetable 2.0
- Meat, lean 2.0
- Fat 0.5

Basic Nutritional Values
- Calories 186
  (Calories from Fat 73)
- Total Fat 8 gm
  (Saturated Fat 3.0 gm,
  Polyunsat Fat 0.4 gm,
  Monounsat Fat 3.4 gm)
- Cholesterol 45 mg
- Sodium 269 mg
- Total Carb 13 gm
- Dietary Fiber 3 gm
- Sugars 3 gm
- Protein 16 gm

Stuffed Green Peppers

Lois Stoltzfus
Honey Brook, PA

Makes 6 servings

Prep. Time: 25 minutes
Cooking Time: 3-8 hours
Ideal slow cooker size: 6-qt.
oval, so the peppers can
each sit on the bottom of the
cooker)

6 large green peppers
¾ lb. 85%-lean ground
  beef, browned and
  drained
2 Tbsp. minced onion
⅛ tsp. salt
⅛ tsp. garlic powder
2 cups cooked rice
15-oz. can tomtato sauce
2 oz. (½ cup) reduced-fat
  shredded mozzarella
  cheese

1. Cut peppers in half and
remove seeds.
2. Combine all ingredients
except peppers and cheese.
3. Stuff peppers with
ground beef mixture. Place in
slow cooker.
4. Cover. Cook on low 6-8
hours, or high 3-4 hours.
Sprinkle with cheese during
last 30 minutes.

Exchange List Values
- Starch 1.0
- Vegetable 3.0
- Meat, lean 1.0
- Fat 1.0

Basic Nutritional Values
- Calories 253
  (Calories from Fat 69)
- Total Fat 8 gm
  (Saturated Fat 3.2 gm,
  Polyunsat Fat 0.5 gm,
  Monounsat Fat 2.8 gm)
- Cholesterol 39 mg
- Sodium 585 mg
- Total Carb 30 gm
- Dietary Fiber 5 gm
- Sugars 9 gm
- Protein 17 gm

Shredded Beef for Tacos

Dawn Day
Westminster, CA

Makes 8 servings

Prep. Time: 20 minutes
Cooking Time: 6-8 hours
Ideal slow cooker size: 4-qt.

2-lb. round roast, cut into
  large chunks, trimmed
  of fat
1 large onion, chopped
2 Tbsp. canola oil
2 serrano chilies, chopped
3 garlic cloves, minced
1 tsp. salt
1 cup water

1. Brown meat and onion
in oil. Transfer to slow
cooker.
2. Add chilies, garlic, salt,
and water.
3. Cover. Cook on high 6-8
hours.
4. Pull meat apart with two
forks until shredded.
5. Serve with fresh tortillas, lettuce, tomatoes, cheese,
and guacamole.

Exchange List Values
- Meat, lean 3.0

Basic Nutritional Values
- Calories 184
  (Calories from Fat 79)
- Total Fat 9 gm
  (Saturated Fat 2.1 gm,
  Polyunsat Fat 1.2 gm,
  Monounsat Fat 4.2 gm)
- Cholesterol 64 mg
- Sodium 335 mg
- Total Carb 4 gm
- Dietary Fiber 1 gm
- Sugars 3 gm
- Protein 22 gm

Choose whole grains — barley, bulgur, quinoa, and whole-wheat couscous — as healthier alternatives to traditional starches such as potatoes, white rice, white bread, grits, and pasta.

Tamale Pie

Jeannine Janzen
Elbing, KS

Makes 8 servings

Prep. Time: 20 minutes
Cooking Time: 4 hours
Ideal slow cooker size: 4-qt.

¾ cup cornmeal
1½ cups fat-free milk
1 egg, beaten
1 lb. ground beef, browned
  and drained
1.25 oz. envelope dry chili
  seasoning mix
16-oz. can diced tomatoes
16-oz. can corn, drained
1 cup grated fat-free
  cheddar cheese

1. Combine cornmeal,
milk, and egg.
2. Stir in meat, chili
seasoning mix, tomatoes, and
corn until well blended. Pour
into slow cooker.
3. Cover. Cook on high 1
hour, then on low 3 hours.
4. Sprinkle with cheese.
Cook another 5 minutes until
cheese is melted.

Exchange List Values
- Starch 1.0
- Vegetable 1.0
- Carbohydrate 0.5
- Meat, lean 2.0

Basic Nutritional Values
- Calories 244
  (Calories from Fat 65)
- Total Fat 7 gm
  (Saturated Fat 2.6 gm,
  Polyunsat Fat 0.6 gm,
  Monounsat Fat 2.9 gm)
- Cholesterol 63 mg
- Sodium 500 mg
- Total Carb 25 gm
- Dietary Fiber 3 gm
- Sugars 6 gm
- Protein 20 gm

Mile-High Shredded Beef Sandwiches

Miriam Christophel
Battle Creek, MI

Mary Seielstad
Sparks, NV

Makes 8 servings

Prep. Time: 35 minutes
Cooking Time: 7-9 hours
Ideal slow cooker size: 4-qt.

3-lb. chuck roast, *or* round
  steak, trimmed of fat
2 Tbsp. oil
1 cup chopped onions
½ cup sliced celery
2 cups lower sodium, 98%
  fat-free beef broth
1 garlic clove
¾ cup ketchup
2 Tbsp. brown sugar
2 Tbsp. vinegar
1 tsp. dry mustard
½ tsp. chili powder
3 drops Tabasco sauce
1 bay leaf
¼ tsp. paprika
¼ tsp. garlic powder
1 tsp. Worcestershire sauce

1. In skillet brown both
sides of meat in oil. Add
onions and celery and sauté
briefly. Transfer to slow
cooker. Add broth or bouillon.
2. Cover. Cook on low
6-8 hours, or until tender.
Remove meat from cooker
and cool. Shred beef.
3. Remove vegetables from
cooker and drain, reserving
1½ cups broth. Combine
vegetables and meat.

4. Return shredded meat
and vegetables to cooker. Add
broth and remaining ingredients and combine well.
5. Cover. Cook on high 1
hour. Remove bay leaf.
6. Pile into 8 sandwich rolls
and serve.

Exchange List Values
- Carbohydrate 1.0
- Meat, lean 3.0

Basic Nutritional Values
- Calories 239
  (Calories from Fat 88)
- Total Fat 10 gm
  (Saturated Fat 2.4 gm,
  Polyunsat Fat 1.3 gm,
  Monounsat Fat 4.6 gm)
- Cholesterol 73 mg
- Sodium 444 mg
- Total Carb 12 gm
- Dietary Fiber 1 gm
- Sugars 8 gm
- Protein 25 gm

Pork Main Dishes

Cranberry Pork Roast

Barbara Aston
Ashdown, AR

Makes 9 servings

Prep. Time: 20 minutes
Cooking Time: 8-10 hours
Ideal slow cooker size: 4-qt.

2¾-lb. boneless pork roast, trimmed of fat
1 cup ground, *or* finely chopped cranberries
3 Tbsp. honey
1 tsp. grated orange peel
⅛ tsp. ground cloves
⅛ tsp. ground nutmeg

1. Sprinkle roast with salt and pepper. Place in slow cooker.

2. Combine remaining ingredients. Pour over roast.

3. Cover. Cook on low 8-10 hours.

Exchange List Values
• Carbohydrate 0.5 • Meat, lean 3.0

Basic Nutritional Values
• Calories 214
  (Calories from Fat 81)
• Total Fat 9 gm
  (Saturated Fat 3.5 gm,
  Polyunsat Fat 0.6 gm,
  Monounsat Fat 4.3 gm)
• Cholesterol 63 mg
• Sodium 37 mg
• Total Carb 7 gm
• Dietary Fiber 1 gm
• Sugars 7 gm
• Protein 25 gm

Tip:
  You may want to add a little salt and pepper to this recipe if you generally use them in your diet.

Barbara Jean's Whole Pork Tenderloin

Barbara Jean Fabel
Wausau, WI

Makes 8 servings

Prep. Time: 20 minutes
Cooking Time: 3-5 hours
Ideal slow cooker size: 4- or 5-qt.

½ cup sliced celery
¼ lb. fresh mushrooms, quartered
1 medium onion, sliced
2 Tbsp. margarine
2 1¼-lb. pork tenderloins, trimmed of fat
1 Tbsp. canola oil
¾ tsp. salt
¼ tsp. pepper
½ cup beef broth

½ tsp. sodium-free beef flavored instant bouillon
1 Tbsp. flour

1. Placed celery, mush-rooms, onion, and margarine in slow cooker.
2. Brown tenderloins in skillet in 1 Tbsp. canola oil. Layer over vegetables in slow cooker.
3. Pour beef broth over tenderloins. Sprinkle with salt and pepper.
4. Combine bouillon and flour until smooth. Pour over tenderloins.
5. Cover. Cook on high 3 hours or low 4-5 hours

Exchange List Values
• Meat, lean 4.0

Basic Nutritional Values
• Calories 228
  (Calories from Fat 87)
• Total Fat 10 gm
  (Saturated Fat 2.4 gm,
  Polyunsat Fat 1.9 gm,
  Monounsat Fat 4.3 gm)
• Cholesterol 82 mg
• Sodium 385 mg
• Total Carb 3 gm
• Dietary Fiber 1 gm
• Sugars 2 gm
• Protein 30 gm

Autumn Harvest Pork Loin

Stacy Schmucker Stoltzfus
Enola, PA

Makes 6 servings

Prep. Time: 30 minutes
Cooking Time: 5-6 hours
Ideal slow cooker size: 4-qt.

1 cup cider *or* apple juice
1½-lb. boneless pork loin, trimmed of fat
½ tsp. salt
¼ tsp. pepper
2 large Granny Smith apples, peeled and sliced
1½ whole medium butternut squashes, peeled and cubed
2 Tbsp. brown sugar
¼ tsp. cinnamon
¼ tsp. dried thyme
¼ tsp. dried sage

1. Heat cider in hot skillet. Sear pork loin on all sides in cider.
2. Sprinkle meat with salt and pepper on all sides. Place in slow cooker, along with juices.
3. Combine apples and squash. Sprinkle with sugar and herbs. Stir. Place around pork loin.
4. Cover. Cook on low 5-6 hours.

5. Remove pork from cooker. Let stand 10-15 minutes. Slice into ½"-thick slices.
6. Serve topped with apples and squash.

Exchange List Values
• Starch 1.0
• Fruit 1.0
• Meat, lean 2.0
• Fat 0.5

Basic Nutritional Values
• Calories 280
  (Calories from Fat 68)
• Total Fat 8 gm
  (Saturated Fat 2.7 gm,
  Polyunsat Fat 0.7 gm,
  Monounsat Fat 3.3 gm)
• Cholesterol 63 mg
• Sodium 241 mg
• Total Carb 31 gm
• Dietary Fiber 3 gm
• Sugars 19 gm
• Protein 24 gm

Deep-colored fruits and vegetables — orange, dark green, blue, red — often provide more vitamins and minerals than lighter-colored ones.

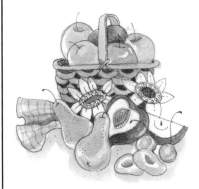

Slow-Cooker Pork Tenderloin

Kathy Hertzler
Lancaster, PA

Makes 6 servings

Prep Time: 5-15 minutes
Cooking Time: 4 hours
Ideal slow-cooker size: 4 qt.

2-lb. pork tenderloin,
 cut in half lengthwise,
 visible fat removed
1 cup water
¾ cup red wine
3 Tbsp. light soy sauce
1 recipe Onion Soup Mix,
 Salt-Free (see recipe on
 page 261)
6 cloves garlic, peeled and
 chopped
freshly ground pepper

1. Place pork tenderloin pieces in slow cooker. Pour water, wine, and soy sauce over pork.
2. Turn pork over in liquid several times to completely moisten.
3. Sprinkle with dry onion soup mix. Top with chopped garlic and pepper.
4. Cover. Cook on low 4 hours.

Tip:
 I mix ½ cup uncooked long-grain white rice and ½ cup uncooked brown rice in a microwavable bowl. Stir in 2½ cups water and ¾ tsp. salt. Cover. Microwave 5 minutes on high, and then 20 minutes on medium. Place finished pork on a large platter and the finished rice alongside, topped with the au jus from the meat. A green salad goes well with this to make a meal.

Exchange List Values
• Carbohydrate 0.5   • Lean Meat 4.0

Basic Nutritional Values
• Calories 220   • Cholesterol 115 mg
 (Calories from Fat 35) • Sodium 370 mg
• Total Fat 4 gm   • Total Carb 6 gm
 (Saturated Fat 1.0 gm, • Dietary Fiber 0 gm
 Polyunsat Fat 0.5 gm,   • Sugars 2 gm
 Monounsat Fat 1.5 gm)   • Protein 37 gm

Flautas with Pork Filling

Donna Lantgen
Rapid City, SD

Makes 8 servings

Prep. Time: 15 minutes
Cooking Time: 4-6 hours
Ideal slow cooker size: 4-qt.

1 lb. pork roast *or* chops,
 cubed
¼ cup chopped onions
4-oz. can diced green
 chilies
7-oz. can green chile salsa
1 tsp. cocoa powder
16-oz. can chili with beans

1. Brown cubed pork in skillet. Drain. Place in slow cooker.
2. Add remaining ingredients except chili.
3. Cover. Cook on low 2-3 hours.
4. Add chili. Cook 2-3 hours longer.
5. Serve on flour tortillas with guacamole dip.

Exchange List Values
• Starch 0.5   • Meat, lean 2.0

Basic Nutritional Values
• Calories 153   • Cholesterol 35 mg
 (Calories from Fat 62) • Sodium 566 mg
• Total Fat 7 gm   • Total Carb 9 gm
 (Saturated Fat 2.8 gm, • Dietary Fiber 3 gm
 Polyunsat Fat 0.5 gm,   • Sugars 2 gm
 Monounsat Fat 3.1 gm)   • Protein 14 gm

Note:
 This is especially good on spinach-herb tortillas.

Barbecued Pork and Beef Sandwiches

Nanci Keatley
Salem, OR

Makes 12 servings

Prep Time: 15-30 minutes
Cooking Time: 9 hours
Ideal slow-cooker size: 6-7 qt.

1 cup onion, finely
 chopped
2 cups green pepper, finely
 chopped
6-oz. can tomato paste
½ cup brown sugar, packed
¼ cup cider vinegar
1 Tbsp. chili powder
1 tsp. salt
2 tsp. Worcestershire sauce
1 tsp. dry mustard
1 tsp. hot sauce

1½ lbs. lean stewing beef
1½ lbs. lean pork cubes
buns, pita bread, *or*
   prepared rice

1. Blend onion, green pepper, tomato paste, brown sugar, vinegar, chili powder, salt, Worcestershire sauce, dry mustard, and hot sauce in slow cooker.

2. When thoroughly mixed, stir in beef and pork pieces.

3. Cover. Cook 8 hours on low.

4. Stir and shred meat before serving.

5. Serve in sandwich buns or pita bread, or over rice.

Exchange List Values
- Carbohydrate 0.5 • Lean Meat 4.0
- Vegetable 1.0

Basic Nutritional Values
- Calories 240
  (Calories from Fat 65)
- Total Fat 7 gm
  (Saturated Fat 3.0 gm,
  Polyunsat Fat 0.5 gm,
  Monounsat Fat 3.5 gm)
- Cholesterol 70 mg
- Sodium 380 mg
- Total Carb 15 gm
- Dietary Fiber 2 gm
- Sugars 12 gm
- Protein 27 gm

Pork Chops Pierre

Genelle Taylor
Perrysburg, OH

Makes 6 servings

Prep. Time: 30-40 minutes
Cooking Time: 4½-6½ hours
Ideal slow cooker size: 3-qt.

6 bone-in, lean pork chops,
   each ½"-thick, totalling
   2 lbs.
½ tsp. salt, *optional*
⅛ tsp. pepper
2 medium onions, chopped
2 ribs celery, chopped
1 large green bell pepper,
   sliced
14-oz. can no-salt-added
   stewed tomatoes
½ cup ketchup
2 Tbsp. cider vinegar
2 Tbsp. brown sugar
2 Tbsp. Worcestershire
   sauce
1 Tbsp. lemon juice
1 beef bouillon cube
2 Tbsp. cornstarch
2 Tbsp. water

1. Place chops in slow cooker. Sprinkle with salt and pepper.

2. Spoon onions, celery, green pepper, and tomatoes over chops.

3. In a small bowl, combine ketchup, vinegar, sugar, Worcestershire sauce, lemon juice, and bouillon cube. Pour over vegetables.

4. Cover. Cook on low 4-6 hours, just until chops are tender but not dry.

5. Remove chops to a platter and keep warm.

6. In a small bowl, mix together cornstarch and water until smooth. Stir into liquid in slow cooker.

7. Cover. Cook on high 30 minutes or until sauce thickens.

Exchange List Values
- Carbohydrate 1.0 • Lean Meat 3.0
- Vegetable 2.0

Basic Nutritional Values
- Calories 250
  (Calories from Fat 55)
- Total Fat 6 gm
  (Saturated Fat 2.5 gm,
  Polyunsat Fat 0.5 gm,
  Monounsat Fat 3.0 gm)
- Cholesterol 65 mg
- Sodium 520 mg
- Total Carb 25 gm
- Dietary Fiber 3 gm
- Sugars 17 gm
- Protein 24 gm

If you're marinating ingredients at room temperature, marinate for no more than two hours for food safety reasons.

Shepherd's Pie

Melanie Thrower
McPherson, KS

Makes 6 servings

Prep. Time: 40 minutes
Cooking Time: 3 hours
Ideal slow cooker size: 3- or 4-qt.

¾ lb. ground pork
1 Tbsp. vinegar
¾ tsp. salt
¼ tsp. hot pepper
1 tsp. paprika
¼ tsp. dried oregano
¼ tsp. black pepper
1 tsp. chili powder
1 small onion, chopped
15-oz. can corn, drained
3 large potatoes, unpeeled
¼ cup fat-free milk
1 tsp. margarine
¼ tsp. salt
dash of pepper
shredded cheese

1. Combine pork, vinegar, and spices. Cook in skillet until brown. Add onion and cook until onions begin to glaze. Spread in bottom of slow cooker.
2. Spread corn over meat.
3. Boil potatoes until soft. Mash with milk, butter, ¼ tsp. salt, and dash of pepper. Spread over meat and corn.
4. Cover. Cook on low 3 hours. Sprinkle top with cheese a few minutes before serving.

Exchange List Values
• Starch 2.0   • Fat 1.0
• Meat, lean 1.0

Basic Nutritional Values
• Calories 269   • Cholesterol 38 mg
  (Calories from Fat 85)   • Sodium 538 mg
• Total Fat 9 gm   • Total Carb 33 gm
  (Saturated Fat 3.2 gm, • Dietary Fiber 4 gm
  Polyunsat Fat 1.3 gm,   • Sugars 5 gm
  Monounsat Fat 4.0 gm) • Protein 15 gm

Variation:
You can substitute ground beef for the pork.

This is my 9-year-old son's favorite dish.

Chalupa

Jeannine Janzen
Elbing, KS

Makes 16 servings

Prep. Time: 10 minutes
Soaking Time: overnight or 12 hours
Cooking Time: 8 hours
Ideal slow cooker size: 5-qt.

3-lb. pork roast, trimmed of fat
1 lb. dry pinto beans
2 garlic cloves, minced
1 Tbsp. ground cumin
1 Tbsp. dried oregano
2 Tbsp. chili powder
1 Tbsp. salt
4-oz. can chopped green chilies
water

1. Cover beans with water and soak overnight in slow cooker.
2. In the morning, remove beans and reserve soaking water. Put roast in bottom of cooker. Add remaining ingredients, including the beans and their soaking water, and more water if needed to cover all the ingredients.
3. Cook on high 1 hour, and then on low 6 hours. Remove meat and shred with two forks. Return meat to slow cooker.
4. Cook on high 1 more hour.
5. Serve over a bed of lettuce. Top with grated cheese and chopped onions and tomatoes.

Exchange List Values
• Starch 1.0   • Meat, lean 2.0

Basic Nutritional Values
• Calories 200   • Cholesterol 38 mg
  (Calories from Fat 55)   • Sodium 501 mg
• Total Fat 6 gm   • Total Carb 16 gm
  (Saturated Fat 2.2 gm, • Dietary Fiber 6 gm
  Polyunsat Fat 0.6 gm,   • Sugars 2 gm
  Monounsat Fat 2.8 gm) • Protein 20 gm

Involve the entire family in healthy cooking. Children are more likely to eat healthy foods when they have a role in preparation.

Zesty Pulled Pork

Sheila Plock
Boalsburg, PA

Makes 10 servings

Prep. Time: 20 minutes
Cooking Time: 4-10 hours
Ideal slow cooker size: 4-qt.

2½- lb. boneless pork
  shoulder roast, *or* pork
  sirloin roast
salt and pepper to taste
½ cup water
3 Tbsp. cider vinegar
2 Tbsp. Worcestershire
  sauce
1 tsp. cumin
1 cup barbecue sauce of
  your choice

1. Trim fat from roast. Fit roast into slow cooker.
2. Season meat with salt and pepper.
3. In a small bowl, combine water, vinegar, Worcestershire sauce, and cumin. Spoon over roast, being careful not to wash off the seasonings.
4. Cover. Cook on low 8-10 hours, or on high 4-5 hours, just until pork is very tender but not dry.
5. Remove meat onto a platter. Discard liquid.
6. Shred meat using 2 forks. Return to slow cooker.
7. Stir in barbecue sauce.
8. Cover. Cook on high 30-45 minutes.
9. Serve on split hamburger buns.

Exchange List Values
• Carbohydrate 1.0 • Lean Meat 3.0

Basic Nutritional Values
• Calories 190 • Cholesterol 70 mg
  (Calories from Fat 25) • Sodium 280 mg
• Total Fat 3 gm • Total Carb 12 gm
  (Saturated Fat 1.0 gm, • Dietary Fiber 0 gm
  Polyunsat Fat 0.5 gm, • Sugars 10 gm
  Monounsat Fat 1.5 gm) • Protein 26 gm

Tangy Pork Chops

Tracy Clark
Mt. Crawford, VA

Lois M. Martin
Lititz, PA

Becky Oswald
Broadway, PA

Makes 4 servings

Prep. Time: 25 minutes
Cooking Time: 5½-6½ hours
Ideal slow cooker size: 4-qt.

4 ½-inch thick pork chops,
  bone in, trimmed of fat
⅛ tsp. pepper
2 medium onions, chopped
2 celery ribs, chopped
1 large green pepper, sliced
14½-oz. can stewed
  tomatoes, no salt added
⅓ cup ketchup
2 Tbsp. cider vinegar
2 Tbsp. brown sugar
2 Tbsp. Worcestershire
  sauce
1 Tbsp. lemon juice
1 reduced-sodium beef
  bouillon cube
2 Tbsp. cornstarch
2 Tbsp. water

1. Place chops in slow cooker. Sprinkle with salt and pepper.
2. Add onions, celery, pepper, and tomatoes.
3. Combine ketchup, vinegar, brown sugar, Worcestershire sauce, lemon juice, and bouillon. Pour over vegetables.
4. Cover. Cook on low 5-6 hours.
5. Combine cornstarch and water until smooth. Stir into slow cooker.
6. Cover. Cook on high 30 minutes, or until thickened.
7. Serve over rice.

Exchange List Values
• Carbohydrate 1.5 • Meat, lean 1.0
• Vegetable 3.0

Basic Nutritional Values
• Calories 254 • Cholesterol 47 mg
  (Calories from Fat 47) • Sodium 546 mg
• Total Fat 5 gm • Total Carb 35 gm
  (Saturated Fat 1.7 gm, • Dietary Fiber 4 gm
  Polyunsat Fat 0.5 gm, • Sugars 20 gm
  Monounsat Fat 2.1 gm) • Protein 19 gm

Variation:
  Use chunks of beef or chicken legs and thighs instead of pork.

Chops and Beans

Mary L. Casey
Scranton, PA

Makes 6 servings

Prep. Time: 20 minutes
Cooking Time: 4-5 hours
Ideal slow cooker size: 4-qt.

2 1-lb. cans pork and beans
¼ cup no-salt-added
    ketchup
2 slices bacon, browned
    and crumbled
½ cup chopped onions,
    sautéed
1 Tbsp. Worcestershire sauce
1 Tbsp. brown sugar
brown sugar substitute to
    equal 1 Tbsp. sugar
6 pork chops, bone in,
    trimmed of fat, a total of
    1½ pounds
2 tsp. prepared mustard
1 Tbsp. brown sugar
2 Tbsp. no-salt-added
    ketchup
one lemon, sliced in rings

1. Combine beans, ¼
cup ketchup, bacon, onions,
Worcestershire sauce, and
brown sugar and substitute
in slow cooker.
2. Brown chops in skillet.
3. In separate bowl, mix
together 2 tsp. mustard, 1
Tbsp. brown sugar, and ¼
cup ketchup.
4. Brush each chop with
sauce, then carefully stack
into cooker, placing a slice of
lemon on each chop. Sub-
merge in bean/bacon mixture.
5. Cover. Cook on low 4-6
hours.

Exchange List Values
- Starch 2.0   • Meat, lean 2.0
- Carbohydrate 0.5 • Fat 0.5

Basic Nutritional Values
- Calories 323   • Cholesterol 55 mg
  (Calories from Fat 73)   • Sodium 790 mg
- Total Fat 8 gm   • Total Carb 40 gm
  (Saturated Fat 2.0 gm,   • Dietary Fiber 8 gm
  Polyunsat Fat 1.0 gm,   • Sugars 20 gm
  Monounsat Fat 3.5 gm)   • Protein 23 gm

Perfect Pork Chops

Brenda Pope
Dundee, OH

Makes 2 servings

Prep. Time: 20 minutes
Cooking Time: 3-4 hours
Ideal slow cooker size: 4-qt.

2 small onions
½ lb. boneless, center
    loin pork chops, frozen,
    trimmed of fat
fresh ground pepper to
    taste
¾ tsp. reduced-sodium
    bouillon granules
¼ cup hot water
2 Tbsp. prepared mustard
    with white wine
fresh parsley sprigs, *or*
    lemon slices, *optional*

1. Cut off ends of onions
and peel. Cut onions in half
crosswise to make 4 thick
wheels. Place in bottom of
slow cooker.
2. Sear both sides of frozen
chops in heavy skillet. Place
in cooker on top of onions.
Sprinkle with pepper.
3. Dissolve bouillon cube
in hot water. Stir in mustard.
Pour into slow cooker.
4. Cover. Cook on high 3-4
hours.
5. Serve topped with fresh
parsley sprigs or lemon slices,
if desired.

Exchange List Values
- Carbohydrate 0.5 • Meat, lean 3.0

Basic Nutritional Values
- Calories 204   • Cholesterol 51 mg
  (Calories from Fat 72)   • Sodium 392 mg
- Total Fat 8 gm   • Total Carb 11 gm
  (Saturated Fat 2.9 gm,   • Dietary Fiber 2 gm
  Polyunsat Fat 0.7 gm,   • Sugars 7 gm
  Monounsat Fat 3.9 gm)   • Protein 22 gm

Make your own salad dressing so you can use healthy oils, such as sunflower, canola, or soybean oil.

Pork and Cabbage Dinner

Mrs. Paul Gray
Beatrice, NE

Makes 8 servings

Prep. Time: 25 minutes
Cooking Time: 5-6 hours
Ideal slow cooker size: 4- or 5-qt.

2 lbs. pork steaks, *or* chops, *or* shoulder, bone-in, trimmed of fat
¾ cup chopped onions
¼ cup chopped fresh parsley, *or* 2 Tbsp. dried parsley
4 cups shredded cabbage
1 tsp. salt
⅛ tsp. pepper
½ tsp. caraway seeds
⅛ tsp. allspice
½ cup beef broth
2 medium cooking apples, cored and sliced ¼-inch thick

1. Place pork in slow cooker. Layer onions, parsley, and cabbage over pork.
2. Combine salt, pepper, caraway seeds, and allspice. Sprinkle over cabbage. Pour broth over cabbage.
3. Cover. Cook on low 5-6 hours.
4. Add apple slices 30 minutes before serving.

Exchange List Values
• Fruit 0.5 • Meat, lean 2.0
• Vegetable 1.0

Basic Nutritional Values
• Calories 149 • Cholesterol 47 mg
(Calories from Fat 44) • Sodium 382 mg
• Total Fat 5 gm • Total Carb 9 gm
(Saturated Fat 1.7 gm, • Dietary Fiber 2 gm
Polyunsat Fat 0.4 gm, • Sugars 6 gm
Monounsat Fat 2.1 gm) • Protein 18 gm

Creamy Ham Topping (for baked potatoes)

Judy Buller
Bluffton, OH

Makes 12 servings

Prep. Time: 20 minutes
Cooking Time: 1-2 hours
Ideal slow cooker size: 4-qt.

2 Tbsp. margarine
¼ cup flour
2 cups fat-free milk
¼ cup fat-free half-and-half
1 Tbsp. chopped parsley
1 Tbsp. sodium-free chicken bouillon granules
½ tsp. Italian seasoning
2 cups diced cooked ham
¼ cup grated Romano cheese
1 cup sliced mushrooms

1. Melt butter in saucepan. Stir in flour. Add milk and half-and-half.
2. Stir in remaining ingredients (except shredded cheese, and sour cream). Pour into slow cooker.
3. Cover. Cook on low 1-2 hours.
4. Serve over baked potatoes. Top with shredded cheese and sour cream.

Exchange List Values
• Carbohydrate 0.5 • Meat, lean 1.0

Basic Nutritional Values
• Calories 93 • Cholesterol 17 mg
(Calories from Fat 36) • Sodium 386 mg
• Total Fat 4 gm • Total Carb 5 gm
(Saturated Fat 1.3 gm, • Dietary Fiber 0 gm
Polyunsat Fat 0.8 gm, • Sugars 3 gm
Monounsat Fat 1.6 gm) • Protein 9 gm

Black Beans with Ham

Colleen Heatwole
Burton, MI

Makes 10 servings

Prep. Time: 10 minutes
Soaking Time: 8 hours
Cooking Time: 10-12 hours
Ideal slow cooker size: 5-qt.

4 cups dry black beans
1 cup diced ham
1 tsp. cumin
½-1 cup minced onion
2 garlic cloves, minced
3 bay leaves
1 qt. fresh diced tomatoes
1 Tbsp. brown sugar

1. Cover black beans with water and soak for 8 hours, or over night. Drain and pour beans into slow cooker.
2. Add all remaining ingredients and stir well. Cover with water.
3. Cover cooker. Cook on low 10-12 hours.
4. Serve over rice.

Exchange List Values
- Starch 3.0
- Meat, very lean 1.0
- Vegetable 1.0

Basic Nutritional Values
- Calories 302
- Cholesterol 8 mg
- (Calories from Fat 19)
- Sodium 196 mg
- Total Fat 2 gm
- Total Carb 51 gm
- (Saturated Fat 0.5 gm,
- Dietary Fiber 18 gm
- Polyunsat Fat 0.6 gm,
- Sugars 8 gm
- Monounsat Fat 0.5 gm)
- Protein 21 gm

Note:
This is our favorite black bean recipe. We make it frequently in the winter.

Ham and Corn Slow-Cooker Casserole

Vicki Dinkel
Sharon Springs, KS

Makes 8 servings

Prep. Time: 25 minutes
Cooking Time: 4-8 hours
Ideal slow cooker size: 4- or 5-qt.

¼ cup canola oil
1 small green bell pepper, chopped
1 medium onion, chopped
½ cup flour
½ tsp. paprika
½ tsp. pepper
¼ tsp. dried thyme
1 tsp. dry mustard
4 cups fat-free milk
8-oz. can cream-style corn
2 cups diced, slightly cooked potatoes
3 cups diced cooked extra-lean, reduced-sodium ham
3 oz. shredded reduced-fat sharp cheddar cheese

1. Sauté green pepper and onion in canola oil in skillet.
2. Stir in flour and seasonings.
3. Gradually stir in milk and cook until thickened. Pour into slow cooker.
4. Stir in remaining ingredients.
5. Cover. Cook on low 8 hours or high 4 hours.

Exchange List Values
- Starch 1.0
- Meat, lean 2.0
- Milk, fat-free 0.5
- Fat 0.5

Basic Nutritional Values
- Calories 255
- Cholesterol 34 mg
- (Calories from Fat 95)
- Sodium 596 mg
- Total Fat 11 gm
- Total Carb 24 gm
- (Saturated Fat 2.3 gm,
- Dietary Fiber 2 gm
- Polyunsat Fat 2.4 gm,
- Sugars 11 gm
- Monounsat Fat 5.3 gm)
- Protein 18 gm

Consider adding fruit to your entrées. Try pairing apples with pork or cranberries with chicken.

Ham and Scalloped Potatoes

Penny Blosser, Beavercreek, OH
Jo Haberkamp, Fairbank, IA
Ruth Hofstetter, Versailles, MO
Rachel Kauffman, Alto, MI
Mary E. Martin, Goshen, IN
Brenda Pope, Dundee, OH
Joyce Slaymaker, Strasburg, PA

Makes 8 servings

Prep. Time: 25 minutes
Cooking Time: 4-10 hours
Ideal slow cooker size: 4- or 5-qt.

6-8 (1 lb. total) slices ham
8 medium potatoes, thinly sliced
2 medium onions, thinly sliced
1 cup reduced-fat grated cheddar, *or* American, cheese
10¾-oz. can 98% fat-free, reduced-sodium cream of celery, *or* mushroom, soup
paprika, to garnish

1. Put half of ham, potatoes, and onions in slow cooker. Sprinkle with cheese. Repeat layers.
2. Spoon soup over top. Sprinkle with paprika.
3. Cover. Cook on low 8-10 hours, or high 4 hours.

Exchange List Values
- Starch 2.0
- Meat, lean 2.0

Basic Nutritional Values
- Calories 229
  (Calories from Fat 45)
- Total Fat 5 gm
  (Saturated Fat 2.5 gm,
  Polyunsat Fat 0.6 gm,
  Monounsat Fat 1.4 gm)
- Cholesterol 36 mg
- Sodium 733 mg
- Total Carb 32 gm
- Dietary Fiber 3 gm
- Sugars 7 gm
- Protein 17 gm

Tip:
You may want to add salt and pepper to taste if you generally use them in your diet.

Variation:
If you like a lot of creamy sauce with your ham and potatoes, stir ¾ soup can of milk into the soup before pouring it over the layers.
Alma Z. Weaver
Ephrata, PA

Schnitz und Knepp

Jean Robinson
Cinnaminson, NJ

Makes 12 servings

Soaking Time: 2-3 hours
Prep. Time: 20 minutes
Cooking Time: 5¼ hours
Ideal slow cooker size: 5-qt.

Schnitz:
1 qt. dried sweet apples
3 lbs. extra-lean, lower sodium, boneless ham slices, cut into 2" cubes
2 Tbsp. brown sugar
1 cinnamon stick

Knepp (Dumplings):
2 cups flour
4 tsp. baking powder
1 egg, well beaten
3 Tbsp. melted margarine
scant ½ cup fat free milk
¼ tsp. pepper

1. Cover apples with water in large bowl and let soak for a few hours.

2. Meanwhile, place ham in slow cooker. Cover with water.
3. Cover cooker. Cook on high 2 hours.
4. Add apples and water in which they have been soaking.
5. Add brown sugar and cinnamon stick. Mix until dissolved.
6. Cover. Cook on low 3 hours.
7. Combine dumpling ingredients in bowl. Drop into hot liquid in cooker by tablespoonfuls. Turn to high. Cover. Do not lift lid for 15 minutes.
8. Serve piping hot on a large platter.

Exchange List Values
- Starch 1.5
- Fruit 1.0
- Meat, lean 2.0

Basic Nutritional Values
- Calories 293
  (Calories from Fat 48)
- Total Fat 5 gm
  (Saturated Fat 1.4 gm,
  Polyunsat Fat 1.4 gm,
  Monounsat Fat 2.1 gm)
- Cholesterol 63 mg
- Sodium 980 mg
- Total Carb 41 gm
- Dietary Fiber 3 gm
- Sugars 19 gm
- Protein 20 gm

Note:
This was my grandmother's recipe and she had no slow cooker. Schnitz und Knepp cooked on the back of the woodstove till the quilting was done.
I was allowed to drop in the dumplings.

Ham in Cider

Dorothy M. Van Deest
Memphis, TN

Makes 8 servings

Prep. Time: 20 minutes
Cooking Time: 8½-10½ hours
Ideal slow cooker size: 4- or 5-qt.

3-lb. boneless, precooked extra-lean, lower sodium ham, trimmed of fat
4 cups sweet cider, *or* apple juice
¼ cup brown sugar
brown sugar substitute to equal ¼ cup sugar
2 tsp. dry mustard
1 tsp. ground cloves
1 cup golden raisins

1. Place ham and cider in slow cooker.
2. Cover. Cook on low 8-10 hours.
3. Remove ham from cider and place in baking pan.
4. Make a paste of sugar, mustard, cloves, and a little hot cider. Brush over ham. Pour ½ cup of juice from slow cooker into baking pan. Stir in raisins.
5. Bake at 375° for 30 minutes, until the paste has turned into a glaze.

Exchange List Values
• Carbohydrate 2.0 • Meat, very lean 3.0

Basic Nutritional Values
• Calories 255
(Calories from Fat 26)
• Total Fat 3 gm
(Saturated Fat 1.0 gm,
Polyunsat Fat 0.6 gm,
Monounsat Fat 1.0 gm)
• Cholesterol 67 mg
• Sodium 1194 mg
• Total Carb 31 gm
• Dietary Fiber 1 gm
• Sugars 28 gm
• Protein 27 gm

Sweet-Sour Pork

Mary W. Stauffer
Ephrata, PA

Makes 6 servings

Prep. Time: 30 minutes
Cooking Time: 5-7 hours
Ideal slow cooker size: 4-qt.

2 lbs. boneless pork shoulder, cut in strips, trimmed of fat
1 green bell pepper, cut in strips
half a medium onion, thinly sliced
¾ cup shredded carrots
2 Tbsp. coarsely chopped sweet pickles
2 Tbsp. brown sugar
brown sugar substitute to equal 1 Tbsp. sugar
2 Tbsp. cornstarch
¼ cup water
1 cup pineapple juice (reserved from pineapple chunks)
¼ cup cider vinegar
1 Tbsp. soy sauce
2 cups (20 oz. can) pineapple chunks, canned in juice, juice reserved

1. Place pork strips in slow cooker.
2. Add green pepper, onion, carrots, and pickles.
3. In bowl, mix together brown sugar and cornstarch. Add water, pineapple syrup, vinegar, and soy sauce. Stir until smooth.
4. Pour over ingredients in slow cooker.
5. Cover. Cook on low 5-7

hours. One hour before serving, add pineapple chunks. Stir.
6. Serve over buttered noodles with an additional dash of vinegar or garlic to taste.

Exchange List Values
• Fruit 1.0
• Carbohydrate 0.5
• Vegetable 1.0
• Meat, lean 3.0

Basic Nutritional Values
• Calories 270
(Calories from Fat 74)
• Total Fat 8 gm
(Saturated Fat 2.8 gm,
Polyunsat Fat 0.8 gm,
Monounsat Fat 3.8 gm)
• Cholesterol 75 mg
• Sodium 285 mg
• Total Carb 27 gm
• Dietary Fiber 2 gm
• Sugars 21 gm
• Protein 22 gm

Sausage-Potato Slow Cooker Dinner

Deborah Swartz
Grottoes, VA

Makes 8 servings

Prep. Time: 25 minutes
Cooking Time: 3-9 hours
Ideal slow cooker size: 4- or 5-qt.

1 cup water
½ tsp. cream of tartar
6 medium potatoes, unpeeled, thinly sliced
¾ lb. sausage, casings removed and browned
1 onion, chopped
¼ cup flour
salt to taste
pepper to taste
1½ cups grated fat-free cheddar cheese, *divided*
1 Tbsp. margarine

10¾-oz. can 98% fat-free, reduced-sodium cream of mushroom soup

1. Combine water and cream of tartar. Toss sliced potatoes in water. Drain.

2. Layer potatoes, sausage, onion, flour, a sprinkling of salt and pepper, and half of cheddar cheese in slow cooker. Repeat layers until ingredients are used.

3. Dot butter over top. Pour soup over all.

4. Cover. Cook on low 7-9 hours or on high 3-4 hours.

5. Sprinkle reserved cheese over top just before serving.

Exchange List Values
- Starch 2.0
- Fat 0.5
- Meat, medium fat 1.0

Basic Nutritional Values
- Calories 262
- (Calories from Fat 77)
- Total Fat 9 gm
- (Saturated Fat 2.8 gm,
- Polyunsat Fat 1.5 gm,
- Monounsat Fat 3.6 gm)
- Cholesterol 19 mg
- Sodium 579 mg
- Total Carb 32 gm
- Dietary Fiber 3 gm
- Sugars 5 gm
- Protein 15 gm

Election Lunch
Alix Nancy Botsford
Seminole, OK

Makes 12 servings

Prep. Time: 25 minutes
Cooking Time: 2-4 hours
Ideal slow cooker size: 4- or 5-qt.

2 Tbsp. olive oil
1 large onion, chopped
1 lb. sausage, cut into thin slices, *or* casings removed and crumbled
1 rib celery, sliced
1 Tbsp. Worcestershire sauce
1½ tsp. dry mustard
2 Tbsp. honey
sugar substitute to equal 1 Tbsp. sugar
10-oz. can tomatoes with green chili peppers
1-lb. can lima *or* butter beans, drained, with liquid reserved
1-lb. can red kidney beans, drained, with liquid reserved
1-lb. can garbanzo beans, drained, rinsed

1. Brown onion and sausage in oil.

2. Combine ingredients in 6-qt. slow cooker, or divide between 2 4-qt. cookers and stir to combine.

3. Add reserved juice from lima and kidney beans if there's enough room in the cookers.

4. Cover. Cook on low 2-4 hours.

Exchange List Values
- Starch 1.5
- Fat 0.5
- Meat, medium fat 1.0

Basic Nutritional Values
- Calories 204
- (Calories from Fat 79)
- Total Fat 9 gm
- (Saturated Fat 2.4 gm,
- Polyunsat Fat 1.3 gm,
- Monounsat Fat 4.3 gm)
- Cholesterol 14 mg
- Sodium 613 mg
- Total Carb 23 gm
- Dietary Fiber 5 gm
- Sugars 8 gm
- Protein 9 gm

Note:
I mixed up this hearty stew the night before Election Day and took it to the voting site the next morning. I plugged it in, and all day long we could smell the stew cooking. I work at a very sparsely populated, country polling place and ended up giving out the recipe and little water-cup samples to many voters!

I have four different sizes of slow cookers. One is very tiny, with only an on-and-off switch, for keeping cheese sauce hot. One I use for heating gravy. Another I often use to keep mashed potatoes warm.

If you plan to drink alcohol, be sure you will be eating too.

Rice and Beans with Sausage

Marcia S. Myer
Manheim, PA

Makes 8 servings

Prep. Time: 20 minutes
Cooking Time: 4-6 hours
Ideal slow cooker size: 4-qt.

3 celery ribs, chopped
1 onion, chopped
2 garlic cloves, minced
1¾ cups tomato juice
2 16-oz. cans kidney beans, drained
¾ tsp. dried oregano
¾ tsp. dried thyme
¼ tsp. red pepper flakes
¼ tsp. pepper
½ lb. fully-cooked smoked turkey sausage, *or* kielbasa, cut into ¼" slices
3 cups cooked rice
shredded cheese, *optional*

1. Combine all ingredients except rice and shredded cheese in slow cooker.
2. Cover. Cook on low 4-6 hours.
3. Serve over rice. Garnish with shredded cheese, if you wish.

Exchange List Values
- Starch 2.5
- Meat, lean 1.0
- Vegetable 1.0

Basic Nutritional Values
- Calories 241
  (Calories from Fat 33)
- Total Fat 4 gm
  (Saturated Fat 1.0 gm,
  Polyunsat Fat 0.8 gm,
  Monounsat Fat 0.8 gm)
- Cholesterol 18 mg
- Sodium 611 mg
- Total Carb 42 gm
- Dietary Fiber 6 gm
- Sugars 6 gm
- Protein 13 gm

Golden Autumn Stew

Naomi E. Fast
Hesston, KS

Makes 10 servings

Prep. Time: 40 minutes
Cooking Time: 6 hours
Ideal slow cooker size: 4- or 5-qt.

2 cups cubed Yukon gold potatoes
2 cups cubed, peeled sweet potatoes
2 cups cubed, peeled butternut squash
1 cup cubed, peeled rutabaga
1 cup diced carrots
1 cup sliced celery
1 lb. low-fat smoked sausage
2 cups apple juice *or* cider
1 tart apple, thinly sliced
salt to taste
pepper to taste
1 Tbsp. sugar *or* honey

1. Combine vegetables in slow cooker.
2. Place ring of sausage on top.
3. Add apple juice and apple slices.
4. Cover. Cook on high 2 hours and on low 4 hours, or until vegetables are tender. Do not stir.
5. To serve, remove sausage ring. Season with salt, pepper, and sugar as desired. Place vegetables in bowl. Slice meat into rings and place on top.

Exchange List Values
- Starch 1.0
- Fruit 0.5
- Vegetable 1.0
- Meat, lean 1.0

Basic Nutritional Values
- Calories 172
  (Calories from Fat 21)
- Total Fat 2 gm
  (Saturated Fat 0.8 gm,
  Polyunsat Fat 0.9 gm,
  Monounsat Fat 0.5 gm)
- Cholesterol 19 mg
- Sodium 413 mg
- Total Carb 31 gm
- Dietary Fiber 3 gm
- Sugars 15 gm
- Protein 7 gm

Tip:
Don't omit the rutabaga! Get acquainted with its rich uniqueness. It will surprise and please your taste buds.

Polish Kraut 'n' Apples

Lori Berezovsky
Salina, KS

Marie Morucci,
Glen Lyon, PA

Makes 6 servings

Prep. Time: 25 minutes
Cooking Time: 3-7 hours
Ideal slow cooker size: 4-qt.

1 lb. fresh, *or* canned, sauerkraut
1 lb. lean low-fat, smoked Polish sausage
3 tart cooking apples, unpeeled, thinly sliced
2 Tbsp. brown sugar
brown sugar substitute to equal 3 Tbsp. sugar
⅛ tsp. pepper
½ tsp. caraway seeds, *optional*
¾ cup apple juice, *or* cider

1. Rinse sauerkraut and squeeze dry. Place half in slow cooker.

2. Cut sausage into 2-inch lengths and add to cooker.

3. Continue to layer remaining ingredients in slow cooker in order given. Top with remaining sauerkraut. Do not stir.

4. Cover. Cook on high 3-3½ hours, or low 6-7 hours. Stir before serving.

Exchange List Values
- Fruit 1.0
- Meat, lean 1.0
- Carbohydrate 1.0

Basic Nutritional Values
- Calories 195
  (Calories from Fat 33)
- Total Fat 4 gm
  (Saturated Fat 1.4 gm,
  Polyunsat Fat 0.3 gm,
  Monounsat Fat 1.9 gm)
- Cholesterol 35 mg
- Sodium 945 mg
- Total Carb 31 gm
- Dietary Fiber 4 gm
- Sugars 20 gm
- Protein 10 gm

Simple Kielbasa and Cabbage

Mary Ann Lefever
Lancaster, PA

Makes 6 servings

Prep. Time: 15 minutes
Cooking Time: 8 hours
Ideal slow cooker size: 4- or 5-qt.

½ lb. kielbasa cut into 2"-thick chunks
4 large white potatoes, cut into chunks
1-lb. head green cabbage, shredded
4 cups whole tomatoes
onion, thinly sliced, *optional*

1. Layer kielbasa, then potatoes, and then cabbage into slow cooker.

2. Pour tomatoes over top.

3. Top with sliced onions if you wish.

4. Cover. Cook on high 8 hours, or until meat is cooked through and vegetables are as tender as you like them.

Exchange List Values
- Starch 2.0
- High-Fat Meat 1.0
- Vegetable 1.0

Basic Nutritional Values
- Calories 285
  (Calories from Fat 100)
- Total Fat 11 gm
  (Saturated Fat 3.5 gm,
  Polyunsat Fat 1.5 gm,
  Monounsat Fat 4.5 gm)
- Cholesterol 25 mg
- Sodium 370 mg
- Total Carb 39 gm
- Dietary Fiber 6 gm
- Sugars 9 gm
- Protein 10 gm

Kielbasa and Cabbage

Barbara McGinnis
Jupiter, FL

Makes 6 servings

Prep. Time: 35 minutes
Cooking Time: 7-8 hours
Ideal slow cooker size: 4- or 5-qt.

1½ lb.-head green cabbage, shredded
2 medium onions, chopped
3 medium red potatoes, peeled and cubed
1 red bell pepper, chopped
2 garlic cloves, minced
⅔ cup dry white wine
1 lb. low-fat Polish kielbasa, cut into 3-inch pieces
28-oz. can diced no-added-salt tomatoes with juice
1 Tbsp. Dijon mustard
¾ tsp. caraway seeds
½ tsp. pepper

1. Combine all ingredients in slow cooker.

2. Cover. Cook on low 7-8 hours, or until cabbage is tender.

Exchange List Values
- Starch 0.5
- Vegetable 3.0
- Carbohydrate 0.5
- Meat, lean 1.0

Basic Nutritional Values
- Calories 226
  (Calories from Fat 39)
- Total Fat 4 gm
  (Saturated Fat 1.4 gm,
  Polyunsat Fat 0.6 gm,
  Monounsat Fat 2.0 gm)
- Cholesterol 35 mg
- Sodium 781 mg
- Total Carb 34 gm
- Dietary Fiber 7 gm
- Sugars 15 gm
- Protein 14 gm

Aunt Lavina's Sauerkraut

Pat Unternahrer
Wayland, IA

Makes 12 servings

Prep. Time: 20 minutes
Cooking Time: 3-6 hours
Ideal slow cooker size: 4-qt.

2 lbs. smoked low-fat sausage, cut into 1-inch pieces
2 Tbsp. water, *or* oil
2 bell peppers, chopped
2 onions, sliced
½ lb. sliced fresh mushrooms
1 qt. sauerkraut, drained
2 14½-oz. cans no-added-salt diced tomatoes with green peppers
½ tsp. pepper
2 Tbsp. brown sugar

1. Place sausage in slow cooker. Heat on low while you prepare other ingredients.
2. Sauté peppers, onions, and mushrooms in small amount of water or oil in saucepan.
3. Combine all ingredients in slow cooker.
4. Cover. Cook on low 5-6 hours, or high 3-4 hours.
5. Serve with mashed potatoes.

Exchange List Values
• Carbohydrate 0.5 • Meat, lean 1.0
• Vegetable 2.0

Basic Nutritional Values
• Calories 163   • Cholesterol 32 mg
  (Calories from Fat 34) • Sodium 984 mg
• Total Fat 4 gm   • Total Carb 21 gm
  (Saturated Fat 1.4 gm, • Dietary Fiber 4 gm
  Polyunsat Fat 1.5 gm, • Sugars 11 gm
  Monounsat Fat 0.8 gm) • Protein 12 gm

Chops and Kraut

Willard E. Roth
Elkhart, IN

Makes 6 servings

Prep. Time: 15 minutes
Cooking Time: 6 hours
Ideal slow cooker size: 4-qt.

1-lb. bag fresh sauerkraut, drained and rinsed
⅓ cup water
2 large Vidalia onions, sliced
6 (¼ lb. each) pork chops, bone-in, trimmed of fat

1. Make 3 layers in well-greased cooker: kraut, onions, and chops. Pour water over top.
2. Cover. Cook on low 6 hours.

Exchange List Values
• Vegetable 2.0   • Meat, lean 2.0

Basic Nutritional Values
• Calories 156   • Cholesterol 47 mg
  (Calories from Fat 43) • Sodium 336 mg
• Total Fat 5 gm   • Total Carb 10 gm
  (Saturated Fat 1.7 gm, • Dietary Fiber 3 gm
  Polyunsat Fat 0.4 gm, • Sugars 6 gm
  Monounsat Fat 2.1 gm) • Protein 18 gm

Smothered Lentils

Tracey B. Stenger
Gretna, LA

Makes 6 servings

Prep. Time: 25 minutes
Cooking Time: 8 hours
Ideal slow cooker size: 4-qt.

2 cups dry lentils, rinsed and sorted
1 medium onion, chopped
½ cup chopped celery
2 garlic cloves, minced
1 cup ham, cooked and chopped
½ cup chopped carrots
1 cup diced fresh tomatoes
1 tsp. dried marjoram
1 tsp. ground coriander
3 cups water

1. Combine all ingredients in slow cooker.
2. Cover. Cook on low 8 hours, but check lentils after 5 hours of cooking. If they've absorbed all the water, stir in 1 more cup water.

Exchange List Values
• Starch 2.0   • Meat, very lean 2.0
• Vegetable 1.0

Basic Nutritional Values
• Calories 239   • Cholesterol 13 mg
  (Calories from Fat 19) • Sodium 333 mg
• Total Fat 2 gm   • Total Carb 36 gm
  (Saturated Fat 0.5 gm, • Dietary Fiber 14 gm
  Polyunsat Fat 0.5 gm, • Sugars 6 gm
  Monounsat Fat 0.7 gm) • Protein 21 gm

Tip:
  You may want to add salt and pepper if you regularly use them in your diet.

Green Beans and Sausage

Alma Weaver
Ephrata, PA

Makes 6 servings

Prep. Time: 20 minutes
Cooking Time: 4-6 hours
Ideal slow cooker size: 4-qt.

1 qt. green beans, cut into
   2-inch pieces
1 carrot, chopped
1 small green pepper,
   chopped
8-oz. can no-added-salt
   tomato sauce
¼ tsp. dried thyme
¼ tsp. salt
½ lb. bulk pork sausage,
   browned and drained

1. Combine all ingredients except sausage in slow cooker.
2. Cover. Cook on high 3-4 hours. Add sausage and cook another 2 hours on low.

Exchange List Values
• Vegetable 2.0   • Meat, medium fat 1.0

Basic Nutritional Values
• Calories 114   • Cholesterol 14 mg
  (Calories from Fat 53)   • Sodium 350 mg
• Total Fat 6 gm   • Total Carb 11 gm
  (Saturated Fat 2.0 gm,   • Dietary Fiber 4 gm
  Polyunsat Fat 0.8 gm,   • Sugars 5 gm
  Monounsat Fat 2.5 gm)   • Protein 6 gm

Ham Balls

Jo Haberkamp
Fairbank, IA

Makes 24 servings

Prep. Time: 45 minutes
Cooking Time: 4-5 hours
Ideal slow cooker size: 6-qt.

Ham Balls:
  3 eggs
  3 cups crushed graham
    crackers
  2 cups milk
  2 tsp. dried minced
    onion
  ¼ tsp. pepper
  2 lbs. extra-lean,
    reduced-sodium
    ground ham
  1½ lbs. 90%-lean ground
    beef
  1½ lbs. lean ground pork

Topping:
  ½ cup no-salt-added
    ketchup
  ¼ cup water
  ½ cup brown sugar
  ¼ cup plus 2 Tbsp.
    vinegar
  ½ tsp. dry mustard

1. Beat eggs slightly in large bowl. Add graham crackers, milk, minced onion, pepper, and ground meats. Mix well.
2. Form into 24 balls, using ½ cup measuring cup for each ball.
3. Combine topping ingredients.
4. Layer meat balls and topping in greased slow cooker.
5. Cover. Cook on high 1 hour. Reduce heat to low and cook 3-4 hours more.

Exchange List Values
• Carbohydrate 1.0   • Meat, medium fat 2.0

Basic Nutritional Values
• Calories 220   • Cholesterol 82 mg
  (Calories from Fat 63)   • Sodium 429 mg
• Total Fat 7 gm   • Total Carb 17 gm
  (Saturated Fat 2.5 gm,   • Dietary Fiber 0 gm
  Polyunsat Fat 0.9 gm,   • Sugars 10 gm
  Monounsat Fat 2.9 gm)   • Protein 21 gm

Using leftover foods for a recipe saves time. If the leftovers are seasoned, reduce the amount of salt in the recipe.

Chicken Main Dishes

Frances' Roast Chicken

Frances Schrag
Newton, KS

Makes 6 servings

Prep. Time: 15 minutes
Cooking Time: 4-10 hours
Ideal slow cooker size: 4- or 5-qt.

3-lb. whole frying chicken
half an onion, chopped
1 rib celery, chopped
salt to taste
pepper to taste
½ tsp. poultry seasoning
¼ tsp. dried basil

1. Sprinkle chicken cavity with salt, pepper, and poultry seasoning. Put onion and celery inside cavity. Put chicken in slow cooker.

Sprinkle with basil.
2. Cover. Cook on low 8-10 hours, or high 4-6 hours.
3. Remove skin from chicken and discard liquid.

Exchange List Values
• Meat, lean 3.0

Basic Nutritional Values
• Calories 140
  (Calories from Fat 48)
• Total Fat 5 gm
  (Saturated Fat 1.4 gm,
  Polyunsat Fat 1.2 gm,
  Monounsat Fat 1.9 gm)
• Cholesterol 65 mg
• Sodium 56 mg
• Total Carb 0 gm
• Dietary Fiber 0 gm
• Sugars 0 gm
• Protein 21 gm

Donna's Cooked Chicken

Donna Treloar
Gaston, IN

Makes 7 servings

Prep. Time: 10 minutes
Cooking Time: 4 hours
Ideal slow cooker size: 5-qt.

1 medium onion, sliced
2 ½-lb. boneless, skinless
  chicken breasts
½ tsp. seasoned salt
¼ tsp. pepper
½ tsp. garlic powder

1. Layer onion in bottom of slow cooker. Add chicken and sprinkle with seasoned salt, pepper, and garlic powder.
2. Cook on low 4 hours or until done but not dry.

3. Use in stir-fries, chicken salads, or casseroles, slice for sandwiches, shred for enchiladas, or cut up and freeze for later use.

Exchange List Values
- Meat, very lean 4.0

Basic Nutritional Values
- Calories 138
- (Calories from Fat 24)
- Total Fat 3 gm
- (Saturated Fat 0.7 gm, Polyunsat Fat 0.6 gm, Monounsat Fat 0.9 gm)
- Cholesterol 67 mg
- Sodium 131 mg
- Total Carb 1 gm
- Dietary Fiber 0 gm
- Sugars 1 gm
- Protein 25 gm

Variation:
Splash chicken with 2 Tbsp. light soy sauce before cooking.

Chicken in a Pot

Carolyn Baer,
Conrath, WI

Evie Hershey
Atglen, PA

Judy Koczo
Piano, IL

Mary Puskar
Forest Hill, MD

Mary Wheatley
Mashpee, MA

Makes 6 servings

Prep. Time: 20 minutes
Cooking Time: 3½-10 hours
Ideal slow cooker size: 5-qt.

2 medium carrots, sliced
2 medium onions, sliced
2 celery ribs, cut in 1-inch pieces
3 lb. chicken, whole *or* cut up, skin removed

¾ tsp. salt
½ tsp. dried coarse black pepper
1 tsp. dried basil
½ cup water, chicken broth, *or* white cooking wine

1. Place vegetables in bottom of slow cooker. Place chicken on top of vegetables. Add seasonings and water.
2. Cover. Cook on low 8-10 hours, or high 3½ hours (use 1 cup liquid if cooking on high).
3. This is a great foundation for soups: chicken vegetable, chicken noodle, chicken rice, chicken corn, and other favorites.

Exchange List Values
- Vegetable 1.0
- Meat, lean 3.0

Basic Nutritional Values
- Calories 172
- (Calories from Fat 49)
- Total Fat 5 gm
- (Saturated Fat 1.5 gm, Polyunsat Fat 1.3 gm, Monounsat Fat 1.9 gm)
- Cholesterol 65 mg
- Sodium 381 mg
- Total Carb 8 gm
- Dietary Fiber 2 gm
- Sugars 4 gm
- Protein 22 gm

Note:
To make this a full meal, add 2 medium-sized potatoes, quartered, to vegetables before cooking.

Another Chicken in a Pot

Jennifer J. Gehman
Harrisburg, PA

Makes 6 servings

Prep. Time: 20 minutes
Cooking Time: 3½-10 hours
Ideal slow cooker size: 4- or 5-qt.

1-lb. bag baby carrots
1 small onion, diced
10 oz. pkg. frozen, thawed green beans
3-lb. whole chicken, cut into serving-size pieces, skin and fat removed
½ tsp. salt
½ tsp. black pepper
½ cup chicken broth
¼ cup white wine
½-1 tsp. dried basil

1. Put carrots, onion, and beans on bottom of slow cooker. Add chicken. Top with salt, pepper, broth, and wine. Sprinkle with basil.
2. Cover. Cook on low 8-10 hours, or high 3½-5 hours.

Exchange List Values
- Vegetable 2.0
- Meat, lean 3.0

Basic Nutritional Values
- Calories 194
- (Calories from Fat 51)
- Total Fat 6 gm
- (Saturated Fat 1.5 gm, Polyunsat Fat 1.4 gm, Monounsat Fat 2.0 gm)
- Cholesterol 66 mg
- Sodium 434 mg
- Total Carb 12 gm
- Dietary Fiber 4 gm
- Sugars 6 gm
- Protein 23 gm

Don't let diabetes stop you from living life to the fullest.

Savory Slow-Cooker Chicken

Sara Harter Fredette
Williamsburg, MA

Makes 4 servings

Prep. Time: 25 minutes
Cooking Time: 8-10 hours
Ideal slow cooker size: 4- or 5-qt.

2½ lbs. chicken pieces, skinned
1 lb. fresh tomatoes, chopped, *or* 15-oz. can stewed tomatoes
2 Tbsp. white wine
1 bay leaf
¼ tsp. pepper
2 garlic cloves, minced
1 onion, chopped
½ cup chicken broth
1 tsp. dried thyme
¼ tsp. salt
2 cups broccoli, cut into bite-sized pieces

1. Combine all ingredients except broccoli in slow cooker.
2. Cover. Cook on low 8-10 hours.
3. Add broccoli 30 minutes before serving.

Exchange List Values
• Vegetable 2.0   • Meat, lean 3.0

Basic Nutritional Values
• Calories 230   • Cholesterol 82 mg
  (Calories from Fat 67) • Sodium 427 mg
• Total Fat 7 gm   • Total Carb 11 gm
  (Saturated Fat 1.9 gm,   • Dietary Fiber 3 gm
  Polyunsat Fat 1.8 gm,   • Sugars 7 gm
  Monounsat Fat 2.5 gm) • Protein 30 gm

Chicken and Vegetables

Rosanne Hankins
Stevensville, MD

Makes 6 servings

Prep. Time: 20 minutes
Cooking Time: 3½-8½ hours
Ideal slow cooker size: 4- or 5-qt.

3 lb. chicken, cut up, skin and visible fat removed
salt to taste
pepper to taste
1 bay leaf
2 tsp. lemon juice
¼ cup diced onions
¼ cup diced celery
1 lb. frozen mixed vegetables including corn

1. Sprinkle salt and pepper over chicken and place chicken in slow cooker. Add bay leaf and lemon juice.
2. Cover. Cook on low 6-8 hours, or high 3-5 hours. Remove chicken from bones. Reserve liquid, skimming fat.
3. Cook ½ cup liquid, celery and onions in microwave on high for 2 minutes. Add frozen vegetables and microwave until cooked through.
4. Return all ingredients to slow cooker and cook on high 30 minutes.
5. Serve over cooked rice.

Exchange List Values
• Vegetable 2.0   • Meat, lean 3.0

Basic Nutritional Values
• Calories 187   • Cholesterol 65 mg
  (Calories from Fat 49) • Sodium 105 mg
• Total Fat 5 gm   • Total Carb 11 gm
  (Saturated Fat 1.4 gm,   • Dietary Fiber 2 gm
  Polyunsat Fat 1.3 gm,   • Sugars 3 gm
  Monounsat Fat 1.9 gm) • Protein 24 gm

Baked Chicken Breasts

Janice Crist
Quinter, KS
Tracy Supcoe
Barclay, MD

Makes 6 servings

Prep. Time: 15 minutes
Cooking Time: 8-10 hours
Ideal slow cooker size: 4-qt.

3 whole chicken breasts, halved
10¾-oz. can 98% fat-free, reduced sodium cream of chicken soup
½ cup dry sherry
1 tsp. dried tarragon, *or* rosemary
1 tsp. Worcestershire sauce
¼ tsp. garlic powder
4-oz. can sliced mushrooms, drained

1. Place chicken breasts in slow cooker.
2. In saucepan, combine remaining ingredients. Heat until smooth and hot. Pour over chicken.
3. Cover. Cook on low 8-10 hours.

Exchange List Values
- Carbohydrate 0.5
- Fat 0.5
- Meat, very lean 4.0

Basic Nutritional Values
- Calories 214
  (Calories from Fat 40)
- Total Fat 4 gm
  (Saturated Fat 1.3 gm,
  Polyunsat Fat 1.2 gm,
  Monounsat Fat 1.3 gm)
- Cholesterol 88 mg
- Sodium 339 mg
- Total Carb 7 gm
- Dietary Fiber 1 gm
- Sugars 2 gm
- Protein 34 gm

Chicken in Wine

Mary Seielstad
Sparks, NV

Makes 6 servings

Prep. Time: 10 minutes
Cooking Time: 6-8 hours
Ideal slow cooker size: 4-qt.

2 lbs. chicken breasts,
  trimmed of skin and fat
10¾-oz. can 98% fat-free,
  reduced-sodium cream
  of mushroom soup
10¾-oz. can French onion
  soup
1 cup dry white wine, *or*
  chicken broth

1. Put chicken in slow cooker.
2. Combine soups and wine. Pour over chicken.
3. Cover. Cook on low 6-8 hours.
4. Serve over rice, pasta, or potatoes.

Exchange List Values
- Carbohydrate 0.5
- Meat, very lean 5.0

Basic Nutritional Values
- Calories 225
  (Calories from Fat 47)
- Total Fat 5 gm
  (Saturated Fat 1.4 gm,
  Polyunsat Fat 1.2 gm,
  Monounsat Fat 1.6 gm)
- Cholesterol 91 mg
- Sodium 645 mg
- Total Carb 7 gm
- Dietary Fiber 1 gm
- Sugars 3 gm
- Protein 35 gm

Creamy Chicken and Noodles

Rhonda Burgoon
Collingswood, NJ

Makes 6 servings

Prep. Time: 25 minutes
Cooking Time: 4½-9 hours
Ideal slow cooker size: 4-qt.

2 cups sliced carrots
1½ cups chopped onions
1 cup sliced celery
2 Tbsp. snipped fresh
  parsley
bay leaf
3 medium-sized chicken
  legs and thighs (about
  2 lbs.), skin removed
2 10¾-oz. cans 98% fat-free,
  reduced-sodium cream of
  chicken soup
½ cup water
1 tsp. dried thyme
¼ tsp. salt
¼ tsp. pepper
1 cup frozen peas
8 oz. dry wide noodles,
  cooked

1. Place carrots, onions, celery, parsley, and bay leaf in bottom of slow cooker.
2. Place chicken on top of vegetables.
3. Combine soup, water, thyme, salt, and pepper. Pour over chicken and vegetables.
4. Cover. Cook on low 8-9 hours or high 4-4½ hours.
5. Remove chicken from slow cooker. Cool slightly. Remove from bones, cut into bite-sized pieces and return to slow cooker.
6. Remove and discard bay leaf.
7. Stir peas into mixture in slow cooker. Allow to cook for 5-10 more minutes.
8. Pour over cooked noodles. Toss gently to combine.
9. Serve with crusty bread and a salad.

Exchange List Values
- Starch 2.0
- Carbohydrate 0.5
- Vegetable 2.0
- Meat, lean 2.0

Basic Nutritional Values
- Calories 357
  (Calories from Fat 71)
- Total Fat 8 gm
  (Saturated Fat 2.4 gm,
  Polyunsat Fat 2.3 gm,
  Monounsat Fat 2.3 gm)
- Cholesterol 87 mg
- Sodium 614 mg
- Total Carb 48 gm
- Dietary Fiber 5 gm
- Sugars 9 gm
- Protein 22 gm

Chicken in Mushroom Gravy

Rosemarie Fitzgerald
Gibsonia, PA
Audrey L. Kneer
WIlliamsfield, IL

Makes 6 servings

Prep. Time: 10 minutes
Cooking Time: 7-9 hours
Ideal slow cooker size: 4-qt.

6 (5 oz. each) boneless, skinless chicken-breast halves
salt and pepper to taste
¼ cup dry white wine, *or* chicken broth
10¾-oz. can 98% fat-free, reduced-sodium cream of mushroom soup
4-oz. can sliced mushrooms, drained

1. Place chicken in slow cooker. Season with salt and pepper.
2. Combine wine and soup. Pour over chicken. Top with mushrooms.
3. Cover. Cook on low 7-9 hours.

Exchange List Values
• Carbohydrate 0.5 • Fat 0.5
• Meat, very lean 4.0

Basic Nutritional Values
• Calories 204 • Cholesterol 85 mg
(Calories from Fat 40) • Sodium 320 mg
• Total Fat 4 gm • Total Carb 6 gm
(Saturated Fat 1.4 gm, • Dietary Fiber 1 gm
Polyunsat Fat 1.0 gm, • Sugars 1 gm
Monounsat Fat 1.3 gm) • Protein 34 gm

Mushroom Chicken in Sour Cream Sauce

Lavina Hochstedler
Grand Blanc, MI
Joyce Shackelford
Green Bay, WI

Makes 6 servings

Prep. Time: 15 minutes
Cooking Time: 5-8 hours
Ideal slow cooker size: 4-qt.

¼ tsp. salt
¼ tsp. pepper
½ tsp. paprika
¼ tsp. lemon pepper
1 tsp. garlic powder
6 skinless, bone-in chicken breast halves
10¾-oz. can 98% fat-free, reduced-sodium cream of mushroom soup
8-oz. container fat-free sour cream
½ cup dry white wine *or* chicken broth
½ lb. fresh mushrooms, sliced

1. Combine salt, pepper, paprika, lemon pepper, and garlic powder. Rub over chicken. Place in slow cooker.
2. Combine soup, sour cream, and wine or broth. Stir in mushrooms. Pour over chicken.
3. Cover. Cook on low 6-8 hours or high 5 hours.

Exchange List Values
• Carbohydrate 1.0 • Meat, very lean 4.0

Basic Nutritional Values
• Calories 217 • Cholesterol 76 mg
(Calories from Fat 37) • Sodium 407 mg
• Total Fat 4 gm • Total Carb 12 gm
(Saturated Fat 1.2 gm, • Dietary Fiber 1 gm
Polyunsat Fat 0.9 gm, • Sugars 4 gm
Monounsat Fat 1.2 gm) • Protein 30 gm

Note:
Serve over potatoes, rice, or couscous. Delicious accompanied with broccoli-cauliflower salad and applesauce.

Chicken Azteca

Katrine Rose
Woodbridge, VA

Makes 12 servings

Prep. Time: 10 minutes
Cooking Time: 2-6 hours
Ideal slow cooker size: 5- or 6-qt.

2 15-oz. cans black beans, drained
4 cups frozen corn kernels
2 garlic cloves, minced
¾ tsp. ground cumin
2 cups chunky salsa, *divided*
10 skinless, boneless chicken-breast halves
12-oz. fat-free cream cheese, cubed

1. Combine beans, corn, garlic, cumin, and half of salsa in slow cooker.
2. Arrange chicken breasts over top. Pour remaining salsa over top.
3. Cover. Cook on high 2-3 hours or on low 4-6 hours.

4. Remove chicken and cut into bite-sized pieces. Return to cooker.

5. Stir in cream cheese. Cook on high until cream cheese melts.

6. Spoon chicken and sauce over cooked rice.

Exchange List Values
- Starch 1.5
- Meat, very lean 4.0

Basic Nutritional Values
- Calories 252
  (Calories from Fat 27)
- Total Fat 3 gm
  (Saturated Fat 0.8 gm,
  Polyunsat Fat 0.8 gm,
  Monounsat Fat 0.9 gm)
- Cholesterol 64 mg
- Sodium 366 mg
- Total Carb 24 gm
- Dietary Fiber 5 gm
- Sugars 4 gm
- Protein 33 gm

Tex-Mex Chicken and Rice
Kelly Amos
Pittsboro, NC

Makes 8 servings

Prep. Time: 25 minutes
Cooking Time: 4-4½ hours
Ideal slow cooker size: 4- or 5-qt.

1 cup converted uncooked white rice
28-oz. can diced peeled tomatoes
6-oz. can tomato paste
3 cups hot water
1 pkg. dry taco seasoning mix
4 whole boneless, skinless chicken breasts, uncooked and cut into ½" cubes
2 medium onions, chopped

1 green pepper, chopped
4-oz. can diced green chilies
1 tsp. garlic powder
½ tsp. pepper

1. Combine all ingredients except chilies and seasonings in large slow cooker.

2. Cover. Cook on low 4-4½ hours, or until rice is tender and chicken is cooked.

3. Stir in green chilies and seasonings and serve.

Exchange List Values
- Starch 1.5
- Vegetable 3.0
- Meat, very lean 3.0

Basic Nutritional Values
- Calories 300
  (Calories from Fat 32)
- Total Fat 4 gm
  (Saturated Fat 0.8 gm,
  Polyunsat Fat 0.9 gm,
  Monounsat Fat 1.1 gm)
- Cholesterol 73 mg
- Sodium 656 mg
- Total Carb 34 gm
- Dietary Fiber 4 gm
- Sugars 7 gm
- Protein 32 gm

Tamale Chicken
Jeanne Allen
Rye, CO

Makes 8 servings

Prep. Time: 20 minutes
Cooking Time: 3-4 hours
Ideal slow cooker size: 4- or 5-qt.

1 medium onion, chopped
4-oz. can chopped green chilies
1 Tbsp. canola oil
10¾-oz. can 98% fat-free, reduced-sodium cream of chicken soup
1 cup fat-free sour cream
1 cup sliced ripe olives

1 cup chopped no-added-salt stewed tomatoes
1¼ cups shredded fat-free cheddar cheese, *divided*
8 chicken breast halves, cooked and chopped
16-oz. can beef tamales, chopped
1 tsp. chili powder
1 tsp. garlic powder
1 tsp. pepper

1. Sauté onion and chilies in oil in skillet.

2. Combine all ingredients except ¼ cup shredded cheese. Pour into slow cooker.

3. Top with remaining cheese.

4. Cover. Cook on high 3-4 hours.

Exchange List Values
- Starch 0.5
- Carbohydrate 0.5
- Vegetable 1.0
- Meat, lean 4.0
- Fat 0.5

Basic Nutritional Values
- Calories 341
  (Calories from Fat 98)
- Total Fat 11 gm
  (Saturated Fat 2.7 gm,
  Polyunsat Fat 2.1 gm,
  Monounsat Fat 4.9 gm)
- Cholesterol 87 mg
- Sodium 848 mg
- Total Carb 21 gm
- Dietary Fiber 3 gm
- Sugars 5 gm
- Protein 37 gm

Note:
Pass chopped fresh tomatoes, shredded lettuce, sour cream, salsa, and or guacamole as toppings.

Wanda's Chicken and Rice Casserole

Wanda Roth
Napoleon, OH

Makes 8 servings

Prep. Time: 15 minutes
Cooking Time: 3-4 hours
Ideal slow cooker size: 4- or 5-qt.

1 cup long-grain rice, uncooked
3 cups water
2 tsp. chicken bouillon granules
10¾-oz can 98% fat-free, reduced-sodium cream of chicken soup
16-oz. bag frozen broccoli
2 cups chopped, cooked chicken
½ tsp. garlic powder
¼ tsp. onion salt
1 cup grated fat-free cheddar cheese

1. Combine all ingredients in slow cooker.
2. Cook on high 3-4 hours.

Exchange List Values
- Starch 1.5
- Meat, lean 1.0
- Vegetable 1.0

Basic Nutritional Values
- Calories 214
  (Calories from Fat 33)
- Total Fat 4 gm
  (Saturated Fat 1.0 gm,
  Polyunsat Fat 1.0 gm,
  Monounsat Fat 1.1 gm)
- Cholesterol 36 mg
- Sodium 559 mg
- Total Carb 26 gm
- Dietary Fiber 2 gm
- Sugars 3 gm
- Protein 19 gm

Note:
If casserole is too runny, remove lid from slow cooker for 15 minutes while continuing to cook on high.

Sharon's Chicken and Rice Casserole

Sharon Anders
Alburtis, PA

Makes 4 servings

Prep. Time: 15 minutes
Cooking Time: 4-6 hours
Ideal slow cooker size: 3- or 4-qt.

10¾-oz. can cream of celery soup
2-oz. can sliced mushrooms, drained
½ cup uncooked long grain rice
4 chicken-breast halves, skinned and boned
1 Tbsp. sodium free dried onion soup mix (see recipe on page 261)

1. Combine soup, mushrooms, and rice in greased slow cooker. Mix well.
2. Layer chicken breasts on top of mixture. Sprinkle with onion soup mix.
3. Cover. Cook on low 4-6 hours.

Exchange List Values
- Starch 2.0
- Fat 1.0
- Meat, very lean 4.0

Basic Nutritional Values
- Calories 330
  (Calories from Fat 71)
- Total Fat 8 gm
  (Saturated Fat 2.4 gm,
  Polyunsat Fat 2.5 gm,
  Monounsat Fat 2.0 gm)
- Cholesterol 86 mg
- Sodium 677 mg
- Total Carb 26 gm
- Dietary Fiber 2 gm
- Sugars 2 gm
- Protein 35 gm

Scalloped Chicken

Carolyn W. Carmichael
Berkeley Heights, NJ

Makes 4 servings

Prep. Time: 15 minutes
Cooking Time: 4-10 hours
Ideal slow cooker size: 4-qt.

5-oz. pkg. scalloped potatoes
scalloped potatoes dry seasoning pack
2 chicken-breast halves
2 chicken legs
10-oz. pkg. frozen peas
2 cups water

1. Put potatoes, seasoning pack, chicken, and peas in slow cooker. Pour water over all.
2. Cover. Cook on low 8-10 hours, or high 4 hours.

Exchange List Values
- Starch 2.0
- Meat, lean 3.0

Basic Nutritional Values
- Calories 336
  (Calories from Fat 64)
- Total Fat 7 gm
  (Saturated Fat 2.0 gm,
  Polyunsat Fat 2.1 gm,
  Monounsat Fat 2.1 gm)
- Cholesterol 87 mg
- Sodium 861 mg
- Total Carb 34 gm
- Dietary Fiber 5 gm
- Sugars 5 gm
- Protein 35 gm

Wild Rice Hot Dish

Barbara Tenney
Delta, PA

Makes 10 side dish servings

Prep. Time: 25 minutes
Cooking Time: 4-6 hours
Ideal slow cooker size: 4-qt.

2 cups wild rice, uncooked
½ cup slivered almonds
½ cup chopped onions
½ cup chopped celery
8-oz. can mushrooms, drained
2 cups chopped, cooked chicken
6 cups reduced-sodium, 98% fat-free chicken broth
¼ tsp. pepper
¼ tsp. garlic powder
1 Tbsp. parsley

1. Wash and drain rice.
2. Combine all ingredients in slow cooker. Mix well.
3. Cover. Cook on low 4-6 hours, or until rice is finished. Do not remove lid before rice has cooked 4 hours.

Exchange List Values
- Starch 2.0
- Meat, lean 1.0
- Fat 0.5

Basic Nutritional Values
- Calories 227
  (Calories from Fat 51)
- Total Fat 6 gm
  (Saturated Fat 0.8 gm,
  Polyunsat Fat 1.4 gm,
  Monounsat Fat 2.7 gm)
- Cholesterol 25 mg
- Sodium 403 mg
- Total Carb 28 gm
- Dietary Fiber 4 gm
- Sugars 2 gm
- Protein 17 gm

Autumn Chicken and Veggies

Nanci Keatley
Salem, OR

Makes 6 servings

Prep. Time: 15 minutes
Cooking Time: 4-6 hours
Ideal slow-cooker size: 6 qt.

2 yellow onions, chopped
2 parsnips, cut into ½"-thick slices
3 carrots, cut into ½"-thick slices
1 lb. celery root, cut into chunks
½ tsp. salt
¼-½ tsp. pepper
6 boneless skinless chicken breast halves
1 tsp. dried tarragon
1 cup fat-free, low-sodium chicken broth
½ cup white wine

1. Place vegetables in slow cooker.
2. Lay chicken pieces over vegetables.
3. Season with salt and pepper. Sprinkle with tarragon.
4. Pour broth and wine around the chicken pieces, so as not to disturb the seasonings.
5. Cover. Cook on low 4-6 hours, or until vegetables and chicken are tender and done to your liking.

Exchange List Values
- Starch 0.5
- Vegetable 2.0
- Lean Meat 3.0

Basic Nutritional Values
- Calories 230
  (Calories from Fat 30)
- Total Fat 4 gm
  (Saturated Fat 1.0 gm,
  Polyunsat Fat 1.0 gm,
  Monounsat Fat 1.0 gm)
- Cholesterol 75 mg
- Sodium 435 mg
- Total Carb 19 gm
- Dietary Fiber 4 gm
- Sugars 6 gm
- Protein 29 gm

Tip:
We like this with mashed potatoes or some good French bread.

Eat a variety of fruits and vegetables for a greater mix of vitamins, minerals, and other nutrients.

Chicken and Vegetables

Jeanne Heyerly
Chenoa, IL

Makes 2 servings

Prep. Time: 25 minutes
Cooking Time: 8-9 hours
Ideal slow cooker size: 4-qt.

2 medium potatoes, quartered
2-3 carrots, sliced
5 oz. frozen chicken breasts
1 frozen drumstick
salt and pepper to taste
1 medium onion, chopped
2 garlic cloves, minced
1 cup shredded cabbage
2 tsp. salt-free bouillon
2 cups water

1. Place potatoes and carrots in slow cooker. Layer chicken on top. Sprinkle with salt, pepper, onion, and garlic. Top with cabbage.
2. Combine bouillon powder with water. Carefully pour bouillon mixture around the edge.
3. Cover. Cook on low 8-9 hours.

Exchange List Values
• Starch 2.0   • Meat, lean 2.0
• Vegetable 3.0

Basic Nutritional Values
• Calories 335   • Cholesterol 62 mg
(Calories from Fat 30) • Sodium 129 mg
• Total Fat 3 gm   • Total Carb 48 gm
(Saturated Fat 0.8 gm, • Dietary Fiber 8 gm
Polyunsat Fat 1.0 gm, • Sugars 14 gm
Monounsat Fat 1.0 gm) • Protein 28 gm

California Chicken

Shirley Sears
Tiskilwa, IL

Makes 6 servings

Prep. Time: 20 minutes
Cooking Time: 8½-9½ hours
Ideal slow cooker size: 4-qt.

3-lb. chicken, quartered, skin removed, trimmed of visible fat
1 cup orange juice
⅓ cup chili sauce
2 Tbsp. light soy sauce
1 Tbsp. molasses
1 tsp. dry mustard
¼ tsp. garlic powder
¼ tsp. onion powder
2 Tbsp. chopped green peppers
3 medium oranges, peeled and separated into slices

1. Arrange chicken in slow cooker.
2. In separate bowl, combine juice, chili sauce, soy sauce, molasses, dry mustard, garlic, and onion powder. Pour over chicken.
3. Cover. Cook on low 8-9 hours.
4. Stir in green peppers and oranges. Heat 30 minutes longer.

Exchange List Values
• Fruit 1.0   • Meat, lean 3.0
• Vegetable 1.0

Basic Nutritional Values
• Calories 224   • Cholesterol 65 mg
(Calories from Fat 50) • Sodium 426 mg
• Total Fat 6 gm   • Total Carb 20 gm
(Saturated Fat 1.5 gm, • Dietary Fiber 2 gm
Polyunsat Fat 1.3 gm, • Sugars 15 gm
Monounsat Fat 1.9 gm) • Protein 24 gm

Variation:
Stir 1 tsp. curry powder in with sauces and seasonings. Stir 1 small can pineapple chunks and juice in with green peppers and oranges.

Dad's Spicy Chicken Curry

Tom & Sue Ruth
Lancaster, PA

Makes 8 servings

Prep. Time: 25 minutes
Cooking Time: 6-8 hours
Ideal slow cooker size: 4- or 5-qt.

4 lbs. chicken pieces, with bones, trimmed of skin and fat
water
2 medium onions, diced
10-oz. pkg. frozen chopped spinach, thawed and squeezed dry
1 cup plain low-fat yogurt
2-3 diced red potatoes
1 tsp. salt
1 tsp. garlic powder
1 tsp. ground ginger
1 tsp. ground cumin
1 tsp. ground coriander
1 tsp. pepper
1 tsp. ground cloves
1 tsp. ground cardamom

1 tsp. ground cinnamon
½ tsp. chili powder
1 tsp. red pepper flakes
3 tsp. turmeric

1. Place chicken in large slow cooker. Cover with water.
2. Cover. Cook on high 2 hours, or until tender.
3. Drain chicken. Remove from slow cooker. Cool briefly and cut/shred into small pieces. Return to slow cooker.
4. Add remaining ingredients.
5. Cover. Cook on low 4-6 hours, or until potatoes are tender.

Exchange List Values
• Carbohydrate 1.0 • Meat, lean 3.0

Basic Nutritional Values
• Calories 221
 (Calories from Fat 56)
• Total Fat 6 gm
 (Saturated Fat 1.8 gm,
 Polyunsat Fat 1.4 gm,
 Monounsat Fat 2.1 gm)
• Cholesterol 67 mg
• Sodium 402 mg
• Total Carb 16 gm
• Dietary Fiber 3 gm
• Sugars 4 gm
• Protein 25 gm

Note:
Serve on rice. Accompany with fresh mango slices or mango chutney.

Variation:
Substitute 5 tsp. curry powder for the garlic, ginger, cumin, coriander, and pepper.

Orange Chicken Leg Quarters
Kimberly Jensen
Bailey, CO

Makes 5 servings

Prep. Time: 35 minutes
Cooking Time: 6-7 hours
Ideal slow cooker size: 4-qt.

4 chicken drumsticks, visible fat removed
4 chicken thighs, visible fat removed
1 cup green and red bell pepper strips
½ cup chicken broth
½ cup orange juice
½ cup no-salt-added ketchup
2 Tbsp. light soy sauce
1 Tbsp. light molasses
1 Tbsp. prepared mustard
¼ tsp. garlic powder
11-oz. can mandarin oranges
2 tsp. cornstarch
1 cup frozen peas
2 green onions, sliced

1. Place chicken in slow cooker. Top with pepper strips.
2. Combine broth, juice, ketchup, soy sauce, molasses, mustard, and garlic salt. Pour over chicken.
3. Cover. Cook on low 6-7 hours.
4. Remove chicken and vegetables from slow cooker. Keep warm.
5. Measure out 1 cup of cooking sauce. Put in saucepan and bring to boil. Discard remaining cooking sauce.
6. Drain oranges, reserving 1 Tbsp. juice. Stir cornstarch into reserved juice. Add to boiling sauce in pan.
7. Add peas to sauce and cook, stirring for 2-3 minutes until sauce thickens and peas are warm. Stir in oranges.
8. Arrange chicken pieces on platter of cooked rice, fried cellophane noodles, or lo mein noodles. Pour orange sauce over all. Top with sliced green onions.

Exchange List Values
• Carbohydrate 1.5 • Meat, lean 3.0

Basic Nutritional Values
• Calories 285
 (Calories from Fat 77)
• Total Fat 9 gm
 (Saturated Fat 2.3 gm,
 Polyunsat Fat 2.0 gm,
 Monounsat Fat 3.1 gm)
• Cholesterol 90 mg
• Sodium 382 mg
• Total Carb 21 gm
• Dietary Fiber 3 gm
• Sugars 14 gm
• Protein 30 gm

Exercise with someone. It's more fun that way, and you can encourage each other when your motivation fails you.

Creamy Nutmeg Chicken

Amber Swarey
Donalds, SC

Makes 6 servings

Prep. Time: 30 minutes
Cooking Time: 3 hours
Ideal slow cooker size: 4-qt.

6 boneless chicken breast halves, skin and visible fat removed
1 Tbsp. canola oil
¼ cup chopped onions
¼ cup minced parsley
2 10¾-oz. cans 98% fat-free, reduced-sodium cream of mushroom soup
½ cup fat-free sour cream
½ cup fat-free milk
1 Tbsp. ground nutmeg
¼ tsp. sage
¼ tsp. dried thyme
¼ tsp. crushed rosemary

1. Brown chicken in skillet in oil. Reserve drippings and place chicken in slow cooker.
2. Sauté onions and parsley in drippings until onions are tender.
3. Stir in remaining ingredients. Mix well. Pour over chicken.
4. Cover. Cook on low 3 hours, or until juices run clear.

Exchange List Values
• Carbohydrate 1.0   • Fat 1.0
• Meat, very lean 4.0

Basic Nutritional Values
• Calories 264   • Cholesterol 83 mg
  (Calories from Fat 69) • Sodium 495 mg
• Total Fat 8 gm   • Total Carb 15 gm
  (Saturated Fat 1.9 gm, • Dietary Fiber 1 gm
  Polyunsat Fat 2.1 gm,   • Sugars 5 gm
  Monounsat Fat 2.8 gm)   • Protein 31 gm

Orange Chicken and Sweet Potatoes

Kimberlee Greenawalt
Harrisonburg, VA

Makes 6 servings

Prep. Time: 25 minutes
Cooking Time: 3-10 hours
Ideal slow cooker size: 4-qt.

2 (5½ oz. each) sweet potatoes, peeled and sliced
3 whole boneless skinless chicken breasts, halved, all visible fat removed
⅔ cup flour
1 tsp. nutmeg
½ tsp. cinnamon
10¾-oz. can 98% fat-free, reduced-sodium cream of chicken soup
4-oz. can sliced mushrooms, drained
½ cup orange juice
½ tsp. grated orange rind
2 tsp. brown sugar
3 Tbsp. flour

1. Place sweet potatoes in bottom of slow cooker.
2. Rinse chicken breasts and pat dry. Combine flour, nutmeg, and cinnamon.

Thoroughly coat chicken in flour mixture. Place on top of sweet potatoes.
3. Combine soup with remaining ingredients. Stir well. Pour over chicken breasts.
4. Cover. Cook on low 8-10 hours, or high 3-4 hours.
5. Serve over rice.

Exchange List Values
• Starch 2.0   • Meat, very lean 4.0
• Carbohydrate 0.5

Basic Nutritional Values
• Calories 337   • Cholesterol 88 mg
  (Calories from Fat 44) • Sodium 335 mg
• Total Fat 5 gm   • Total Carb 34 gm
  (Saturated Fat 1.4 gm, • Dietary Fiber 3 gm
  Polyunsat Fat 1.3 gm,   • Sugars 8 gm
  Monounsat Fat 1.4 gm)   • Protein 36 gm

Sweet and Sour Chicken

Bernice A. Esau
North Newton, KS

Makes 6 servings

Prep. Time: 20 minutes
Cooking Time: 8-10 hours
Ideal slow cooker size: 4-qt.

1½ cups sliced carrots
1 large green pepper, chopped
1 medium onion, chopped
2 Tbsp. quick-cooking tapioca
2½ lbs. chicken, cut into serving-size pieces, skin removed, trimmed of fat
8-oz. can pineapple chunks in juice

3 Tbsp. brown sugar
brown sugar substitute to
    equal 1½ Tbsp. sugar
⅓ cup vinegar
1 Tbsp. soy sauce
½ tsp. instant chicken
    bouillon
¼ tsp. garlic powder
½ tsp. freshly grated ginger
⅛ tsp. salt

1. Place vegetables in bottom of slow cooker. Sprinkle with tapioca. Add chicken.
2. In separate bowl, combine pineapple, brown sugar, vinegar, soy sauce, bouillon, garlic powder, ginger, and salt. Pour over chicken.
3. Cover. Cook on low 8-10 hours.

Exchange List Values
- Fruit 0.5
- Vegetable 1.0
- Carbohydrate 0.5
- Meat, lean 2.0

Basic Nutritional Values
- Calories 208
  (Calories from Fat 41)
- Total Fat 5 gm
  (Saturated Fat 1.2 gm,
  Polyunsat Fat 1.1 gm,
  Monounsat Fat 1.6 gm)
- Cholesterol 54 mg
- Sodium 365 mg
- Total Carb 23 gm
- Dietary Fiber 2 gm
- Sugars 16 gm
- Protein 19 gm

Chicken with Applesauce
Kelly Amos
Pittsboro, NC

Makes 4 servings

Prep. Time: 20 minutes
Cooking Time: 2-3 hours
Ideal slow cooker size: 4-qt.

4 boneless, skinless
    chicken breast halves
salt to taste
pepper to taste
2 Tbsp. oil
2 cups applesauce,
    unsweetened
¼ cup barbecue sauce
½ tsp. poultry seasoning
2 tsp. honey
½ tsp. lemon juice

1. Season chicken with salt and pepper. Brown in oil for 5 minutes per side.
2. Cut up chicken into 1" chunks and transfer to slow cooker.
3. Combine remaining ingredients. Pour over chicken and mix together well.
4. Cover. Cook on high 2-3 hours, or until chicken is tender.

Exchange List Values
- Fruit 1.0
- Fat 2.0
- Meat, very lean 4.0

Basic Nutritional Values
- Calories 301
  (Calories from Fat 94)
- Total Fat 10 gm
  (Saturated Fat 1.5 gm,
  Polyunsat Fat 2.9 gm,
  Monounsat Fat 5.3 gm)
- Cholesterol 84 mg
- Sodium 199 mg
- Total Carb 19 gm
- Dietary Fiber 2 gm
- Sugars 16 gm
- Protein 32 gm

Maui Chicken
John D. Allen
Rye, CO

Makes 6 servings

Prep. Time: 20 minutes
Cooking Time: 4-6 hours
Ideal slow cooker size: 4-qt.

6 boneless skinless chicken
    breast halves, trimmed
    of fat
2 Tbsp. oil
14½-oz. can chicken broth
20-oz. can pineapple
    chunks
¼ cup vinegar
2 Tbsp. brown sugar
2 tsp. soy sauce
1 garlic clove, minced
1 medium green bell
    pepper, chopped
3 Tbsp. cornstarch
¼ cup water

1. Brown chicken in oil. Transfer chicken to slow cooker.
2. Combine remaining ingredients. Pour over chicken.
3. Cover. Cook on high 4-6 hours.

Exchange List Values
- Fruit 1.0
- Meat, very lean 4.0
- Carbohydrate 0.5
- Fat 1.5

Basic Nutritional Values
- Calories 305
  (Calories from Fat 75)
- Total Fat 8 gm
  (Saturated Fat 1.4 gm,
  Polyunsat Fat 2.2 gm,
  Monounsat Fat 4.0 gm)
- Cholesterol 82 mg
- Sodium 601 mg
- Total Carb 25 gm
- Dietary Fiber 1 gm
- Sugars 19 gm
- Protein 32 gm

Ann's Chicken Cacciatore

Ann Driscoll
Albuquerque, NM

Makes 8 servings

Prep. Time: 25 minutes
Cooking Time: 3-9 hours
Ideal slow cooker size: 4-qt.

1 large onion, thinly sliced
3 lb. chicken, cut up, skin removed, trimmed of fat
2 6-oz. cans tomato paste
4-oz. can sliced mushrooms, drained
1 tsp. salt
¼ cup dry white wine
¼ tsp. pepper
1-2 garlic cloves, minced
1-2 tsp. dried oregano
½ tsp. dried basil
½ tsp. celery seed, *optional*
1 bay leaf

1. Place onion in slow cooker. Add chicken.
2. Combine remaining ingredients. Pour over chicken.
3. Cover. Cook on low 7-9 hours, or high 3-4 hours.

Exchange List Values
• Vegetable 3.0   • Meat, lean 2.0

Basic Nutritional Values
• Calories 161   • Cholesterol 49 mg
(Calories from Fat 40)   • Sodium 405 mg
• Total Fat 4 gm   • Total Carb 12 gm
(Saturated Fat 1.1 gm,   • Dietary Fiber 3 gm
Polyunsat Fat 1.1 gm,   • Sugars 3 gm
Monounsat Fat 1.5 gm)   • Protein 19 gm

Chicken and Sausage Cacciatore

Joyce Kaut
Rochester, NY

Makes 6 servings

Prep. Time: 30 minutes
Cooking Time: 8 hours
Ideal slow cooker size: 4-qt.

1 large green pepper, sliced in 1" strips
1 cup sliced mushrooms
1 medium onion, sliced in rings
1 lb. skinless, boneless chicken breasts, browned
1 lb. lean sweet Italian turkey sausage, browned
½ tsp. dried oregano
½ tsp. dried basil
2 Tbsp. Italian seasoning (see recipe on page 260)
1½ cups no-added-salt tomato sauce

1. Layer vegetables in slow cooker.
2. Top with meat.
3. Sprinkle with oregano, basil, and Italian seasoning mix.
4. Top with tomato sauce.
5. Cover. Cook on low 8 hours.
6. Remove cover during last 30 minutes of cooking time to allow sauce to cook-off and thicken.

Exchange List Values
• Vegetable 2.0   • Meat, lean 4.0

Basic Nutritional Values
• Calories 278   • Cholesterol 105 mg
(Calories from Fat 100)   • Sodium 547 mg
• Total Fat 11 gm   • Total Carb 10 gm
(Saturated Fat 3.1 gm,   • Dietary Fiber 2 gm
Polyunsat Fat 1.5 gm,   • Sugars 6 gm
Monounsat Fat 2.3 gm)   • Protein 34 gm

Braised Chicken with Summer Tomatoes

Karen Ceneviva
Seymour, CT

Makes 7 servings

Prep. Time: 30 minutes
Cooking Time: 3-4 hours
Ideal slow-cooker size: 6 qt.

4½-lb. chicken cut into 8 pieces (save back and wings for making soup another day), skin removed
salt and pepper to taste
¼ cup extra-virgin olive oil, *divided*
1 large yellow onion, chopped
10 cloves garlic, peeled
½ cup wine vinegar
1½ cups chicken broth
4 fresh tarragon sprigs, *or* 2 Tbsp. finely chopped fresh tarragon leaves
6-8 medium (about 3½ lbs.) tomatoes, chopped

1. Season chicken to taste with salt and pepper.
2. Place 2 Tbsp. oil in large skillet. Brown chicken, a few pieces at a time, over

medium-high heat in skillet.

3. When both sides of each piece of chicken are browned, remove from skillet and keep warm on platter.

4. Add remaining 2 Tbsp. oil to skillet. Stir in chopped onion. Sauté over medium heat about 8 minutes.

5. Add garlic and sauté about 5 minutes. Add vinegar and simmer 1 minute.

6. Carefully pour oil/vinegar/onion/garlic mixture into slow cooker. Place chicken on top.

7. Tuck tarragon sprigs around chicken pieces, or sprinkle with chopped tarragon. Spoon chopped tomatoes over top.

8. Cover. Cook on low 3-4 hours, or until chicken is tender.

Exchange List Values

- Vegetable 3.0   • Fat 1.5
- Lean Meat 4.0

Basic Nutritional Values

- Calories 325   • Cholesterol 90 mg
  (Calories from Fat 135) • Sodium 445 mg
- Total Fat 15 gm   • Total Carb 14 gm
  (Saturated Fat 3.0 gm, • Dietary Fiber 3 gm
  Polyunsat Fat 2.5 gm,   • Sugars 8 gm
  Monounsat Fat 8.0 gm)   • Protein 33 gm

Coq au Vín

Kimberlee Greenawalt
Harrisonburg, VA

Makes 6 servings

Prep. Time: 20 minutes
Cooking Time: 6¼-8¼ hours
Ideal slow cooker size: 4-qt.

2 cups frozen pearl onions, thawed
4 thick slices bacon, fried, drained, patted dry, and crumbled
1 cup sliced button mushrooms
1 garlic clove, minced
1 tsp. dried thyme leaves
⅛ tsp. black pepper
6 (5 oz. each) boneless, skinless chicken-breast halves, trimmed of fat
½ cup dry red wine
¾ cup chicken broth
¼ cup tomato paste
3 Tbsp. flour

1. Layer ingredients in slow cooker in the following order: onions, bacon, mushrooms, garlic, thyme, pepper, chicken, wine, broth.

2. Cover. Cook on low 6-8 hours.

3. Remove chicken and vegetables. Cover and keep warm.

4. Ladle ½ cup cooking liquid into small bowl. Cool slightly. Turn slow cooker to high and cover.

5. Mix reserved liquid, tomato paste, and flour until smooth. Return mixture to slow cooker, cover, and cook 15 minutes, or until thickened.

6. Serve chicken, vegetables, and sauce over noodles.

Exchange List Values

- Vegetable 2.0   • Fat 1.5
- Meat, very lean 4.0

Basic Nutritional Values

- Calories 258   • Cholesterol 91 mg
  (Calories from Fat 66) • Sodium 388 mg
- Total Fat 7 gm   • Total Carb 10 gm
  (Saturated Fat 2.2 gm, • Dietary Fiber 2 gm
  Polyunsat Fat 1.2 gm,   • Sugars 4 gm
  Monounsat Fat 2.9 gm)   • Protein 36 gm

Lemon Garlic Chicken

Cindy Krestynick
Glen Lyon, PA

Makes 6 servings

Prep. Time: 25 minutes
Cooking Time: 2½-5½ hours
Ideal slow cooker size: 4-qt.

1 tsp. dried oregano
½ tsp. seasoned salt
¼ tsp. pepper
6 (5 oz. each) chicken-breast halves, skinned and rinsed
2 Tbsp. canola oil
¼ cup water
3 Tbsp. lemon juice
2 garlic cloves, minced
1 tsp. chicken bouillon granules
1 Tbsp. minced fresh parsley

1. Combine oregano, salt, and pepper. Rub all of mixture into chicken. Brown chicken in canola oil in skillet. Transfer to slow cooker.

2. Place water, lemon juice, garlic, and bouillon cubes in skillet. Bring to boil, loosening browned bits from skillet. Pour over chicken.

3. Cover. Cook on high 2-2½ hours, or low 4-5 hours.

4. Add parsley and baste chicken. Cover. Cook on high 15-30 minutes, until chicken is tender.

Exchange List Values
• Meat, very lean 4.0 • Fat 1.5

Basic Nutritional Values
• Calories 210   • Cholesterol 84 mg
  (Calories from Fat 71) • Sodium 283 mg
• Total Fat 8 gm   • Total Carb 1 gm
  (Saturated Fat 1.2 gm, • Dietary Fiber 0 gm
  Polyunsat Fat 2.1 gm, • Sugars 1 gm
  Monounsat Fat 3.8 gm) • Protein 32 gm

Chicken Cordon Bleu

Melanie Thrower
McPherson, KS

Makes 6 servings

Prep. Time: 40 minutes
Cooking Time: 4 hours
Ideal slow cooker size: 4-qt.

3 (1½ lb.) whole boneless, skinless chicken breasts
6 (½ oz. per slice) pieces thinly sliced ham
6 (½ oz. per slice) thin slices reduced-fat Swiss cheese
salt and pepper to taste
6 slices bacon, fried, drained, and patted dry
¼ cup water
1 tsp. salt-free chicken bouillon powder
½ cup white cooking wine
1 tsp. cornstarch
¼ cup cold water

1. Flatten chicken to ⅛-¼-inch thickness. Place a slice of ham and a slice of cheese on top of each flattened breast. Sprinkle with salt and pepper. Roll up and wrap with strip of bacon. Secure with toothpick. Place in slow cooker.

2. Combine ¼ cup water, granules, and wine. Pour into slow cooker.

3. Cover. Cook on high 4 hours.

4. Combine cornstarch and ¼ cup cold water. Add to slow cooker. Cook until sauce thickens.

Exchange List Values
• Meat, very lean 5.0 • Fat 1.0

Basic Nutritional Values
• Calories 231   • Cholesterol 86 mg
  (Calories from Fat 77) • Sodium 424 mg
• Total Fat 9 gm   • Total Carb 1 gm
  (Saturated Fat 3.1 gm, • Dietary Fiber 0 gm
  Polyunsat Fat 1.1 gm, • Sugars 0 gm
  Monounsat Fat 3.3 gm) • Protein 35 gm

Marcy's Barbecued Chicken

Marcy Engle
Harrisonburg, VA

Makes 6 servings

Prep. Time: 20 minutes
Cooking Time: 5 hours
Ideal slow cooker size: 4-qt.

2 lbs. chicken pieces, skin and visible fat removed
¼ cup flour
1 cup ketchup
2 cups water
⅓ cup Worcestershire sauce
1 tsp. chili powder
½ tsp. salt
½ tsp. pepper
2 drops Tabasco sauce
¼ tsp. garlic salt
¼ tsp. onion salt

1. Dust chicken with flour. Transfer to slow cooker.

2. Combine remaining ingredients. Pour over chicken.

3. Cover. Cook on low 5 hours.

Exchange List Values
• Carbohydrate 1.5 • Meat, lean 2.0

Basic Nutritional Values
• Calories 219   • Cholesterol 66 mg
  (Calories from Fat 37)   • Sodium 348 mg
• Total Fat 4 gm   • Total Carb 20 gm
  (Saturated Fat 1.1 gm,   • Dietary Fiber 1 gm
  Polyunsat Fat 0.9 gm,   • Sugars 14 gm
  Monounsat Fat 1.4 gm)   • Protein 24 gm

Chicken and Seafood Gumbo

Dianna Milhizer
Brighton, MI

Makes 12 servings

Prep. Time: 25 minutes
Cooking Time: 10-12 hours
Ideal slow cooker size: 5- or 6-qt.

1 cup chopped celery
1 cup chopped onions
½ cup chopped green
　peppers
¼ cup olive oil
¼ cup, plus 1 Tbsp., flour
6 cups 100% fat-free,
　30-50% lower sodium
　chicken broth
2 lbs. chicken, cut up, skin
　and visible fat removed

3 bay leaves
1½ cups sliced okra
12-oz. can diced tomatoes
1 tsp. Tabasco sauce
salt and pepper to taste
1 lb. ready-to-eat shrimp
½ cup snipped fresh
　parsley

1. Sauté celery, onions, and peppers in oil. Blend in flour and chicken stock until smooth. Cook 5 minutes. Pour into slow cooker.

2. Add remaining ingredients except seafood and parsley.

3. Cover. Cook on low 10-12 hours.

4. One hour before serving add shrimp and parsley.

5. Remove bay leaves before serving.

Exchange List Values
• Vegetable 2.0 • Meat, lean 2.0

Basic Nutritional Values
• Calories 162   • Cholesterol 95 mg
  (Calories from Fat 61)   • Sodium 424 mg
• Total Fat 7 gm   • Total Carb 7 gm
  (Saturated Fat 1.2 gm,   • Dietary Fiber 1 gm
  Polyunsat Fat 1.0 gm,   • Sugars 3 gm
  Monounsat Fat 4.0 gm)   • Protein 17 gm

Tracy's Barbecued Chicken Wings

Tracy Supcoe
Barclay, MD

Makes 8 servings

Prep. Time: 35 minutes
Cooking Time: 5-6 hours
Ideal slow cooker size: 4-qt.

4-lb. chicken wings, skin
　removed
2 large onions, chopped
2 6-oz. cans tomato paste
2 large garlic cloves, minced
¼ cup Worcestershire sauce
¼ cup cider vinegar
¼ cup brown sugar
brown sugar substitute to
　equal 2 Tbsp. sugar
½ cup sweet pickle relish
½ cup red, *or* white, wine
¼ tsp. salt
2 tsp. dry mustard

1. Cut off wing tips. Cut wings at joint. Place in slow cooker.

2. Combine remaining ingredients. Add to slow cooker. Stir.

3. Cover. Cook on low 5-6 hours.

Exchange List Values
• Carbohydrate 0.5 • Meat, lean 2.0
• Vegetable 3.0

Basic Nutritional Values
• Calories 226   • Cholesterol 44 mg
  (Calories from Fat 45)   • Sodium 369 mg
• Total Fat 5 gm   • Total Carb 27 gm
  (Saturated Fat 1.2 gm,   • Dietary Fiber 3 gm
  Polyunsat Fat 1.1 gm,   • Sugars 19 gm
  Monounsat Fat 1.5 gm)   • Protein 19 gm

When choosing high-fat ingredients, such as cheese, pick the most flavorful option and use less.

Szechuan-Style Chicken and Broccoli

Jane Meiser
Harrisonburg, VA

Makes 4 servings

Prep. Time: 30 minutes
Cooking Time: 1½-3 hours
Ideal slow cooker size: 4-qt.

2 whole boneless, skinless
    chicken breasts
1 Tbsp. canola oil
½ cup picante sauce
2 Tbsp. light soy sauce
½ tsp. sugar
2 tsp. quick-cooking
    tapioca
1 medium onion, chopped
2 garlic cloves, minced
½ tsp. ground ginger
2 cups broccoli florets
1 medium red bell pepper,
    sliced

1. Cut chicken into 1" cubes
and brown lightly in oil in
skillet. Place in slow cooker.
2. Stir in remaining
ingredients.
3. Cover. Cook on high
1-1½ hours or on low 2-3
hours.

Exchange List Values
- Vegetable 2.0   • Fat 1.0
- Meat, very lean 4.0

Basic Nutritional Values
- Calories 254   • Cholesterol 84 mg
  (Calories from Fat 64) • Sodium 619 mg
- Total Fat 7 gm   • Total Carb 12 gm
  (Saturated Fat 1.2 gm, • Dietary Fiber 3 gm
  Polyunsat Fat 1.9 gm,   • Sugars 7 gm
  Monounsat Fat 3.2 gm)   • Protein 35 gm

Chicken Casablanca

Joyce Kaut
Rochester, NY

Makes 8 servings

Prep. Time: 35 minutes
Cooking Time: 4-6 hours
Ideal slow cooker size: 4- or 5-qt.

2 Tbsp. canola oil
2 large onions, sliced
1 tsp. ground ginger
3 garlic cloves, minced
3 large carrots, diced
2 large potatoes, unpeeled,
    diced
3 lbs. skinless chicken
    pieces
½ tsp. ground cumin
½ tsp. salt
½ tsp. pepper
¼ tsp. cinnamon
2 Tbsp. raisins
14½-oz. can chopped
    tomatoes
3 small zucchini, sliced
15-oz. can garbanzo beans,
    drained
2 Tbsp. chopped parsley

1. Sauté onions, ginger, and
garlic in oil in skillet. (Reserve
oil.) Transfer to slow cooker.
Add carrots and potatoes.
2. Brown chicken over
medium heat in reserved oil.

Transfer to slow cooker. Mix
gently with vegetables.
3. Combine seasonings in
separate bowl. Sprinkle over
chicken and vegetables. Add
raisins and tomatoes.
4. Cover. Cook on high 4-6
hours.
5. Add sliced zucchini,
beans, and parsley 30 minutes before serving.
6. Serve over cooked rice
or couscous.

Exchange List Values
- Starch 2.0   • Meat, lean 3.0
- Vegetable 2.0   • Fat 0.5

Basic Nutritional Values
- Calories 395   • Cholesterol 87 mg
  (Calories from Fat 93) • Sodium 390 mg
- Total Fat 10 gm   • Total Carb 40 gm
  (Saturated Fat 1.9 gm, • Dietary Fiber 8 gm
  Polyunsat Fat 2.9 gm,   • Sugars 12 gm
  Monounsat Fat 4.3 gm)   • Protein 36 gm

Variation:
Add ½ tsp. turmeric and
¼ tsp. cayenne pepper to
Step 3.

Michelle Mann
Mt. Joy, PA

Anything that raises your pulse and makes you breathe harder—swimming, walking, jogging, dancing, or biking—is aerobic. Find something you enjoy and do it for 30 minutes, three or four times a week.

Greek Chicken

Judy Govotsos
Monrovia, MD

Makes 6 servings

Prep. Time: 25 minutes
Cooking Time: 5-10 hours
Ideal slow cooker size: 4-qt.

4 potatoes, unpeeled,
　quartered
2 lbs. chicken pieces,
　trimmed of skin and fat
2 large onions, quartered
1 whole bulb garlic, cloves
　minced
3 tsp. dried oregano
¾ tsp. salt
½ tsp. pepper
1 Tbsp. olive oil

1. Place potatoes in bottom of slow cooker. Add chicken, onions, and garlic. Sprinkle with seasonings. Top with oil.

2. Cover. Cook on high 5-6 hours, or on low 9-10 hours.

Exchange List Values
- Starch 1.5
- Vegetable 2.0
- Meat, lean 2.0

Basic Nutritional Values
- Calories 278
  (Calories from Fat 56)
- Total Fat 6 gm
  (Saturated Fat 1.3 gm,
  Polyunsat Fat 1.1 gm,
  Monounsat Fat 3.0 gm)
- Cholesterol 65 mg
- Sodium 358 mg
- Total Carb 29 gm
- Dietary Fiber 4 gm
- Sugars 9 gm
- Protein 27 gm

Cathy's Chicken Creole

Cathy Boshart
Lebanon, PA

Makes 6 servings

Prep. Time: 20 minutes
Cooking Time: 3-4 hours
Ideal slow cooker size: 4-qt.

2 Tbsp. canola oil
half a medium green
　pepper, chopped
2 medium onions, chopped
½ cup chopped celery
1 lb. 4 oz.-can tomatoes
½ tsp. pepper
¾ tsp. salt, *or* your choice
　of dried herbs
⅛ tsp. red pepper
1 cup water
2 Tbsp. cornstarch
1 tsp. sugar
1½ Tbsp. cold water
2 cups cooked, cubed
　chicken
6 green, *or* black, olives,
　sliced
½ cup sliced mushrooms

1. Put oil in slow cooker. Add green pepper, onions, and celery. Turn on high until vegetables are hot.

2. Add tomatoes, pepper, salt and 1 cup water.

3. Cover. Cook on high while preparing remaining ingredients.

4. Combine cornstarch and sugar. Add 1½ Tbsp. cold water and make a smooth paste. Stir into mixture in slow cooker. Add chicken, olives, and mushrooms.

5. Cover. Cook on low 2-3 hours.

Exchange List Values
- Vegetable 2.0
- Meat, lean 2.0
- Fat 0.5

Basic Nutritional Values
- Calories 190
  (Calories from Fat 79)
- Total Fat 9 gm
  (Saturated Fat 1.3 gm,
  Polyunsat Fat 2.3 gm,
  Monounsat Fat 4.3 gm)
- Cholesterol 42 mg
- Sodium 521 mg
- Total Carb 13 gm
- Dietary Fiber 3 gm
- Sugars 7 gm
- Protein 15 gm

Mulligan Stew

Carol Ambrose
Ripon, CA

Makes 8 servings

Prep. Time: 25 minutes
Cooking Time: 7 hours
Ideal slow cooker size: 5- or 6-qt.

3-lb. stewing chicken, cut up,
   trimmed of skin and fat
½ tsp. salt
1 oz. salt pork, *or* bacon,
   cut in 1-inch squares
4 cups tomatoes, peeled
   and chopped
2 cups fresh corn
1 cup coarsely chopped
   potatoes
10-oz. pkg. frozen lima
   beans
½ cup chopped onions
1 tsp. salt
¼ tsp. pepper
dash of cayenne pepper

1. Place chicken in slow
cooker. Add water to cover.
Add 1½ tsp. salt.
2. Cover. Cook on low 2
hours. Add more water if
needed.
3. Add remaining ingredi-
ents. Simmer on low 5 hours
longer.

Exchange List Values
- Starch 1.0   • Meat, lean 2.0
- Vegetable 1.0   • Fat 0.5

Basic Nutritional Values
- Calories 241   • Cholesterol 52 mg
  (Calories from Fat 68)   • Sodium 563 mg
- Total Fat 8 gm   • Total Carb 24 gm
  (Saturated Fat 2.2 gm,   • Dietary Fiber 5 gm
  Polyunsat Fat 1.5 gm,   • Sugars 5 gm
  Monounsat Fat 3.0 gm)   • Protein 21 gm

Notes:
   1. The flavor improves if
the stew is refrigerated and
reheated the next day. May
also be made in advance and
frozen.
   2. You can debone the
chicken after the first cooking
for 2 hours. Stir chicken
pieces back into cooker with
other ingredients and continue with directions above.

Gran's Big Potluck

Carol Ambrose
Ripon, CA

Makes 10 servings

Prep. Time: 20 minutes
Cooking Time: 10-12 hours
Ideal slow cooker size: 5- or 6-qt.

2½ lb. stewing hen, cut
   into pieces, trimmed of
   skin and fat
½ lb. stewing beef, cubed,
   trimmed of skin and fat
½-lb. veal shoulder, cubed,
   trimmed of fat
1½ qts. water
½ lb. small red potatoes,
   cubed
½ lb. onions, halved
1 cup sliced carrots
1 cup chopped celery
1 medium green pepper,
   chopped
1 lb. pkg. frozen lima beans

---

1 cup okra, sliced, fresh *or*
   frozen
1 cup frozen corn
8-oz. can whole tomatoes
   with juice
15-oz. can tomato purée
1 tsp. salt
¼-½ tsp. pepper
1 tsp. dry mustard
½ tsp. chili powder
¼ cup chopped fresh
   parsley

1. Combine all ingredients
except last 5 seasonings in
one very large slow cooker, or
divide between two medium-
sized ones.
2. Cover. Cook on low
10-12 hours. Add seasonings
during last hour of cooking.

Exchange List Values
- Starch 1.0   • Meat, lean 2.0
- Vegetable 2.0

Basic Nutritional Values
- Calories 242   • Cholesterol 63 mg
  (Calories from Fat 42)   • Sodium 535 mg
- Total Fat 5 gm   • Total Carb 26 gm
  (Saturated Fat 1.2 gm,   • Dietary Fiber 6 gm
  Polyunsat Fat 0.9 gm,   • Sugars 7 gm
  Monounsat Fat 1.6 gm)   • Protein 25 gm

Note:
   You may want to debone
the chicken and mix it back
into the cooker before serving
the meal.

Drink plenty of water. You should try to drink eight 8-oz. glasses each day.

Sunday Chicken Stew with Dumplings

Kathy Hertzler
Lancaster, PA

Makes 6 servings

Prep. Time: 40 minutes
Cooking Time: 6½-7½ hours
Ideal slow-cooker size: 5 qt.

½ cup flour
¼ tsp. salt
½ tsp. white pepper
3-lb. broiler/fryer chicken, cut up and skin removed
2 Tbsp. olive oil
3 cups fat-free, low-sodium chicken broth
6 large carrots, cut in 1"-thick pieces
2 celery ribs, cut into ½"-thick slices
1 large sweet onion, chopped into ½"-thick slices
1-2 tsp. dried rosemary
1½ cups frozen peas

Dumplings:
1 cup flour
½ tsp. dried rosemary
2 tsp. baking powder
¼ tsp. salt
1 egg, beaten
½ cup 1% milk

1. To prepare chicken, combine flour, salt, and pepper in a large resealable plastic bag.

2. Add chicken, a few pieces at a time. Shake to coat.

3. In a large skillet, brown chicken in olive oil, a few pieces at a time.

4. When all the chicken is brown, gradually add broth to skillet while bringing to a boil. Stir up the browned, flavorful bits sticking to the skillet.

5. In a 5-quart slow cooker, layer in carrots, celery, and onion. Sprinkle with rosemary.

6. Add chicken. Carefully add hot broth.

7. Cover. Cook 6-7 hours on low, or until chicken juice runs clear, vegetables are tender, and stew is bubbling.

8. Stir in peas.

9. To make the dumplings, combine flour, crushed rosemary, baking powder, and salt in a small bowl.

10. In a separate bowl combine egg and milk.

11. Stir wet ingredients into dry ingredients until just combined.

12. Drop by spoonfuls into simmering chicken mixture.

13. Cover. Cook on high 25-30 minutes, or until a toothpick inserted in dumpling comes out clean. Check the dumplings at 25 minutes; otherwise, do not lift the cover while simmering.

14. Serve a "scoop" of dumpling topped with vegetables and broth, with a piece of chicken on the side.

Tip:
The dumplings cook best if you use an oval, or wide, more shallow slow cooker.

Exchange List Values
- Starch 2.0
- Vegetable 2.0
- Lean Meat 3.0
- Fat 1.0

Basic Nutritional Values
- Calories 400 (Calories from Fat 110)
- Total Fat 12 gm (Saturated Fat 2.5 gm, Polyunsat Fat 2.0 gm, Monounsat Fat 6.0 gm)
- Cholesterol 95 mg
- Sodium 540 mg
- Total Carb 42 gm
- Dietary Fiber 5 gm
- Sugars 10 gm
- Protein 31 gm

Chicken and Stuffing

Janice Yoskovich
Carmichaels, PA
Jo Ellen Moore
Pendleton, IN

Makes 16 servings

Prep. Time: 35 minutes
Cooking Time: 4½-5 hours
Ideal slow cooker size: 6-qt.

2½ tsp. salt-free chicken
   bouillon powder
2½ cups water
¼ cup canola oil
½ cup chopped onions
½ cup chopped celery
4-oz. can mushrooms,
   stems and pieces,
   drained
¼ cup dried parsley flakes
1½ tsp. rubbed sage
1 tsp. poultry seasoning
½ tsp. salt
½ tsp. pepper
12 cups day-old bread
   cubes (½-inch pieces)
2 eggs
10¾-oz. can 98% fat-free,
   reduced-sodium cream
   of chicken soup
5 cups cubed cooked
   chicken

1. Combine all ingredients
except bread, eggs, soup, and
chicken in saucepan. Simmer
for 10 minutes.

2. Place bread cubes in
large bowl.

3. Combine eggs and soup.
Stir into broth mixture until
smooth. Pour over bread and
toss well.

4. Layer half of stuffing
and then half of chicken into
very large slow cooker (or
two medium-sized cookers).
Repeat layers.

5. Cover. Cook on low
4½-5 hours.

Exchange List Values
- Starch 1.0
- Fat 0.5
- Meat, lean 2.0

Basic Nutritional Values
- Calories 215
  (Calories from Fat 78)
- Total Fat 9 gm
  (Saturated Fat 1.6 gm,
  Polyunsat Fat 2.5 gm,
  Monounsat Fat 3.7 gm)
- Cholesterol 67 mg
- Sodium 362 mg
- Total Carb 16 gm
- Dietary Fiber 1 gm
- Sugars 2 gm
- Protein 16 gm

Barbecue Chicken for Buns

Linda Sluiter
Schererville, IN

Makes 20 servings

Prep. Time: 25 minutes
Cooking Time: 8 hours
Ideal slow cooker size: 4-qt.

6 cups diced cooked
   chicken
2 cups chopped celery
1 cup chopped onions
1 cup chopped green
   peppers
2 Tbsp. canola oil
2 cups ketchup
2 cups water
2 Tbsp. brown sugar
4 Tbsp. vinegar
2 tsp. dry mustard
1 tsp. pepper
½ tsp. salt

1. Combine all ingredients
in slow cooker.

2. Cover. Cook on low 8
hours.

3. Stir chicken until it
shreds.

4. Pile into steak rolls and
serve.

Exchange List Values
- Carbohydrate 0.5
- Meat, lean 2.0

Basic Nutritional Values
- Calories 131
  (Calories from Fat 43)
- Total Fat 5 gm
  (Saturated Fat 1.0 gm,
  Polyunsat Fat 1.1 gm,
  Monounsat Fat 1.9 gm)
- Cholesterol 37 mg
- Sodium 391 mg
- Total Carb 10 gm
- Dietary Fiber 1 gm
- Sugars 5 gm
- Protein 13 gm

Onions or garlic can increase the flavor of a dish without adding too many calories.

Chicken Reuben Bake

Gail Bush
Landenberg, PA

Makes 6 servings

Prep. Time: 10 minutes
Cooking Time: 6-8 hours
Ideal slow cooker size: 4-qt.

4 boneless, skinless chicken-breast halves
1-lb. bag sauerkraut, drained and rinsed
4-5 (1 oz. each) slices Swiss cheese
¾ cup fat-free Thousand Island salad dressing
2 Tbsp. chopped fresh parsley

1. Place chicken in slow cooker. Layer sauerkraut over chicken. Add cheese. Top with salad dressing. Sprinkle with parsley.
2. Cover. Cook on low 6-8 hours.

Exchange List Values
• Carbohydrate 1.0   • Meat, very lean 4.0

Basic Nutritional Values
• Calories 217
(Calories from Fat 41)
• Total Fat 5 gm
(Saturated Fat 2.0 gm,
Polyunsat Fat 0.6 gm,
Monounsat Fat 1.4 gm)
• Cholesterol 63 mg
• Sodium 693 mg
• Total Carb 13 gm
• Dietary Fiber 2 gm
• Sugars 6 gm
• Protein 28 gm

Turkey in a Pot

Dorothy M. Pittman
Pickens, SC

Makes 12 servings

Prep. Time: 15 minutes
Cooking Time: 6 hours
Standing Time: 10 minutes
Ideal Slow Cooker Size: 6-qt.

4-5 lb. turkey breast, skin removed
1 medium onion, chopped
1 rib celery, chopped
¼ cup melted margarine
1½ cups chicken broth

1. Wash turkey breast. Pat dry. Put onion and celery in cavity. Place in greased slow cooker.
2. Pour margarine over turkey. Pour broth around turkey.
3. Cover. Cook on high 6 hours. Let stand 10 minutes before carving.

Exchange List Values
• Meat, very lean 4.0   • Fat 0.5

Basic Nutritional Values
• Calories 160
(Calories from Fat 45)
• Total Fat 5 gm
(Saturated Fat 0.8 gm,
Polyunsat Fat 1.3 gm,
Monounsat Fat 1.8 gm)
• Cholesterol 70 mg
• Sodium 287 mg
• Total Carb 1 gm
• Dietary Fiber 0 gm
• Sugars 1 gm
• Protein 26 gm

Optional:
You may wish to season the recipe with salt and lemon-pepper seasoning to taste, if your diet permits.

Turkey Breast

Barbara Katrine Rose
Woodbridge, VA

Makes 8 servings

Prep. Time: 10 minutes
Cooking Time: 3-4 hours
Ideal slow cooker size: 6-qt.

4½ lb. boneless turkey breast, skin removed
¼ cup apple cider, *or* juice
1 tsp. salt
¼ tsp. pepper

1. Put turkey breast in slow cooker. Drizzle apple cider over turkey. Sprinkle on both sides with salt and pepper.
2. Cover. Cook on high 3-4 hours.
3. Remove turkey breast. Let stand for 15 minutes before slicing.

Exchange List Values
• Meat, very lean 4.0

Basic Nutritional Values
• Calories 150
(Calories from Fat 10)
• Total Fat 1 gm
(Saturated Fat 0.0 gm,
Polyunsat Fat 0.0 gm,
Monounsat Fat 0.0 gm)
• Cholesterol 89 mg
• Sodium 252 mg
• Total Carb 1 gm
• Dietary Fiber 0 gm
• Sugars 1 gm
• Protein 33 gm

Slow Cooker Turkey Breast

Liz Ann Yoder
Hartville, OH

Makes 12 servings

Prep. Time: 15 minutes
Cooking Time: 9-10 hours
Ideal slow cooker size: 6- or 7-qt.

**6-lb. turkey breast, skin
  and visible fat removed**
2 tsp. oil
salt and pepper to taste
1 onion, quartered
4 garlic cloves, peeled
½ cup water

1. Rinse turkey and pat dry with paper towels.
2. Rub oil over turkey. Sprinkle with salt and pepper. Place, meaty side up, in large slow cooker.
3. Place onion and garlic around sides of cooker.
4. Cover. Cook on low 9-10 hours, or until meat thermometer stuck in meaty part of breast registers 170°.
5. Remove from slow cooker and let stand 10 minutes before slicing.

Exchange List Values
• Meat, very lean 5.0

Basic Nutritional Values
• Calories 187 • Cholesterol 107 mg
  (Calories from Fat 16) • Sodium 68 mg
• Total Fat 2 gm • Total Carb 1 gm
  (Saturated Fat 0.4 gm, • Dietary Fiber 0 gm
  Polyunsat Fat 0.5 gm, • Sugars 1 gm
  Monounsat Fat 0.6 gm) • Protein 39 gm

Variations:

1. Add carrot chunks and chopped celery to Step 3 to add more flavor to the turkey broth.
2. Reserve broth for soups, or thicken with flour-water paste and serve as gravy over sliced turkey.
3. Debone turkey and freeze in pint-sized containers for future use.

Turkey Breast with Orange Sauce

Jean Butzer
Batavia, NY

Makes 6 servings

Prep. Time: 15 minutes
Cooking Time: 7-8 hours
Ideal slow cooker size: 4- or 5-qt.

1 large onion, chopped
3 garlic cloves, minced
1 tsp. dried rosemary
½ tsp. pepper
**2-lb. boneless, skinless
  turkey breast**
1½ cups orange juice

1. Place onions in slow cooker.
2. Combine garlic, rosemary, and pepper.
3. Make gashes in turkey, about ¾ of the way through at 2" intervals. Stuff with herb mixture. Place turkey in slow cooker.
4. Pour juice over turkey.
5. Cover. Cook on low 7-8 hours, or until turkey is no longer pink in center.

Exchange List Values
• Fruit 0.5 • Meat, very lean 4.0

Basic Nutritional Values
• Calories 178 • Cholesterol 81 mg
  (Calories from Fat 8) • Sodium 53 mg
• Total Fat 1 gm • Total Carb 10 gm
  (Saturated Fat 0.3 gm, • Dietary Fiber 1 gm
  Polyunsat Fat 0.3 gm, • Sugars 9 gm
  Monounsat Fat 0.2 gm) • Protein 30 gm

Note:
This very easy, impressive-looking and -tasting recipe is perfect for company.

Stuffed Turkey Breast

Jean Butzer
Batavia, NY

Makes 12 servings

Prep. Time: 40 minutes
Cooking Time: 7-9 hours
Ideal slow cooker size: 5- or 6-qt.

¼ cup margarine, melted
**1 small onion, finely
  chopped**
½ cup finely chopped celery
**2½-oz. pkg. croutons with
  real bacon bits**
1 cup chicken broth
2 Tbsp. fresh minced parsley
½ tsp. poultry seasoning
**1 whole uncooked turkey
  breast, *or* 2 halves (about
  5 lbs.), skin and visible
  fat removed**
salt to taste
pepper to taste
**2 24" × 26" pieces of
  cheesecloth**
dry white wine

1. Combine margarine, onion, celery, croutons, broth, parsley, and poultry seasoning.

2. Cut turkey breast in thick slices from breastbone to rib cage, leaving slices attached to bone (crosswise across breast).

3. Sprinkle turkey with salt and pepper.

4. Soak cheesecloth in wine. Place turkey on cheesecloth. Stuff bread mixture into slits between turkey slices. Fold one end of cheesecloth over the other to cover meat. Place on metal rack or trivet in 5- or 6-qt. slow cooker.

5. Cover. Cook on low 7-9 hours or until tender. Pour additional wine over turkey during cooking.

6. Remove from pot and remove cheesecloth immediately. If browner breast is preferred, remove from pot and brown in 400° oven for 15-20 minutes. Let stand 10 minutes before slicing through and serving.

Exchange List Values
- Starch 0.5   • Fat 0.5
- Meat, very lean 5.0

Basic Nutritional Values
- Calories 216   • Cholesterol 89 mg
  (Calories from Fat 57)   • Sodium 341 mg
- Total Fat 6 gm   • Total Carb 5 gm
  (Saturated Fat 1.0 gm,   • Dietary Fiber 1 gm
  Polyunsat Fat 1.4 gm,   • Sugars 1 gm
  Monounsat Fat 2.4 gm)   • Protein 34 gm

Variation:
Thicken the drippings after the turkey is removed from the cooker, if you wish, for gravy. Mix together 3 Tbsp. cornstarch and ¼ cup cold water. When smooth, stir into broth left in the cooker. Turn cooker to high and stir until cornstarch paste is dissolved. Allow to cook for about 10 minutes, until broth is thickened and smooth.

Slow Cooker Turkey and Dressing

Carol Sherwood
Batavia, NY

Makes 8 servings

Prep. Time: 15 minutes
Cooking Time: 5-6 hours
Ideal slow cooker size: 5- or 6-qt.

8-oz. pkg. herb flavored stuffing mix
½ cup hot water
2 Tbsp. butter, softened
1 onion, chopped
½ cup chopped celery
¼ cup dried cranberries
3-lb. boneless turkey breast
¼ tsp. dried basil
½ tsp. pepper

1. Spread dry stuffing mix in greased slow cooker.

2. Add water, butter, onion, celery, and cranberries. Mix well.

3. Sprinkle turkey breast with basil, and pepper. Place over stuffing mixture.

4. Cover. Cook on low 5-6 hours, or until turkey is done but not dry.

5. Remove turkey. Slice and set aside.

6. Gently stir stuffing and allow to sit for 5 minutes before serving.

7. Place stuffing on platter, topped with sliced turkey.

Exchange List Values
- Starch 2.0   • Meat, very lean 4.0

Basic Nutritional Values
- Calories 307   • Cholesterol 99 mg
  (Calories from Fat 34)   • Sodium 488 mg
- Total Fat 4 gm   • Total Carb 26 gm
  (Saturated Fat 2.1 gm,   • Dietary Fiber 3 gm
  Polyunsat Fat 0.3 gm,   • Sugars 5 gm
  Monounsat Fat 1.0 gm)   • Protein 37 gm

Turkey Meat Loaf and Potatoes

Lizzie Weaver
Ephrata, PA

Makes 7 servings

Prep. Time: 25 minutes
Cooking Time: 4-5 hours
Standing Time: 10 minutes
Ideal slow cooker size: 4-qt.

2 lbs. lean ground turkey
1½ cups soft bread
  crumbs, *or* uncooked
  oatmeal (quick *or* rolled)
2 eggs, slightly beaten
1 small onion, chopped
1 tsp. salt
1 tsp. dry mustard
¼ cup ketchup
¼ cup fat-free evaporated
  milk
6 medium-sized potatoes,
  quartered

1. Before you make the
Meat Loaf, make handles
to lift the finished Loaf
out of your slow cooker,
trouble-free! Tear 4 strips
of aluminum foil, each 18"
long × 2" wide. Space them
spoke-fashion in the slow
cooker, with both ends of
each strip sticking out over
the edges of the cooker to act
as handles.

2. Combine all Meat Loaf
ingredients, except potatoes,
in large bowl.
3. Form mixture into loaf
and fit into slow cooker,
centered over the foil strips.
4. Place potatoes around
meat.
5. Cover. (Ends of foil strips
will stick out of cooker, but
that's okay.) Cook on high 4-5
hours, or until potatoes are
soft.
6. Gently lift up on ends of
foil strips to hoist Meat Loaf
out of the cooker and onto a
platter.
7. Allow to stand 10
minutes before slicing.

Tip:
    Serve with green vegetable
and coleslaw.

Exchange List Values
- Starch 2.5   • Fat 0.5
- Lean Meat 4.0

Basic Nutritional Values
• Calories 380	• Cholesterol 145 mg
(Calories from Fat 115)	• Sodium 605 mg
• Total Fat 13 gm	• Total Carb 35 gm
(Saturated Fat 3.0 gm,	• Dietary Fiber 3 gm
Polyunsat Fat 4.0 gm,	• Sugars 6 gm
Monounsat Fat 4.5 gm)	• Protein 32 gm

Zucchini and Turkey Dish

Dolores Kratz
Souderton, PA

Makes 6 servings

Prep. Time: 25 minutes
Cooking Time: 8-9 hours
Ideal slow cooker size: 3- or 4-qt.

3 cups sliced zucchini
1 small onion, chopped
¼ tsp. salt
1 cup cubed cooked turkey
2 fresh tomatoes, sliced,
  or 14½-oz. can diced
  tomatoes
½ tsp. dried oregano
1 tsp. dried basil
¼ cup freshly grated
  Parmesan cheese
6 Tbsp. shredded
  provolone cheese
¾ cup Pepperidge Farms
  stuffing

1. Combine zucchini,
onion, salt, turkey, tomatoes,
oregano, and basil in slow
cooker. Mix well.
2. Top with cheeses and
stuffing.
3. Cover. Cook on low 8-9
hours.

Exchange List Values
- Starch 0.5   • Meat, lean 1.0
- Vegetable 1.0

Basic Nutritional Values
• Calories 128	• Cholesterol 23 mg
(Calories from Fat 39)	• Sodium 312 mg
• Total Fat 4 gm	• Total Carb 12 gm
(Saturated Fat 2.3 gm,	• Dietary Fiber 2 gm
Polyunsat Fat 0.5 gm,	• Sugars 4 gm
Monounsat Fat 1.2 gm)	• Protein 11 gm

For meatloaf and meatball recipes, try substituting whole-grain bread or cooked brown rice in place of some meat.

Turkey Cacciatore

Dorothy VanDeest
Memphis, TN

Makes 6 servings

Prep. Time: 15 minutes
Cooking Time: 4 hours
Ideal slow cooker size: 4-qt.

2½ cups chopped cooked
   turkey
¾ tsp. salt
dash pepper
1 Tbsp. dried onion flakes
1 green pepper, minced
1 clove garlic, minced
15-oz. can whole tomatoes,
   mashed
4-oz. can sliced
   mushrooms, drained
2 tsp. tomato paste
1 bay leaf
¼ tsp. dried thyme
2 Tbsp. finely chopped
   pimento

   1. Combine all ingredients
well in slow cooker.
   2. Cover. Cook on low 4
hours.
   3. Serve over rice or pasta.
Or drain off most liquid and
serve in taco shells.

Exchange List Values
• Vegetable 1.0   • Lean Meat 2.0

Basic Nutritional Values
• Calories 135   • Cholesterol 45 mg
 (Calories from Fat 25) • Sodium 520 mg
• Total Fat 3 gm   • Total Carb 7 gm
 (Saturated Fat 1.0 gm, • Dietary Fiber 2 gm
 Polyunsat Fat 1.0 gm,   • Sugars 3 gm
 Monounsat Fat 0.5 gm)   • Protein 19 gm

Slow-Cooked Turkey Dinner

Miriam Nolt, New Holland, PA

Makes 6 servings

Prep. Time: 20 minutes
Cooking Time: 7½ hours
Ideal slow cooker size: 4- or 5-qt.

1 onion, diced
6 (15 oz. total) small red
   potatoes, quartered
2 cups sliced carrots
1½ lbs. boneless, skinless
   turkey thighs
¼ cup flour
2 Tbsp. salt-free dry onion
   soup mix (see recipe on
   page 261)
10¾-oz. can 98% fat-free,
   reduced-sodium cream
   of mushroom soup
⅔ cup fat-free, reduced-
   sodium chicken broth

   1. Place vegetables in
bottom of slow cooker.
   2. Place turkey thighs over
vegetables.
   3. Combine remaining
ingredients. Pour over turkey.
   4. Cover. Cook on high 30
minutes. Reduce heat to low
and cook 7 hours.

Exchange List Values
• Starch 1.5   • Meat, lean 2.0
• Vegetable 1.0

Basic Nutritional Values
• Calories 274   • Cholesterol 61 mg
 (Calories from Fat 58) • Sodium 571 mg
• Total Fat 6 gm   • Total Carb 29 gm
 (Saturated Fat 2.2 gm, • Dietary Fiber 4 gm
 Polyunsat Fat 1.9 gm,   • Sugars 6 gm
 Monounsat Fat 1.4 gm)   • Protein 25 gm

Barbecued Turkey Legs

Barbara Walker
Sturgis, SC

Makes 6 servings

Prep. Time: 10 minutes
Cooking Time: 5-7 hours
Ideal slow cooker size: 4- or 5-qt.

4 small skinless turkey
   drumsticks
¼-½ tsp. pepper
¼ cup molasses
¼ cup vinegar
½ cup ketchup
3 Tbsp. Worcestershire
   sauce
¾ tsp. hickory smoke
2 Tbsp. instant minced
   onion

   1. Sprinkle turkey with
salt and pepper. Place in slow
cooker.
   2. Combine remaining
ingredients. Pour over turkey.
   3. Cover. Cook on low 5-7
hours.

Exchange List Values
• Carbohydrate 1.0   • Meat, lean 4.0

Basic Nutritional Values
• Calories 319   • Cholesterol 112 mg
 (Calories from Fat 87) • Sodium 445 mg
• Total Fat 10 gm   • Total Carb 18 gm
 (Saturated Fat 3.2 gm, • Dietary Fiber 0 gm
 Polyunsat Fat 2.9 gm,   • Sugars 13 gm
 Monounsat Fat 2.2 gm)   • Protein 38 gm

Barbecued Turkey Cutlets

Maricarol Magill
Freehold, NJ

Makes 8 servings

Prep. Time: 15 minutes
Cooking Time: 4 hours
Ideal slow cooker size: 4 qt.

2 lbs. turkey cutlets, approximately 6-8 cutlets
¼ cup molasses
¼ cup cider vinegar
¼ cup ketchup
3 Tbsp. Worcestershire sauce
1 tsp. garlic salt
3 Tbsp. chopped onion
2 Tbsp. brown sugar
¼ tsp. pepper

1. Place turkey cutlets in slow cooker.
2. Combine remaining ingredients. Pour over turkey.
3. Cover. Cook on low 4 hours.

Exchange List Values
• Carbohydrate 1.0 • Meat, very lean 3.0

Basic Nutritional Values
• Calories 155
(Calories from Fat 5)
• Total Fat 1 gm
(Saturated Fat 0.2 gm,
Polyunsat Fat 0.2 gm,
Monounsat Fat 0.1 gm)
• Cholesterol 61 mg
• Sodium 365 mg
• Total Carb 14 gm
• Dietary Fiber 0 gm
• Sugars 12 gm
• Protein 22 gm

Turkey and Sweet Potato Casserole

Michele Ruvola
Selden, NY

Makes 4 servings

Prep. Time: 20 minutes
Cooking Time: 8-10 hours
Ideal slow cooker size: 4-qt.

3 medium (6¼-6½ oz. each) sweet potatoes, peeled, cut into 2" pieces
10-oz. pkg. frozen cut green beans
1½ lbs. turkey cutlets
12-oz. jar home-style turkey gravy
2 Tbsp. flour
1 tsp. parsley flakes
½ tsp. dried rosemary
⅛ tsp. pepper

1. Layer sweet potatoes, green beans, and turkey in slow cooker.
2. Combine remaining ingredients until smooth. Pour over mixture in slow cooker.
3. Cover. Cook on low 8-10 hours.
4. Remove turkey and vegetables and keep warm. Stir sauce. Serve with sauce over meat and vegetables, or with sauce in a gravy boat.

Exchange List Values
• Starch 2.0
• Vegetable 1.0
• Meat, very lean 4.0

Basic Nutritional Values
• Calories 318
(Calories from Fat 24)
• Total Fat 3 gm
(Saturated Fat 0.3 gm,
Polyunsat Fat 0.7 gm,
Monounsat Fat 0.9 gm)
• Cholesterol 93 mg
• Sodium 473 mg
• Total Carb 35 gm
• Dietary Fiber 4 gm
• Sugars 7 gm
• Protein 37 gm

Tip:
    Serve with biscuits and cranberry sauce.

Turkey Sloppy Joes

Marla Folkerts
Holland, OH

Makes 6 servings

Prep. Time: 20 minutes
Cooking Time: 4½-6 hours
Ideal slow cooker size: 4-qt.

1 red onion, chopped
1 bell pepper, chopped
1½ lbs. boneless turkey, finely chopped
1 cup no-salt-added ketchup
½ tsp. salt
1 garlic clove, minced
1 tsp. Dijon-style mustard
⅛ tsp. pepper
6 (1½ oz. each) multigrain sandwich rolls

1. Place onion, sweet pepper, and turkey in slow cooker.
2. Combine ketchup, salt, garlic, mustard, and pepper. Pour over turkey mixture. Mix well.
3. Cover. Cook on low 4½-6 hours.
4. Serve on homemade bread or sandwich rolls.

Exchange List Values

- Starch 1.5
- Meat, lean 1.0
- Vegetable 3.0
- Fat 0.5

Basic Nutritional Values

- Calories 271
  (Calories from Fat 49)
- Total Fat 5 gm
  (Saturated Fat 1.6 gm,
  Polyunsat Fat 1.3 gm,
  Monounsat Fat 1.8 gm)
- Cholesterol 40 mg
- Sodium 457 mg
- Total Carb 36 gm
- Dietary Fiber 3 gm
- Sugars 16 gm
- Protein 21 gm

Savory Turkey Meatballs in Italian Sauce

Marla Folkerts
Holland, OH

Makes 8 servings

Prep. Time: 40 minutes
Cooking Time: 6-8 hours
Ideal slow cooker size: 4-qt.

28-oz. can crushed
  tomatoes
1 Tbsp. red wine vinegar
1 medium onion, finely
  chopped
2 garlic cloves, minced
¼ tsp. Italian herb
  seasoning
1 tsp. dried basil
1 lb. ground turkey
⅛ tsp. garlic powder
⅛ tsp. black pepper
⅓ cup dried parsley
2 egg whites
¼ tsp. dried minced onion
⅓ cup quick oats
¼ cup grated Parmesan
  cheese
¼ cup flour
2 Tbsp. canola oil

1. Combine tomatoes, vinegar, onions, garlic, Italian seasonings, and basil in slow cooker. Turn to low.

2. Combine remaining ingredients, except flour and oil. Form into 1" balls. Dredge each ball in flour. Brown in oil in skillet over medium heat. Drain. Transfer to slow cooker. Stir into sauce.

3. Cover. Cook on low 6-8 hours.

Exchange List Values

- Starch 0.5
- Meat, lean 2.0
- Vegetable 2.0
- Fat 0.5

Basic Nutritional Values

- Calories 226
  (Calories from Fat 94)
- Total Fat 10 gm
  (Saturated Fat 2.4 gm,
  Polyunsat Fat 2.5 gm,
  Monounsat Fat 4.5 gm)
- Cholesterol 46 mg
- Sodium 402 mg
- Total Carb 16 gm
- Dietary Fiber 3 gm
- Sugars 7 gm
- Protein 17 gm

Note:
  The meatballs and sauce freeze well.

Tricia's Cranberry Turkey Meatballs

Shirley Unternahrer Hinh
Wayland, IA

Makes 12 servings

Prep. Time: 35 minutes
Cooking Time: 3½ hours
Ideal slow cooker size: 4-qt.

16-oz. can jelled cranberry
  sauce
½ cup ketchup *or* barbecue
  sauce
1 egg
1 lb. ground turkey
¼ cup chopped onion
1 tsp. salt
¼ tsp. black pepper
1-2 tsp. grated orange peel,
  optional

1. Combine cranberry sauce and ketchup in slow cooker.

2. Cover. Cook on high until sauce is mixed.

3. Combine remaining ingredients. Shape into 24 balls.

4. Cook over medium heat in skillet for 8-10 minutes, or just until browned. Add to sauce in slow cooker.

5. Cover. Cook on low 3 hours.

Exchange List Values

- Carbohydrate 1.0
- Meat, lean 1.0

Basic Nutritional Values

- Calories 134
  (Calories from Fat 34)
- Total Fat 4 gm
  (Saturated Fat 0.9 gm,
  Polyunsat Fat 0.9 gm,
  Monounsat Fat 1.4 gm)
- Cholesterol 28 mg
- Sodium 353 mg
- Total Carb 18 gm
- Dietary Fiber 1 gm
- Sugars 15 gm
- Protein 8 gm

Tip:
  Serve with rice and a steamed vegetable.

Turkey Meatballs and Gravy

Betty Sue Good
Broadway, VA

Makes 10 servings

Prep. Time: 35 minutes
Cooking Time: 3-8 hours
Ideal slow cooker size: 4-qt.

2 eggs, beaten
¾ cup bread crumbs
½ cup finely chopped onions
½ cup finely chopped celery
2 Tbsp. chopped fresh
   parsley
¼ tsp. pepper
⅛ tsp. garlic powder
1½ lbs. ground turkey
1½ Tbsp. canola oil
10¾-oz. can 99% fat-free,
   reduced-sodium cream
   of mushroom soup
1 cup water
⅞-oz. pkg. turkey gravy mix
½ tsp. dried thyme
2 bay leaves

1. Combine eggs, bread
crumbs, onions, celery,
parsley, pepper, garlic powder, and meat. Shape into ¾"
balls.
2. Brown meat balls in oil
in skillet. Drain meatballs
and pat dry. Transfer to slow
cooker.
3. Combine soup, water,
dry gravy mix, thyme,
and bay leaves. Pour over
meatballs.
4. Cover. Cook on low
6-8 hours or high 3-4 hours.
Discard bay leaves before
serving.

Exchange List Values
- Starch 0.5
- Carbohydrate 0.5
- Meat, lean 2.0
- Fat 0.5

Basic Nutritional Values
- Calories 212
  (Calories from Fat 97)
- Total Fat 11 gm
  (Saturated Fat 2.5 gm,
  Polyunsat Fat 2.7 gm,
  Monounsat Fat 4.4 gm)
- Cholesterol 94 mg
- Sodium 365 mg
- Total Carb 11 gm
- Dietary Fiber 1 gm
- Sugars 2 gm
- Protein 17 gm

Tip:
   Serve over mashed potatoes
or buttered noodles.

Sausage, Beans, and Rice

Janie Steele
Moore, OK

Makes 6 servings

Prep. Time: 15 minutes
Cooking Time: 2-3 hours
Ideal slow-cooker size: 4 qt.

½ lb. lean smoked turkey
   sausage, cut in bite-size
   pieces
1 onion, chopped
1 green pepper, chopped
1 clove garlic, chopped
2 15-oz. cans kidney beans,
   drained
15-oz. can no-salt-added
   stewed tomatoes with
   juice
salt, *or* garlic powder, to
   taste
black pepper to taste
3 cups cooked brown rice
hot sauce

1. Combine all ingredients
but rice and hot sauce in slow
cooker.
2. Cook on high 2-3 hours,
or until vegetables are tender
and dish is heated through.
3. Serve over rice. Pass the
hot sauce so each person can
add what they'd like.

Exchange List Values
- Starch 3.0
- Vegetable 1.0
- Lean Meat 1.0

Basic Nutritional Values
- Calories 330
  (Calories from Fat 30)
- Total Fat 4 gm
  (Saturated Fat 1.5 gm,
  Polyunsat Fat 1.0 gm,
  Monounsat Fat 1.0 gm)
- Cholesterol 25 mg
- Sodium 565 mg
- Total Carb 55 gm
- Dietary Fiber 10 gm
- Sugars 7 gm
- Protein 18 gm

Beans and Other Main Dishes

New England Baked Beans

Mary Wheatley
Mashpee, MA
Jean Butzer
Batavia, NY

Makes 8 servings

Prep. Time: 20 minutes
Cooking Time: 14½-16½ hours
Ideal slow cooker size: 4-qt.

1 lb. dried Great Northern,
    pea, *or* navy beans
2 oz. salt pork, sliced
1 qt. water
1 tsp. salt
1 Tbsp. brown sugar
½ cup molasses
½ tsp. dry mustard
½ tsp. baking soda
1 onion, coarsely chopped
5 cups water

1. Wash beans and remove any stones or shriveled beans.
2. Meanwhile, simmer salt pork in 1 quart water in saucepan for 10 minutes. Drain. Do not reserve liquid.
3. Combine all ingredients in slow cooker.
4. Cook on high until contents come to boil. Turn to low. Cook 14-16 hours, or until beans are tender.

Exchange List Values
- Starch 2.0
- Carbohydrate 1.0

Basic Nutritional Values
- Calories 269
  (Calories from Fat 41)
- Total Fat 5 gm
  (Saturated Fat 1.6 gm,
  Polyunsat Fat 0.7 gm,
  Monounsat Fat 1.9 gm)
- Cholesterol 4 mg
- Sodium 444 mg
- Total Carb 47 gm
- Dietary Fiber 10 gm
- Sugars 18 gm
- Protein 12 gm

Variations:
1. Add ½ tsp. pepper to Step 3.

Rachel Kauffman
Alton, MI

2. Add ¼ cup ketchup to Step 3.

Cheri Jantzen
Houston, TX

Eat more beans (kidney, pinto, garbanzos, etc.)—they're an excellent alternative to meat, providing protein and fiber with no saturated fat or cholesterol.

Famous Baked Beans

Katrine Rose
Woodbridge, VA

Makes 15 servings

Prep. Time: 20 minutes
Cooking Time: 3-6 hours
Ideal slow cooker size: 4- or 5-qt.

1 lb. ground beef
¼ cup minced onions
1 cup no-salt-added ketchup
4 15-oz. cans pork and beans
⅓ cup brown sugar
brown sugar substitute to equal ¼ cup sugar
2 Tbsp. liquid smoke
1 Tbsp. Worcestershire sauce

1. Brown beef and onions in skillet. Drain. Spoon meat and onions into slow cooker.
2. Add remaining ingredients and stir well.
3. Cover. Cook on high 3 hours or on low 5-6 hours.

Exchange List Values
- Starch 1.0
- Meat, lean 1.0
- Carbohydrate 1.0

Basic Nutritional Values
- Calories 207
- Cholesterol 22 mg
- (Calories from Fat 44)
- Sodium 539 mg
- Total Fat 5 gm
- Total Carb 32 gm
- (Saturated Fat 1.2 gm,
- Dietary Fiber 5 gm
- Polyunsat Fat 0.5 gm,
- Sugars 17 gm
- Monounsat Fat 2.0 gm)
- Protein 10 gm

Note:
There are many worthy baked bean recipes, but this recipe is both easy and absolutely delicious. The secret to this recipe is the liquid smoke. I get many requests for this recipe, and some of my friends have added the word "famous" to its name.

Crock-O-Beans

Nanci Keatley
Salem, OR

Makes 12 servings

Prep. Time: 15 minutes
Cooking Time: 6 hours
Ideal slow-cooker size: 6 qt.

15-oz. can tomato purée
1 medium onion, chopped
2 cloves garlic, chopped
1 Tbsp. chili powder
1 Tbsp. dried oregano
1 Tbsp. ground cumin
1 Tbsp. dried parsley
1-2 tsp. hot sauce, to taste
15-oz. can black beans, drained and rinsed
15-oz. can kidney beans, drained and rinsed
15-oz. can garbanzo beans, drained and rinsed
2 15-oz. cans vegetarian baked beans
15-oz. can whole-kernel corn

1. Place tomato purée, onion, garlic, and seasonings in slow cooker. Stir together well.
2. Add each can of beans, stirring well after each addition. Stir in corn.
3. Cover and cook on low 6 hours.

Exchange List Values
- Starch 2.0
- Lean Meat 1.0
- Vegetable 1.0

Basic Nutritional Values
- Calories 220
- Cholesterol 0 mg)
- (Calories from Fat 15)
- Sodium 270 mg
- Total Fat 2 gm
- Total Carb 41 gm
- (Saturated Fat 0 gm,
- Dietary Fiber 11 gm
- Polyunsat Fat 0.5 gm,
- Sugars 8 gm
- Monounsat Fat 0 gm
- Protein 12 gm

Make one meal today free of meat and cheese. Your heart will thank you.

Barbecued Lima Beans

Hazel L. Propst
Oxford, PA

Makes 20 servings

Soaking Time: 12 hours or overnight
Prep. Time: 15 minutes
Cooking Time: 5-11 hours
Ideal slow cooker size: 4- or 5-qt.

1½ lbs. dried lima beans
6 cups water
2¼ cups chopped onions
½ cup brown sugar
brown sugar substitute to equal 6 Tbsp. sugar
1½ cups ketchup
13 drops Tabasco sauce
½ cup dark corn syrup
1 tsp. salt
¼ lb. bacon, diced

1. Soak washed beans in water overnight. Do not drain.
2. Add onion. Bring to boil. Simmer 30-60 minutes, or until beans are tender. Drain beans, reserving liquid.
3. Combine all ingredients except bean liquid in slow cooker. Mix well. Pour in enough liquid so that beans are barely covered.
4. Cover. Cook on low 10 hours, or high 4-6 hours. Stir occasionally.

Exchange List Values
- Starch 1.0
- Vegetable 1.0
- Carbohydrate 1.0
- Fat 0.5

Basic Nutritional Values
- Calories 195
  (Calories from Fat 27)
- Total Fat 3 gm
  (Saturated Fat 0.9 gm,
  Polyunsat Fat 0.4 gm,
  Monounsat Fat 1.2 gm)
- Cholesterol 4 mg
- Sodium 393 mg
- Total Carb 36 gm
- Dietary Fiber 7 gm
- Sugars 15 gm
- Protein 8 gm

Refried Beans with Bacon

Arlene Wengerd
Millersburg, OH

Makes 8 servings

Prep. Time: 20 minutes
Cooking Time: 5½ hours
Ideal slow cooker size: 4-qt.

2 cups dried red, *or* pinto, beans
6 cups water
2 garlic cloves, minced
1 large tomato, peeled, seeded, and chopped
1 tsp. salt
2 oz. bacon

1. Combine beans, water, garlic, tomato, and salt in slow cooker.
2. Cover. Cook on high 5 hours, stirring occasionally. When the beans become soft, drain off some liquid.
3. While the beans cook, brown bacon in skillet. Drain, reserving drippings. Crumble bacon. Add half of bacon and 1½ Tbsp. drippings to beans. Stir.
4. Mash or purée beans with a food processor. Fry the mashed bean mixture in the remaining bacon drippings. Add more salt to taste.
5. To serve, sprinkle the remaining bacon and shredded cheese on top of beans.

Exchange List Values
- Starch 1.5
- Fat 0.5
- Meat, very lean 1.0

Basic Nutritional Values
- Calories 171
  (Calories from Fat 34)
- Total Fat 4 gm
  (Saturated Fat 1.2 gm,
  Polyunsat Fat 0.6 gm,
  Monounsat Fat 1.5 gm)
- Cholesterol 5 mg
- Sodium 354 mg
- Total Carb 26 gm
- Dietary Fiber 9 gm
- Sugars 3 gm
- Protein 9 gm

Variations:
1. Instead of draining off liquid, add ⅓ cup dry minute rice and continue cooking about 20 minutes. Add a dash of hot sauce and a dollop of sour cream to individual servings.
2. Instead of frying the mashed bean mixture, place several spoonfuls on flour tortillas, roll up, and serve.

Susan McClure
Dayton, VA

Red Beans and Pasta

Naomi E. Fast, Hesston, KS

Makes 8 servings

Prep. Time: 20 minutes
Cooking Time: 3-4 hours
Ideal slow cooker size: 4- or 5-qt.

3 14.5-oz. cans fat-free, reduced-sodium chicken broth
½ tsp. ground cumin
1 Tbsp. chili powder
1 garlic clove, minced
8 oz. uncooked spiral pasta
half a large green pepper, diced
half a large red pepper, diced
1 medium onion, diced
15-oz. can red beans, rinsed and drained
chopped fresh parsley
chopped fresh cilantro

1. Combine broth, cumin, chili powder, and garlic in slow cooker.
2. Cover. Cook on high until mixture comes to boil.
3. Add pasta, vegetables, and beans. Stir together well.
4. Cover. Cook on low 3-4 hours.
5. Add parsley or cilantro before serving.

Exchange List Values
• Starch 2.0   • Vegetable 1.0

Basic Nutritional Values
• Calories 180
 (Calories from Fat 9)
• Total Fat 1 gm
 (Saturated Fat 0.0 gm,
 Polyunsat Fat 0.4 gm,
 Monounsat Fat 0.2 gm)
• Cholesterol 0 mg
• Sodium 448 mg
• Total Carb 34 gm
• Dietary Fiber 4 gm
• Sugars 4 gm
• Protein 9 gm

Red Beans and Sausage

Margaret A. Moffitt, Bartlett, TN

Makes 10 servings

Soaking Time: 8 hours
Prep. Time: 20 minutes
Cooking Time: 10-12 hours
Ideal slow cooker size: 4- or 5-qt.

1-lb. pkg. dried red beans
water
4 oz. smoked sausage
½ tsp. salt
1 tsp. pepper
3-4 cups water
6-oz. can tomato paste
8-oz. can tomato sauce
4 garlic cloves, minced

1. Soak beans for 8 hours. Drain. Discard soaking water.
2. Mix together all ingredients in slow cooker.
3. Cover. Cook on low 10-12 hours, or until beans are soft.

Exchange List Values
• Starch 1.5   • Meat, lean 1.0
• Vegetable 1.0

Basic Nutritional Values
• Calories 198
 (Calories from Fat 36)
• Total Fat 4 gm
 (Saturated Fat 1.2 gm,
 Polyunsat Fat 0.8 gm,
 Monounsat Fat 1.5 gm)
• Cholesterol 7 mg
• Sodium 370 mg
• Total Carb 30 gm
• Dietary Fiber 8 gm
• Sugars 4 gm
• Protein 12 gm

Variation:
Use canned red kidney beans. Cook 1 hour on high and then 3 hours on low.

Note:
These beans freeze well.

Party-Time Beans

Beatrice Martin
Goshen, IN

Makes 14 servings

Prep. Time: 30 minutes
Cooking Time: 5-7 hours
Ideal slow cooker size: 6-qt.

1½ cups ketchup
1 onion, chopped
1 green pepper, chopped
1 red pepper, chopped
½ cup water
¼ cup packed brown sugar
brown sugar substitute to equal 2 Tbsp. sugar
2 bay leaves
2-3 tsp. cider vinegar
1 tsp. ground mustard
⅛ tsp. pepper
16-oz. can kidney beans, rinsed and drained
15½-oz. can Great Northern beans, rinsed and drained
15-oz. can lima beans, rinsed and drained
15-oz. can black beans, rinsed and drained
15½-oz. can black-eyed peas, rinsed and drained

1. Combine first 10 ingredients in slow cooker. Mix well.
2. Add remaining ingredients. Mix well.
3. Cover. Cook on low 5-7 hours, or until onion and peppers are tender.
4. Remove bay leaves before serving.

Exchange List Values
• Starch 1.5   • Carbohydrate 0.5

Basic Nutritional Values

- Calories 172
  (Calories from Fat 7)
- Total Fat 1 gm
  (Saturated Fat 0.1 gm,
  Polyunsat Fat 0.2 gm,
  Monounsat Fat 0.0 gm)
- Cholesterol 0 mg
- Sodium 493 mg
- Total Carb 35 gm
- Dietary Fiber 8 gm
- Sugars 11 gm
- Protein 9 gm

Scandinavian Beans

Virginia Bender
Dover, DE

Makes 8 servings

Prep. Time: 10 minutes
Soaking Time: 8 hours
Cooking Time: 6½-8 hours
Ideal slow cooker size: 4- or 5-qt.

1 lb. dried pinto beans
6 cups water
¼ lb. bacon, *or* 1 ham hock
1 onion, chopped
2-3 garlic cloves, minced
¼ tsp. pepper
¼ tsp. salt
2 Tbsp. molasses
1 cup ketchup
Tabasco to taste
1 tsp. Worcestershire
**   sauce**
¼ cup brown sugar
brown sugar substitute to
**   equal ¼ cup sugar**
⅓ cup cider vinegar
¼ tsp. dry mustard

1. Soak beans in water in soup pot for 8 hours. Bring beans to boil and cook 1½~2 hours, or until soft. Drain, reserving liquid.

2. Combine all ingredients in slow cooker, using just enough bean liquid to cover everything.

3. Cook on low 5-6 hours.

Exchange List Values

- Starch 2.0
- Carbohydrate 1.0
- Vegetable 1.0
- Fat 1.0

Basic Nutritional Values

- Calories 305
  (Calories from Fat 65)
- Total Fat 7 gm
  (Saturated Fat 2.2 gm,
  Polyunsat Fat 0.9 gm,
  Monounsat Fat 3.0 gm)
- Cholesterol 10 mg
- Sodium 564 mg
- Total Carb 51 gm
- Dietary Fiber 11 gm
- Sugars 18 gm
- Protein 12 gm

New Mexico Pinto Beans

John D. Allen
Rye, CO

Makes 10 servings

Soaking Time: overnight
Prep. Time: 10 minutes
Cooking Time: 6-10 hours
Ideal slow cooker size: 4-qt.

2½ cups dried pinto beans
3 qts. water
½ cup ham, *or* salt pork,
**   diced**
2 garlic cloves, crushed
1 tsp. crushed red chili
**   peppers, *optional***

1. Sort beans. Discard pebbles, shriveled beans, and floaters. Wash beans under running water. Place in saucepan, cover with 3 quarts water, and soak overnight.

2. Drain beans and discard soaking water. Pour beans into slow cooker. Cover with fresh water.

3. Add meat, garlic, chili, salt, and pepper. Cook on low 6-10 hours, or until beans are soft.

Exchange List Values

- Starch 1.5
- Meat, very lean 1.0

Basic Nutritional Values

- Calories 145
  (Calories from Fat 8)
- Total Fat 1 gm
  (Saturated Fat 0.2 gm,
  Polyunsat Fat 0.2 gm,
  Monounsat Fat 0.3 gm)
- Cholesterol 4 mg
- Sodium 95 mg
- Total Carb 25 gm
- Dietary Fiber 8 gm
- Sugars 2 gm
- Protein 10 gm

Serving meals family-style tempts people to overeat. Avoid putting bowls or casserole dishes on the table.

Calico Beans

Alice Miller
Stuarts Draft, VA

Makes 12 servings

Prep. Time: 25 minutes
Cooking Time: 3-4 hours
Ideal slow cooker size: 6-qt.

½ lb. ground beef
¼ lb. bacon, chopped
½ cup chopped onions
½ cup no-added-salt
    ketchup
⅓ cup brown sugar
brown sugar substitute to
    equal 3 Tbsp. sugar
2 Tbsp. sugar
1 Tbsp. vinegar
1 tsp. dry mustard
16-oz. can pork and beans,
    undrained
16-oz. can red kidney
    beans, undrained
16-oz. can yellow limas,
    undrained
16-oz. can navy beans,
    undrained

1. Brown ground beef, bacon, and onions together in skillet. Drain. Spoon meat and onions into slow cooker.
2. Stir ketchup, brown sugar, sugar, vinegar, mustard, and salt. Mix together well. Add to slow cooker.
3. Pour beans into slow cooker and combine all ingredients thoroughly.
4. Cover. Cook on high 3-4 hours.

Exchange List Values
• Starch 2.5   • Meat, lean 1.0

Basic Nutritional Values
• Calories 233   • Cholesterol 15 mg
  (Calories from Fat 39)   • Sodium 620 mg
• Total Fat 4 gm   • Total Carb 37 gm
  (Saturated Fat 1.3 gm,   • Dietary Fiber 7 gm
  Polyunsat Fat 0.5 gm,   • Sugars 16 gm
  Monounsat Fat 1.7 gm)   • Protein 12 gm

New Orleans Red Beans

Cheri Jantzen
Houston, TX

Makes 6 servings

Soaking Time: 1 hour
Prep. Time: 15 minutes
Cooking Time: 9-11 hours
Ideal slow cooker size: 4-qt.

2 cups dried kidney beans
5 cups water
8 oz. low-fat smoked
    sausage, diced
2 medium onions, chopped
2 cloves garlic, minced
¼ tsp. salt

1. Wash and sort beans. In saucepan, combine beans and water. Boil 2 minutes. Remove from heat. Soak 1 hour.
2. Brown sausage slowly in a skillet. If needed, use non-fat cooking spray. Add onions and garlic and sauté until tender.
3. Combine all ingredients, including the bean water, in slow cooker.
4. Cover. Cook on low 8-10 hours. During last 20 minutes of cooking, stir frequently and mash lightly with spoon.

Exchange List Values
• Starch 2.5   • Meat, very lean 1.0
• Vegetable 1.0

Basic Nutritional Values
• Calories 260   • Cholesterol 16 mg
  (Calories from Fat 23)   • Sodium 422 mg
• Total Fat 3 gm   • Total Carb 42 gm
  (Saturated Fat 0.8 gm,   • Dietary Fiber 10 gm
  Polyunsat Fat 1.1 gm,   • Sugars 8 gm
  Monounsat Fat 0.5 gm)   • Protein 18 gm

Tip:
    Serve over hot cooked rice.

Four Beans and Sausage

Mary Seielstad
Sparks, NV

Makes 8 servings

Prep. Time: 30 minutes
Cooking Time: 4-10 hours
Ideal slow cooker size: 5-qt.

15-oz. can Great Northern
    beans, drained
15½-oz. can black beans,
    rinsed and drained
16-oz. can red kidney
    beans, drained
15-oz. can butter beans,
    drained
1½ cups no-salt-added
    ketchup
½ cup chopped onions
1 green pepper, chopped
1 lb. low-fat smoked
    sausage, cooked and cut
    into ½-inch slices
2 Tbsp. brown sugar
brown sugar substitute to
    equal 1 Tbsp. sugar
2 garlic cloves, minced

1 tsp. Worcestershire sauce
½ tsp. dry mustard
½ tsp. Tabasco sauce

1. Combine all ingredients in slow cooker.
2. Cover. Cook on low 9-10 hours, or high 4-5 hours.

Exchange List Values
- Starch 2.0
- Meat, lean 1.0
- Carbohydrate 1.5

Basic Nutritional Values
- Calories 328
- Cholesterol 24 mg
- (Calories from Fat 31)
- Sodium 764 mg
- Total Fat 3 gm
- Total Carb 56 gm
- (Saturated Fat 1.2 gm,
- Dietary Fiber 11 gm
- Polyunsat Fat 1.4 gm,
- Sugars 22 gm
- Monounsat Fat 0.7 gm)
- Protein 19 gm

Pioneer Beans
Kay Magruder
Seminole, OK

Makes 8 servings

Prep. Time: 10 minutes
Cooking Time: 8-9 hours
Ideal slow cooker size: 4-qt.

1 lb. dry lima beans
1 bunch green onions, chopped
3 tsp. salt-free beef bouillon powder
6 cups water
1 lb. low-fat smoked sausage
½ tsp. garlic powder
¾ tsp. Tabasco sauce

1. Combine all ingredients in slow cooker. Mix well.
2. Cover. Cook on high 8-9 hours, or until beans are soft but not mushy.

Exchange List Values
- Starch 2.5
- Meat, very lean 2.0

Basic Nutritional Values
- Calories 252
- Cholesterol 24 mg
- (Calories from Fat 28)
- Sodium 487 mg
- Total Fat 3 gm
- Total Carb 38 gm
- (Saturated Fat 1.1 gm,
- Dietary Fiber 10 gm
- Polyunsat Fat 1.3 gm,
- Sugars 7 gm
- Monounsat Fat 0.7 gm)
- Protein 18 gm

Tip:
Serve with homemade bread and butter.

At least half of the starches you eat should be whole-wheat or whole-grain options.

Cowboy Beans
Sharon Timpe
Mequon, WI

Makes 12 servings

Prep. Time: 25 minutes
Cooking Time: 3-7 hours
Ideal slow cooker size: 5- or 6-qt.

6 slices bacon, cut in pieces
½ cup onions, chopped
1 garlic clove, minced
16-oz. can baked beans
16-oz. can kidney beans, drained
15-oz. can butter beans *or* pinto beans, drained
2 Tbsp. dill pickle relish *or* chopped dill pickles
⅓ cup chili sauce *or* ketchup
2 tsp. Worcestershire sauce
¼ cup brown sugar
brown sugar substitute to equal 2 Tbsp. sugar
⅛ tsp. hot pepper sauce, *optional*

1. Lightly brown bacon, onions, and garlic in skillet. Drain.
2. Combine all ingredients in slow cooker. Mix well.
3. Cover. Cook on low 5-7 hours or high 3-4 hours.

Exchange List Values
- Starch 1.0
- Fat 0.5
- Carbohydrate 0.5

Basic Nutritional Values
- Calories 138
- Cholesterol 3 mg
- (Calories from Fat 17)
- Sodium 441 mg
- Total Fat 2 gm
- Total Carb 25 gm
- (Saturated Fat 0.6 gm,
- Dietary Fiber 5 gm
- Polyunsat Fat 0.3 gm,
- Sugars 9 gm
- Monounsat Fat 0.7 gm)
- Protein 7 gm

Creole Black Beans

Joyce Kaut
Rochester, NY

Makes 8 servings

Prep. Time: 25 minutes
Cooking Time: 4-8 hours
Ideal slow cooker size: 4-qt.

14 oz. low-fat smoked
   sausage, sliced in
   ½" pieces, browned
3 15-oz. cans black beans,
   drained
1½ cups chopped onions
1½ cups chopped green
   peppers
1½ cups chopped celery
4 garlic cloves, minced
2 tsp. dried thyme
1½ tsp. dried oregano
1½ tsp. pepper
1 tsp. salt-free chicken
   bouillon powder
3 bay leaves
8-oz. can no-added-salt
   tomato sauce
1 cup water

1. Combine all ingredients
in slow cooker.
2. Cover. Cook on low 8
hours or on high 4 hours.
3. Remove bay leaves.

Exchange List Values

- Starch 1.5   • Meat, lean 1.0
- Vegetable 2.0

Basic Nutritional Values

- Calories 223   • Cholesterol 21 mg
  (Calories from Fat 27) • Sodium 566 mg
- Total Fat 3 gm   • Total Carb 34 gm
  (Saturated Fat 1.0 gm, • Dietary Fiber 10 gm
  Polyunsat Fat 1.2 gm, • Sugars 9 gm
  Monounsat Fat 0.6 gm) • Protein 15 gm

Variation:
   You may substitute a 14½-
oz. can of stewed tomatoes for
the tomato sauce.

Tip:
   Serve over rice, with a
salad and fresh fruit for
dessert.

Pizza Beans

Kelly Amos
Pittsboro, NC

Makes 6 servings

Prep. Time: 20 minutes
Cooking Time: 7-9 hours
Ideal slow cooker size: 4-qt.

16-oz. can pinto beans,
   drained
16-oz. can kidney beans,
   drained
2.25-oz. can ripe olives
   sliced, drained
28-oz. can no-added-
   salt stewed *or* whole
   tomatoes
¾ lb. bulk lean Italian
   turkey sausage
1 Tbsp. oil
1 green pepper, chopped
1 medium onion, chopped
1 garlic clove, minced
1 tsp. dried oregano
1 tsp. dried basil

1. Combine beans, olives,
and tomatoes in slow cooker.
   2. Brown sausage in ½
Tbsp. oil in skillet. Drain.
Transfer sausage to slow
cooker.
   3. Sauté green pepper in
½ Tbsp. oil for 1 minute,
stirring constantly. Add
onions and continue stirring
until onions start to become
translucent. Add garlic and
cook 1 more minute. Transfer
to slow cooker.
   4. Stir in seasonings.
   5. Cover. Cook on low 7-9
hours.
   6. To serve, sprinkle with
Parmesan cheese.

Exchange List Values

- Starch 1.5   • Meat, lean 2.0
- Vegetable 3.0   • Fat 1.0

Basic Nutritional Values

- Calories 335   • Cholesterol 45 mg
  (Calories from Fat 104) • Sodium 632 mg
- Total Fat 12 gm   • Total Carb 39 gm
  (Saturated Fat 2.2 gm, • Dietary Fiber 10 gm
  Polyunsat Fat 2.0 gm, • Sugars 8 gm
  Monounsat Fat 3.7 gm) • Protein 23 gm

Variation:
   For a thicker soup, 20 minutes before serving remove
¼ cup liquid from cooker
and add 1 Tbsp. cornstarch.
Stir until dissolved. Return
to soup. Cook on high for 15
minutes, or until thickened.

Keep track of the total grams of fiber you eat today—you should get around 25-35 grams a day.

Cajun Sausage and Beans

Melanie Thrower
McPherson, KS

Makes 6 servings

Prep. Time: 15 minutes
Cooking Time: 8 hours
Ideal slow cooker size: 4-qt.

1 lb. low-fat smoked
  sausage, sliced into
  ¼-inch pieces
16-oz. can no-salt-added
  red kidney beans
16-oz. can crushed
  tomatoes with green
  chilies
1 cup chopped celery
half an onion, chopped
2 Tbsp. Italian seasoning
Tabasco sauce to taste

1. Combine all ingredients
in slow cooker.
2. Cover. Cook on low 8
hours.
3. Serve over rice or as a
thick zesty soup.

Exchange List Values

- Starch 1.0   • Meat, lean 1.0
- Vegetable 1.0

Basic Nutritional Values

- Calories 158   • Cholesterol 18 mg
  (Calories from Fat 22)   • Sodium 588 mg
- Total Fat 2 gm   • Total Carb 23 gm
  (Saturated Fat 0.8 gm,   • Dietary Fiber 7 gm
  Polyunsat Fat 1.0 gm,   • Sugars 7 gm
  Monounsat Fat 0.5 gm)   • Protein 11 gm

Beans with Rice

Miriam Christophel
Battle Creek, MI

Makes 8 servings

Soaking Time: overnight
Prep. Time: 25 minutes
Cooking Time: 14-17 hours
Soaking Time: 8 hours
Ideal slow cooker size: 5- or 6-qt.

3 cups dried small red
  beans
8 cups water
3 garlic cloves, minced
1 large onion, chopped
8 cups fresh water
1 ham hock
½ cup ketchup
½ tsp. salt
pinch of pepper
1½-2 tsp. ground cumin
1 Tbsp. parsley
1-2 bay leaves

1. Soak beans overnight
in 8 cups water. Drain. Place
soaked beans in slow cooker
with garlic, onion, 8 cups
fresh water, and ham
hock.
2. Cover. Cook on
high 12-14 hours.
3. Take ham
hocks out of
cooker and
allow to cool.
Remove meat
from bones.
Remove
and discard
visible fat
and skin. Cut
up and return
to slow cooker.

Add remaining ingredients.
  4. Cover. Cook on high 2-3
hours.

Exchange List Values

- Starch 1.5   • Fat 0.5

Basic Nutritional Values

- Calories 148   • Cholesterol 4 mg
  (Calories from Fat 25)   • Sodium 382 mg
- Total Fat 3 gm   • Total Carb 24 gm
  (Saturated Fat 0.8 gm,   • Dietary Fiber 6 gm
  Polyunsat Fat 0.5 gm,   • Sugars 5 gm
  Monounsat Fat 1.0 gm)   • Protein 8 gm

Tip:
  Serve over rice with a
dollop of sour cream.

Six-Bean Barbecued Beans

Gladys Longacre
Susquehanna, PA

Makes 24 (½ cup) servings

Prep. Time: 25 minutes
Cooking Time: 4-6 hours
Ideal slow cooker size: 6-qt.

1-lb. can kidney beans, drained
1-lb. can pinto beans, drained
1-lb. can Great Northern beans, drained
1-lb. can butter beans, drained
1-lb. can navy beans, drained
1-lb. can pork and beans
¼ cup barbecue sauce
⅓ cup prepared mustard
⅓ cup ketchup
2 Tbsp. Worcestershire sauce
1 small onion, chopped
1 small bell pepper, chopped
2 Tbsp. molasses
½ cup brown sugar
brown sugar substitute to equal ¼ cup sugar

1. Mix together all ingredients in slow cooker.
2. Cook on low 4-6 hours.

Exchange List Values
• Starch 1.5

Basic Nutritional Values
• Calories 122   • Cholesterol 1 mg
 (Calories from Fat 6) • Sodium 322 mg
• Total Fat 1 gm   • Total Carb 24 gm
 (Saturated Fat 0.1 gm, • Dietary Fiber 6 gm
 Polyunsat Fat 0.2 gm, • Sugars 7 gm
 Monounsat Fat 0.2 gm) • Protein 6 gm

Four-Bean Medley

Sharon Brubaker
Myerstown, PA

Makes 8 servings

Prep. Time: 20 minutes
Cooking Time: 6-8 hours
Ideal slow cooker size: 4- or 5-qt.

8 bacon slices, diced and browned until crisp
2 medium onions, chopped
6 Tbsp. brown sugar
brown sugar substitute to equal 3 Tbsp. sugar
½ cup vinegar
1 tsp. dry mustard
½ tsp. garlic powder
16-oz. can baked beans, undrained
16-oz. can kidney beans, drained
15½-oz. can butter beans, drained
14½-oz. can green beans, drained
2 Tbsp. ketchup

1. Mix together all ingredients. Pour into slow cooker.
2. Cover. Cook on low 6-8 hours.

Exchange List Values
• Starch 2.0   • Vegetable 1.0
• Carbohydrate 0.5   • Fat 0.5

Basic Nutritional Values
• Calories 242   • Cholesterol 5 mg
 (Calories from Fat 34) • Sodium 619 mg
• Total Fat 4 gm   • Total Carb 44 gm
 (Saturated Fat 1.1 gm, • Dietary Fiber 9 gm
 Polyunsat Fat 0.6 gm, • Sugars 19 gm
 Monounsat Fat 1.5 gm) • Protein 11 gm

Main Dish Baked Beans

Sue Pennington
Bridgewater, VA

Makes 8 servings

Prep. Time: 20 minutes
Cooking Time: 4-8 hours
Ideal slow cooker size: 4-qt.

1 lb. ground beef
28-oz. can baked beans
8-oz. can pineapple tidbits packed in juice, drained
4½-oz. can sliced mushrooms, drained
1 large onion, chopped
1 large green pepper, chopped
½ cup Phyllis' Homemade Barbecue Sauce (see recipe on page 261)
2 Tbsp. light soy sauce
1 clove garlic, minced
¼ tsp. pepper

1. Brown ground beef in skillet. Drain. Place in slow cooker.
2. Stir in remaining ingredients. Mix well.
3. Cover. Cook on low 4-8 hours, or until bubbly. Serve in soup bowls.

Exchange List Values
• Starch 1.0   • Meat, lean 1.0
• Carbohydrate 0.5   • Fat 1.0
• Vegetable 1.0

Basic Nutritional Values
• Calories 238   • Cholesterol 34 mg
 (Calories from Fat 58) • Sodium 663 mg
• Total Fat 6 gm   • Total Carb 31 gm
 (Saturated Fat 2.4 gm, • Dietary Fiber 7 gm
 Polyunsat Fat 0.5 gm, • Sugars 13 gm
 Monounsat Fat 2.6 gm) • Protein 17 gm

Slow Cooker Kidney Beans

Jeanette Oberholtzer
Manheim, PA

Makes 12 servings

Prep. Time: 20 minutes
Cooking Time: 6-7 hours
Ideal slow cooker size: 4-qt.

2 30-oz. cans kidney beans,
   rinsed and drained
28-oz. can no-salt-added
   diced tomatoes, drained
2 medium red bell
   peppers, chopped
1 cup ketchup
¼ cup brown sugar
brown sugar substitute to
   equal 2 Tbsp. sugar
2 Tbsp. honey
2 Tbsp. molasses
1 Tbsp. Worcestershire sauce
1 tsp. dry mustard
2 medium red apples,
   cored and chopped

1. Combine all ingredients,
except apples, in slow cooker.
2. Cover. Cook on low 4-5
hours.
3. Stir in apples.
4. Cover. Cook 2 more
hours.

Exchange List Values
- Starch 1.5
- Vegetable 1.0
- Carbohydrate 1.0

Basic Nutritional Values
- Calories 216
  (Calories from Fat 8)
- Total Fat 1 gm
  (Saturated Fat 0.0 gm,
  Polyunsat Fat 0.4 gm,
  Monounsat Fat 0.1 gm)
- Cholesterol 0 mg
- Sodium 445 mg
- Total Carb 46 gm
- Dietary Fiber 9 gm
- Sugars 20 gm
- Protein 10 gm

Sweet and Sour Beans

Julette Leaman
Harrisonburg, VA

Makes 8 servings

Prep. Time: 20 minutes
Cooking Time: 3 hours
Ideal slow cooker size: 4- or 5-qt.

5 slices bacon
4 medium onions, cut in
   rings
¼ cup brown sugar
brown sugar substitute to
   equal 2 Tbsp. sugar
1 tsp. dry mustard
½ tsp. salt
¼ cup cider vinegar
1-lb. can green beans,
   drained
2 1-lb. cans butter beans,
   drained
2 14.8-oz. cans baked
   beans, no-added-salt

1. Brown bacon in
skillet and crumble.
Drain all but 3 tsp.
bacon drippings.
Stir in onions,
brown sugar,
mustard, salt, and
vinegar. Simmer
20 minutes.
2. Combine
all ingredients in
slow cooker.

3. Cover. Cook on low 3
hours.

Exchange List Values
- Starch 2.0
- Carbohydrate 1.0
- Vegetable 1.0
- Meat, lean 1.0

Basic Nutritional Values
- Calories 289
  (Calories from Fat 40)
- Total Fat 4 gm
  (Saturated Fat 1.5 gm,
  Polyunsat Fat 0.7 gm,
  Monounsat Fat 1.7 gm)
- Cholesterol 5 mg
- Sodium 519 mg
- Total Carb 51 gm
- Dietary Fiber 13 gm
- Sugars 22 gm
- Protein 13 gm

Eggplant, which is low in carbohydrates, is a healthy starch and a great meat alternative.

Fruity Baked Bean Casserole

Elaine Unruh
Minneapolis, MN

Makes 8 servings

Prep. Time: 25 minutes
Cooking Time: 2-3 hours
Ideal slow cooker size: 4- or 5-qt.

½ lb. bacon
3 medium onions, chopped
cooking spray
16-oz. can lima beans, drained
16-oz. can kidney beans, drained
16-oz. can baked beans
14.8-oz. can no-added-salt baked beans
15½-oz. can pineapple chunks, canned in juice
2 Tbsp. brown sugar
brown sugar substitute to equal 2 Tbsp. sugar
¼ cup cider vinegar
2 Tbsp. molasses
½ cup ketchup
2 Tbsp. prepared mustard
½ tsp. garlic powder
1 medium green pepper, chopped

1. Cook bacon in skillet. Crumble. Place bacon in slow cooker. Rinse skillet.
2. Sauté onions in non-stick skillet with cooking spray until soft. Drain. Add to bacon in slow cooker.
3. Add beans and pineapple to cooker. Mix well.
4. Combine brown sugar, vinegar, molasses, ketchup, mustard, garlic powder and green pepper. Mix well. Stir into mixture in slow cooker.
5. Cover. Cook on high 2-3 hours.

Exchange List Values
- Starch 2.5
- Fruit 0.5
- Carbohydrate 1.0
- Vegetable 1.0

Basic Nutritional Values
- Calories 350 (Calories from Fat 46)
- Total Fat 5 gm (Saturated Fat 1.5 gm, Polyunsat Fat 0.9 gm, Monounsat Fat 2.0 gm)
- Cholesterol 7 mg
- Sodium 577 mg
- Total Carb 65 gm
- Dietary Fiber 13 gm
- Sugars 32 gm
- Protein 15 gm

Apple Bean Bake

Barbara A. Yoder
Goshen, IN

Makes 12 servings

Prep. Time: 25 minutes
Cooking Time: 2-4 hours
Ideal slow cooker size: 4- or 5-qt.

4 Tbsp. margarine
2 large Granny Smith apples, unpeeled, cubed
¼ cup brown sugar
brown sugar substitute to equal 2 Tbsp. sugar
2 Tbsp. sugar
white sugar substitute to equal 1 Tbsp. sugar
½ cup no-added-salt ketchup
1 tsp. cinnamon
1 Tbsp. molasses
24-oz. can Great Northern beans, undrained
24-oz. can pinto beans, undrained

1. Melt butter in skillet. Add apples and cook until tender.
2. Stir in brown sugar and sugar. Cook until they melt. Stir in ketchup, cinnamon, and molasses.
3. Add beans and ham chunks. Mix well. Pour into slow cooker.
4. Cover. Cook on high 2-4 hours.

Exchange List Values
- Starch 1.0
- Fruit 0.5
- Carbohydrate 0.5
- Fat 1.0

Basic Nutritional Values
- Calories 195 (Calories from Fat 44)
- Total Fat 5 gm (Saturated Fat 0.8 gm, Polyunsat Fat 1.5 gm, Monounsat Fat 1.8 gm)
- Cholesterol 0 mg
- Sodium 399 mg
- Total Carb 32 gm
- Dietary Fiber 6 gm
- Sugars 17 gm
- Protein 6 gm

Legumes are rich in vitamins and minerals. Try adding beans or lentils to soups and salads.

Ann's Boston Baked Beans

Ann Driscoll
Albuquerque, MN

Makes 20 servings

Prep. Time: 20 minutes
Cooking Time: 6-8 hours
Ideal slow cooker size: 4- or 5-qt.

---

1 cup raisins
2 small onions, diced
2 tart apples, unpeeled, diced
1 cup chili sauce
1 cup chopped extra-lean, reduced-sodium ham
1-lb.-15-oz. can baked beans
2 14.8-oz. cans no-added-salt baked beans
3 tsp. dry mustard
½ cup sweet pickle relish

1. Mix together all ingredients.
2. Cover. Cook on low 6-8 hours.

Exchange List Values
- Starch 1.0
- Carbohydrate 0.5
- Fruit 0.5

Basic Nutritional Values
- Calories 148
  (Calories from Fat 6)
- Total Fat 1 gm
  (Saturated Fat 0.1 gm,
  Polyunsat Fat 0.2 gm,
  Monounsat Fat 0.1 gm)
- Cholesterol 3 mg
- Sodium 443 mg
- Total Carb 32 gm
- Dietary Fiber 6 gm
- Sugars 16 gm
- Protein 6 gm

Pheasant a la Elizabeth

Elizabeth L. Richards
Rapid City, SD

Makes 8 servings

Marinating Time: 2-4 hours
Prep. Time: 30 minutes
Cooking Time: 6-8 hours
Ideal slow cooker size: 4-qt.

---

6 half boneless, skinless pheasant breasts, 6½ oz. each, cubed
¾ cup teriyaki sauce
⅓ cup flour
1½ tsp. garlic salt
pepper to taste
2 Tbsp. olive oil
1 large onion, sliced
12-oz. can beer
¾ cup fresh mushrooms, sliced

1. Marinate pheasant in teriyaki sauce for 2-4 hours. Remove breasts from teriyaki sauce and discard sauce.
2. Combine flour, garlic salt, and pepper in a shallow bowl. Dredge pheasant in flour mixture.
3. Brown floured breasts in olive oil in skillet. Add onion and sauté for 3 minutes, stirring frequently. Transfer to slow cooker.
3. Add beer and mushrooms.
4. Cover. Cook on low 6-8 hours.

Exchange List Values
- Carbohydrate 0.5
- Meat, lean 4.0

Basic Nutritional Values
- Calories 260
  (Calories from Fat 75)
- Total Fat 8 gm
  (Saturated Fat 0.5 gm,
  Polyunsat Fat 1.3 gm,
  Monounsat Fat 3.9 gm)
- Cholesterol 92 mg
- Sodium 357 mg
- Total Carb 10 gm
- Dietary Fiber 1 gm
- Sugars 5 gm
- Protein 34 gm

Variation:
Instead of pheasant, use chicken.

Pot-Roasted Rabbit

Donna Treloar, Gaston, IN

Makes 6 servings

Prep. Time: 20 minutes
Cooking Time: 10-12 hours
Ideal slow cooker size: 4-qt.

2 onions, sliced
4-lb. roasting rabbit,
    skinned
1 garlic clove, sliced
2 bay leaves
1 whole clove
1 cup hot water
2 Tbsp. soy sauce
2 Tbsp. flour
½ cup cold water

1. Place onion in bottom of slow cooker.
2. Rub rabbit with salt and pepper. Insert garlic in cavity. Place rabbit in slow cooker.
3. Add bay leaves, clove, hot water, and soy sauce.
4. Cover. Cook on low 10-12 hours.
5. Remove rabbit and thicken gravy by stirring 2 Tbsp. flour blended into ½ cup water into simmering juices in cooker. Continue stirring until gravy thickens. Cut rabbit into serving-size pieces and serve with gravy.

Exchange List Values
• Carbohydrate 0.5 • Meat, lean 5.0

Basic Nutritional Values
• Calories 294
  (Calories from Fat 97)
• Total Fat 11 gm
  (Saturated Fat 3.2 gm,
  Polyunsat Fat 2.1 gm,
  Monounsat Fat 2.9 gm)
• Cholesterol 110 mg
• Sodium 390 mg
• Total Carb 7 gm
• Dietary Fiber 1 gm
• Sugars 4 gm
• Protein 40 gm

Venison Steak

Eleanor Glick
Bird-In-Hand, PA

Makes 4 servings

Prep Time: 15-20 minutes
Cooking Time: 5 hours
Ideal slow-cooker size: 2-qt.

1 Tbsp. olive oil
1 lb. venison tenderloin
    steak, cubed
1 large onion, chopped
½ tsp. garlic salt
½ tsp. garlic powder
1 large bell pepper, diced
1 tsp. soy sauce
1 Tbsp. brown sugar
1 Tbsp. chili powder
1 cup V8, *or* home-canned
    tomato, juice

1. In a skillet, brown steak and onion with garlic salt and powder.
2. Add chopped pepper, soy sauce, brown sugar, and chili powder to slow cooker.
3. Transfer steak and onion to slow-cooker.
4. Pour juice over top. Cover. Cook 5 hours on low.

Tip:
Cube meat while it's partially frozen and you'll find it's easier to cut.

Exchange List Values
• Vegetable 3.0   • Lean Meat 3.0

Basic Nutritional Values
• Calories 225
  (Calories from Fat 55)
• Total Fat 6 gm
  (Saturated Fat 1.5 gm,
  Polyunsat Fat 0.5 gm,
  Monounsat Fat 3.0 gm)
• Cholesterol 75 mg
• Sodium 410 mg
• Total Carb 15 gm
• Dietary Fiber 3 gm
• Sugars 10 gm
• Protein 27 gm

Venison Roast

Colleen Heatwole
Burton, MI

Makes 10 servings

Marinating Time: 8 hours or
*   more*
Prep. Time: 15 minutes
Cooking Time: 10-12 hours
Ideal slow cooker size: 4- or 5-qt.

3-lb. venison roast
¼ cup vinegar
2 garlic cloves, minced
1 tsp. salt
½ cup chopped onions
15-oz. can no-added-salt
    tomato sauce
1 Tbsp. ground mustard
1 pkg. brown gravy mix
½ tsp. salt
¼ cup water

1. Place venison in deep bowl. Combine vinegar, garlic, and salt. Pour over venison. Add enough cold water to cover venison. Marinate for at least 8 hours in refrigerator.
2. Rinse and drain venison. Place in slow cooker.
3. Combine remaining ingredients and pour over venison.
4. Cover. Cook on low 10-12 hours.

Tip:
Serve with a green salad, potatoes, and rolls to make a complete meal. There is usually a lot of sauce, so make plenty of potatoes, noodles, or rice. This is an easy meal to have for a Saturday dinner

with guests or extended family.

Exchange List Values
- Vegetable 1.0
- Meat, very lean 4.0

Basic Nutritional Values
- Calories 186
  (Calories from Fat 31)
- Total Fat 3 gm
  (Saturated Fat 1.4 gm,
  Polyunsat Fat 0.7 gm,
  Monounsat Fat 0.7 gm)
- Cholesterol 115 mg
- Sodium 530 mg
- Total Carb 5 gm
- Dietary Fiber 1 gm
- Sugars 4 gm
- Protein 31 gm

Note:
The sauce on this roast works well for any meat.

Venison in Sauce

Anona M. Teel
Bangor, PA

Makes 12 sandwiches

Marinating Time: 6-8 hours
Prep. Time: 25 minutes
Cooking Time: 8-10 hours
Ideal slow cooker size: 5-qt.

3-4-lb. venison roast
¼ cup vinegar
2 garlic cloves, minced
¼ tsp. salt
cold water
2 Tbsp. oil
1 large onion, sliced
half a green bell pepper, sliced

2 ribs celery, sliced
1-2 garlic cloves, minced
1½-2 tsp. salt
¼ tsp. pepper
½ tsp. dried oregano
¼ cup ketchup
1 cup tomato juice

1. Combine vinegar, garlic cloves, and ¼ tsp. salt. Pour over venison. Add water until meat is covered. Marinate 6-8 hours.
2. Cut meat into pieces. Brown in oil in skillet. Place in slow cooker.
3. Mix remaining ingredients together; then pour into cooker. Stir in meat.
4. Cover. Cook on low 8-10 hours.
5. Using two forks, pull the meat apart and then stir it through the sauce.
6. Serve on sandwich rolls, or over rice or pasta.

Exchange List Values
- Vegetable 1.0
- Fat 1.0
- Meat, very lean 3.0

Basic Nutritional Values
- Calories 176
  (Calories from Fat 46)
- Total Fat 5 gm
  (Saturated Fat 1.4 gm,
  Polyunsat Fat 1.3 gm,
  Monounsat Fat 2.0 gm)
- Cholesterol 96 mg
- Sodium 429 mg
- Total Carb 5 gm
- Dietary Fiber 1 gm
- Sugars 3 gm
- Protein 26 gm

Baked Lamb Shanks

Irma H. Schoen
Windsor, CT

Makes 6 servings

Prep. Time: 20 minutes
Cooking Time: 4-10 hours
Ideal slow cooker size: 4-qt.

1 medium onion, thinly sliced
2 small carrots, cut in thin strips
1 rib celery, chopped
3 (1 lb. each) lamb shanks, cracked, trimmed of fat
1-2 cloves garlic, split
⅛ tsp. salt
¼ tsp. pepper
1 tsp. dried oregano
1 tsp. dried thyme
2 bay leaves, crumbled
½ cup dry white wine
8-oz. can tomato sauce

1. Place onions, carrots, and celery in slow cooker.
2. Rub lamb with garlic and season with salt and pepper. Add to slow cooker.
3. Mix remaining ingredients together in separate bowl and add to meat and vegetables.
4. Cover. Cook on low 8-10 hours, or high 4-6 hours.

Exchange List Values
- Vegetable 1.0
- Fat 0.5
- Meat, very lean 4.0

Basic Nutritional Values
- Calories 182
  (Calories from Fat 44)
- Total Fat 5 gm
  (Saturated Fat 1.7 gm,
  Polyunsat Fat 0.3 gm,
  Monounsat Fat 2.1 gm)
- Cholesterol 83 mg
- Sodium 386 mg
- Total Carb 7 gm
- Dietary Fiber 2 gm
- Sugars 4 gm
- Protein 26 gm

A registered dietitian can help you create the right meal plan for you, and your health insurance company may even cover the sessions!

Herbed Lamb Stew

Jan Mast
Lancaster, PA

Makes 6 servings

Prep Time: 20-30 minutes
Cooking Time: 8-10 hours
Ideal slow-cooker size: 6-qt.

1½ lbs. lean lamb, cut into
   1-2" cubes
1 Tbsp. oil
2 medium onions, chopped
4 cups fat-free, low-sodium
   beef broth
3 medium potatoes, peeled
   and thinly sliced
½ tsp. salt
¼ tsp. pepper
¼ tsp. celery seed
¼ tsp. dried marjoram
¼ tsp. dried thyme
10-oz. pkg. frozen peas
6 Tbsp. flour
½ cup cold water

1. Brown lamb cubes in skillet in oil over medium-high heat. Do in two batches so that cubes brown and don't just steam.
2. Transfer browned meat to slow cooker.
3. Add remaining ingredients except peas, flour, and water.
4. Cover. Cook on low 8 to 10 hours, or just until meat is tender.
5. Stir in peas.
6. In a small bowl, dissolve flour in water. When smooth, stir into pot.
7. Cover. Turn cooker to high and cook an additional 15 to 20 minutes, or until broth thickens.

Exchange List Values
• Starch 2.0   • Lean Meat 4.0

Basic Nutritional Values
• Calories 325   • Cholesterol 75 mg
  (Calories from Fat 80)   • Sodium 590 mg
• Total Fat 9 gm   • Total Carb 32 gm
  (Saturated Fat 2.5 gm,   • Dietary Fiber 4 gm
  Polyunsat Fat 1.5 gm,   • Sugars 6 gm
  Monounsat Fat 4.0 gm)   • Protein 30 gm

Lamb Stew

Dottie Schmidt
Kansas City, MO

Makes 6 servings

Prep. Time: 30 minutes
Cooking Time: 8-10 hours
Ideal slow cooker size: 4-qt.

2 lbs. lamb, cubed
½ tsp. sugar
2 Tbsp. oil
2 tsp. salt
¼ tsp. pepper
¼ cup flour
2 cups water
¾ cup red cooking wine
¼ tsp. powdered garlic
2 tsp. Worcestershire sauce
6 medium carrots, sliced
4 small onions, quartered
4 ribs celery, sliced
3 medium potatoes,
   unpeeled, diced

1. Sprinkle lamb with sugar. Brown in oil in skillet.
2. Remove lamb and place in cooker, reserving drippings.
3. Stir salt, pepper, and flour into drippings until smooth. Stir in water and wine, until smooth, stirring until broth simmers and thickens.
4. Pour into cooker. Add remaining ingredients and stir until well mixed.
5. Cover. Cook on low 8-10 hours.

Tip:
   Serve with crusty bread.

Exchange List Values
• Starch 1.5   • Meat, lean 4.0
• Vegetable 2.0

Basic Nutritional Values
• Calories 388   • Cholesterol 98 mg
  (Calories from Fat 116)   • Sodium 943 mg
• Total Fat 13 gm   • Total Carb 32 gm
  (Saturated Fat 3.2 gm,   • Dietary Fiber 5 gm
  Polyunsat Fat 2.3 gm,   • Sugars 9 gm
  Monounsat Fat 5.9 gm)   • Protein 35 gm

Lamb Chops

Shirley Sears
Tiskilwa, IL

Makes 8 servings

Prep. Time: 15 minutes
Cooking Time: 4-6 hours
Ideal slow cooker size: 4-qt.

1 medium onion, sliced
1 tsp. dried oregano
½ tsp. dried thyme
½ tsp. garlic powder
¼ tsp. salt
⅛ tsp. pepper
8 loin lamb chops (1¾-2
   lbs.), bone-in, trimmed
   of visible fat
2 garlic cloves, minced
¼ cup water

1. Place onion in slow cooker.

2. Combine oregano, thyme, garlic powder, salt, and pepper. Rub over lamb chops. Place in slow cooker. Top with garlic.

3. Pour water down along the side of crock, so as not to disturb the rub on the chops.

4. Cover. Cook on low 4-6 hours.

Exchange List Values

• Meat, lean 2.0

Basic Nutritional Values

• Calories 117
(Calories from Fat 44)
• Total Fat 5 gm
(Saturated Fat 1.7 gm,
Polyunsat Fat 0.3 gm,
Monounsat Fat 2.1 gm)
• Cholesterol 48 mg
• Sodium 116 mg
• Total Carb 2 gm
• Dietary Fiber 0 gm
• Sugars 1 gm
• Protein 15 gm

Herbed Potato Fish Bake

Barbara Sparks
Glen Burnie, MD

Makes 4 servings

Prep. Time: 25 minutes
Cooking Time: 1-2 hours
Ideal slow cooker size: 4-qt.

10¾-oz. can cream of
  celery soup
½ cup water
1-lb. perch fillet, fresh *or*
  thawed
2 cups cooked, diced
  potatoes
¼ cup freshly grated
  Parmesan cheese
1 Tbsp. chopped parsley
½ tsp. dried basil
¼ tsp. dried oregano

1. Combine soup and water. Pour half in slow cooker.

2. Lay fillet on top. Place potatoes on fillet. Pour remaining soup mix over top.

3. Combine cheese and herbs. Sprinkle over ingredients in slow cooker.

4. Cover. Cook on high 1-2 hours, being careful not to overcook fish.

Exchange List Values

• Starch 1.0   • Meat, lean 3.0
• Carbohydrate 0.5

Basic Nutritional Values

• Calories 269
(Calories from Fat 73)
• Total Fat 8 gm
(Saturated Fat 2.8 gm,
Polyunsat Fat 2.3 gm,
Monounsat Fat 2.2 gm)
• Cholesterol 56 mg
• Sodium 696 mg
• Total Carb 22 gm
• Dietary Fiber 2 gm
• Sugars 2 gm
• Protein 26 gm

Shrimp Marinara

Jan Mast
Lancaster, PA

Makes 6 servings

Prep Time: 10-15 minutes
Cooking Time: 6-7 hours
Ideal slow-cooker size: 4 qt.

6-oz. can no-salt-added
  tomato paste
2 Tbsp. dried parsley
1 cloves garlic, minced
¼ tsp. pepper
½ tsp. dried basil

1 tsp. dried oregano
scant ½ tsp. garlic salt
2 14½-oz. cans no-salt-
  added diced tomatoes
1 lb. cooked shrimp,
  peeled
cooked spaghetti
grated Parmesan cheese,
  optional

1. In slow-cooker combine tomato paste, parsley, garlic, pepper, basil, oregano, salt, garlic salt, and 1 can of diced tomatoes.

2. Cook on low 6-7 hours.

3. Turn to high and add shrimp.

4. If you'd like the sauce to have more tomatoes, stir in remaining can of tomatoes.

5. Cover and cook an additional 15-20 minutes.

6. Serve over cooked spaghetti. Garnish with grated Parmesan cheese if you wish.

Exchange List Values

• Vegetable 2.0   • Lean Meat 1.0

Basic Nutritional Values

• Calories 95
(Calories from Fat 10)
• Total Fat 1 gm
(Saturated Fat 0 gm,
Polyunsat Fat 0 gm
Monounsat Fat 0 gm
  Cholesterol 80 mg),
  Sodium 550 mg
• Total Carb 12 gm
• Dietary Fiber 3 gm
• Sugars 7 gm
• Protein 11 gm

What's your best weapon in the fight against diabetes? Exercise!

Shrimp Jambalaya

Karen Ashworth
Duenweg, MO

Makes 8 servings

Prep. Time: 25 minutes
Cooking Time: 1½ hours
Ideal slow cooker size: 4-qt.

2 Tbsp. margarine
2 medium onions, chopped
2 green bell peppers, chopped
3 ribs celery, chopped
1 cup chopped extra-lean, lower-sodium cooked ham
2 garlic cloves, chopped
1½ cups minute rice
1½ cups 99% fat-free, lower-sodium beef broth
28-oz. can chopped tomatoes
2 Tbsp. chopped parsley
1 tsp. dried basil
½ tsp. dried thyme
¼ tsp. pepper
⅛ tsp. cayenne pepper
1 lb. shelled, deveined, medium-size shrimp
1 Tbsp. chopped parsley

1. Melt margarine in slow cooker set on high. Add onions, peppers, celery, ham, and garlic. Cook 30 minutes.

2. Add rice. Cover and cook 15 minutes.

3. Add broth, tomatoes, 2 Tbsp. parsley, and remaining seasonings. Cover and cook on high 1 hour.

4. Add shrimp. Cook on high 30 minutes, or until liquid is absorbed.

5. Garnish with parsley.

Exchange List Values

- Starch 1.0
- Vegetable 2.0
- Meat, lean 1.0
- Fat 0.5

Basic Nutritional Values

- Calories 205
  (Calories from Fat 36)
- Total Fat 4 gm
  (Saturated Fat 0.8 gm,
  Polyunsat Fat 1.3 gm,
  Monounsat Fat 1.5 gm)
- Cholesterol 95 mg
- Sodium 529 mg
- Total Carb 26 gm
- Dietary Fiber 3 gm
- Sugars 7 gm
- Protein 16 gm

Jambalaya

Doris M. Coyle-Zipp
South Ozone Park, NY

Makes 6 servings

Prep. Time: 30 minutes
Cooking Time: 2½-4 hours
Ideal slow cooker size: 4-qt.

3½-4-lb. roasting chicken, trimmed of skin and fat, cut up
3 onions, diced
1 carrot, sliced
3-4 garlic cloves, minced
1 tsp. dried oregano
1 tsp. dried basil
½ tsp. salt
⅛ tsp. white pepper
14-oz. can crushed tomatoes
1 lb. shelled raw shrimp
2 cups cooked rice

1. Combine all ingredients except shrimp and rice in slow cooker.

2. Cover. Cook on low 2-3½ hours, or until chicken is tender.

3. Add shrimp and rice.

4. Cover. Cook on high 15-20 minutes, or until shrimp are done.

Exchange List Values

- Starch 1.0
- Vegetable 3.0
- Meat, lean 4.0

Basic Nutritional Values

- Calories 354
  (Calories from Fat 65)
- Total Fat 7 gm
  (Saturated Fat 1.9 gm,
  Polyunsat Fat 1.8 gm,
  Monounsat Fat 2.4 gm)
- Cholesterol 192 mg
- Sodium 589 mg
- Total Carb 29 gm
- Dietary Fiber 4 gm
- Sugars 9 gm
- Protein 41 gm

Shrimp Creole

Carol Findling
Princeton, IL

Makes 10 servings

Prep. Time: 30 minutes
Cooking Time: 6-8 hours
Ideal slow cooker size: 4- or 5-qt.

¼ cup canola oil
⅓ cup flour
1¾ cups sliced onions
1 cup diced green bell
   peppers
1 cup diced celery
1½ large carrots, shredded
2¾-lb. can tomatoes
¾ cup water
½ tsp. dried thyme
1 garlic clove, minced
pinch of rosemary
1 Tbsp. sugar
3 bay leaves
1 Tbsp. Worcestershire
   sauce
¾ tsp. salt
⅛ tsp. dried oregano
2 lbs. shelled shrimp,
   deveined

1. Combine canola oil and flour in a skillet. Brown, stirring constantly. Add onions, green peppers, celery, and carrots. Cook 5-10 minutes. Transfer to slow cooker.
2. Add remaining ingredients, except shrimp, and stir well.
3. Cover. Cook on low 6-8 hours.
4. Add shrimp during last hour.

Exchange List Values
- Vegetable 3.0
- Fat 1.0
- Meat, very lean 2.0

Basic Nutritional Values
- Calories 187
- Cholesterol 140 mg
- (Calories from Fat 59)
- Sodium 563 mg
- Total Fat 7 gm
- Total Carb 15 gm
- (Saturated Fat 0.6 gm,
- Dietary Fiber 3 gm
- Polyunsat Fat 2.1 gm,
- Sugars 8 gm
- Monounsat Fat 3.4 gm)
- Protein 17 gm

Seafood Gumbo

Barbara Katrine Rose
Woodbridge, VA

Makes 6 servings

Prep. Time: 40 minutes
Cooking Time: 2½-3 hours
Ideal slow cooker size: 4- or 5-qt.

3 Tbsp. canola oil, *divided*
1 lb. okra, sliced
¼ cup flour
1 bunch green onions,
   sliced
½ cup chopped celery
2 garlic cloves, minced
16-oz. can tomatoes and
   juice
1 bay leaf
1 Tbsp. chopped fresh
   parsley
1 fresh thyme sprig
½ tsp. salt
½-1 tsp. red pepper
3-5 cups water, depending
   upon the consistency
   you like

1 lb. peeled, deveined fresh
   shrimp
½ lb. fresh crabmeat

1. Sauté okra in 1 Tbsp. canola oil until okra is lightly browned. Transfer to slow cooker.
2. Combine remaining 2 Tbsp. canola oil and flour in skillet. Cook over medium heat, stirring constantly until roux is the color of chocolate, 20-25 minutes.
3. Stir in green onions, celery, and garlic. Cook until vegetables are tender. Add to slow cooker.
4. Gently stir in tomatoes with juice, bay leaf, parsley, thyme, salt, red pepper, and water.
5. Cover. Cook on high 2 hours.
6. Add shrimp, crab, and additional water if you wish. Cover. Cook an additional 30-60 minutes on high, until shrimp is cooked and crab is heated.

Exchange List Values
- Vegetable 3.0
- Fat 1.5
- Meat, very lean 2.0

Basic Nutritional Values
- Calories 221
- Cholesterol 148 mg
- (Calories from Fat 75)
- Sodium 548 mg
- Total Fat 8 gm
- Total Carb 15 gm
- (Saturated Fat 0.7 gm,
- Dietary Fiber 3 gm
- Polyunsat Fat 2.6 gm,
- Sugars 5 gm
- Monounsat Fat 4.3 gm)
- Protein 22 gm

Skipping meals only makes you hungrier and can cause you to overeat at the next meal.

Curried Shrimp

Charlotte Shaffer
East Earl, PA

Makes 5 servings

Prep. Time: 10 minutes
Cooking Time: 4-6 hours
Ideal slow cooker size: 3- or 4-qt.

1 small onion, chopped
2 cups cooked shrimp
1½ tsp. curry powder
10¾-oz. can 98% fat-free,
    lower-sodium cream of
    mushroom soup
1 cup fat-free sour cream

1. Combine all ingredients except sour cream in slow cooker.
2. Cover. Cook on low 4-6 hours.
3. Ten minutes before serving, stir in sour cream.

Exchange List Values

- Carbohydrate 1.0   • Meat, very lean 2.0

Basic Nutritional Values

- Calories 130
  (Calories from Fat 16)
- Total Fat 2 gm
  (Saturated Fat 0.6 gm,
  Polyunsat Fat 0.5 gm,
  Monounsat Fat 0.4 gm)
- Cholesterol 92 mg
- Sodium 390 mg
- Total Carb 15 gm
- Dietary Fiber 1 gm
- Sugars 5 gm
- Protein 12 gm

Tip:
  Serve over rice or puff pastry.

Seafood Medley

Susan Alexander
Baltimore, MD

Makes 12 servings

Prep. Time: 10 minutes
Cooking Time: 3-4 hours
Ideal slow cooker size: 4-qt.

1 lb. peeled and deveined
    shrimp
1 lb. crabmeat
1 lb. bay scallops
2 10¾-oz. cans cream of
    celery soup
2 soup cans fat-free milk
3 tsp. margarine
1 tsp. Old Bay seasoning
¼ tsp. pepper

1. Layer shrimp, crab, and scallops in slow cooker.
2. Combine soup and milk. Pour over seafood.
3. Mix together margarine and spices and pour over top.
4. Cover. Cook on low 3-4 hours.

Exchange List Values

- Carbohydrate 0.5   • Fat 0.5
- Meat, very lean 3.0

Basic Nutritional Values

- Calories 168
  (Calories from Fat 51)
- Total Fat 6 gm
  (Saturated Fat 1.6 gm,
  Polyunsat Fat 2.1 gm,
  Monounsat Fat 1.5 gm)
- Cholesterol 106 mg
- Sodium 679 mg
- Total Carb 7 gm
- Dietary Fiber 0 gm
- Sugars 3 gm
- Protein 20 gm

Salmon Cheese Casserole

Wanda S. Curtin
Bradenton, FL

Makes 6 servings

Prep. Time: 15 minutes
Cooking Time: 3-4 hours
Ideal slow cooker size: 4-qt.

14¾-oz. can salmon,
    no added salt, liquid
    reserved
4-oz. can mushrooms,
    drained
1½ cups bread crumbs
2 eggs, beaten
½ cup grated reduced-fat
    cheddar cheese
1 Tbsp. lemon juice
1 Tbsp. minced onion

1. Flake fish in bowl, removing bones.
2. Stir in remaining ingredients. Pour into lightly greased slow cooker.
3. Cover. Cook on low 3-4 hours.

Exchange List Values

- Starch 1.5   • Meat, medium fat 2.0

Basic Nutritional Values

- Calories 257
  (Calories from Fat 85)
- Total Fat 9 gm
  (Saturated Fat 2.9 gm,
  Polyunsat Fat 2.2 gm,
  Monounsat Fat 3.0 gm)
- Cholesterol 116 mg
- Sodium 442 mg
- Total Carb 21 gm
- Dietary Fiber 1 gm
- Sugars 2 gm
- Protein 23 gm

Eat salmon—it has a type of fat that's great for your heart.

Company Seafood Pasta

Jennifer Yoder Sommers
Harrisonburg, VA

Makes 8 servings

Prep. Time: 35 minutes
Cooking Time: 1-2 hours
Ideal slow cooker size: 4-qt.

2 cups fat-free sour cream
1¼ cups shredded reduced-
    fat Monterey Jack cheese
1 Tbsp. light, soft tub
    margarine, melted
½ lb. fresh crabmeat
⅛ tsp. pepper
½ lb. bay scallops, lightly
    cooked
1 lb. medium shrimp,
    cooked and peeled
4 cups cooked linguine
fresh parsley, for garnish

1. Combine sour cream,
cheese and margarine in slow
cooker.
2. Stir in remaining
ingredients, except linguine.
3. Cover. Cook on low 1-2
hours.
4. Serve immediately over
linguine. Garnish with fresh
parsley.

Exchange List Values
• Starch 2.0   • Meat, lean 3.0

Basic Nutritional Values
• Calories 308   • Cholesterol 127 mg
  (Calories from Fat 59) • Sodium 449 mg
• Total Fat 7 gm   • Total Carb 31 gm
  (Saturated Fat 3.1 gm, • Dietary Fiber 1 gm
  Polyunsat Fat 1.1 gm,   • Sugars 5 gm
  Monounsat Fat 2.1 gm)   • Protein 29 gm

Tuna Barbecue

Esther Martin
Ephrata, PA

Makes 4 servings

Prep. Time: 20 minutes
Cooking Time: 4-10 hours
Ideal slow cooker size: 3- or 4-qt.

12-oz. can tuna, packed in
    water, drained
2 cups no-salt-added
    tomato juice
1 medium green bell
    pepper, finely chopped
2 Tbsp. onion flakes
2 Tbsp. Worcestershire
    sauce
3 Tbsp. vinegar
2 Tbsp. sugar
1 Tbsp. prepared mustard
1 rib celery, chopped
dash chili powder
½ tsp. cinnamon
dash hot sauce, *optional*

1. Combine all ingredients
in slow cooker.
2. Cover. Cook on low 8-10
hours, or high 4-5 hours. If
mixture becomes too dry
while cooking, add ½ cup
tomato juice.
3. Serve on buns.

Exchange List Values
• Carbohydrate 0.5   • Meat, very lean 2.0
• Vegetable 2.0

Basic Nutritional Values
• Calories 162   • Cholesterol 23 mg
  (Calories from Fat 8)   • Sodium 423 mg
• Total Fat 1 gm   • Total Carb 18 gm
  (Saturated Fat 0.2 gm, • Dietary Fiber 2 gm
  Polyunsat Fat 0.3 gm,   • Sugars 14 gm
  Monounsat Fat 0.3 gm)   • Protein 21 gm

Tuna Noodle Casserole

Leona Miller
Millersburg, OH

Makes 6 servings

Prep. Time: 20 minutes
Cooking Time: 3-9 hours
Ideal slow cooker size: 4-qt.

2 6½-oz. cans water-packed
    tuna, drained
2 10½-oz. cans 98% fat-
    free, lower sodium
    cream of mushroom
    soup
1 cup milk
2 Tbsp. dried parsley
10-oz. pkg. frozen mixed
    vegetables, thawed
8-oz. pkg. noodles, cooked
    and drained
½ cup toasted sliced
    almonds

1. Combine tuna, soup,
milk, parsley, and vegetables.
Fold in noodles. Pour into
greased slow cooker. Top with
almonds.
2. Cover. Cook on low 7-9
hours, or high 3-4 hours.

Exchange List Values
• Starch 2.0   • Meat, lean 3.0
• Carbohydrate 1.0

Basic Nutritional Values
• Calories 395   • Cholesterol 21 mg
  (Calories from Fat 101) • Sodium 637 mg
• Total Fat 11 gm   • Total Carb 46 gm
  (Saturated Fat 1.9 gm, • Dietary Fiber 5 gm
  Polyunsat Fat 2.5 gm,   • Sugars 8 gm
  Monounsat Fat 5.7 gm)   • Protein 27 gm

Tempeh-Stuffed Peppers

Sara Harter Fredette
Williamsburg, MA

Makes 4 servings

Prep. Time: 35 minutes
Cooking Time: 3-8 hours
Ideal slow cooker size: 6-qt.
  oval, so the peppers can each
  sit on the bottom of slow
  cooker

4 oz. tempeh, cubed
1 garlic clove, minced
2 14½-oz. cans diced no-
  salt-added tomatoes
2 tsp. soy sauce
¼ cup chopped onions
1½ cups cooked rice
1 cup shredded fat-free
  cheddar cheese
Tabasco sauce, *optional*
4 green, red, *or* yellow, bell
  peppers, with tops sliced
  off and seeds removed
¼ cup shredded fat-free
  cheddar cheese

1. Steam tempeh 10
minutes in saucepan. Mash in
bowl with the garlic, half the
tomatoes, and soy sauce.
2. Stir in onions, rice, ½
cup cheese, and Tabasco
sauce. Stuff into peppers.
3. Place peppers in slow
cooker. Pour remaining half
of tomatoes over peppers.
4. Cover. Cook on low 6-8
hours, or high 3-4 hours. Top
with remaining cheese in last
30 minutes.

Exchange List Values
- Starch 2.0
- Meat, lean 1.0
- Vegetable 3.0

Basic Nutritional Values
- Calories 266
- (Calories from Fat 26)
- Total Fat 3 gm
- (Saturated Fat 0.1 gm,
- Polyunsat Fat 1.5 gm,
- Monounsat Fat 0.6 gm)
- Cholesterol 4 mg
- Sodium 510 mg
- Total Carb 42 gm
- Dietary Fiber 6 gm
- Sugars 17 gm
- Protein 21 gm

Barbecued Lentils

Sue Hamilton
Minooka, IL

Makes 8 servings

Prep. Time: 10 minutes
Cooking Time: 6-8 hours
Ideal slow cooker size: 4-qt.

2 cups Phyllis' Homemade
  Barbecue Sauce (see
  recipe on page 261)
3½ cups water
1 lb. dry lentils
9.7-oz. pkg. vegetarian hot
  dogs, sliced

1. Combine all ingredients
in slow cooker.
2. Cover. Cook on low 6-8
hours.

Exchange List Values
- Starch 2.0
- Meat, very lean 2.0
- Vegetable 2.0

Basic Nutritional Values
- Calories 270
- (Calories from Fat 9)
- Total Fat 1 gm
- (Saturated Fat 0.1 gm,
- Polyunsat Fat 0.5 gm,
- Monounsat Fat 0.2 gm)
- Cholesterol 0 mg
- Sodium 464 mg
- Total Carb 43 gm
- Dietary Fiber 15 gm
- Sugars 12 gm
- Protein 23 gm

Minestra Di Ceci

Jeanette Oberholtzer
Manheim, PA

Makes 8 servings

Soaking Time: 8 hours
Prep. Time: 20 minutes
Cooking Time: 5½-6 hours
Ideal slow cooker size: 4-qt.

1 lb. dry chickpeas
1 sprig fresh rosemary
10 leaves fresh sage
1 Tbsp. salt
1-2 large garlic cloves,
  minced
1 tsp. olive oil
1 cup small dry pasta,
  your choice of shape

1. Wash chickpeas. Place in
slow cooker. Soak for 8 hours
in full pot of water, along
with rosemary, sage, and salt.
2. Drain water. Remove
herbs.
3. Refill slow cooker with
water to 1" above peas.
4. Cover. Cook on low 5
hours.
5. Sauté garlic in olive oil
in skillet until clear.
6. Purée half of peas, along
with several cups of broth
from cooker, in blender.
Return purée to slow cooker.
Add garlic and oil.
7. Boil pasta in saucepan
until al dente, about 5 minutes. Drain. Add to beans.
8. Cover. Cook on high
30-60 minutes, or until pasta
is tender and heated through,
but not mushy.

Exchange List Values
- Starch 2.5
- Meat, very lean 1.0

Basic Nutritional Values
- Calories 236
  (Calories from Fat 34)
- Total Fat 4 gm
  (Saturated Fat 0.4 gm,
  Polyunsat Fat 1.5 gm,
  Monounsat Fat 1.1 gm)
- Cholesterol 0 mg
- Sodium 445 mg
- Total Carb 40 gm
- Dietary Fiber 9 gm
- Sugars 7 gm
- Protein 12 gm

Variation:
Add ½ tsp. black pepper to Step 1, if you like.

Slow Cooker Macaroni
Lisa F. Good
Harrisonburg, VA

Makes 6 servings

Prep. Time: 10 minutes
Cooking Time: 3-4 hours
Ideal slow cooker size: 4-qt.

1½ **cups dry macaroni**
1½ **Tbsp. light, soft tub margarine**
6 **oz. light Velveeta cheese, sliced**
2 **cups fat-free milk**
1 **cup fat-free half-and-half**

1. Combine macaroni, and butter.
2. Layer cheese over top.
3. Pour in milk and half-and-half.
4. Cover. Cook on high 3-4 hours, or until macaroni is soft.

Exchange List Values
- Starch 1.0
- Milk, fat-free 1.0
- Fat 1.0

Basic Nutritional Values
- Calories 208
  (Calories from Fat 45)
- Total Fat 5 gm
  (Saturated Fat 2.5 gm,
  Polyunsat Fat 0.5 gm,
  Monounsat Fat 1.6 gm)
- Cholesterol 15 mg
- Sodium 555 mg
- Total Carb 27 gm
- Dietary Fiber 0 gm
- Sugars 12 gm
- Protein 14 gm

Gourmet Spaghetti Sauce
Doris Perkins
Mashpee, MA

Makes 20 servings

Prep. Time: 25 minutes
Cooking Time: 4-5 hours
Ideal slow cooker size: 6-qt.

2 **slices bacon**
1¼ **lbs. ground beef**
½ **lb. ground pork**
1 **cup chopped onions**
½ **cup chopped green bell pepper**
3 **garlic cloves, minced**
2 **2-lb. 3-oz. cans Italian tomatoes**
2 **6-oz. cans tomato paste**
1 **cup dry red wine,** *or* **water**
2½ **tsp. dried oregano**
2½ **tsp. dried basil**
1 **bay leaf, crumbled**
¾ **cup water**
¼ **cup chopped fresh parsley**
1 **tsp. dried thyme**
1 **tsp. salt**
¼ **tsp. pepper**
¼ **cup dry red wine,** *or* **water**

1. Brown bacon in skillet until crisp. Drain. Remove and crumble.
2. Add ground beef and pork. Crumble and cook until brown. Stir in onions, green peppers, and garlic. Cook 10 minutes.
3. Drain fat and pat dry with paper towel.
4. Pour tomatoes into slow cooker and crush with back of spoon.
5. Add all other ingredients, except ¼ cup wine, in slow cooker.
6. Cover. Bring to boil on high. Reduce heat to low for 3-4 hours.
7. During last 30 minutes, stir in ¼ cup red wine or water.

Exchange List Values
- Vegetable 2.0
- Meat, medium fat 1.0

Basic Nutritional Values
- Calories 115
  (Calories from Fat 46)
- Total Fat 5 gm
  (Saturated Fat 1.8 gm,
  Polyunsat Fat 0.4 gm,
  Monounsat Fat 2.2 gm)
- Cholesterol 25 mg
- Sodium 309 mg
- Total Carb 9 gm
- Dietary Fiber 2 gm
- Sugars 4 gm
- Protein 9 gm

The key to weight loss is simple: burn more calories than you eat.

Chunky Spaghetti Sauce

Patti Boston
Newark, OH

Makes 12 cups

Prep. Time: 25 minutes
Cooking Time: 3½-8 hours
Ideal slow cooker size: 4-qt.

1 lb. ground beef, browned and drained
½ lb. bulk sausage, browned and drained
14½-oz. can no-added-salt Italian tomatoes with basil
15-oz. can Italian tomato sauce
1 medium onion, chopped
1 green pepper, chopped
8-oz. can sliced mushrooms
½ cup dry red wine
2 tsp. sugar
1 tsp. minced garlic
1½ tsp. dried basil

1. Combine all ingredients in slow cooker.
2. Cover. Cook on high 3½-4 hours, or low 7-8 hours.

Exchange List Values
• Vegetable 2.0   • Meat, medium fat 1.0

Basic Nutritional Values
• Calories 134
  (Calories from Fat 61)
• Total Fat 7 gm
  (Saturated Fat 2.5 gm,
  Polyunsat Fat 0.5 gm,
  Monounsat Fat 2.9 gm)
• Cholesterol 30 mg
• Sodium 397 mg
• Total Carb 8 gm
• Dietary Fiber 2 gm
• Sugars 4 gm
• Protein 11 gm

Variations:
1. For added texture and zest, add 3 fresh, medium-sized tomatoes, chopped, and

4 large fresh basil leaves, torn. Stir in 1 tsp. salt and ½ tsp. pepper.
2. To any leftover sauce, add chickpeas or kidney beans and serve chili!

Spaghetti Sauce

Colleen Heatwole
Burton, MI

Makes 15 servings

Prep Time: 30-35 minutes
Cooking Time: 4 hours
Ideal slow-cooker size: 1 7-qt., or 2 4-qt. cookers

1½ lbs. 90%-lean ground beef, cooked and drained
3 onions, coarsely chopped
1 red bell pepper, coarsely chopped
1 green pepper, coarsely chopped
4 cloves garlic, minced
2 28-oz. cans diced tomatoes
14½-oz. can diced tomatoes
2 14½-oz. cans fat-free, low-sodium beef broth
2 Tbsp. sugar
2 tsp. dried basil

2 tsp. dried oregano
1 tsp. salt
2 6-oz. cans tomato paste, no salt added

1. Combine all ingredients except tomato paste in slow cooker.
2. Cook for 3½ hours on high. Stir in tomato paste.
3. Cover and cook an additional 30 minutes.

Exchange List Values
• Vegetable 3.0   • Fat 0.5
• Lean Meat 1.0

Basic Nutritional Values
• Calories 140
  (Calories from Fat 35)
• Total Fat 4 gm
  (Saturated Fat 1.5 gm,
  Polyunsat Fat 0 gm
  Monounsat Fat 1.5 gm)
• Cholesterol 25 mg
• Sodium 475 mg
• Total Carb 15 gm
• Dietary Fiber 3 gm
• Sugars 9 gm
• Protein 12 gm

Just for today, add up the calories from all your beverages, including alcohol. Pay special attention to serving sizes, since many sodas and juice bottles contain 2 servings, but the calories listed are for 1 serving.

Sausage-Beef Spaghetti Sauce

Jeannine Janzen
Elbing, KS

Makes 20 servings

Prep. Time: 20 minutes
Cooking Time: 6½ hours
Ideal slow cooker size: 4-qt.

1 lb. ground beef
1 lb. Italian sausage, sliced
2 28-oz. cans crushed
   tomatoes
¾ can (28-oz. tomato can)
   water
2 tsp. garlic powder
1 tsp. pepper
2 Tbsp. parsley
2 Tbsp. dried oregano
2 12-oz. cans tomato paste
2 12-oz. cans tomato purée

1. Brown ground beef and sausage in skillet. Drain. Transfer to large slow cooker.
2. Add crushed tomatoes, water, garlic powder, pepper, parsley, and oregano.
3. Cover. Cook on high 30 minutes. Add tomato paste and tomato purée. Cook on low 6 hours.

Exchange List Values
• Vegetable 3.0,   Meat, high fat 1.0

Basic Nutritional Values
• Calories 176   • Cholesterol 27 mg
  (Calories from Fat 71) • Sodium 408 mg
• Total Fat 8 gm   • Total Carb 17 gm
  (Saturated Fat 2.7 gm, • Dietary Fiber 4 gm
  Polyunsat Fat 0.8 gm,   • Sugars 6 gm
  Monounsat Fat 3.1 gm)   • Protein 10 gm

Mom's Meatballs

Mary C. Casey
Scranton, PA

Makes 10 servings

Prep. Time: 45 minutes
Cooking Time: 4-5 hours
Ideal slow cooker size: 4- or 5-qt.

Sauce:
2 Tbsp. canola oil
¼-½ cup chopped onions
3 garlic cloves, minced
29-oz. can tomato purée
29-oz. can water
12-oz. can tomato paste
12-oz. can water
1 Tbsp. sugar
2 tsp. dried oregano
¼ tsp. Italian seasoning
½ tsp. dried basil
⅛ tsp. pepper
¼ cup diced green
   peppers

Meatballs:
1 lb. 85%-lean ground
   beef
1 egg
2 Tbsp. water
¾ cup Italian bread
   crumbs
⅛ tsp. black
   pepper
⅛ tsp. salt
1 Tbsp.
   canola
   oil

1. Sauté onions and garlic in oil in saucepan.
2. Combine all sauce ingredients in slow cooker.

---

3. Cover. Cook on low.
4. Mix together all meatball ingredients except oil. Form into small meatballs, then brown on all sides in oil in saucepan. Drain on paper towels. Add to sauce.
5. Cover. Cook on low 4-5 hours.

Exchange List Values
• Starch 0.5   fat 1.0
• Vegetable 3.0   • Fat 1.0
• Meat, medium

Basic Nutritional Values
• Calories 221   • Cholesterol 48 mg
  (Calories from Fat 91) • Sodium 540 mg
• Total Fat 10 gm   • Total Carb 22 gm
  (Saturated Fat 2.4 gm, • Dietary Fiber 4 gm
  Polyunsat Fat 1.7 gm,   • Sugars 7 gm
  Monounsat Fat 4.9 gm)   • Protein 13 gm

Nancy's Spaghetti Sauce

Nancy Graves
Manhattan, KS

Makes 6 servings

Prep. Time: 25 minutes
Cooking Time: 3 hours
Ideal slow cooker size: 4-qt.

¼ cup minced onion
garlic powder, to taste
3 cups chopped fresh
  tomatoes
6-oz. can tomato paste
½ tsp. salt
dash of pepper
½ tsp. dried basil
1 bay leaf
1 chopped green bell
  pepper
1 lb. ground beef, browned
  and drained
4-oz. can sliced
  mushrooms, undrained

1. Combine all ingredients
in slow cooker.
2. Cover. Cook on low 3
hours.

Exchange List Values
• Vegetable 2.0   • Fat 0.5
• Meat, lean 2.0

Basic Nutritional Values
• Calories 186   • Cholesterol 45 mg
  (Calories from Fat 75) • Sodium 372 mg
• Total Fat 8 gm   • Total Carb 12 gm
  (Saturated Fat 3.0 gm, • Dietary Fiber 3 gm
  Polyunsat Fat 0.5 gm,   • Sugars 4 gm
  Monounsat Fat 3.4 gm)   • Protein 17 gm

Pasta Sauce with Meat and Veggies

Marla Folkerts
Holland, OH

Makes 6 servings

Prep. Time: 35 minutes
Cooking Time: 7-8 hours
Ideal slow cooker size: 4-qt.

½ lb. ground turkey,
  browned and drained
½ lb. ground beef,
  browned and drained
1 rib celery, chopped
2 medium carrots, chopped
1 garlic clove, minced
1 medium onion, chopped
28-oz. can diced tomatoes
  with juice
¼ tsp. salt
¼ tsp. dried thyme
6-oz. can tomato paste
⅛ tsp. pepper

1. Combine turkey, beef,
celery, carrots, garlic, and
onion in slow cooker.
2. Add remaining ingredi-
ents. Mix well.
3. Cover. Cook on low 7-8
hours.

Exchange List Values
• Vegetable 3.0   • Fat 0.5
• Meat, lean 2.0

Basic Nutritional Values
• Calories 200   • Cholesterol 50 mg
  (Calories from Fat 72) • Sodium 391 mg
• Total Fat 8 gm   • Total Carb 16 gm
  (Saturated Fat 2.4 gm, • Dietary Fiber 4 gm
  Polyunsat Fat 1.3 gm,   • Sugars 7 gm
  Monounsat Fat 3.1 gm)   • Protein 17 gm

Katelyn's Spaghetti Sauce

Katelyn Bailey
Mechanicsburg, PA

Makes 12 servings

Prep. Time: 25 minutes
Cooking Time: 8-10 hours
Ideal slow cooker size: 4- or 5-qt.

1 lb. ground beef, browned
  and drained
¾ cup chopped onions
1 garlic clove, minced
3 Tbsp. oil
2 6-oz. cans tomato paste
1 Tbsp. sugar
1½ tsp. salt
1-1½ tsp. dried oregano
½ tsp. pepper
1 bay leaf
2 qts. chopped fresh
  tomatoes, *or* tomato
  sauce

1. Combine all ingredients
in slow cooker.
2. Cover. Cook on low
8-10 hours. Remove bay leaf
before serving.

Exchange List Values
• Vegetable 3.0   • Fat 0.5
• Meat, lean 1.0

Basic Nutritional Values
• Calories 151   • Cholesterol 22 mg
  (Calories from Fat 71) • Sodium 342 mg
• Total Fat 8 gm   • Total Carb 13 gm
  (Saturated Fat 1.7 gm, • Dietary Fiber 3 gm
  Polyunsat Fat 1.4 gm,   • Sugars 6 gm
  Monounsat Fat 3.8 gm)   • Protein 9 gm

Note:
This sauce freezes well

Meat Sauce for Spaghetti

Esther Lehman
Croghan, NY

Makes 10 servings

Prep. Time: 35 minutes
Cooking Time: 8¼-10¼ hours
Ideal slow cooker size: 4- or 5-qt.

1 lb. ground beef, browned
2 28-oz. cans tomatoes
2 medium onions, quartered
2 medium carrots, cut into chunks
2 garlic cloves, minced
6-oz. can tomato paste
2 Tbsp. chopped fresh parsley
1 bay leaf
1 Tbsp. sugar
1 tsp. dried basil
½ tsp. salt
½ tsp. dried oregano
dash pepper
2 Tbsp. cold water
2 Tbsp. cornstarch

1. Place meat in slow cooker.
2. In blender, combine 1 can tomatoes, onions, carrots, and garlic. Cover and blend until finely chopped. Stir into meat.
3. Cut up the remaining can of tomatoes. Stir into meat mixture. Add tomato paste, parsley, bay leaf, sugar, basil, salt, oregano, and pepper. Mix well.
4. Cover. Cook on low 8-10 hours.
5. To serve, turn to high.

Remove bay leaf. Cover and heat until bubbly, about 10 minutes.
6. Combine water and cornstarch. Stir into tomato mixture. Cook 10 minutes longer.

Exchange List Values
- Vegetable 3.0
- Fat 0.5
- Meat, lean 1.0

Basic Nutritional Values
- Calories 151
- (Calories from Fat 46)
- Total Fat 5 gm
- (Saturated Fat 1.8 gm, Polyunsat Fat 0.4 gm, Monounsat Fat 2.1 gm)
- Cholesterol 27 mg
- Sodium 403 mg
- Total Carb 17 gm
- Dietary Fiber 3 gm
- Sugars 8 gm
- Protein 11 gm

Italian Vegetable Pasta Sauce

Sherril Bieberly
Sauna, KS

Makes 20, ½ cup servings

Prep. Time: 20 minutes
Cooking Time: 5-18 hours
Ideal slow cooker size: 4- or 5-qt.

3 Tbsp. olive oil
1 cup packed chopped fresh parsley
3 ribs celery, chopped
1 medium onion, chopped
2 garlic cloves, minced
2-inch sprig fresh rosemary, *or* ½ tsp. dried rosemary
2 small fresh sage leaves, *or* ½ tsp. dried sage
32-oz. can tomato sauce
32-oz. can chopped tomatoes
1 small dried hot chili pepper
¼ lb. fresh mushrooms, sliced
½ tsp. salt

1. Heat oil in skillet. Add parsley, celery, onion, garlic, rosemary, and sage. Sauté until vegetables are tender. Place in slow cooker.
2. Add tomatoes, chili pepper, mushrooms, and salt.
3. Cover. Cook on low 12-18 hours, or on high 5-6 hours.

Exchange List Values
- Vegetable 1.0
- Fat 0.5

Basic Nutritional Values
- Calories 49
- (Calories from Fat 20)
- Total Fat 2 gm
- (Saturated Fat 0.3 gm, Polyunsat Fat 0.3 gm, Monounsat Fat 1.5 gm)
- Cholesterol 0 mg
- Sodium 402 mg
- Total Carb 7 gm
- Dietary Fiber 2 gm
- Sugars 4 gm
- Protein 1 gm

Variation:
Add 2 lbs. browned ground beef to olive oil and sautéed vegetables. Continue with recipe.

Use less meat and double the vegetables in a stir-fry, pasta dish, or stew.

Louise's Vegetable Spaghetti Sauce

Louise Stackhouse
Benton, PA

Makes 6 servings

Prep. Time: 20 minutes
Cooking Time: 8-10 hours
Ideal slow cooker size: 4-qt.

6 fresh medium tomatoes, peeled and crushed
1 medium onion, chopped
2 medium green peppers, chopped
2 cloves garlic, minced
½ tsp. dried basil
½ tsp. dried oregano
¼ tsp. salt
2 Tbsp. sugar
sweetener substitute to equal 1 Tbsp. sugar

1. Combine all ingredients in slow cooker.
2. Cover. Cook on low 8-10 hours. If the sauce is too watery for your liking, stir in a 6-oz. can of tomato paste during the last hour of cooking.

Exchange List Values
• Vegetable 3.0

Basic Nutritional Values
• Calories 69
(Calories from Fat 6)
• Total Fat 1 gm
(Saturated Fat 0.0 gm,
Polyunsat Fat 0.2 gm,
Monounsat Fat 0.1 gm)
• Cholesterol 0 mg
• Sodium 113 mg
• Total Carb 16 gm
• Dietary Fiber 3 gm
• Sugars 11 gm
• Protein 2 gm

Easy-Does-It Spaghetti

Rachel Kauffman
Alto, MI
Lois Stoltzfus
Honey Brook, PA
Deb Unternahrer
Wayland, IA

Makes 12 servings

Prep. Time: 25 minutes
Cooking Time: 3½-8½ hours
Ideal slow cooker size: 4-qt.

2 lbs. 85%-lean ground chuck, browned and drained
1 cup chopped onions
2 cloves garlic, minced
2 15-oz. cans no-salt-added tomato sauce
3 tsp. Italian seasoning (see recipe on page 260)
¼ tsp. pepper
2 4-oz. cans sliced mushrooms, drained
6 cups tomato juice
16-oz. dry spaghetti, broken into 4-5-inch pieces

1. Combine all ingredients except spaghetti and cheese in 4-quart (or larger) slow cooker.
2. Cover. Cook on low 6-8 hours, or high 3-5 hours.

3. Turn to high during last 30 minutes and stir in dry spaghetti. If spaghetti is not fully cooked, continue cooking for 10 minute intervals, checking to make sure it is not becoming over-cooked.

Exchange List Values
• Starch 2.0
• Vegetable 2.0
• Meat, lean 2.0

Basic Nutritional Values
• Calories 328
(Calories from Fat 78)
• Total Fat 9 gm
(Saturated Fat 3.0 gm,
Polyunsat Fat 0.6 gm,
Monounsat Fat 3.5 gm)
• Cholesterol 45 mg
• Sodium 547 mg
• Total Carb 42 gm
• Dietary Fiber 3 gm
• Sugars 10 gm
• Protein 22 gm

Variation:
Add 1 tsp. dry mustard and ½ tsp. allspice in Step 1.
Kathy Hertzler
Lancaster, PA

If someone you love has diabetes, you can help by learning about the disease, talking about your feelings (because diabetes affects you, too!), offering practical help, and getting help if needed.

Pizza Rice

Sue Hamilton
Minooka, IL

Makes 14 servings

Prep. Time: 10 minutes
Cooking Time: 3-6 hours
Ideal slow cooker size: 3- or 4-qt.

2 cups raw brown rice
2 cups chunky pizza sauce
1 cup water
7-oz. can mushrooms, drained and rinsed
3 oz. turkey pepperoni, sliced
1 cup grated reduced-fat cheddar cheese

1. Combine rice, sauce, water, mushrooms, and pepperoni in slow cooker. Stir.
2. Cover. Cook on low 4-6 hours, or on high 3-5 hours.
3. Sprinkle with cheese before serving.

Exchange List Values
- Starch 1.5
- Fat 0.5

Basic Nutritional Values
- Calories 151
  (Calories from Fat 30)
- Total Fat 3 gm
  (Saturated Fat 1.4 gm,
  Polyunsat Fat 0.5 gm,
  Monounsat Fat 0.9 gm)
- Cholesterol 14 mg
- Sodium 365 mg
- Total Carb 24 gm
- Dietary Fiber 1 gm
- Sugars 2 gm
- Protein 7 gm

Pizza in a Pot

Marianne J. Troyer
Millersburg, OH

Makes 8 servings

Prep. Time: 25 minutes
Cooking Time: 8-9 hours
Ideal slow cooker size: 4-qt.

1 lb. bulk lean sweet Italian turkey sausage, browned and drained
28-oz. can crushed tomatoes
15½-oz. can chili beans
2¼-oz. can sliced black olives, drained
1 medium onion, chopped
1 small green bell pepper, chopped
2 garlic cloves, minced
¼ cup grated Parmesan cheese
1 Tbsp. quick-cooking tapioca
1 Tbsp. dried basil
1 bay leaf

1. Combine all ingredients in slow cooker.
2. Cover. Cook on low 8-9 hours.
3. Discard bay leaf. Stir well.

Exchange List Values
- Starch 1.0
- Vegetable 2.0
- Meat, lean 2.0
- Fat 0.5

Basic Nutritional Values
- Calories 251
  (Calories from Fat 87)
- Total Fat 10 gm
  (Saturated Fat 2.8 gm,
  Polyunsat Fat 1.1 gm,
  Monounsat Fat 2.3 gm)
- Cholesterol 49 mg
- Sodium 937 mg
- Total Carb 23 gm
- Dietary Fiber 7 gm
- Sugars 8 gm
- Protein 18 gm

Tip:
Serve over pasta. Top with mozzarella cheese.

Soups

Nancy's Vegetable Beef Soup

Nancy Graves
Manhattan, KS

Makes 8 servings

Prep. Time: 25 minutes
Cooking Time: 8 hours
Ideal slow cooker size: 5- or 6-qt.

2-lb. roast, cubed, *or* 2 lbs. stewing meat
15-oz. can corn
15-oz. can green beans
1-lb. bag frozen peas
40-oz. can no-added-salt stewed tomatoes
5 tsp. salt-free beef bouillon powder
Tabasco, to taste
½ tsp. salt

1. Combine all ingredients in slow cooker. Do not drain vegetables.
2. Add water to fill slow cooker to within 3 inches of top
3. Cover. Cook on low 8 hours, or until meat is tender and vegetables are soft.

Exchange List Values
• Starch 1.0   • Meat, lean 2.0
• Vegetable 2.0

Basic Nutritional Values
• Calories 229   • Cholesterol 56 mg
 (Calories from Fat 46) • Sodium 545 mg
• Total Fat 5 gm   • Total Carb 24 gm
 (Saturated Fat 1.4 gm, • Dietary Fiber 6 gm
 Polyunsat Fat 0.5 gm, • Sugars 10 gm
 Monounsat Fat 2.2 gm) • Protein 23 gm

Variation:
 Add 1 large onion, sliced, 2 cups sliced carrots, and ¾ cup pearl barley to mixture before cooking.

Frances' Hearty Vegetable Soup

Frances Schrag,
Newton, KS

Makes 10 servings

Prep. Time: 40 minutes
Cooking Time: 8 hours
Ideal slow cooker size: 6-qt.

1 lb. round steak, cut into ½-inch pieces
14½-oz. can diced tomatoes
3 cups water
2 potatoes, peeled and cubed
2 onions, sliced
3 celery ribs, sliced
2 carrots, sliced
3 beef bouillon cubes
½ tsp. dried basil
½ tsp. dried oregano
¼ tsp. pepper
1½ cups frozen mixed vegetables

1. Combine first 3 ingredients in slow cooker.

2. Cover. Cook on high 6 hours.

3. Add remaining ingredients. Cover and cook on high 2 hours more, or until meat and vegetables are tender.

Exchange List Values
- Starch 0.5
- Vegetable 1.0
- Meat, lean 1.0

Basic Nutritional Values
- Calories 117
  (Calories from Fat 20)
- Total Fat 2 gm
  (Saturated Fat 0.7 gm,
  Polyunsat Fat 0.2 gm,
  Monounsat Fat 0.9 gm)
- Cholesterol 26 mg
- Sodium 405 mg
- Total Carb 14 gm
- Dietary Fiber 3 gm
- Sugars 5 gm
- Protein 11 gm

Variation:

Cut salt back to ½ tsp. Increase dried basil to 1 tsp. and dried oregano to 1 tsp.

Tracy Clark
Mt. Crawford, VA

Hearty Bean and Vegetable Soup

Jewel Showalter
Landisville, PA

Makes 8 servings

Prep. Time: 20-25 minutes
Cooking Time: 6-8 hours
Ideal slow cooker size: 5-qt.)

2 medium onions, sliced
2 garlic cloves, minced
2 Tbsp. olive oil
6 cups fat-free, lower-
   sodium vegetable broth
2 cups water

1 small head cabbage,
   chopped
2 large red potatoes,
   chopped
2 cups chopped celery
2 cups chopped carrots
4 cups frozen corn
2 tsp. dried basil
1 tsp. dried marjoram
¼ tsp. dried oregano
½ tsp. pepper
2 15-oz. cans navy beans,
   drained

1. Sauté onions and garlic in oil in skillet. Transfer to large slow cooker.

2. Add remaining ingredients. Mix together well.

3. Cover. Cook on low 6-8 hours.

Variation:

Add 2-3 cups cooked and cut-up chicken 30 minutes before serving if you wish.

Note:

I discovered this recipe after my husband's heart attack. It's a great nutritious soup using only a little fat.

Exchange List Values
- Starch 2.5
- Vegetable 3.0
- Fat 0.5

Basic Nutritional Values
- Calories 305
  (Calories from Fat 40)
- Total Fat 4.5 gm
  (Saturated Fat 0.5 gm,
  Polyunsat Fat 1.0 gm,
  Monounsat Fat 2.5 gm)
- Cholesterol 0 mg
- Sodium 590 mg
- Total Carb 58 gm
- Dietary Fiber 13 gm
- Sugars 10 gm
- Protein 12 gm

Anona's Beef Vegetable Soup

Anona M. Teel
Bangor, PA

Makes 6 servings

Prep. Time: 35 minutes
Cooking Time: 8-10 hours
Ideal slow cooker size: 4-qt.

1-1½ lb. soup bone
1 lb. stewing beef cubes
1½ qts. cold water
½ tsp. salt
¾ cup diced celery
¾ cup diced carrots
¾ cup diced potatoes
¾ cup diced onion
1 cup frozen mixed
   vegetables of your choice
1-lb. can tomatoes
⅛ tsp. pepper
1 Tbsp. chopped dried
   parsley

1. Put all ingredients in slow cooker.

2. Cover. Cook on low 8-10 hours. Remove bone before serving.

Exchange List Values
- Starch 0.5
- Vegetable 1.0
- Meat, lean 1.0

Basic Nutritional Values
- Calories 134
  (Calories from Fat 28)
- Total Fat 3 gm
  (Saturated Fat 0.9 gm,
  Polyunsat Fat 0.3 gm,
  Monounsat Fat 1.4 gm)
- Cholesterol 38 mg
- Sodium 407 mg
- Total Carb 13 gm
- Dietary Fiber 3 gm
- Sugars 6 gm
- Protein 14 gm

"Absent Cook" Stew

Kathy Hertzler
Lancaster, PA

Makes 6 servings

Prep. Time: 35 minutes
Cooking Time: 10-12 hours
Ideal slow cooker size: 4-qt.

2 lbs. stewing beef, cubed
2-3 carrots, sliced
1 onion, chopped
3 large potatoes, cubed
3 ribs celery, sliced
10¾-oz. can tomato soup
1 soup can water
⅛ tsp. salt
dash of pepper
2 Tbsp. vinegar

1. Combine all ingredients in slow cooker.
2. Cover. Cook on low 10-12 hours.

Exchange List Values

- Starch 2.0
- Meat, lean 2.0
- Vegetable 1.0

Basic Nutritional Values

- Calories 314
  (Calories from Fat 59)
- Total Fat 7 gm
  (Saturated Fat 2.0 gm,
  Polyunsat Fat 0.8 gm,
  Monounsat Fat 2.9 gm)
- Cholesterol 75 mg
- Sodium 427 mg
- Total Carb 35 gm
- Dietary Fiber 5 gm
- Sugars 9 gm
- Protein 28 gm

Tuscan Beef Stew

Karen Ceneviva
Seymour, CT

Makes 8 servings

Prep Time: 5-10 minutes
Cooking Time: 4-9 hours
Ideal slow-cooker size: 3½ qt.

10½-oz. can tomato soup
10½-oz. can fat-free, low-sodium beef broth
½ cup water
1 tsp. Italian seasoning (see recipe on page 260)
½ tsp. garlic powder
14½-oz. can Italian diced tomatoes
¾ lb. carrot chunks (1" pieces)
2 lbs. stewing beef, cut into 1" cubes
2 15½-oz. cans cannellini beans, rinsed and drained

1. Mix all ingredients, except beans, in slow-cooker.
2. Cover. Cook on high 4-5 hours, or on low 8-9 hours, or until vegetables and beef are tender.
3. Stir in beans. Cover. Cook on high for final 10 minutes of cooking time.

Exchange List Values

- Starch 1.0
- Lean Meat 4.0
- Vegetable 1.0

Basic Nutritional Values

- Calories 260
  (Calories from Fat 45)
- Total Fat 5 gm
  (Saturated Fat 2.0 gm,
  Polyunsat Fat 0.5 gm,
  Monounsat Fat 2.5 gm)
- Cholesterol 60 mg
- Sodium 495 mg
- Total Carb 25 gm
- Dietary Fiber 6 gm
- Sugars 6 gm
- Protein 29 gm

Lilli's Vegetable Beef Soup

Lilli Peters
Dodge City, KS

Makes 12 servings

Prep. Time: 45 minutes
Cooking Time: 8-10 hours
Ideal slow cooker size: 4- or 5-qt.

3 lbs. stewing meat, cut in 1-inch pieces
2 Tbsp. canola oil
4 potatoes, cubed
4 carrots, sliced
3 ribs celery, sliced
14-oz. can diced tomatoes
14-oz. can Italian tomatoes, crushed
2 medium onions, chopped
2 wedges cabbage, sliced thinly
2 tsp. salt-free beef bouillon powder
2 Tbsp. fresh parsley
1 tsp. seasoned salt
1 tsp. garlic salt
½ tsp. pepper
water

1. Brown meat in oil in skillet. Drain.
2. Combine all ingredients except water in large slow cooker. Cover with water.
3. Cover. Cook on low 8-10 hours.

Exchange List Values

- Starch 0.5
- Meat, lean 2.0
- Vegetable 2.0
- Fat 0.5

Basic Nutritional Values

- Calories 223
  (Calories from Fat 61)
- Total Fat 7 gm
  (Saturated Fat 1.5 gm,
  Polyunsat Fat 1.0 gm,
  Monounsat Fat 3.4 gm)
- Cholesterol 56 mg
- Sodium 465 mg
- Total Carb 20 gm
- Dietary Fiber 4 gm
- Sugars 7 gm
- Protein 21 gm

Vegetable Beef Borscht

Jeanne Heyerly
Chenoa, IL

Makes 8 servings

Prep. Time: 40 minutes
Cooking Time: 8-10 hours
Ideal slow cooker size: 5-qt.

1 lb. beef roast, cooked
  and cubed
half a head of cabbage,
  sliced thin
3 medium potatoes, diced
4 carrots, sliced
1 large onion, diced
1 cup tomatoes, diced
1 cup corn
1 cup green beans
2 cups 98% fat-free, lower
  sodium beef broth
2 cups tomato juice
¼ tsp. garlic powder
¼ tsp. dill seed
½ tsp. pepper
water
sour cream

1. Mix together all ingredients except water and sour cream. Add water to fill slow cooker three-quarters full.
2. Cover. Cook on low 8-10 hours.
3. Top individual servings with sour cream.

Exchange List Values

- Starch 1.0
- Vegetable 3.0
- Meat, lean 1.0

Basic Nutritional Values

- Calories 185
  (Calories from Fat 25)
- Total Fat 3 gm
  (Saturated Fat 0.7 gm,
  Polyunsat Fat 0.4 gm,
  Monounsat Fat 1.1 gm)
- Cholesterol 28 mg
- Sodium 434 mg
- Total Carb 29 gm
- Dietary Fiber 6 gm
- Sugars 10 gm
- Protein 14 gm

Variation:

Add 1 cup diced cooked red beets during the last half hour of cooking.

Southwestern Bean Soup with Cornmeal Dumplings

Melba Eshleman
Manheim, PA

Makes 8 servings

Prep. Time: 50 minutes
Cooking Time: 4½-12½ hours
Ideal slow cooker size: 4- or 5-qt.

15½-oz. can red kidney
  beans, rinsed and
  drained
15½-oz. can black beans,
  pinto beans, *or* Great
  Northern beans, rinsed
  and drained
3 cups water
14½-oz. can Mexican-style
  stewed tomatoes
10-oz. pkg. frozen whole-
  kernel corn, thawed
1 cup sliced carrots
1 cup chopped onions

4-oz. can chopped green
  chilies
3 tsp. sodium-free instant
  bouillon powder (any
  flavor)
1-2 tsp. chili powder
2 cloves garlic, minced

Dumplings:
  ⅓ cup flour
  ¼ cup yellow cornmeal
  1 tsp. baking powder
  dash of pepper
  1 egg white, beaten
  2 Tbsp. milk
  1 Tbsp. oil

1. Combine 11 soup ingredients in slow cooker.
2. Cover. Cook on low 10-12 hours or high 4-5 hours.
3. Make dumplings by mixing together flour, cornmeal, baking powder, and pepper.
4. Combine egg white, milk, and oil. Add to flour mixture. Stir with fork until just combined.
5. At the end of the soup's cooking time, turn slow cooker to high. Drop dumpling mixture by rounded teaspoonfuls to make 8 mounds atop the soup.
6. Cover. Cook for 30 minutes without lifting the lid.

Exchange List Values

- Starch 2.0
- Vegetable 2.0

Basic Nutritional Values

- Calories 197
  (Calories from Fat 13)
- Total Fat 1 gm
  (Saturated Fat 0.2 gm,
  Polyunsat Fat 0.6 gm,
  Monounsat Fat 0.5 gm)
- Cholesterol 0 mg
- Sodium 367 mg
- Total Carb 39 gm
- Dietary Fiber 8 gm
- Sugars 6 gm
- Protein 9 gm

Beef Dumpling Soup

Barbara Walker
Sturgis, SD

Makes 6 servings

Prep. Time: 35 minutes
Cooking Time: 4½-6½ hours
Ideal slow cooker size: 4-qt.

1 lb. beef stewing meat, trimmed of visible fat, cubed
1 recipe onion soup mix, dry, salt-free (see recipe on page 261)
6 cups hot water
2 carrots, shredded
1 celery rib, finely chopped
1 tomato, peeled and chopped
2 cloves garlic
½ tsp. dried basil
¼ tsp. dill weed
1 cup buttermilk biscuit mix
1 Tbsp. finely chopped parsley
6 Tbsp. fat-free milk

1. Place meat in slow cooker. Sprinkle with onion soup mix. Pour water over meat.
2. Add carrots, celery, tomato, garlic, basil and dill weed.
3. Cover. Cook on low 4-6 hours, or until meat is tender.
4. Combine biscuit mix and parsley. Stir in milk with fork until moistened. Drop dumplings by teaspoonfuls into pot.
5. Cover. Cook on high 30 minutes without lifting the lid.

Exchange List Values

- Starch 1.0
- Vegetable 1.0
- Meat, lean 1.0
- Fat 0.5

Basic Nutritional Values

- Calories 206
- (Calories from Fat 57)
- Total Fat 6 gm
- (Saturated Fat 0.9 gm, Polyunsat Fat 1.4 gm, Monounsat Fat 2.6 gm)
- Cholesterol 38 mg
- Sodium 329 mg
- Total Carb 22 gm
- Dietary Fiber 2 gm
- Sugars 6 gm
- Protein 15 gm

Winter's Night Beef Soup

Kimberly Jensen
Bailey, CO

Makes 12 servings

Prep. Time: 40 minutes
Cooking Time: 6½ hours
Ideal slow cooker size: 5-qt.

1 lb. boneless chuck, cut in ½-inch cubes
1-2 Tbsp. oil
28-oz. can tomatoes
2 tsp. garlic powder
2 carrots, sliced
2 ribs celery, sliced
4 cups water
½ cup red wine
1 small onion, coarsely chopped
4 beef bouillon cubes
1 tsp. pepper
1 tsp. dried oregano
½ tsp. dried thyme
1 bay leaf
¼-½ cup dry couscous

1. Brown beef cubes in oil in skillet.
2. Place vegetables in bottom of slow cooker. Add beef.
3. Combine all other ingredients in separate bowl except couscous. Pour over ingredients in slow cooker.
4. Cover. Cook on low 6 hours. Stir in couscous. Cover and cook 30 minutes.

Exchange List Values

- Vegetable 2.0
- Meat, lean 1.0

Basic Nutritional Values

- Calories 88
- (Calories from Fat 25)
- Total Fat 3 gm
- (Saturated Fat 0.5 gm, Polyunsat Fat 0.5 gm, Monounsat Fat 1.4 gm)
- Cholesterol 19 mg
- Sodium 461 mg
- Total Carb 9 gm
- Dietary Fiber 2 gm
- Sugars 4 gm
- Protein 8 gm

Variation:
Add zucchini or mushrooms to the rest of the vegetables before cooking.

Seek support from family, friends, and coworkers.

Old-Fashioned Vegetable Beef Soup

Pam Hochstedler
Kalona, IA

Makes 10 servings

Prep. Time: 40 minutes
Cooking Time: 6-9 hours
Ideal slow cooker size: 4-qt.

1 lb. beef short ribs,
   trimmed of fat
2 qts. water
1 tsp. salt
½ tsp. celery salt
1 small onion, chopped
1 cup diced carrots
½ cup diced celery
2 cups diced potatoes
1-lb. can whole kernel
   corn, undrained
1-lb. can diced tomatoes
   and juice

1. Combine meat, water, salt, celery salt, onion, carrots, and celery in slow cooker.
2. Cover. Cook on low 4-6 hours.
3. Debone meat, cut into bite-sized pieces, and return to pot.
4. Add potatoes, corn, and tomatoes.
5. Cover and cook on high 2-3 hours.

Exchange List Values
• Starch 0.5   • Fat 0.5
• Vegetable 1.0

Basic Nutritional Values
• Calories 99   • Cholesterol 11 mg
  (Calories from Fat 24)   • Sodium 413 mg
• Total Fat 3 gm   • Total Carb 13 gm
  (Saturated Fat 1.0 gm,   • Dietary Fiber 3 gm
  Polyunsat Fat 0.3 gm,   • Sugars 6 gm
  Monounsat Fat 1.0 gm)   • Protein 6 gm

Green Chile Corn Chowder

Kelly Amos
Pittsboro, NC

Makes 8 servings

Prep. Time: 20 minutes
Cooking Time: 7-8 hours
Ideal slow cooker size: 4-qt.

16-oz. can cream-style corn
3 potatoes, peeled and
   diced
2 Tbsp. chopped fresh
   chives
4-oz. can diced green
   chilies, drained
2-oz. jar chopped
   pimentos, drained
½ cup chopped cooked ham
2 10½-oz. cans 100% fat-
   free, lower sodium
   chicken broth
pepper to taste
Tabasco sauce
   to taste
1 cup fat-free
   milk

1. Combine all ingredients except milk and cheese in slow cooker.
2. Cover. Cook on low 7-8 hours or until potatoes are tender.
3. Stir in milk. Heat until hot.

Exchange List Values
• Starch 1.5

Basic Nutritional Values
• Calories 124   • Cholesterol 7 mg
  (Calories from Fat 16)   • Sodium 563 mg
• Total Fat 2 gm   • Total Carb 21 gm
  (Saturated Fat 0.5 gm,   • Dietary Fiber 2 gm
  Polyunsat Fat 0.3 gm,   • Sugars 7 gm
  Monounsat Fat 0.7 gm)   • Protein 6 gm

Tip:
   Top individual servings with cheese. Serve with bread.

Three-Bean Chili

Chris Kaczynski
Schenectady, NY

Makes 12 servings

Prep. Time: 30 minutes
Cooking Time: 8-10 hours
Ideal slow cooker size: 5- or 6-qt.

2 lbs. ground beef
2 medium onions, diced
16-oz. jar medium salsa
2 pkgs. dry chili seasoning
2 16-oz. cans red kidney beans, drained
2 16-oz. cans black beans, drained
2 16-oz. cans white kidney, or garbanzo, beans drained
28-oz. can crushed tomatoes
16-oz. can diced tomatoes
2 tsp. sugar

1. Brown beef and onions in skillet.
2. Combine all ingredients in 6-qt. slow cooker, or in 2 4- or 5-qt. cookers.
3. Cover. Cook on low 8-10 hours.

Exchange List Values

- Starch 2.5
- Meat, lean 2.0
- Vegetable 2.0
- Fat 0.5

Basic Nutritional Values

- Calories 381
- Cholesterol 45 mg
- (Calories from Fat 80)
- Sodium 717 mg
- Total Fat 9 gm
- Total Carb 47 gm
- (Saturated Fat 3.1 gm,
- Dietary Fiber 14 gm
- Polyunsat Fat 0.7 gm,
- Sugars 9 gm
- Monounsat Fat 3.4 gm)
- Protein 29 gm

Note:

This recipe can be cut in half without injuring the flavor, if you don't have a cooker large enough to handle the full amount.

Tip:

Serve in bowls with chopped raw onion and grated cheese on top.

Country Auction Chili Soup

Clara Newswanger
Gordonville, PA

Makes 20 servings

Prep. Time: 20 minutes
Cooking Time: 4-8 hours
Ideal slow cooker size: 5- or 6-qt.

1½ lbs. ground beef
¼ cup chopped onions
½ cup flour
1 Tbsp. chili powder
1 tsp. salt
6 cups water
2 cups ketchup
⅓ cup brown sugar
3 15.5-oz. cans kidney beans, undrained

1. Brown ground beef and onions in skillet. Drain. Spoon meat mixture into slow cooker.
2. Stir flour into meat and onions. Add seasonings.
3. Slowly stir in water. Add ketchup, brown sugar, and beans.
4. Cover. Cook on high 4 hours or low 8 hours.

Exchange List Values

- Starch 1.0
- Meat, lean 1.0
- Vegetable 1.0

Basic Nutritional Values

- Calories 163
- Cholesterol 20 mg
- (Calories from Fat 35)
- Sodium 655 mg
- Total Fat 4 gm
- Total Carb 23 gm
- (Saturated Fat 1.4 gm,
- Dietary Fiber 3 gm
- Polyunsat Fat 0.3 gm,
- Sugars 8 gm
- Monounsat Fat 1.5 gm)
- Protein 10 gm

Texican Chili

Becky Oswald
Broadway, VA

Makes 15 servings

Prep. Time: 35 minutes
Cooking Time: 9-10 hours
Ideal slow cooker size: 5- or 6-qt.

8 bacon strips, diced
2½ lbs. beef stewing meat, cubed
28-oz. can stewed tomatoes
14½-oz. can stewed tomatoes
8-oz. can tomato sauce
8-oz. can no-added-salt tomato sauce
16-oz. can kidney beans, rinsed and drained
2 cups sliced carrots
1 medium onion, chopped
1 cup chopped celery
½ cup chopped green pepper
¼ cup minced fresh parsley
1 Tbsp. chili powder
½ tsp. ground cumin
¼ tsp. pepper

1. Cook bacon in skillet until crisp. Drain on paper towel.
2. Brown beef in bacon drippings in skillet.
3. Combine all ingredients in slow cooker.
4. Cover. Cook on low 9-10 hours, or until meat is tender. Stir occasionally.

Exchange List Values
- Starch 0.5
- Meat, lean 1.0
- Vegetable 2.0
- Fat 0.5

Basic Nutritional Values
- Calories 165
  (Calories from Fat 44)
- Total Fat 5 gm
  (Saturated Fat 1.5 gm,
  Polyunsat Fat 0.5 gm,
  Monounsat Fat 2.2 gm)
- Cholesterol 40 mg
- Sodium 434 mg
- Total Carb 15 gm
- Dietary Fiber 3 gm
- Sugars 6 gm
- Protein 16 gm

Forgotten Minestrone

Phyllis Attig
Reynolds, IL

Makes 8 servings

Prep. Time: 30 minutes
Cooking Time: 7¾-9¾ hours
Ideal slow cooker size: 4- or 5-qt.

1 lb. beef stewing meat, all visible fat removed
6 cups water
28-oz. can tomatoes, diced, undrained
1 beef bouillon cube
1 medium onion, chopped
2 Tbsp. dried parsley
¼ tsp. salt
1½ tsp. dried thyme
½ tsp. pepper
1 medium zucchini, thinly sliced
2 cups finely chopped cabbage
16-oz. can garbanzo beans, drained
1 cup uncooked small pasta, such as macaroni
3 Tbsp. freshly grated Parmesan cheese

1. Combine beef, water, tomatoes, bouillon, onion, parsley, salt, thyme, and pepper.
2. Cover. Cook on low 7-9 hours, or until meat is tender.
3. Stir in zucchini, cabbage, beans, and macaroni. Cover and cook on high 30-45 minutes, or until vegetables are tender.
4. Sprinkle individual servings with Parmesan cheese.

Exchange List Values
- Starch 1.0
- Meat, lean 2.0
- Vegetable 2.0

Basic Nutritional Values
- Calories 235
  (Calories from Fat 47)
- Total Fat 5 gm
  (Saturated Fat 1.5 gm,
  Polyunsat Fat 0.8 gm,
  Monounsat Fat 2.0 gm)
- Cholesterol 44 mg
- Sodium 489 mg
- Total Carb 27 gm
- Dietary Fiber 5 gm
- Sugars 8 gm
- Protein 20 gm

Use salsa or hot sauce to add heat and flavor to a low-fat, low-sodium meal.

Slow-Cooker Minestrone

Dorothy Shank
Sterling, IL

Makes 8 servings

Prep. Time: 30 minutes
Cooking Time: 4-12 hours
Ideal slow cooker size: 4-qt.

3 cups water
1½ lbs. stewing meat, cut into bite-sized pieces, fat removed
1 medium onion, diced
4 carrots, diced
14½-oz. can tomatoes
¾ tsp. salt
10-oz. pkg. frozen mixed vegetables
1 Tbsp. dried basil
½ cup dry vermicelli
1 tsp. dried oregano
grated Parmesan cheese

1. Combine all ingredients except cheese in slow cooker. Stir well.
2. Cover. Cook on low 10-12 hours, or on high 4-5 hours.
3. Top individual servings with Parmesan cheese.

Exchange List Values
• Starch 1.0   • Meat, lean 1.0
• Vegetable 2.0

Basic Nutritional Values
• Calories 183   • Cholesterol 42 mg
  (Calories from Fat 33) • Sodium 413 mg
• Total Fat 4 gm   • Total Carb 21 gm
  (Saturated Fat 1.0 gm, • Dietary Fiber 4 gm
  Polyunsat Fat 0.4 gm, • Sugars 7 gm
  Monounsat Fat 1.6 gm) • Protein 17 gm

Hearty Alphabet Soup

Maryann Markano
Wilmington, DE

Makes 6 servings

Prep. Time: 15 minutes
Cooking Time: 6½-8½ hours
Ideal slow cooker size: 4-qt.

½ lb. beef stewing meat, *or* round steak, cubed, all visible fat removed
14½-oz. can stewed tomatoes
8-oz. can tomato sauce
1 cup water
1 recipe salt-free, dry onion soup mix (see recipe on page 261)
10-oz. pkg. frozen vegetables, partially thawed
½ cup uncooked alphabet noodles

1. Combine meat, tomatoes, tomato sauce, water, and soup mix in slow cooker.
2. Cover. Cook on low 6-8 hours. Turn to high.
3. Stir in vegetables and noodles. Add more water if mixture is too dry and thick.
4. Cover. Cook on high 30 minutes, or until vegetables are tender.

Exchange List Values
• Starch 1.0   • Meat, lean 1.0
• Vegetable 2.0

Basic Nutritional Values
• Calories 165   • Cholesterol 19 mg
  (Calories from Fat 17) • Sodium 443 mg
• Total Fat 2 gm   • Total Carb 28 gm
  (Saturated Fat 0.5 gm, • Dietary Fiber 3 gm
  Polyunsat Fat 0.3 gm, • Sugars 8 gm
  Monounsat Fat 0.8 gm) • Protein 10 gm

Easy Hamburger Vegetable Soup

Winifred Paul, Scottdale, PA

Makes 10 servings

Prep. Time: 20 minutes
Cooking Time: 8-10 hours
Ideal slow cooker size: 5-qt.

1 lb. 90%-lean ground beef
1 tsp. canola oil
1 cup chopped onions
15-oz. can kidney beans, *or* butter beans, undrained
1 cup sliced carrots
¼ cup long-grain rice, uncooked
1 qt. stewed tomatoes
3½ cups water
4 reduced-sodium beef bouillon cubes
1 Tbsp. parsley flakes
⅛ tsp. pepper
¼ tsp. dried basil
1 bay leaf

Take advantage of ready-to-eat and easy-to-prepare vegetables at the supermarket to make healthy cooking easier.

1. Brown ground beef in skillet in oil. Stir frequently to break up clumps of meat. Cook until meat is no longer pink. Drain off drippings.

2. Place meat in cooker, along with all other ingredients.

3. Cover. Cook on low 8-10 hours.

Exchange List Values
- Starch 0.5
- Lean Meat 1.0
- Vegetable 2.0
- Fat 0.5

Basic Nutritional Values
- Calories 170
  (Calories from Fat 40)
- Total Fat 4.5 gm
  (Saturated Fat 1.5 gm,
  Polyunsat Fat 0 gm,
  Monounsat Fat 2.0 gm)
- Cholesterol 25 mg
- Sodium 595 mg
- Total Carb 20 gm
- Dietary Fiber 4 gm
- Sugars 6 gm
- Protein 13 gm

Meatball Stew

Barbara Hershey
Lititz, PA

Makes 8 servings

Prep Time: 1 hour (includes preparing and baking meatballs)
Cooking Time: 4-5 hours
Ideal slow-cooker size: 4- or 6-qt.

Meatballs
2 lbs. 90%-lean ground beef
2 eggs, beaten
2 Tbsp. dried onion
⅔ cup bread crumbs
½ cup milk
½ tsp. salt
¼ tsp. pepper
1 tsp. Dijon mustard
2 tsp. Worcestershire sauce

6 medium potatoes, unpeeled if you wish, and diced fine
1 large onion, sliced
8 medium carrots, sliced
4 cups vegetable juice
1 tsp. dried basil
1 tsp. dried oregano
½ tsp. pepper

1. In a bowl, thoroughly mix meatball ingredients together. Form into 1" balls.

2. Place meatballs on a lightly greased rimmed baking sheet. Bake at 400° for 20 minutes.

3. Meanwhile, to make stew, prepare potatoes, onion, and carrots. Place in slow cooker.

4. When finished baking, remove meatballs from pan. Blot dry with paper towels to remove excess fat.

5. Place meatballs on top of vegetables in slow cooker.

6. In a large bowl, combine vegetable juice and seasonings. Pour over meatballs and vegetables in slow cooker.

7. Cover cooker. Cook on high 4 to 5 hours, or until vegetables are tender.

Tips:
1. You can speed up the preparation of this dish by using frozen meatballs, either your own, or store-bought ones.

2. If you will be gone more hours than the time required to cook the slow-cooker dish that you want to make, you can cook that recipe in your slow-cooker overnight on low. I've done this many times. In the morning I put the slow-cooker crock, now full of the cooked food, into the refrigerator. When I get home, I reheat the food in my microwave.

Exchange List Values
- Starch 2.0
- Lean Meat 3.0
- Vegetable 3.0
- Fat 1.0

Basic Nutritional Values
- Calories 405
  (Calories from Fat 100)
- Total Fat 11 gm
  (Saturated Fat 4.0 gm,
  Polyunsat Fat 1.0 gm,
  Monounsat Fat 4.5 gm)
- Cholesterol 115 mg
- Sodium 595 mg
- Total Carb 45 gm
- Dietary Fiber 6 gm
- Sugars 12 gm
- Protein 30 gm

Hamburger Vegetable Soup

Donna Conto
Saylorsburg, PA

Makes 8 servings

Prep. Time: 35 minutes
Cooking Time: 5 hours
Ideal slow cooker size: 4-qt.

½ lb. ground beef,
   browned, drained, and
   patted dry with a paper
   towel
1 beef bouillon cube,
   crushed
5 tsp. salt-free beef
   bouillon powder
16-oz. can tomatoes
1 large onion, diced
¾ cup sliced celery
1 medium carrot, diced
1 garlic clove, minced
1 bay leaf
½ tsp. salt
⅛ tsp. pepper
10-oz. pkg. frozen peas
3 Tbsp. chopped parsley

   1. Combine all ingredients
except peas and parsley in
slow cooker.
   2. Cover. Cook on low 5
hours.
   3. Stir in peas during last
hour.
   4. Garnish with parsley
before serving.

Exchange List Values
• Vegetable 2.0   • Meat, lean 1.0

Basic Nutritional Values
• Calories 107   • Cholesterol 17 mg
  (Calories from Fat 28) • Sodium 431 mg
• Total Fat 3 gm   • Total Carb 12 gm
  (Saturated Fat 1.1 gm, • Dietary Fiber 3 gm
  Polyunsat Fat 0.2 gm, • Sugars 7 gm
  Monounsat Fat 1.3 gm) • Protein 8 gm

Quick and Easy Italian Vegetable Beef Soup

Lisa Warren
Parkesburg, PA

Makes 10 servings

Prep. Time: 35 minutes
Cooking Time: 6-8 hours
Ideal slow cooker size: 4-qt.

¾ lb. 85%-lean ground
   beef, *or* turkey, browned
   and drained
3 carrots, sliced
4 potatoes, peeled and cubed
1 small onion, diced
1 tsp. garlic powder
1 tsp. Italian seasoning
½ tsp. salt
¼ tsp. pepper
15-oz. can diced Italian
   tomatoes, *or* 2 fresh
   tomatoes, chopped
6-oz. can Italian-flavored
   tomato paste

4½ cups water
1 quart 99% fat-free, lower
   sodium beef broth

   1. Combine all ingredients
in slow cooker.
   2. Cover. Cook on high 6-8
hours, or until potatoes and
carrots are tender.

Exchange List Values
• Starch 0.5   • Meat, lean 1.0
• Vegetable 2.0

Basic Nutritional Values
• Calories 138   • Cholesterol 20 mg
  (Calories from Fat 34) • Sodium 423 mg
• Total Fat 4 gm   • Total Carb 17 gm
  (Saturated Fat 1.4 gm, • Dietary Fiber 3 gm
  Polyunsat Fat 0.3 gm, • Sugars 4 gm
  Monounsat Fat 1.5 gm) • Protein 9 gm

Buy no-salt-added canned goods, or rinse canned vegetables and beans to reduce the sodium content.

Naturally Colorful Vegetable Soup

Darla Sathre
Baxter, MN

Makes 6 servings

Prep. Time: 20-30 minutes
Cooking Time: 8-10 hours
Ideal slow cooker size: 4-qt.

15-oz. can whole-kernel
  corn, undrained
2 cups frozen peas
16-oz. can kidney beans,
  undrained
14½-oz. can diced tomatoes
  with juice
15-oz. can no-salt-added
  tomato sauce
½ lb. baby carrots, halved
  lengthwise
1 onion, chopped
6 cloves garlic, thinly sliced
2 tsp. Italian herb
  seasoning
1 tsp. dried marjoram
1 tsp. dried basil

1. Put all ingredients into
slow cooker. Stir well.
2. Cover. Cook on high 1-2
hours. Then cook on low 8-9
hours, or until carrots and
onions are as tender as you
like them.

Exchange List Values
• Starch 2.0   • Vegetable 2.0

Basic Nutritional Values
• Calories 210   Cholesterol 0 mg),
  (Calories from Fat 15)   Sodium 565 mg
• Total Fat 2 gm   • Total Carb 43 gm
  (Saturated Fat 0 gm,   • Dietary Fiber 12 gm
  Polyunsat Fat 0.5 gm, • Sugars 13 gm
  Monounsat Fat 0 gm   • Protein 10 gm

Spicy Beef Vegetable Stew

Melissa Raber
Millersburg, OH

Makes 12 servings

Prep. Time: 25 minutes
Cooking Time: 8 hours
Ideal slow cooker size: 4-qt.

¾ lb. ground beef
1 cup chopped onions
30-oz. jar meatless
  spaghetti sauce
3½ cups water
1 lb. frozen mixed
  vegetables
10-oz. can diced tomatoes
  with green chilies
1 cup sliced celery
1 tsp. salt-free beef
  bouillon powder
1 tsp. pepper

1. Cook beef and onion in
skillet until meat is no longer
pink. Drain. Transfer to slow
cooker.
2. Stir in remaining
ingredients.
3. Cover. Cook on low 8
hours.

Exchange List Values
• Starch 0.5   • Meat, lean 1.0
• Vegetable 2.0

Basic Nutritional Values
• Calories 150   • Cholesterol 17 mg
  (Calories from Fat 44) • Sodium 489 mg
• Total Fat 5 gm   • Total Carb 17 gm
  (Saturated Fat 1.4 gm, • Dietary Fiber 3 gm
  Polyunsat Fat 0.7 gm,   • Sugars 10 gm
  Monounsat Fat 1.9 gm) • Protein 8 gm

Hearty Beef and Cabbage Soup

Carolyn Mathias
Williamsville, NY

Makes 8 servings

Prep. Time: 30 minutes
Cooking Time: 4 hours
Ideal slow cooker size: 4-qt.

⅔ lb. (about 11 oz.) ground
  beef
1 medium onion, chopped
40-oz. can tomatoes
2 cups water
15-oz. can kidney beans
½ tsp. pepper
1 Tbsp. chili powder
½ cup chopped celery
2 cups thinly sliced
  cabbage

1. Sauté beef in skillet.
Drain.
2. Combine all ingredients
except cabbage in slow
cooker.
3. Cover. Cook on low 3
hours. Add cabbage. Cook on
high 30-60 minutes longer.

Exchange List Values
• Starch 0.5   • Meat, lean 1.0
• Vegetable 2.0

Basic Nutritional Values
• Calories 150   • Cholesterol 22 mg
  (Calories from Fat 40) • Sodium 507 mg
• Total Fat 4 gm   • Total Carb 18 gm
  (Saturated Fat 1.5 gm, • Dietary Fiber 5 gm
  Polyunsat Fat 0.4 gm,   • Sugars 8 gm
  Monounsat Fat 1.7 gm) • Protein 12 gm

Hamburger Soup with Barley

Becky Oswald
Broadway, VA

Makes 10 servings

Prep. Time: 30 minutes
Cooking Time: 3-8 hours
Ideal slow cooker size: 4-qt.

¾ lb. 85%-lean ground beef
1 medium onion, chopped
2 14½-oz. cans beef consomme
1¾ cup water
2 tsp. sodium-free beef bouillon powder
28-oz. can no-added-salt diced, tomatoes
3 carrots, sliced
3 celery ribs, sliced
8 Tbsp. barley
1 bay leaf
1 tsp. dried thyme
1 Tbsp. dried parsley
½ tsp. pepper

1. Brown beef and onion in skillet. Drain.
2. Combine all ingredients in slow cooker.
3. Cover. Cook on high 3 hours, or low 6-8 hours.

Exchange List Values
• Starch 1.0   • Meat, lean 1.0
• Vegetable 1.0

Basic Nutritional Values
• Calories 154   • Cholesterol 22 mg
(Calories from Fat 34)   • Sodium 623 mg
• Total Fat 4 gm   • Total Carb 20 gm
(Saturated Fat 1.4 gm,   • Dietary Fiber 4 gm
Polyunsat Fat 0.3 gm,   • Sugars 6 gm
Monounsat Fat 1.5 gm)   • Protein 11 gm

Russian Red-Lentil Soup

Naomi E. Fast
Hesston, KS

Makes 8 servings

Prep. Time: 25 minutes
Cooking Time: 4-5 hours
Ideal slow cooker size: 5- or 6-qt.

1 Tbsp. canola oil
1 large onion, chopped
3 cloves garlic, minced
½ cup diced, dried apricots
1½ cups dried red lentils
½ tsp. cumin
½ tsp. dried thyme
3 cups water
2 14½-oz. cans chicken *or* vegetable broth
14½-oz. can diced tomatoes
1 Tbsp. honey
½ tsp. coarsely ground black pepper
2 Tbsp. chopped fresh mint
1½ cups plain yogurt

1. Combine all ingredients except mint and yogurt in slow cooker.
2. Cover. Heat on high until soup starts to simmer, then turn to low and cook 3-4 hours.
3. Add mint and dollop of yogurt to each bowl of soup.

Exchange List Values
• Starch 1.5   • Vegetable 1.0
• Fruit 1.0   • Meat, very lean 1.0

Basic Nutritional Values
• Calories 244   • Cholesterol 8 mg
(Calories from Fat 37)   • Sodium 587 mg
• Total Fat 4 gm   • Total Carb 42 gm
(Saturated Fat 1.2 gm,   • Dietary Fiber 10 gm
Polyunsat Fat 0.8 gm,   • Sugars 21 gm
Monounsat Fat 1.5 gm)   • Protein 13 gm

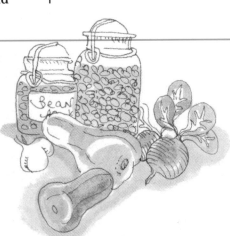

Prepare double batches of healthy dishes. Store the leftovers so you have an easy, nutritious meal on hand for later.

Hamburger Lentil Soup

Juanita Marner
Shipshewana, IN

Makes 8 servings

Prep. Time: 40 minutes
Cooking Time: 4-10 hours
Ideal slow cooker size: 4-qt.

½ lb. 85%-lean ground beef
½ cup chopped onions
4 carrots, diced
3 ribs celery, diced
1 garlic clove, minced
1 qt. no-salt-added tomato juice
1½ tsp. salt
2 cups dry lentils, washed with stones removed
1 qt. water
½ tsp. dried marjoram
1 Tbsp. brown sugar

1. Brown ground beef and onion in skillet. Drain.
2. Combine all ingredients in slow cooker.
3. Cover. Cook on low 8-10 hours, or high 4-6 hours.

Exchange List Values

- Starch 2.0
- Meat, lean 1.0
- Vegetable 2.0

Basic Nutritional Values

- Calories 247
  (Calories from Fat 32)
- Total Fat 4 gm
  (Saturated Fat 1.2 gm,
  Polyunsat Fat 0.4 gm,
  Monounsat Fat 1.4 gm)
- Cholesterol 17 mg
- Sodium 508 mg
- Total Carb 38 gm
- Dietary Fiber 12 gm
- Sugars 10 gm
- Protein 18 gm

Vegetable Soup with Noodles

Glenda S. Weaver
New Holland, PA

Makes 8 servings

Prep. Time: 25 minutes
Cooking Time: 2-6 hours
Ideal slow cooker size: 4-qt.

2 cups water
2 tsp. sodium-free beef bouillon powder
1 onion, chopped
⅔ lb. 85%-lean ground beef
¼ cup ketchup
⅛ tsp. celery salt
½ cup uncooked noodles
16 oz. pkg. frozen mixed vegetables
2 cups tomato juice

1. Dissolve bouillon cubes in water.
2. Brown onion and beef in skillet. Drain.
3. Combine all ingredients in slow cooker.
4. Cover. Cook on low 6 hours, or on high 2-3 hours, until vegetables are tender.

Exchange List Values

- Starch 0.5
- Meat, lean 1.0
- Vegetable 2.0

Basic Nutritional Values

- Calories 135
  (Calories from Fat 37)
- Total Fat 4 gm
  (Saturated Fat 1.5 gm,
  Polyunsat Fat 0.2 gm,
  Monounsat Fat 1.7 gm)
- Cholesterol 25 mg
- Sodium 374 mg
- Total Carb 16 gm
- Dietary Fiber 2 gm
- Sugars 7 gm
- Protein 10 gm

Dottie's Creamy Steak Soup

Debbie Zeida
Mashpee, MA

Makes 8 servings

Prep. Time: 30 minutes
Cooking Time: 8-10 hours
Ideal slow cooker size: 4-qt.

½ lb. 85%-lean ground beef
half a large onion, chopped
12-oz. can low-sodium V8 vegetable juice
3 medium potatoes, diced
10¾-oz. can 98% fat-free, reduced-sodium cream of mushroom soup
10¾-oz. can cream of celery soup
16-oz. pkg. frozen mixed vegetables
½-¾ tsp. pepper

1. Sauté beef and onions in skillet. Drain.
2. Combine all ingredients in slow cooker.
3. Cover. Cook on low 8-10 hours.

Exchange List Values

- Starch 1.0
- Meat, lean 1.0
- Vegetable 2.0
- Fat 0.5

Basic Nutritional Values

- Calories 202
  (Calories from Fat 54)
- Total Fat 6 gm
  (Saturated Fat 2.2 gm,
  Polyunsat Fat 1.2 gm,
  Monounsat Fat 1.8 gm)
- Cholesterol 19 mg
- Sodium 506 mg
- Total Carb 28 gm
- Dietary Fiber 4 gm
- Sugars 7 gm
- Protein 10 gm

Sausage Bean Soup

Janie Steele
Moore, OK

Makes 10 servings

Prep. Time: 40 minutes
Soaking Time: 8 hours
Cooking Time: 9-9½ hours
Ideal slow cooker size: 5- or 6-qt.

1-lb. pkg. dried Great
  Northern beans
28-oz. can whole tomatoes
2 8-oz. cans no-salt-added
  tomato sauce
2 large onions, chopped
3 cloves garlic, minced
¼-½ tsp. pepper, according
  to your taste preference
3 celery ribs, sliced
bell pepper, sliced
large ham bone, all skin
  and visible fat removed
  (yield 6 oz. ham)
1-2 lbs. low-fat smoked
  sausage links, sliced

1. Cover beans with water
and soak for 8 hours. Rinse
and drain.
2. Place beans in 6-qt.
cooker and cover with water.
2. Combine all other
ingredients, except sausage, in
large bowl. Stir into beans in
slow cooker.
3. Cover. Cook on high
1-1½ hours. Reduce to low.
Cook 7 hours.
4. Remove ham bone or
hock and debone. Stir ham
pieces back into soup.
5. Add sausage links.
6. Cover. Cook on low
1 hour.

Exchange List Values
• Starch 2.0   • Meat, lean 1.0
• Vegetable 2.0

Basic Nutritional Values
• Calories 276   • Cholesterol 29 mg
  (Calories from Fat 34) • Sodium 760 mg
• Total Fat 4 gm   • Total Carb 41 gm
  (Saturated Fat 1.3 gm, • Dietary Fiber 11 gm
  Polyunsat Fat 1.2 gm,   • Sugars 12 gm
  Monounsat Fat 1.0 gm)   • Protein 21 gm

Note:
  For enhanced flavor, brown
sausage before adding to soup.

Taco Soup with Black Beans

Alexa Slonin
Harrisonburg, VA

Makes 8 servings

Prep. Time: 25 minutes
Cooking Time: 4-6 hours
Ideal slow cooker size: 4-qt.

¾ lb. 90%-lean ground beef,
  browned and drained
28-oz. can crushed
  tomatoes
1 small onion, chopped
¼-½ cup water
15¼-oz. can corn, drained
  and rinsed
15-oz. can no-salt-added
  black beans, undrained
15½-oz. can no-salt-added
  red kidney beans,
  undrained

1 envelope dry Hidden
  Valley Ranch Dressing
  mix
2 Tbsp. low-sodium taco
  seasoning mix
tortilla chips for garnish
grated cheese for garnish
fat-free sour cream for
  garnish

1. Combine all ingredients
except chips, shredded
cheese, and sour cream in
slow cooker.
2. Cover. Cook on low 4-6
hours.
3. Garnish individual
servings with chips, cheese,
and sour cream.

Exchange List Values
• Starch 1.5   • Meat, very lean 2.0
• Vegetable 2.0

Basic Nutritional Values
• Calories 247   • Cholesterol 26 mg
  (Calories from Fat 41) • Sodium 652 mg
• Total Fat 5 gm   • Total Carb 35 gm
  (Saturated Fat 1.5 gm, • Dietary Fiber 9 gm
  Polyunsat Fat 0.6 gm,   • Sugars 9 gm
  Monounsat Fat 1.7 gm)   • Protein 17 gm

Cut back on high-sodium ingredients — bacon, ham, pickles, and olives — in your recipes.

Santa Fe Soup

Carla Koslowsky
Hillsboro, KS

Makes 8 servings

Prep. Time: 20 minutes
Cooking Time: 3 hours
Ideal slow cooker size: 4-qt.

8 oz. sharp fat-free
  cheddar cheese, cubed
¾ lb. 90%-lean ground
  beef, browned and
  drained
15¼-oz. can corn,
  undrained
15-oz. can no-added-salt
  kidney beans, undrained
14½-oz. can diced tomatoes
  with green chilies
14½-oz. can no-added-salt
  stewed tomatoes
2 Tbsp. low-sodium taco
  seasoning mix (see
  recipe on page 261)

1. Combine all ingredients
except chips or tortillas in
slow cooker.
2. Cover. Cook on high 3
hours.

Exchange List Values
- Starch 1.0   • Meat, lean 2.0
- Vegetable 1.0

Basic Nutritional Values
- Calories 215   • Cholesterol 29 mg
- (Calories from Fat 40)   • Sodium 617 mg
- Total Fat 4 gm   • Total Carb 22 gm
- (Saturated Fat 1.5 gm,   • Dietary Fiber 5 gm
- Polyunsat Fat 0.5 gm,   • Sugars 8 gm
- Monounsat Fat 1.7 gm)   • Protein 22 gm

Taco Soup with Whole Tomatoes

Marla Folkerts
Holland, OH

Makes 8 servings

Prep. Time: 15 minutes
Cooking Time: 4-6 hours
Ideal slow cooker size: 4-qt.

⅔ lb. 85%-lean ground
  beef
½ cup chopped onions
28-oz. can whole tomatoes
  with juice
14-oz. can kidney beans
  with juice
1 7-oz. can corn with juice
8-oz. can no-salt-added
  tomato sauce
2 Tbsp. low-sodium dry
  taco seasoning (see
  recipe on page 261)
1-2 cups water
pepper to taste
1 cup fat-free grated
  cheddar cheese
taco *or* corn chips, garnish

1. Brown beef and onions
in skillet. Drain.
2. Combine all ingredients
except cheese and chips in
slow cooker.
3. Cover. Cook on low 4-6
hours.
4. Ladle into bowls. Top
with cheese and serve with
taco/corn chips.

Exchange List Values
- Starch 1.0   • Meat, lean 1.0
- Vegetable 1.0   • Fat 0.5

Basic Nutritional Values
- Calories 191   • Cholesterol 24 mg
- (Calories from Fat 44)   • Sodium 612 mg
- Total Fat 5 gm   • Total Carb 22 gm
- (Saturated Fat 1.6 gm,   • Dietary Fiber 5 gm
- Polyunsat Fat 0.5 gm,   • Sugars 10 gm
- Monounsat Fat 1.9 gm)   • Protein 16 gm

Norma's Vegetarian Chili

Kathy Hertzler
Lancaster, PA

Makes 10 servings

Prep. Time: 25 minutes
Cooking Time: 8½ hours
Ideal slow cooker size: 5- or 6-qt.

2 Tbsp. canola oil
2 cups minced celery
1½ cups chopped green
  pepper
1 cup minced onions
4 garlic cloves, minced
5½ cups no-salt-added
  stewed tomatoes
2 1-lb. cans kidney beans,
  undrained
1½ cups raisins
¼ cup wine vinegar
1 Tbsp. chopped parsley
1 tsp. salt
1½ tsp. dried oregano
1½ tsp. cumin
¼ tsp. pepper
¼ tsp. Tabasco sauce
1 bay leaf
¾ cup unsalted cashews
1 cup grated cheese,
  optional

1. Combine all ingredients
except cashews and cheese in
slow cooker.
2. Cover. Simmer on low
for 8 hours. Add cashews and
simmer 30 minutes.
3. Garnish individual
servings with grated cheese.

Exchange List Values
• Starch 1.0   • Vegetable 3.0
• Fruit 1.0   • Fat 1.5

Basic Nutritional Values
• Calories 279   • Cholesterol 0 mg
  (Calories from Fat 77) • Sodium 603 mg
• Total Fat 9 gm   • Total Carb 47 gm
  (Saturated Fat 1.4 gm, • Dietary Fiber 7 gm
  Polyunsat Fat 2.0 gm,   • Sugars 22 gm
  Monounsat Fat 4.7 gm)   • Protein 9 gm

Vegetarian Tex-Mex Chili

Joleen Albrecht
Gladstone, MI

Makes 8 servings

Prep Time: 10-15 minutes
Cooking Time: 2-4 hours
Ideal slow-cooker size: 5 qt.

15½-oz. can kidney beans,
  rinsed and drained
19-oz. can black bean soup
15½-oz. can garbanzo
  beans, rinsed and
  drained
16-oz. can vegetarian
  baked beans
15-oz. can whole-kernel
  corn, drained
14½-oz. can chopped
  tomatoes
1 green bell pepper,
  chopped
1 onion, chopped
2 ribs celery, chopped
2 cloves garlic, chopped
1 Tbsp. chili powder
1 Tbsp. dried oregano
1 Tbsp. dried parsley
1 Tbsp. dried basil
1½ tsp. Tabasco, *optional*
sour cream, *optional*
shredded cheddar cheese,
  optional
tortilla chips, *optional*

1. Combine all beans, soup,
and all vegetables in slow
cooker.
2. Stir in chili powder,
oregano, parsley, basil and
optional Tabasco.
3. Cover. Cook on high 2 to
3 hours, or on low 4 hours.
4. If you wish, garnish
individual servings of chili
with sour cream, shredded
cheese, and tortilla chips.

Exchange List Values
• Starch 2.5   • Lean Meat (Protein) 1.0
• Vegetable 1.0

Basic Nutritional Values
• Calories 260   • Cholesterol 0 mg
  (Calories from Fat 20) • Sodium 530 mg
• Total Fat 2 gm   • Total Carb 49 gm
  (Saturated Fat 0 gm,   • Dietary Fiber 13 gm
  Polyunsat Fat 1.0 gm,   • Sugars 9 gm
  Monounsat Fat 0 gm)   • Protein 14 gm

Easy Chili

Sheryl Shenk
Harrisonburg, VA

Makes 12 servings

Prep. Time: 20 minutes
Cooking Time: 3-8 hours
Ideal slow cooker size: 5-qt.

1 lb. ground beef
1 onion, chopped
1 medium green pepper,
  chopped
½ tsp. salt
1 Tbsp. chili powder
2 tsp. Worcestershire sauce
29-oz. can no-added-salt
  tomato sauce
3 16-oz. cans kidney beans,
  drained

14½-oz. can crushed, *or* stewed, tomatoes
6-oz. can tomato paste
4 oz. fat-free grated cheddar cheese

1. Brown meat in skillet. Add onion and green pepper halfway through browning process. Drain. Pour into slow cooker.
2. Stir in remaining ingredients except cheese.
3. Cover. Cook on high 3 hours, or low 7-8 hours.
4. Serve in bowls topped with cheddar cheese.

Exchange List Values
- Starch 1.0
- Vegetable 3.0
- Meat, lean 1.0
- Fat 0.5

Basic Nutritional Values
- Calories 232
  (Calories from Fat 41)
- Total Fat 5 gm
  (Saturated Fat 1.5 gm,
  Polyunsat Fat 0.5 gm,
  Monounsat Fat 1.8 gm)
- Cholesterol 23 mg
- Sodium 456 mg
- Total Carb 30 gm
- Dietary Fiber 8 gm
- Sugars 9 gm
- Protein 18 gm

Note:
This chili can be served over cooked rice.

Trail Chili
Jeanne Allen
Rye, CO

Makes 10 servings

Prep. Time: 20 minutes
Cooking Time: 4½-6½ hours
Ideal slow cooker size: 4- or 5-qt.

1½ lbs. 90%-lean ground beef
1 large onion, diced

28-oz. can diced tomatoes
2 8-oz. cans tomato purée
16-oz. cans kidney beans, undrained
4-oz. can diced green chilies
1 cup water
2 garlic cloves, minced
2 Tbsp. mild chili powder
½ tsp. salt
2 tsp. ground cumin
1 tsp. pepper

1. Brown beef and onion in skillet. Drain. Place in slow cooker on high.
2. Stir in remaining ingredients. Cook on high 30 minutes.
3. Reduce heat to low. Cook 4-6 hours.

Exchange List Values
- Starch 0.5
- Vegetable 2.0
- Meat, lean 2.0

Basic Nutritional Values
- Calories 195
  (Calories from Fat 57)
- Total Fat 6 gm
  (Saturated Fat 2.3 gm,
  Polyunsat Fat 0.5 gm,
  Monounsat Fat 2.6 gm)
- Cholesterol 41 mg
- Sodium 545 mg
- Total Carb 17 gm
- Dietary Fiber 4 gm
- Sugars 8 gm
- Protein 18 gm

Note:
Top individual servings with shredded cheese. Serve with taco chips.

Chipotle Chili
Karen Ceneviva
Seymour, CT

Makes 8 servings

Prep Time: 10-15 minutes
Cooking Time: 4-9 hours
Ideal slow-cooker size: 3½ qt.

16-oz. jar chipotle chunky salsa
1 cup water
2 tsp. chili powder
1 large onion, chopped
2 lbs. stewing beef, cut into ½" pieces
19-oz. can red kidney beans, rinsed and drained

1. Stir all ingredients together in slow cooker.
2. Cover. Cook on high 4-5 hours or on low 8-9 hours, until beef is fork-tender.

Exchange List Values
- Starch 1.0
- Lean Meat 3.0

Basic Nutritional Values
- Calories 220
  (Calories from Fat 45)
- Total Fat 5 gm
  (Saturated Fat 2.0 gm,
  Polyunsat Fat 0.5 gm,
  Monounsat Fat 2.5 gm)
- Cholesterol 60 mg
- Sodium 385 mg
- Total Carb 17 gm
- Dietary Fiber 5 gm
- Sugars 3 gm
- Protein 27 gm

Instead of rice or potatoes, try couscous or quinoa [KEEN-wa], whole grains that cook fast, are easy to make, and taste great!

Quick and Easy Chili

Nan Decker
Albuquerque, NM

Makes 6 servings

Prep. Time: 20 minutes
Cooking Time: 4-5 hours
Ideal slow cooker size: 4- or 3-qt.

1 lb. ground beef
1 onion, chopped
16-oz. can stewed tomatoes
11½-oz. can Hot V8 juice
2 15-oz. cans pinto beans,
  drained and rinsed
¼-½ cup water
¼ tsp. cayenne pepper
1 Tbsp. chili powder

1. Crumble ground beef in microwave-safe casserole. Add onion. Microwave, covered, on high 15 minutes. Drain. Break meat into pieces.
2. Combine all ingredients in slow cooker.
3. Cook on low 4-5 hours.

Exchange List Values
- Starch 1.5
- Vegetable 2.0
- Meat, lean 2.0
- Fat 0.5

Basic Nutritional Values
- Calories 302
  (Calories from Fat 76)
- Total Fat 8 gm
  (Saturated Fat 3.0 gm,
  Polyunsat Fat 0.7 gm,
  Monounsat Fat 3.5 gm)
- Cholesterol 45 mg
- Sodium 539 mg
- Total Carb 34 gm
- Dietary Fiber 10 gm
- Sugars 7 gm
- Protein 23 gm

Suggested garnishes:
  sour cream
  chopped green onions
  grated cheese
  sliced ripe olives

Pirate Stew

Nancy Graves, Manhattan, KS

Makes 6 servings

Prep. Time: 20 minutes
Cooking Time: 6 hours
Ideal slow cooker size: 4-qt.

¾ cup sliced onion
1 lb. ground beef
¼ cup uncooked, long-grain
  rice
3 cups diced raw potatoes
1 cup diced celery
2 cups canned kidney
  beans, drained
½ tsp. salt
⅛ tsp. pepper
¼ tsp. chili powder
¼ tsp. Worcestershire sauce
1 cup tomato sauce
½ cup water

1. Brown onions and ground beef in skillet. Drain.
2. Layer ingredients in slow cooker in order given.
3. Cover. Cook on low 6 hours, or until potatoes and rice are cooked.

Exchange List Values
- Starch 2.0
- Vegetable 1.0
- Meat, lean 2.0
- Fat 0.5

Basic Nutritional Values
- Calories 310
  (Calories from Fat 73)
- Total Fat 8 gm
  (Saturated Fat 3.0 gm,
  Polyunsat Fat 0.5 gm,
  Monounsat Fat 3.4 gm)
- Cholesterol 45 mg
- Sodium 611 mg
- Total Carb 38 gm
- Dietary Fiber 7 gm
- Sugars 6 gm
- Protein 22 gm

Variation:
  Add a layer of 2 cups sliced carrots between potatoes and celery.
  Katrine Rose
  Woodbridge, VA

Corn Chili

Gladys Longacre, Susquehanna, PA

Makes 6 servings

Prep. Time: 25 minutes
Cooking Time: 5-6 hours
Ideal slow cooker size: 4-qt.

1 lb. ground beef
½ cup chopped onions
½ cup chopped green
  peppers
¼ tsp. salt
⅛ tsp. pepper
¼ tsp. dried thyme
14½-oz. can diced tomatoes
  with Italian herbs
6-oz. can tomato paste,
  diluted with 1 can water
2 cups frozen whole kernel
  corn
16-oz. can kidney beans
1 Tbsp. chili powder

1. Sauté ground beef, onions, and green peppers in deep saucepan. Drain and season with salt, pepper, and thyme.
2. Stir in tomatoes, tomato paste, and corn. Heat until corn is thawed. Add kidney beans and chili powder. Pour into slow cooker.
3. Cover. Cook on low 5-6 hours.

Exchange List Values
- Starch 1.5
- Vegetable 2.0
- Meat, lean 2.0

Basic Nutritional Values
- Calories 281
  (Calories from Fat 78)
- Total Fat 9 gm
  (Saturated Fat 3.1 gm,
  Polyunsat Fat 0.7 gm,
  Monounsat Fat 3.5 gm)
- Cholesterol 45 mg
- Sodium 574 mg
- Total Carb 33 gm
- Dietary Fiber 7 gm
- Sugars 7 gm
- Protein 21 gm

Dorothea's Slow-Cooker Chili

Dorothea K. Ladd
Ballston Lake, NY

Makes 8 servings

Prep. Time: 20 minutes
Cooking Time: 8-10 hours
Ideal slow cooker size: 4-qt.

1 lb. ground beef
¼ lb. bulk pork sausage
1 large onion, chopped
1 large green pepper, chopped
2-3 ribs celery, chopped
2 15½-oz. cans kidney beans, drained and rinsed
¼-½ cup water
29-oz. can no-added-salt tomato purée
6-oz. can tomato paste
2 cloves garlic, minced
2 Tbsp. chili powder
½ tsp. salt

1. Brown ground beef and sausage in skillet. Drain.
2. Combine all ingredients in slow cooker.
3. Cover. Cook on low 8-10 hours.

Exchange List Values
- Starch 1.5
- Vegetable 3.0
- Meat, lean 2.0

Basic Nutritional Values
- Calories 298
  (Calories from Fat 80)
- Total Fat 9 gm
  (Saturated Fat 3.0 gm,
  Polyunsat Fat 1.0 gm,
  Monounsat Fat 3.6 gm)
- Cholesterol 39 mg
- Sodium 453 mg
- Total Carb 35 gm
- Dietary Fiber 9 gm
- Sugars 10 gm
- Protein 22 gm

Variations:
1. For extra flavor, add 1 tsp. cayenne pepper.
2. For more zest, use mild or hot Italian sausage instead of regular pork sausage.
3. Top individual servings with shredded sharp cheddar cheese.

White Bean Chili

Tracey Stenger
Gretna, LA

Makes 12 servings

Prep. Time: 25 minutes
Cooking Time: 8-10 hours
Ideal slow cooker size: 6-qt.

1 lb. ground beef, browned and drained
1 lb. ground turkey, browned and drained
3 bell peppers, chopped
2 onions, chopped
4 garlic cloves, minced
2 14½-oz. cans 98% fat-free, lower-sodium chicken, *or* vegetable, broth
15½-oz. can butter beans, rinsed and drained
15-oz. can black-eyed peas, rinsed and drained
15-oz. can garbanzo beans, rinsed and drained
15-oz. can navy beans, rinsed and drained
4-oz. can chopped green chilies
2 Tbsp. chili powder
3 tsp. ground cumin
2 tsp. dried oregano
2 tsp. paprika
½ tsp. salt
½ tsp. pepper

1. Combine all ingredients in slow cooker.
2. Cover. Cook on low 8-10 hours.

Exchange List Values
- Starch 1.5
- Vegetable 1.0
- Meat, lean 2.0
- Fat 0.5

Basic Nutritional Values
- Calories 282
  (Calories from Fat 79)
- Total Fat 9 gm
  (Saturated Fat 2.5 gm,
  Polyunsat Fat 1.6 gm,
  Monounsat Fat 3.3 gm)
- Cholesterol 50 mg
- Sodium 570 mg
- Total Carb 28 gm
- Dietary Fiber 8 gm
- Sugars 6 gm
- Protein 24 gm

Chili for Twenty

Janie Steele
Moore, OK

Makes 20 servings

Prep. Time: 25 minutes
Cooking Time: 3-4 hours
*Ideal slow cooker size: use
2 slow cookers approx.
4-5-quarts each*

3 lbs. 85%-lean ground
  beef
3 onions, minced
3 green peppers, minced
2 garlic cloves, minced
4 16-oz. cans Italian-style
  tomatoes
4 16-oz. cans kidney beans,
  drained
10-oz. can diced tomatoes
  and chilies
2 6-oz. cans tomato paste
1 cup water
1¼ tsp. salt
1 tsp. pepper
3 whole cloves
2 bay leaves
2 Tbsp. chili powder

1. Brown meat, onions, and
peppers in soup pot on top of
stove. Drain.
2. Combine all ingredients
in large bowl. Divide among
several medium-sized slow
cookers.
3. Cover. Cook on low 3-4
hours.

Exchange List Values
• Starch 1.0   • Meat, lean 2.0
• Vegetable 2.0

Basic Nutritional Values
• Calories 243   • Cholesterol 40 mg
  (Calories from Fat 69) • Sodium 547 mg
• Total Fat 8 gm   • Total Carb 25 gm
  (Saturated Fat 2.7 gm, • Dietary Fiber 7 gm
  Polyunsat Fat 0.6 gm,   • Sugars 7 gm
  Monounsat Fat 3.1 gm)   • Protein 20 gm

Crab Soup

Susan Alexander
Baltimore, MD

Makes 10 servings

Prep. Time: 30 minutes
Cooking Time: 8-10 hours
Ideal slow cooker size: 5-qt.

1 lb. carrots, sliced
½ bunch celery, sliced
1 large onion, diced
2 10-oz. bags frozen mixed
  vegetables
12-oz. can no-added-salt
  tomato juice
8 oz. extra-lean, lower
  sodium ham
1 lb. beef, cubed
6 slices bacon, chopped
¼ tsp. pepper
1 Tbsp. Old Bay seasoning
1 lb. claw crabmeat

1. Combine all ingredients
except seasonings and crabmeat in large slow cooker.

Pour in water until cooker is
half-full.
2. Add spices. Stir in
thoroughly. Put crab on top.
3. Cover. Cook on low 8-10
hours.
4. Stir well and serve.

Exchange List Values
• Starch 0.5   • Meat, lean 2.0
• Vegetable 2.0

Basic Nutritional Values
• Calories 199   • Cholesterol 74 mg
  (Calories from Fat 44) • Sodium 649 mg
• Total Fat 5 gm   • Total Carb 17 gm
  (Saturated Fat 1.5 gm, • Dietary Fiber 4 gm
  Polyunsat Fat 0.7 gm,   • Sugars 8 gm
  Monounsat Fat 2.0 gm)   • Protein 23 gm

Corn and Shrimp Chowder

Naomi E. Fast
Hesston, KS

Makes 6 servings

Prep. Time: 20 minutes
Cooking Time: 3-4 hours
Ideal slow cooker size: 4- or 5-qt.

4 slices bacon, diced
1 cup chopped onions
2 cups diced, unpeeled red
  potatoes
2 10-oz. pkgs. frozen corn
1 tsp. Worcestershire sauce
½ tsp. paprika
½ tsp. salt
⅛ tsp. pepper
2 6-oz. cans shrimp
2 cups water
2 Tbsp. light, soft tub
  margarine

*Use puréed, cooked vegetables to thicken soups
and stews to add flavor and nutrients.*

12-oz. can fat-free
  evaporated milk
chopped chives

1. Fry bacon in skillet until lightly crisp. Add onions to drippings and sauté until transparent. Using slotted spoon, transfer bacon and onions to slow cooker.
2. Add remaining ingredients to cooker except milk and chives.
3. Cover. Cook on low 3-4 hours, adding milk and chives 30 minutes before end of cooking time.

Tip:
  Delicious served with broccoli salad.

Exchange List Values
- Starch 3.0
- Milk, fat-free 0.5
- Meat, very lean 1.0
- Fat 0.5

Basic Nutritional Values
- Calories 331
  (Calories from Fat 50)
- Total Fat 6 gm
  (Saturated Fat 0.9 gm,
  Polyunsat Fat 1.2 gm,
  Monounsat Fat 2.1 gm)
- Cholesterol 102 mg
- Sodium 488 mg
- Total Carb 49 gm
- Dietary Fiber 5 gm
- Sugars 11 gm
- Protein 24 gm

Note:
  I learned to make this recipe in a 7th grade home economics class. It made an impression on my father who liked seafood very much. The recipe calls only for canned shrimp, but I often increase the taste appeal with extra cooked shrimp.
  I frequently use frozen hash brown potatoes for speedy preparation. There is no difference in the taste.

Special Seafood Chowder

Dorothea K. Ladd
Ballston Lake, NY

Makes 10 servings

Prep. Time: 20 minutes
Cooking Time: 6 hours
Ideal slow cooker size: 4-qt.

½ cup chopped onions
1 Tbsp. canola oil
1 lb. fresh *or* frozen cod, *or*
  haddock
4 cups diced potatoes
15-oz. can creamed corn
½ tsp. salt
dash pepper
2 cups water
1 pint fat-free half-and-half

1. Sauté onions in butter in skillet until transparent but not brown.
2. Cut fish into ¾-inch cubes. Combine fish, onions, potatoes, corn, seasonings, and water in slow cooker.
3. Cover. Cook on low 6 hours, until potatoes are tender.
4. Add half-and-half during last hour.

Exchange List Values
- Carbohydrate 1.5
- Meat, lean 1.0

Basic Nutritional Values
- Calories 172
  (Calories from Fat 25)
- Total Fat 3 gm
  (Saturated Fat 0.5 gm,
  Polyunsat Fat 0.6 gm,
  Monounsat Fat 0.9 gm)
- Cholesterol 29 mg
- Sodium 381 mg
- Total Carb 24 gm
- Dietary Fiber 2 gm
- Sugars 8 gm
- Protein 12 gm

Manhattan Clam Chowder

Joyce Slaymaker
Strasburg, PA
Louise Stackhouse
Benton, PA

Makes 8 servings

Prep. Time: 25 minutes
Cooking Time: 8-10 hours
Ideal slow cooker size: 4-qt.

¼ lb. bacon, diced and fried
1 large onion, chopped
2 carrots, thinly sliced
3 ribs celery, sliced
1 Tbsp. dried parsley
  flakes
1-lb. 12-oz. can tomatoes
⅛ tsp. salt
2 8-oz. cans clams with
  liquid
2 whole peppercorns
1 bay leaf
1½ tsp. dried crushed thyme
3 medium potatoes, cubed

1. Combine all ingredients in slow cooker.
2. Cover. Cook on low 8-10 hours.

Exchange List Values
- Starch 0.5
- Vegetable 2.0
- Meat, lean 1.0

Basic Nutritional Values
- Calories 151
  (Calories from Fat 25)
- Total Fat 3 gm
  (Saturated Fat 0.8 gm,
  Polyunsat Fat 0.6 gm,
  Monounsat Fat 0.9 gm)
- Cholesterol 21 mg
- Sodium 427 mg
- Total Carb 22 gm
- Dietary Fiber 4 gm
- Sugars 8 gm
- Protein 11 gm

Chicken Clam Chowder

Irene Klaeger
Inverness, Fl

Makes 12 servings

Prep. Time: 25 minutes
Cooking Time: 4-9 hours
Ideal slow cooker size: 6-qt.

¼ lb. bacon, diced
¼ lb. extra-lean, lower
   sodium ham, cubed
2 cups chopped onions
2 cups diced celery
¼ tsp. pepper
2 cups diced potatoes
2 cups cooked, diced chicken
4 tsp. sodium-free chicken
   bouillon powder mixed
   with 4 cups water
2 bottles clam juice, *or* 2
   cans clams with juice
1-lb. can whole kernel
   corn, drained and rinsed
¼-½ cup water
¾ cup flour
3 cups fat-free milk
1½ cups fat-free half-and-
   half
4 cups shredded cheddar,
   or Jack, cheese
½ cup heavy cream
2 Tbsp. fresh parsley

1. Sauté bacon, ham,
onions, and celery in skillet
until bacon is crisp and
onions and celery are limp.
Add pepper.

2. Combine all ingredients
in slow cooker except flour,
milk, half-and-half, cheese,
cream, and parsley.

3. Cover. Cook on low 6-8
hours, or on high 3-4 hours.

4. Whisk flour into milk
and half-and-half. Stir into
soup, along with cheese and
parsley. Cook one more hour
on high.

Exchange List Values
• Carbohydrate 1.5   • Meat, lean 2.0

Basic Nutritional Values
• Calories 225	• Cholesterol 34 mg
(Calories from Fat 37)	• Sodium 517 mg
• Total Fat 4 gm	• Total Carb 26 gm
(Saturated Fat 1.3 gm,	• Dietary Fiber 2 gm
Polyunsat Fat 0.8 gm,	• Sugars 9 gm
Monounsat Fat 1.4 gm)	• Protein 21 gm

Chicken Broth

Ruth Conrad Liechty
Goshen, IN

Makes about 6 (1 cup) servings

Prep. Time: 20 minutes
Cooking Time: 4-5 hours
Ideal slow cooker size: 4-qt.

bony chicken pieces from
   2 chickens, skin and
   visible fat removed
1 onion, quartered
3 whole cloves, *optional*
3 ribs celery, cut up
1 carrot, quartered
½ tsp. salt
¼ tsp. pepper
4 cups water

1. Place chicken in slow
cooker.

2. Stud onion with cloves.
Add to slow cooker with other
ingredients.

3. Cover. Cook on high 4-5
hours.

4. Remove chicken and vegetables. Discard vegetables.
Debone chicken. Cut up meat
to equal about 1 cup and add
to broth.

5. Place broth in the refrigerator. After broth is cooled,
skim fat from the surface.
Use as stock for soups.

Exchange List Values
• Meat, lean 1.0

Basic Nutritional Values
• Calories 42	• Cholesterol 19 mg
(Calories from Fat 14)	• Sodium 211 mg
• Total Fat 2 gm	• Total Carb 0 gm
(Saturated Fat 0.4 gm,	• Dietary Fiber 0 gm
Polyunsat Fat 0.4 gm,	• Sugars 0 gm
Monounsat Fat 0.6 gm)	• Protein 6 gm

Replace some of the all-purpose flour in a recipe with whole-wheat flour to increase fiber.

Chicken Noodle Soup

Beth Shank
Wellman, IA

Makes 8 servings

Prep. Time: 15 minutes
Cooking Time: 4-6 hours
Ideal slow cooker size: 4-qt.

5 cups hot water
2 tsp. sodium-free chicken bouillon powder
46-oz. can fat-free, lower sodium chicken broth
2 cups cooked, chopped chicken
4 cups "homestyle" noodles, uncooked
⅓ cup thinly sliced celery, lightly pre-cooked in microwave
⅓ cup shredded carrots

1. Dissolve bouillon in water. Pour into slow cooker.
2. Add remaining ingredients. Mix well.
3. Cover. Cook on low 4-6 hours.

Exchange List Values
• Starch 1.0   • Meat, lean 1.0

Basic Nutritional Values
• Calories 155   • Cholesterol 49 mg
  (Calories from Fat 31)   • Sodium 382 mg
• Total Fat 3 gm   • Total Carb 15 gm
  (Saturated Fat 1.0 gm,   • Dietary Fiber 1 gm
  Polyunsat Fat 0.8 gm,   • Sugars 2 gm
  Monounsat Fat 1.2 gm)   • Protein 14 gm

Chicken Rice Soup

Karen Ceneviva
Seymour, CT

Makes 8 servings

Prep Time: 15 minutes
Cooking Time: 4-8 hours
Ideal slow-cooker size: 3½ qt.

½ cup wild rice, uncooked
½ cup long-grain rice, uncooked
1 tsp. vegetable oil
1 lb. boneless skinless chicken breasts, cut into ¾" cubes
5¼ cups fat-free, low-sodium chicken broth
1 cup celery (about 2 ribs), chopped in ½"-thick pieces
1 medium onion, chopped
2 tsp. dried thyme leaves
¼ tsp. red pepper flakes

1. Mix wild and white rice with oil in slow cooker.
2. Cover. Cook on high 15 minutes.
3. Add chicken, broth, vegetables, and seasonings.

4. Cover. Cook 4-5 hours on high or 7-8 hours on low.

Tip:
A dollop of sour cream sprinkled with finely chopped scallions on top of each individual serving bowl makes a nice finishing touch.

Exchange List Values
• Starch 1.0   • Lean Meat 2.0

Basic Nutritional Values
• Calories 160   • Cholesterol 35 mg
  (Calories from Fat 20)   • Sodium 375 mg
• Total Fat 2 gm   • Total Carb 18 gm
  (Saturated Fat 0 gm,   • Dietary Fiber 1 gm
  Polyunsat Fat 0.5 gm,   • Sugars 2 gm
  Monounsat Fat 1.0 gm)   • Protein 16 gm

Chicken Corn Soup

Eleanor Larson
Glen Lyon, PA

Makes 6 servings

Prep. Time: 25 minutes
Cooking Time: 8-9 hours
Ideal slow cooker size: 4-qt.

2 whole boneless skinless
  chicken breasts, cubed
1 onion, chopped
1 garlic clove, minced
2 carrots, sliced
2 ribs celery, chopped
2 medium potatoes, cubed
1 tsp. mixed dried herbs
⅓ cup tomato sauce
12-oz. can cream-style corn
14-oz. can whole kernel corn
3 tsp. sodium-free chicken
  bouillon powder
3 cups water
¼ cup chopped Italian
  parsley
¼ tsp. pepper

1. Combine all ingredients
except parsley and pepper in
slow cooker.
2. Cover. Cook on low 8-9
hours, or until chicken is
tender.
3. Add parsley and seasonings 30 minutes before serving.

Exchange List Values
• Starch 2.0   • Meat, very lean 3.0
• Vegetable 1.0

Basic Nutritional Values
• Calories 251   • Cholesterol 49 mg
  (Calories from Fat 28) • Sodium 534 mg
• Total Fat 3 gm   • Total Carb 33 gm
  (Saturated Fat 0.6 gm,   • Dietary Fiber 5 gm
  Polyunsat Fat 0.8 gm,   • Sugars 13 gm
  Monounsat Fat 0.9 gm)   • Protein 23 gm

Chili, Chicken, Corn Chowder

Jeanne Allen
Rye, CO

Makes 8 servings

Prep. Time: 20 minutes
Cooking Time: 4 hours
Ideal slow cooker size: 4-qt.

2 Tbsp. canola oil
1 large onion, diced
1 garlic clove, minced
1 rib celery, finely chopped
2 cups frozen corn
2 cups cooked, diced
  chicken
4-oz. can diced green
  chilies
½ tsp. black pepper
2 cups fat-free, lower-
  sodium chicken broth
¼ tsp. salt
1 cup fat-free half-and-half

1. In saucepan, sauté onion,
garlic, and celery in oil until
limp.
2. Stir in corn, chicken, and
chilies. Sauté for 2-3 minutes.
3. Combine all ingredients
except half-and-half in slow
cooker.
4. Cover. Heat on low 4
hours.
5. Stir in half-and-half
before serving. Do not boil,
but be sure cream is heated
through.

Exchange List Values
• Starch 0.5   • Meat, lean 1.0
• Vegetable 1.0   • Fat 1.0

Basic Nutritional Values
• Calories 169   • Cholesterol 33 mg
  (Calories from Fat 60) • Sodium 343 mg
• Total Fat 7 gm   • Total Carb 14 gm
  (Saturated Fat 1.2 gm,   • Dietary Fiber 2 gm
  Polyunsat Fat 1.7 gm,   • Sugars 4 gm
  Monounsat Fat 3.0 gm)   • Protein 13 gm

White Chili

Esther Martin
Ephrata, PA

Makes 8 servings

Prep. Time: 20 minutes
Cooking Time: 4-10 hours
Ideal slow cooker size: 5-qt.

3 15-oz. cans Great
  Northern beans, rinsed
  and drained
8 oz. cooked and shredded
  chicken breasts
1 cup chopped onions
1½ cups chopped yellow,
  red, *or* green bell
  peppers
2 garlic cloves, minced
2 tsp. ground cumin
½ tsp. salt
½ tsp. dried oregano
3½ cups chicken broth

1. Combine all ingredients
except sour cream, cheddar
cheese, and chips in slow
cooker.
2. Cover. Cook on low 8-10
hours, or high 4-5 hours.

Exchange List Values
• Starch 1.5   • Meat, very lean 1.0
• Vegetable 1.0

158

Basic Nutritional Values

- Calories 189
  (Calories from Fat 15)
- Total Fat 2 gm
  (Saturated Fat 0.4 gm,
  Polyunsat Fat 0.5 gm,
  Monounsat Fat 0.5 gm)
- Cholesterol 24 mg
- Sodium 561 mg
- Total Carb 25 gm
- Dietary Fiber 8 gm
- Sugars 5 gm
- Protein 19 gm

Suggested garnishes:
   reduced-fat sour cream
   reduced-fat cheddar
      cheese
   tortilla chips

Black Bean and Butternut Chicken Chili

Colleen Heatwole
Burton, MI

Makes 10 servings

Prep Time: 20 minutes
Cooking Time: 4-5 hours
Ideal slow-cooker size: 5 qt.

1 medium onion, chopped
1 medium red bell sweet
   pepper, chopped
3 cloves garlic, minced
2 Tbsp. olive oil
3 cups fat-free, low-sodium
   chicken broth
2 15-oz. can black beans,
   rinsed and drained
2½ cups cooked chicken,
   cubed

3 cups butternut squash,
   peeled and cubed
14½-oz. can crushed
   tomatoes
2 tsp. dried parsley flakes
1½ tsp. dried oregano
1½ tsp. ground cumin
1 tsp. chili powder
½ tsp. salt

1. In large skillet, sauté onion, red pepper, and garlic in olive oil until tender.
2. Combine sautéed ingredients with all other ingredients in slow cooker.
3. Cover. Cook on low 4-5 hours, or until vegetables are done to your liking.

Exchange List Values

- Starch 1.0
- Vegetable 1.0
- Lean Meat 2.0
- Fat 0.5

Basic Nutritional Values

- Calories 205
  (Calories from Fat 55)
- Total Fat 6 gm
  (Saturated Fat 1.0 gm,
  Polyunsat Fat 1.0 gm,
  Monounsat Fat 3.0 gm)
- Cholesterol 30 mg
- Sodium 420 mg
- Total Carb 23 gm
- Dietary Fiber 7 gm
- Sugars 5 gm
- Protein 17 gm

White Chili Special

Barbara McGinnis
Jupiter, FL

Makes 10 servings

Prep. Time: 45 minutes
Soaking Time: overnight, 12 hours
Cooking Time: 5-12 hours
Ideal slow cooker size: 5-qt.

1 lb. large Great Northern
   beans, soaked overnight
2 lbs. boneless, skinless
   chicken breasts, cut up
1 medium onion, chopped
2 4½-oz. cans chopped
   green chilies
2 tsp. ground cumin
½ tsp. salt
14½-oz. can chicken broth
1 cup water

1. Put soaked beans in medium-sized saucepan and cover with water. Bring to boil and simmer 20 minutes. Discard water.
2. Brown chicken in fat-free cooking spray, in skillet.
3. Combine pre-cooked and drained beans, chicken, and all remaining ingredients in slow cooker.
4. Cover. Cook on low 10-12 hours, or high 5-6 hours.

Exchange List Values

- Starch 2.0
- Meat, very lean 3.0

Basic Nutritional Values

- Calories 258
  (Calories from Fat 28)
- Total Fat 3 gm
  (Saturated Fat 0.9 gm,
  Polyunsat Fat 0.8 gm,
  Monounsat Fat 1.0 gm)
- Cholesterol 55 mg
- Sodium 571 mg
- Total Carb 26 gm
- Dietary Fiber 9 gm
- Sugars 4 gm
- Protein 30 gm

For easy preparation, use store-bought rotisserie chicken in recipes. Remember to remove the skin first.

Chicken Barley Chili

Colleen Heatwole
Burton, MI

Makes 10 servings

Prep Time: 20 minutes
Cooking Time: 6-8 hours
Ideal slow-cooker size: 6 qt.

2 14½-oz. cans tomatoes
16-oz. jar salsa
1 cup quick-cooking barley, uncooked
3 cups water
14½-oz. can fat-free, low-sodium chicken broth
15½-oz. can black beans, rinsed and drained
3 cups cooked chicken, *or* turkey, cubed
15¼-oz. can whole-kernel corn, undrained
1-3 tsp. chili powder
1 tsp. ground cumin
sour cream, *optional*
shredded cheese, *optional*

1. Combine all ingredients except sour cream and cheese in slow cooker.
2. Cover. Cook on low 6-8 hours, or until barley is tender.
3. Serve in individual soup bowls topped with sour cream and shredded cheese.

Exchange List Values
- Starch 1.5
- Lean Meat 2.0
- Vegetable 1.0

Basic Nutritional Values
- Calories 210
- (Calories from Fat 20)
- Total Fat 2.5 gm
- (Saturated Fat 0.5 gm, Polyunsat Fat 1.0 gm, Monounsat Fat 0.5 gm)
- Cholesterol 35 mg
- Sodium 565 mg
- Total Carb 30 gm
- Dietary Fiber 6 gm
- Sugars 5 gm
- Protein 19 gm

Mexican Rice and Bean Soup

Esther J. Mast
East Petersburg, PA

Makes 6 servings

Prep. Time: 25 minutes
Cooking Time: 6 hours
Ideal slow cooker size: 4-qt.

½ cup chopped onions
⅓ cup chopped green bell peppers
1 garlic clove, minced
1 Tbsp. oil
4-oz. pkg. sliced *or* chipped dried beef
18-oz. can no-added-salt tomato juice
15½-oz. can red kidney beans, undrained
1½ cups water
½ cup long-grain rice, uncooked
1 tsp. paprika
½-1 tsp. chili powder
dash of pepper

1. Cook onions, green peppers, and garlic in oil in skillet until vegetables are tender but not brown. Transfer to slow cooker.
2. Tear beef into small pieces and add to slow cooker.
3. Add remaining ingredients. Mix well.
4. Cover. Cook on low 6 hours. Stir before serving.

Exchange List Values
- Starch 1.5
- Fat 0.5
- Vegetable 2.0

Basic Nutritional Values
- Calories 190
- (Calories from Fat 28)
- Total Fat 3 gm
- (Saturated Fat 0.4 gm, Polyunsat Fat 0.9 gm, Monounsat Fat 1.6 gm)
- Cholesterol 15 mg
- Sodium 796 mg
- Total Carb 30 gm
- Dietary Fiber 4 gm
- Sugars 7 gm
- Protein 12 gm

Note:
This is a recipe I fixed often when our sons were growing up. We have all enjoyed it in any season of the year. Serve the soup with a relish tray, cornbread, home-canned fruit, and cookies.

Bell peppers are flavorful and low in calories and carbohydrates. Enjoy them cooked or raw.

Chicken Tortilla Soup

Becky Harder
Monument, CO

Makes 8 servings

Prep. Time: 15 minutes
Cooking Time: 8 hours
Ideal slow cooker size: 4- or 5-qt.

4 boneless skinless chicken
  breast halves
2 15-oz. cans no-salt-added
  black beans, undrained
2 15-oz. cans Mexican
  stewed tomatoes, *or*
  Rotel tomatoes
1 cup salsa of your choice
4-oz. can chopped green
  chilies
14½-oz. can no-added-salt
  tomato sauce
2 oz. (about 24 chips)
  tortilla chips
1 cup fat-free cheddar
  cheese

1. Combine all ingredients
except chips and cheese in
large slow cooker.
2. Cover. Cook on low 8
hours.
3. Just before serving,
remove chicken breasts and
slice into bite-sized pieces.
Stir into soup.
4. To serve, put a handful
of chips in each individual
soup bowl. Ladle soup over
chips. Top with cheese.

Exchange List Values
- Starch 1.0   • Meat, very lean 3.0
- Vegetable 2.0   • Fat 0.5

Basic Nutritional Values
- Calories 263   • Cholesterol 43 mg
  (Calories from Fat 36) • Sodium 793 mg
- Total Fat 4 gm   • Total Carb 29 gm
  (Saturated Fat 0.9 gm, • Dietary Fiber 7 gm
  Polyunsat Fat 0.8 gm,   • Sugars 9 gm
  Monounsat Fat 1.7 gm)   • Protein 28 gm

Southwest Chicken and White Bean Soup

Karen Ceneviva
Seymour, CT

Makes 6 servings

Prep Time: 15 minutes
Cooking Time: 4-10 hours
Ideal slow-cooker size: 3½ qt.

1 Tbsp. vegetable oil
1 lb. boneless skinless
  chicken breasts, cut into
  1" cubes
1¾ cups fat-free, low-
  sodium chicken broth
1 cup chunky salsa
3 cloves garlic, minced
2 Tbsp. cumin
15½-oz. can small
  white beans,
  drained and
  rinsed
1 cup frozen
  corn
1 large onion,
  chopped

1. Heat oil in 10"
skillet over medium
to high heat. Add
chicken and cook until
it is well browned on all
sides. Stir frequently to
prevent sticking.

2. Mix broth, salsa, garlic,
cumin, beans, corn, and
onion in slow cooker. Add
chicken. Stir well.
3. Cover. Cook 8-10 hours
on low or 4-5 hours on high.

Exchange List Values
- Starch 1.0   • Lean Meat 2.0
- Vegetable 1.0   • Fat 0.5

Basic Nutritional Values
- Calories 220   • Cholesterol 45 mg
  (Calories from Fat 45) • Sodium 535 mg
- Total Fat 5 gm   • Total Carb 23 gm
  (Saturated Fat 1.0 gm, • Dietary Fiber 6 gm
  Polyunsat Fat 1.5 gm,   • Sugars 4 gm
  Monounsat Fat 2.5 gm)   • Protein 22 gm

Ham and Potato Chowder

Penny Blosser
Beavercreek, OH

Makes 5 servings

Prep. Time: 25 minutes
Cooking Time: 8 hours
Ideal slow cooker size: 4-qt.

5-oz. pkg. scalloped
 potatoes
sauce mix from potato pkg.
1 cup extra-lean, reduced
 sodium, cooked ham,
 cut into narrow strips
4 tsp. sodium free bouillon
 powder
4 cups water
1 cup chopped celery
⅓ cup chopped onions
pepper to taste
2 cups fat-free half-and-half
⅓ cup flour

1. Combine potatoes, sauce
mix, ham, bouillon powder,
water, celery, onions, and
pepper in slow cooker.
2. Cover. Cook on low 7
hours.
3. Combine half-and-half
and flour. Gradually add to
slow cooker, blending well.
4. Cover. Cook on low up
to 1 hour, stirring occasionally until thickened.

Exchange List Values
• Starch 1.5   • Meat, lean 1.0
• Carbohydrate 1.0

Basic Nutritional Values
• Calories 241   • Cholesterol 21 mg
 (Calories from Fat 29) • Sodium 836 mg
• Total Fat 3 gm   • Total Carb 41 gm
 (Saturated Fat 1.2 gm, • Dietary Fiber 3 gm
 Polyunsat Fat 0.7 gm,   • Sugars 8 gm
 Monounsat Fat 0.2 gm) • Protein 11 gm

Chicken and Ham Gumbo

Barbara Tenney
Delta, PA

Makes 6 servings

Prep. Time: 25 minutes
Cooking Time: 6-8 hours
Ideal slow cooker size: 4-qt.

1½ lbs. boneless, skinless
 chicken thighs
1 Tbsp. oil
10-oz. pkg. frozen okra
½ lb. extra-lean, lower
 sodium ham, chopped
1½ cups coarsely chopped
 onions
1½ cups coarsely chopped
 green peppers
2 10-oz. cans no-added-salt
 cannellini beans, rinsed
 and drained
6 cups low sodium chicken
 broth
2 10-oz. cans diced
 tomatoes with green
 chilies
2 Tbsp. chopped fresh
 cilantro

1. Cut chicken into bite-
sized pieces. Cook in oil in
skillet until no longer pink.
2. Run hot water over okra
until pieces separate easily.

---

3. Combine all ingredients
but cilantro in slow cooker.
4. Cover. Cook on low 6-8
hours. Stir in cilantro before
serving.

Exchange List Values
• Starch 1.0   • Meat, lean 4.0
• Vegetable 3.0

Basic Nutritional Values
• Calories 385   • Cholesterol 96 mg
 (Calories from Fat 120) • Sodium 879 mg
• Total Fat 13 gm   • Total Carb 28 gm
 (Saturated Fat 3.1 gm, • Dietary Fiber 7 gm
 Polyunsat Fat 3.4 gm,   • Sugars 10 gm
 Monounsat Fat 5.2 gm) • Protein 38 gm

Variations:
 1. Stir in ½ cup long-grain,
dry rice with rest of ingredients.
 2. Add ¼ tsp. pepper with
other ingredients.

Easy Southern Brunswick Stew

Barbara Sparks
Glen Burnie, MD

Makes 12 servings

Prep. Time: 20 minutes
Cooking Time: 7-9 hours
Ideal slow cooker size: 4-qt.

2 lbs. pork butt, visible fat
 removed
17-oz. can white corn
1¼ cup ketchup
2 cups diced, cooked
 potatoes
10-oz. pkg. frozen peas
2 10¾-oz. cans reduced-
 sodium tomato soup
hot sauce, *optional*, to taste

1. Place pork in slow cooker.

2. Cover. Cook on low 6-8 hours. Remove meat from bone and shred, removing and discarding all visible fat.

3. Combine all ingredients in slow cooker.

4. Cover. Bring to boil on high. Reduce heat to low and simmer 30 minutes. Add hot sauce if you wish.

Exchange List Values

- Starch 1.0
- Meat, lean 1.0
- Vegetable 2.0
- Fat 0.5

Basic Nutritional Values

- Calories 213
  (Calories from Fat 61)
- Total Fat 7 gm
  (Saturated Fat 2.3 gm,
  Polyunsat Fat 0.9 gm,
  Monounsat Fat 2.6 gm)
- Cholesterol 34 mg
- Sodium 584 mg
- Total Carb 27 gm
- Dietary Fiber 3 gm
- Sugars 9 gm
- Protein 13 gm

Asian Pork Soup

Judi Manos
West Islip, NY

Makes 8 servings

Prep. Time: 25 minutes
Cooking Time: 4-10 hours
Ideal slow cooker size: 5-qt.

½ lb. ground pork
2 garlic cloves, minced
2 medium carrots, cut into matchsticks
4 medium green onions, cut into 1" pieces
2 Tbsp. light soy sauce

½ tsp. gingerroot, chopped
⅛ tsp. pepper
2 14½-oz. cans chicken broth
2½ tsp. sodium-free chicken bouillon powder
2½ cups water
1 cup sliced mushrooms
1 cup bean sprouts

1. Cook meat with garlic in skillet until brown. Drain.

2. Combine all ingredients except mushrooms and sprouts in slow cooker.

3. Cover. Cook on low 7-9 hours or high 3-4 hours.

4. Stir in mushrooms and bean sprouts.

5. Cover. Cook on low 1 hour.

Exchange List Values

- Vegetable 1.0
- Meat, medium fat 1.0

Basic Nutritional Values

- Calories 97
  (Calories from Fat 39)
- Total Fat 4 gm
  (Saturated Fat 1.5 gm,
  Polyunsat Fat 0.4 gm,
  Monounsat Fat 1.8 gm)
- Cholesterol 19 mg
- Sodium 486 mg
- Total Carb 6 gm
- Dietary Fiber 2 gm
- Sugars 3 gm
- Protein 8 gm

Variation:

For added flavor to the pork, add ⅛ tsp. five-spice blend to Step 1.

Joy's Brunswick Stew

Joy Sutter
Iowa City, IA

Makes 8 servings

Prep. Time: 20 minutes
Cooking Time: 4 hours
Ideal slow cooker size: 4-qt.

1 lb. skinless, boneless chicken breasts, cut into bite-sized pieces
2 potatoes, thinly sliced
10¾-oz. can tomato soup
16-oz. can stewed tomatoes
10-oz. pkg. frozen corn
10-oz. pkg. frozen lima beans
3 Tbsp. onion flakes
¼ tsp. salt
⅛ tsp. pepper

1. Combine all ingredients in slow cooker.

2. Cover. Cook on high 2 hours. Reduce to low and cook 2 hours.

Exchange List Values

- Starch 2.0
- Meat, very lean 1.0
- Vegetable 1.0

Basic Nutritional Values

- Calories 220
  (Calories from Fat 21)
- Total Fat 2 gm
  (Saturated Fat 0.6 gm,
  Polyunsat Fat 0.8 gm,
  Monounsat Fat 0.6 gm)
- Cholesterol 34 mg
- Sodium 480 mg
- Total Carb 33 gm
- Dietary Fiber 5 gm
- Sugars 8 gm
- Protein 18 gm

Variation:

For more flavor, add 1 or 2 bay leaves during cooking.

Cut the fat in at least one meal today.

Asian Turkey Chili

Kimberly Jensen
Bailey, CO

Makes 6 servings

Prep. Time: 25 minutes
Cooking Time: 6 hours
Ideal slow cooker size: 4-qt.

2 cups diced yellow onions
1 small red bell pepper,
  diced
1 lb. ground turkey,
  browned
2 Tbsp. minced gingerroot
3 cloves garlic, minced
¼ cup dry sherry
¼ cup hoisin sauce
2 Tbsp. chili powder
2 Tbsp. light soy sauce
1 tsp. sugar
2 cups canned whole
  tomatoes
16 oz. can no-salt-added
  dark red kidney beans,
  undrained

1. Combine all ingredients in slow cooker.
2. Cover. Cook on low 6 hours.
3. Serve topped over chow mein noodles or cooked rice.

Exchange List Values
- Starch 1.0
- Meat, lean 2.0
- Vegetable 2.0
- Fat 1.0

Basic Nutritional Values
- Calories 279
- Cholesterol 56 mg
  (Calories from Fat 93)
- Sodium 612 mg
- Total Fat 10 gm
- Total Carb 26 gm
  (Saturated Fat 2.4 gm,
- Dietary Fiber 8 gm
  Polyunsat Fat 3.5 gm,
- Sugars 12 gm
  Monounsat Fat 3.4 gm)
- Protein 22 gm

Note:
  If you serve this chili over rice, this recipe will yield 12 servings.

Pumpkin Black-Bean Turkey Chili

Rhoda Atzeff
Harrisburg, PA

Makes 10 servings

Prep. Time: 25 minutes
Cooking Time: 7-8 hours
Ideal slow cooker size: 4- or 5-qt.

1 cup chopped onions
1 cup chopped yellow bell
  pepper
3 garlic cloves, minced
2 Tbsp. canola oil
1½ tsp. dried oregano
1½-2 tsp. ground cumin
2 tsp. chili powder
2 15-oz. cans black beans,
  rinsed and drained
2½ cups chopped cooked
  turkey
16-oz. can pumpkin
14½-oz. can diced tomatoes
3 cups 98% fat-free, lower
  sodium chicken broth

1. Sauté onions, yellow pepper, and garlic in oil for 8 minutes, or until soft.
2. Stir in oregano, cumin, and chili powder. Cook 1 minute. Transfer to slow cooker.
3. Add remaining ingredients.

---

4. Cover. Cook on low 7-8 hours.

Exchange List Values
- Starch 1.0
- Meat, lean 1.0
- Vegetable 1.0
- Fat 0.5

Basic Nutritional Values
- Calories 189
- Cholesterol 27 mg
  (Calories from Fat 46)
- Sodium 327 mg
- Total Fat 5 gm
- Total Carb 20 gm
  (Saturated Fat 0.9 gm,
- Dietary Fiber 7 gm
  Polyunsat Fat 1.5 gm,
- Sugars 6 gm
  Monounsat Fat 2.1 gm)
- Protein 17 gm

Best Bean Chili

Carolyn Baer
Conrath, WI

Makes 6 servings

Prep Time: 20-30 minutes
Cooking Time: 5-6 hours
Ideal slow-cooker size: 4-5 qt.

1 lb. 90%-lean ground beef
1½ cups chopped onion
1 cup chopped green bell
  pepper
1 tsp. minced garlic
1 Tbsp. chili powder
1 tsp. ground cumin
15-oz. can red kidney beans,
  rinsed and drained
15-oz. can pinto beans,
  rinsed and drained
14½-oz. can diced Italian-,
  or Mexican-seasoned
  tomatoes
2 14½-oz. cans no-salt-
  added diced Italian-
  seasoned tomatoes
2 Tbsp. brown sugar
1 tsp. unsweetened cocoa
  powder

1. Spray large skillet with cooking spray. Brown beef in skillet over medium heat.

2. Add onions, bell pepper, and garlic to skillet. Cook until just-tender.

3. Transfer contents of skillet to slow cooker.

4. Add seasonings, beans, tomatoes, sugar and cocoa powder.

5. Cover. Cook on low 5-6 hours.

Tip:

Offer a sprinkle of soy sauce and/or ground ginger with individual servings to enhance the flavor of the chili.

Exchange List Values

- Starch 1.0
- Lean Meat 2.0
- Carbohydrate 0.5
- Fat 1.0
- Vegetable 4.0

Basic Nutritional Values

- Calories 355
- Cholesterol 45 mg
- (Calories from Fat 70)
- Sodium 525 mg
- Total Fat 8 gm
- Total Carb 46 gm
- (Saturated Fat 2.5 gm,
- Dietary Fiber 11 gm
- Polyunsat Fat 1.0 gm,
- Sugars 16 gm
- Monounsat Fat 3.0 gm)
- Protein 26 gm

Turkey Chili

Reita F. Yoder
Carlsbad, NM

Makes 8 servings

Prep. Time: 15 minutes
Cooking Time: 6-8 hours
Ideal slow cooker size: 4-qt.

2 lbs. ground turkey, browned and drained
16-oz. can pinto, *or* kidney, beans
2 cups chopped fresh tomatoes
2 cups no-salt-added tomato sauce
1 garlic clove, minced
1 small onion, chopped
16-oz. can Rotel tomatoes
1-oz. pkg. Williams chili seasoning

1. Crumble ground turkey in bottom of slow cooker.

2. Add remaining ingredients. Mix well.

3. Cover. Cook on low 6-8 hours.

Exchange List Values

- Starch 0.5
- Meat, lean 3.0
- Vegetable 2.0
- Fat 0.5

Basic Nutritional Values

- Calories 294
- Cholesterol 84 mg
- (Calories from Fat 106)
- Sodium 633 mg
- Total Fat 12 gm
- Total Carb 19 gm
- (Saturated Fat 2.8 gm,
- Dietary Fiber 5 gm
- Polyunsat Fat 2.9 gm,
- Sugars 9 gm
- Monounsat Fat 4.2 gm)
- Protein 27 gm

Joyce's Slow-Cooked Chili

Joyce Slaymaker
Strasburg, PA

Makes 10 servings

Prep. Time: 20 minutes
Cooking Time: 4-10 hours
Ideal slow cooker size: 4-qt.

2 lbs. ground turkey
2 16-oz. cans kidney beans, rinsed and drained
2 14½-oz. cans diced tomatoes, undrained
8-oz. can tomato sauce
2 medium onions, chopped
1 green pepper, chopped
2 cloves garlic, minced
2 Tbsp. chili powder
1 tsp. pepper

1. Brown ground turkey in skillet. Drain. Transfer to slow cooker.

2. Stir in remaining ingredients.

3. Cover. Cook on low 8-10 hours, or on high 4 hours.

4. Garnish individual servings with cheese.

Exchange List Values

- Starch 1.0
- Meat, lean 2.0
- Vegetable 2.0
- Fat 0.5

Basic Nutritional Values

- Calories 276
- Cholesterol 67 mg
- (Calories from Fat 85)
- Sodium 490 mg
- Total Fat 9 gm
- Total Carb 24 gm
- (Saturated Fat 2.2 gm,
- Dietary Fiber 6 gm
- Polyunsat Fat 2.5 gm,
- Sugars 8 gm
- Monounsat Fat 3.3 gm)
- Protein 25 gm

Sauté with less oil or butter than a recipe calls for. Lower the heat so the food doesn't burn.

Turkey and Corn Chili

Dawn Day
Westminster, CA

Makes 8 servings

Prep. Time: 15 minutes
Cooking Time: 8-9 hours
Ideal slow cooker size: 4-qt.

1 large chopped onion
2 Tbsp. oil
1 lb. ground turkey
3 Tbsp. chili powder
6-oz. can tomato paste
3 1-lb. cans small red
 beans with liquid
1 cup frozen corn

1. Sauté onion in oil in skillet until transparent. Add turkey and salt and brown lightly in skillet.
2. Combine all ingredients in slow cooker. Mix well.
3. Cover. Cook on low 8-9 hours.

Exchange List Values
- Starch 2.0
- Meat, lean 2.0
- Vegetable 1.0
- Fat 0.5

Basic Nutritional Values
- Calories 319
- Cholesterol 42 mg
 (Calories from Fat 91)
- Sodium 678 mg
- Total Fat 10 gm
- Total Carb 37 gm
 (Saturated Fat 1.7 gm,
- Dietary Fiber 9 gm
 Polyunsat Fat 3.0 gm,
- Sugars 7 gm
 Monounsat Fat 4.3 gm)
- Protein 22 gm

Note:
 Ground beef can be used in place of turkey.

Turkey Green Chili Chowder

Colleen Konetzni
Rio Rancho, NM

Makes 12 servings

Prep. Time: 45 minutes
Cooking Time: 6 hours
Ideal slow cooker size: 6-qt.

1 cup chopped celery
1 cup chopped onion
2 Tbsp. butter
3 cups chopped cooked
 turkey
4 cups fat-free, low-sodium
 turkey *or* chicken broth
4 potatoes, peeled *or*
 unpeeled, and cubed
½ cup green chilies,
 chopped
½ cup cubed cheese
2 14¾-oz. cans creamed
 corn
2 cups 1% milk

1. In a skillet, sauté celery and onion in butter until vegetables soften and begin to brown.
2. Place sautéed vegetables, turkey, broth, potatoes, chili, cheese, corn, and milk in slow cooker.
3. Cover. Cook on high 6 hours, or until potatoes are soft.
4. If you wish, mash the Soup a few times with a potato masher to make it thicker.

Exchange List Values
- Starch 1.5
- Lean Meat 2.0

Basic Nutritional Values
- Calories 210
- Cholesterol 40 mg
 (Calories from Fat 55)
- Sodium 405 mg
- Total Fat 6 gm
- Total Carb 23 gm
 (Saturated Fat 3.0 gm,
- Dietary Fiber 2 gm
 Polyunsat Fat 1.0 gm,
- Sugars 8 gm
 Monounsat Fat 1.5 gm)
- Protein 16 gm

Chili Sans Cholesterol

Dolores S. Kratz
Souderton, PA

Makes 4 servings

Prep. Time: 20 minutes
Cooking Time: 6 hours
Ideal slow cooker size: 4-qt.

1 lb. ground turkey
½ cup chopped celery
½ cup chopped onions
8-oz. can tomatoes
15-oz. can no-salt-added
 pinto beans
14½-oz. can diced
 tomatoes
½ tsp. chili powder
¼ tsp. salt
dash pepper

1. Sauté turkey in skillet until browned. Drain.
2. Combine all ingredients in slow cooker.
3. Cover. Cook on low 6 hours.

Exchange List Values
- Starch 1.0
- Meat, lean 3.0
- Vegetable 2.0
- Fat 0.5

Basic Nutritional Values

- Calories 317
  (Calories from Fat 104)
- Total Fat 12 gm
  (Saturated Fat 2.9 gm,
  Polyunsat Fat 3.0 gm,
  Monounsat Fat 4.1 gm)
- Cholesterol 84 mg
- Sodium 578 mg
- Total Carb 24 gm
- Dietary Fiber 7 gm
- Sugars 8 gm
- Protein 29 gm

Pork Chili

Carol Duree
Salina, KS

Makes 5 servings

Prep. Time: 15 minutes
Cooking Time: 4-8 hours
Ideal slow cooker size: 4-qt.

1 lb. boneless pork ribs
2 14½-oz. cans fire-roasted
  diced tomatoes
4¼-oz. cans diced green
  chili peppers, drained
½ cup chopped onion
1 clove garlic, minced
1 Tbsp. chili powder

1. Layer ingredients into
slow cooker in order given.
2. Cover. Cook on high 4
hours or on low 6-8 hours, or
until pork is tender but not
dry.
3. Cut up or shred meat.
Stir through chili and serve.

Notes:
1. You can serve this as
soup, but we especially like it
over rice.
2. You can add a 1-lb. can
of your favorite chili beans 30
minutes before end of cooking
time.

Exchange List Values

- Vegetable 2.0
- Lean Meat 2.0
- Fat 1.0

Basic Nutritional Values

- Calories 180
  (Calories from Fat 65)
- Total Fat 7 gm
  (Saturated Fat 2.5 gm,
  Polyunsat Fat 1.0 gm,
  Monounsat Fat 3.0 gm)
- Cholesterol 55 mg
- Sodium 495 mg
- Total Carb 12 gm
- Dietary Fiber 3 gm
- Sugars 6 gm
- Protein 18 gm

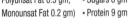

Italian Vegetable Soup

Patti Boston
Newark, OH

Makes 6 servings

Prep. Time: 20 minutes
Cooking Time: 4¾-9¼ hours
Ideal slow cooker size: 4-qt.

3 small carrots, sliced
1 small onion, chopped
2 small potatoes, diced
2 Tbsp. chopped parsley
1 garlic clove, minced
3 tsp. sodium-free beef
  bouillon powder
1¼ tsp. dried basil
¼ tsp. pepper
16-oz. can red kidney
  beans, undrained
3 cups water
14½-oz. can
  stewed
  tomatoes,
  with juice
1 cup diced,
  extra-lean,
  lower sodium
  cooked ham

1. Layer carrots, onions,
potatoes, parsley, garlic, beef
bouillon, basil, salt, pepper,
and kidney beans in slow
cooker. Do not stir. Add
water.
2. Cover. Cook on low 8-9
hours, or on high 4½-5½
hours, until vegetables are
tender.
3. Stir in tomatoes and
ham. Cover and cook on high
10-15 minutes.

Exchange List Values

- Starch 1.5
- Vegetable 2.0

Basic Nutritional Values

- Calories 156
  (Calories from Fat 7)
- Total Fat 1 gm
  (Saturated Fat 0.2 gm,
  Polyunsat Fat 0.3 gm,
  Monounsat Fat 0.2 gm)
- Cholesterol 9 mg
- Sodium 614 mg
- Total Carb 29 gm
- Dietary Fiber 5 gm
- Sugars 8 gm
- Protein 9 gm

Spicy Potato Soup

Sharon Kauffman
Harrisonburg, VA

Makes 8 servings

Prep. Time: 25 minutes
Cooking Time: 5-10 hours
Ideal slow cooker size: 4-qt.

¾ lb. 90%-lean ground
  beef, browned
4 cups cubed peeled
  potatoes
1 small onion, chopped
3 8-oz. cans no-added-salt
  tomato sauce
1 tsp. salt
1½ tsp. pepper
½-1 tsp. hot pepper sauce
water

1. Combine all ingredients
except water in slow cooker.
Add enough water to cover
ingredients.
2. Cover. Cook on low 8-10
hours, or high 5 hours, until
potatoes are tender.

Exchange List Values
- Starch 1.0
- Meat, lean 1.0
- Vegetable 1.0

Basic Nutritional Values
- Calories 152
  (Calories from Fat 32)
- Total Fat 4 gm
  (Saturated Fat 1.4 gm,
  Polyunsat Fat 0.2 gm,
  Monounsat Fat 1.5 gm)
- Cholesterol 26 mg
- Sodium 346 mg
- Total Carb 19 gm
- Dietary Fiber 2 gm
- Sugars 7 gm
- Protein 10 gm

Hearty Potato Sauerkraut Soup

Kathy Hertzler
Lancaster, PA

Makes 8 servings

Prep. Time: 25 minutes
Cooking Time: 10-12 hours
Ideal slow cooker size: 4-qt.

4 tsp. sodium-free chicken
  bouillon powder
4 cups water
10¾-oz. can 98% fat-free,
  reduced-sodium cream
  of mushroom soup
16-oz. can sauerkraut,
  rinsed and drained
8 oz. fresh mushrooms,
  sliced
1 medium potato, cubed
2 medium carrots, peeled
  and sliced
2 ribs celery, chopped
8 oz. low-fat Polish
  kielbasa (smoked), cubed
2 cups chopped cooked
  chicken
2 Tbsp. vinegar
2 tsp. dried dillweed
1½ tsp. pepper

1. Mix together bouillon
powder and water. Pour into
slow cooker.
2. Combine remaining
ingredients in large slow cooker.
3. Cover. Cook on low
10-12 hours.
4. If necessary, skim fat
before serving.

Exchange List Values
- Carbohydrate 1.0
- Vegetable 1.0
- Meat, lean 1.0
- Fat 0.5

Basic Nutritional Values
- Calories 178
  (Calories from Fat 44)
- Total Fat 5 gm
  (Saturated Fat 1.5 gm,
  Polyunsat Fat 1.0 gm,
  Monounsat Fat 1.8 gm)
- Cholesterol 45 mg
- Sodium 664 mg
- Total Carb 17 gm
- Dietary Fiber 3 gm
- Sugars 5 gm
- Protein 16 gm

Sauerkraut Soup

Barbara Tenny
Delta, PA

Makes 10 servings

Prep. Time: 30 minutes
Cooking Time: 8-10 hours
Ideal slow cooker size: 5-qt.

8 oz. low-fat kielbasa, cut
  into ½-inch pieces
5 medium potatoes, cubed
2 large onions, chopped
2 large carrots, cut into
  ¼-inch slices
4 tsp. sodium-free chicken
  bouillon powder
4 cups water
32-oz. can sauerkraut,
  rinsed and drained
6-oz. can tomato paste

1. Combine all ingredients
in large slow cooker. Stir to
combine.
2. Cover. Cook on high 2
hours, and then on low 6-8
hours.

Take a walk after dinner instead of watching TV.

Exchange List Values

- Starch 1.0
- Meat, lean 1.0
- Vegetable 3.0

Basic Nutritional Values

- Calories 188
  (Calories from Fat 22)
- Total Fat 2 gm
  (Saturated Fat 0.8 gm,
  Polyunsat Fat 0.4 gm,
  Monounsat Fat 1.2 gm)
- Cholesterol 21 mg
- Sodium 772 mg
- Total Carb 33 gm
- Dietary Fiber 6 gm
- Sugars 9 gm
- Protein 10 gm

Tip:
Serve with rye bread.

Curried Carrot Soup

Ann Bender
Ft. Defiance, VA

Makes 8 servings

Prep. Time: 30 minutes
Cooking Time: 2½ hours
Ideal slow cooker size: 4-qt.

1 garlic clove, minced
1 large onion, chopped
2 Tbsp. oil
1 Tbsp. butter
1 tsp. curry powder
1 Tbsp. flour
4 cups fat-free, lower-
 sodium chicken broth
6 large carrots, sliced
¼ tsp. salt
¼ tsp. cayenne pepper,
 optional
1½ cups plain yogurt, *or*
 light sour cream

1. In skillet cook minced garlic and onion in oil and butter until limp but not brown.
2. Add curry and flour. Cook 30 seconds. Pour into slow cooker.

3. Add chicken broth and carrots.
4. Cover. Cook on high for about 2 hours, or until carrots are soft.
5. Purée mixture in blender. Season with salt and pepper. Return to slow cooker and keep warm until ready to serve.
6. Add a dollop of yogurt or sour cream to each serving.

Exchange List Values

- Vegetable 2.0
- Fat 1.0

Basic Nutritional Values

- Calories 113
  (Calories from Fat 46)
- Total Fat 5 gm
  (Saturated Fat 1.2 gm,
  Polyunsat Fat 1.1 gm,
  Monounsat Fat 2.5 gm)
- Cholesterol 5 mg
- Sodium 414 mg
- Total Carb 13 gm
- Dietary Fiber 2 gm
- Sugars 7 gm
- Protein 5 gm

Sausage, Tomato, Spinach Soup

Wendy B. Martzall
New Holland, PA

Makes 8 servings

Prep. Time: 15-20 minutes
Cooking Time: 5 hours
*Ideal slow cooker size: 3- to
 4-qt.*

½ lb. loose pork, *or* turkey,
 sausage
1 medium onion, chopped
1 small green bell pepper,
 chopped
28-oz. can diced tomatoes
2 14½-oz. cans fat-free,
 low-sodium beef broth

8-oz. can no-salt-added
 tomato sauce
½ cup picánte sauce
1½ tsp. sugar
1 tsp. dried basil
½ tsp. dried oregano
10-oz. pkg. frozen spinach,
 thawed and squeezed dry
½ cup shredded mozzarella
 cheese

1. Brown sausage with onions and peppers in skillet. (If you use turkey sausage, you'll probably need to add 1-2 Tbsp. oil to the pan.) Stir frequently, breaking up clumps of meat. When no longer pink, drain off drippings.
2. Spoon meat and vegetables into slow cooker.
3. Add all remaining ingredients except spinach and cheese. Stir until well blended.
4. Cover. Cook on low 4¾ hours.
5. Stir spinach into Soup. Cover and continue cooking on low another 15 minutes.
6. Top each individual serving with a sprinkling of mozzarella cheese.

Exchange List Values

- Vegetable 4.0
- High-Fat Meat 1.0

Basic Nutritional Values

- Calories 185
  (Calories from Fat 70)
- Total Fat 8 gm
  (Saturated Fat 2.5 gm,
  Polyunsat Fat 1.0 gm,
  Monounsat Fat 3.0 gm)
- Cholesterol 20 mg
- Sodium 580 mg
- Total Carb 22 gm
- Dietary Fiber 8 gm
- Sugars 11 gm
- Protein 11 gm

Curried Pork and Pea Soup

Kathy Hertzler
Lancaster, PA

Makes 8 servings

Prep. Time: 30 minutes
Cooking Time: 4-12 hours
Ideal slow cooker size: 4-qt.

1½ lb. boneless pork shoulder roast
1 cup yellow *or* green split peas, rinsed and drained
½ cup finely chopped carrots
½ cup finely chopped celery
½ cup finely chopped onions
49½-oz. can (approximately 6 cups) reduced-sodium chicken broth
2 tsp. curry powder
½ tsp. paprika
¼ tsp. ground cumin
¼ tsp. pepper
2 cups torn fresh spinach

1. Trim fat from pork and cut pork into ½-inch pieces.
2. Combine split peas, carrots, celery, and onions in slow cooker.
3. Stir in broth, curry powder, paprika, cumin, and pepper. Stir in pork.
4. Cover. Cook on low 10-12 hours, or on high 4 hours.
5. Stir in spinach. Serve immediately.

Exchange List Values
- Starch 1.0   • Fat 0.5
- Meat, very lean 3.0

Basic Nutritional Values
- Calories 206   • Cholesterol 43 mg
  (Calories from Fat 41)   • Sodium 480 mg
- Total Fat 5 gm   • Total Carb 16 gm
  (Saturated Fat 1.5 gm,   • Dietary Fiber 6 gm
  Polyunsat Fat 0.6 gm,   • Sugars 3 gm
  Monounsat Fat 1.9 gm)   • Protein 24 gm

Ruth's Split Pea Soup

Ruth Conrad Liechty
Goshen, IN

Makes 8 servings

Prep. Time: 20 minutes
Cooking Time: 12 hours
Ideal slow cooker size: 4-qt.

½ lb. bulk sausage, browned and drained
6 cups water
2¼ cups dry split peas
2 medium potatoes, diced
1 onion, chopped
½ tsp. dried marjoram, *or* thyme
½ tsp. pepper

1. Wash and sort dried peas, removing any stones. Then combine all ingredients in slow cooker.
2. Cover. Cook on low 12 hours.

Exchange List Values
- Starch 2.5   • Meat, medium fat 1.0

Basic Nutritional Values
- Calories 257   • Cholesterol 11 mg
  (Calories from Fat 43)   • Sodium 179 mg
- Total Fat 5 gm   • Total Carb 39 gm
  (Saturated Fat 1.5 gm,   • Dietary Fiber 13 gm
  Polyunsat Fat 0.8 gm,   • Sugars 6 gm
  Monounsat Fat 2.0 gm)   • Protein 16 gm

Kelly's Split Pea Soup

Kelly Amos
Pittsboro, NC

Makes 8 servings

Prep. Time: 20 minutes
Cooking Time: 8-9 hours
Ideal slow cooker size: 4-qt.

2 cups dry split peas
2 quarts water
2 onions, chopped
2 carrots, peeled and sliced
4 slices Canadian bacon, chopped
2 Tbsp. sodium-free chicken bouillon powder
¾ tsp. salt
¼-½ tsp. pepper

1. Combine all ingredients in slow cooker.
2. Cover. Cook on low 8-9 hours.

Exchange List Values
- Starch 2.0   • Meat, very lean 1.0

Basic Nutritional Values
- Calories 195   • Cholesterol 7 mg
  (Calories from Fat 14)   • Sodium 411 mg
- Total Fat 2 gm   • Total Carb 32 gm
  (Saturated Fat 0.4 gm,   • Dietary Fiber 11 gm
  Polyunsat Fat 0.3 gm,   • Sugars 7 gm
  Monounsat Fat 0.6 gm)   • Protein 14 gm

Variation:
For a creamier soup, remove half of soup when done and purée. Stir back into rest of soup.

Karen's Split Pea Soup

Karen Stoltzfus
Alto, MI

Makes 6 servings

Prep. Time: 30 minutes
Cooking Time: 7 hours
Ideal slow cooker size: 4- or 5-qt.

2 carrots
2 ribs celery
1 onion
1 parsnip
1 leek (keep 3 inches of green)
1 ripe tomato
6 oz. extra-lean lower-sodium ham, cubed
1¾ cups (1 lb.) dried split peas, washed, with stones removed
2 Tbsp. olive oil
1 bay leaf
1 tsp. dried thyme
4 cups chicken broth
4 cups water
1 tsp. salt
¼ tsp. pepper
2 tsp. chopped fresh parsley

1. Cut all vegetables into ¼-inch pieces and place in slow cooker. Add remaining ingredients except salt, pepper, and parsley.
2. Cover. Cook on high 7 hours.
3. Season soup with salt and pepper. Stir in parsley. Serve immediately.

Exchange List Values
• Starch 2.0   • Meat, lean 1.0
• Vegetable 2.0

Basic Nutritional Values
• Calories 275   • Cholesterol 10 mg
  (Calories from Fat 41) • Sodium 453 mg
• Total Fat 5 gm   • Total Carb 41 gm
  (Saturated Fat 0.7 gm, • Dietary Fiber 14 gm
  Polyunsat Fat 0.7 gm,   • Sugars 7 gm
  Monounsat Fat 2.8 gm)   • Protein 20 gm

Dorothy's Split Pea Soup

Dorothy M. Van Deest
Memphis, TN

Makes 8 servings

Prep. Time: 25 minutes
Cooking Time: 8-10 hours
Ideal slow cooker size: 5-qt.

2 Tbsp. canola oil
1 cup minced onions
8 cups water
2 cups (1 lb.) green split peas, washed and stones removed
4 whole cloves
1 bay leaf
¼ tsp. pepper
6 oz. extra-lean lower-sodium ham, cubed
1 cup finely minced celery
1 cup diced carrots
⅛ tsp. dried marjoram
¾ tsp. salt
⅛ tsp. dried savory

1. Combine all ingredients in slow cooker.
2. Cover. Cook on low 8-10 hours.

Exchange List Values
• Starch 2.0   • Meat, lean 1.0
• Vegetable 1.0

Basic Nutritional Values
• Calories 239   • Cholesterol 10 mg
  (Calories from Fat 40) • Sodium 419 mg
• Total Fat 4 gm   • Total Carb 35 gm
  (Saturated Fat 0.5 gm, • Dietary Fiber 13 gm
  Polyunsat Fat 1.4 gm,   • Sugars 7 gm
  Monounsat Fat 2.3 gm)   • Protein 16 gm

Variation:

For a thick soup, uncover soup after 8-10 hours and turn heat to high. Simmer, stirring occasionally, until the desired consistency is reached.

Rosemarie's Pea Soup

Rosemarie Fitzgerald
Gibsonia, PA
Shirley Sears, Tiskilwa, IL

Makes 6 servings

Prep. Time: 25 minutes
Cooking Time: 6-12 hours
Ideal slow cooker size: 4-qt.

2 cups dried split peas
4 cups water
1 rib celery, chopped
1 cup chopped potatoes
1 large carrot, chopped
1 medium onion, chopped
¼ tsp. dried thyme, *or* marjoram
1 bay leaf
½ tsp. salt
1 garlic clove
½ tsp. dried basil

1. Combine all ingredients in slow cooker.
2. Cover. Cook on low 8-12 hours, or on high 6 hours, until peas are tender.

Exchange List Values
• Starch 2.5   • Vegetable 1.0

Basic Nutritional Values
• Calories 230
(Calories from Fat 7)
• Total Fat 1 gm
(Saturated Fat 0.1 gm,
Polyunsat Fat 0.3 gm,
Monounsat Fat 0.1 gm)
• Cholesterol 0 mg
• Sodium 216 mg
• Total Carb 43 gm
• Dietary Fiber 15 gm
• Sugars 7 gm
• Protein 15 gm

Variations:
For increased flavor, use chicken broth instead of water. Stir in curry powder, coriander, or red pepper flakes to taste.

French Market Soup

Ethel Mumaw, Berlin, OH

Makes 8 servings
(about 2½ quarts total)

Prep. Time: 20 minutes
Cooking Time: 10 hours
Ideal slow cooker size: 4-qt.

2 cups mixed dry beans, washed with stones removed
2 quarts water
1 ham hock, all visible fat removed
1 tsp. salt
¼ tsp. pepper
16-oz. can tomatoes
1 large onion, chopped
1 garlic clove, minced
1 chili pepper, chopped, *or* 1 tsp. chili powder
¼ cup lemon juice

1. Combine all ingredients in slow cooker.
2. Cover. Cook on low 8 hours. Turn to high and cook an additional 2 hours, or until beans are tender.
3. Debone ham, cut meat into bite-sized pieces, and stir back into soup.

Exchange List Values
• Starch 1.5   • Meat, lean 1.0
• Vegetable 1.0

Basic Nutritional Values
• Calories 191
(Calories from Fat 34)
• Total Fat 4 gm
(Saturated Fat 1.3 gm,
Polyunsat Fat 0.6 gm,
Monounsat Fat 1.5 gm)
• Cholesterol 9 mg
• Sodium 488 mg
• Total Carb 29 gm
• Dietary Fiber 7 gm
• Sugars 5 gm
• Protein 12 gm

Nine Bean Soup with Tomatoes

Violette Harris Denney
Carrollton, GA

Makes 8 servings

Prep. Time: 15 minutes
Soaking Time: overnight or 12 hours
Cooking Time: 8 hours
Ideal slow cooker size: 5-qt.

2 cups dry nine-bean soup mix
12 oz. extra-lean, lower sodium ham, diced
1 large onion, chopped
1 garlic clove, minced
2 qts. water
16-oz. can no-added-salt tomatoes, undrained and chopped
10-oz. can tomatoes with green chilies, undrained

1. Sort and wash bean mix. Place in slow cooker. Cover with water 2 inches above beans. Let soak overnight. Drain.
2. Add ham, onion, garlic, and 2 quarts fresh water.
3. Cover. Cook on low 7 hours.
4. Add remaining ingredients and continue cooking on low another hour. Stir occasionally.

Exchange List Values
• Starch 2.0   • Meat, very lean 1.0
• Vegetable 1.0

Basic Nutritional Values

- Calories 231
  (Calories from Fat 14)
- Total Fat 2 gm
  (Saturated Fat 0.4 gm,
  Polyunsat Fat 0.5 gm,
  Monounsat Fat 0.4 gm)
- Cholesterol 20 mg
- Sodium 518 mg
- Total Carb 37 gm
- Dietary Fiber 9 gm
- Sugars 9 gm
- Protein 19 gm

Note:

Bean Soup Mix is a mix of barley pearls, black beans, red beans, pinto beans, navy beans, Great Northern beans, lentils, split peas, and black-eyed peas.

Calico Ham and Bean Soup

Esther Martin
Ephrata, PA

Makes 8 servings

Prep. Time: 25 minutes
Cooking Time: 4-10 hours
Ideal slow cooker size: 5- or 6-qt.

1 lb. dry bean mix, rinsed and drained, with stones removed
6 cups water
2 cups extra-lean, lower-sodium, cubed, cooked ham
1 cup chopped onions
1 cup chopped carrots
1 tsp. dried basil
1 tsp. dried oregano

¾ tsp. salt
¼ tsp. pepper
2 bay leaves
6 cups water
1 tsp. liquid smoke, *optional*

1. Combine beans and 6 cups water in large saucepan. Bring to boil, reduce heat, and simmer uncovered for 10 minutes. Drain, discarding cooking water, and rinse beans.
2. Combine all ingredients in slow cooker.
3. Cover. Cook on low 8-10 hours, or high 4-5 hours. Discard bay leaves before serving.

Exchange List Values

- Starch 2.0
- Vegetable 1.0
- Meat, very lean 1.0

Basic Nutritional Values

- Calories 228
  (Calories from Fat 12)
- Total Fat 1 gm
  (Saturated Fat 0.4 gm,
  Polyunsat Fat 0.5 gm,
  Monounsat Fat 0.3 gm)
- Cholesterol 13 mg
- Sodium 462 mg
- Total Carb 38 gm
- Dietary Fiber 10 gm
- Sugars 6 gm
- Protein 17 gm

Lentil Soup with Ham Bone

Rhoda Atzeff
Harrisburg, PA

Makes 8 servings

Prep. Time: 20 minutes
Cooking Time: 8-9 hours
Ideal slow cooker size: 5-qt.

1 lb. lentils, washed and drained
1 celery rib, chopped
1 large carrot, grated
½ cup chopped onions
1 bay leaf
¼ tsp. dried thyme
7-8 cups water
1 ham bone, skin and visible fat removed
¼-½ tsp. crushed red hot pepper flakes
pepper to taste

1. Combine all ingredients except pepper and salt in slow cooker.
2. Cover. Cook on low 8-9 hours. Remove bay leaf and ham bone. Dice meat from bone and return to cooker.
3. Season to taste with pepper.

Exchange List Values

- Starch 2.0
- Meat, lean 1.0

Basic Nutritional Values

- Calories 220
  (Calories from Fat 17)
- Total Fat 2 gm
  (Saturated Fat 0.5 gm,
  Polyunsat Fat 0.4 gm,
  Monounsat Fat 0.6 gm)
- Cholesterol 12 mg
- Sodium 298 mg
- Total Carb 33 gm
- Dietary Fiber 13 gm
- Sugars 4 gm
- Protein 19 gm

Serving foods with a measuring cup is an easy way to keep track of how much you're eating.

Bean and Herb Soup

LaVerne A. Olson
Willow Street, PA

Makes 6 servings

Prep. Time: 1 hour
Cooking Time: 4 hours
Ideal slow cooker size: 5- or 6-qt.

1½ cups dry mixed beans
5 cups water
6 oz. extra-lean, lower-
  sodium ham
1 cup chopped onions
1 cup chopped celery
1 cup chopped carrots
2-3 cups water
½ tsp. salt
¼-½ tsp. pepper
1-2 tsp. fresh basil, *or*
  ½ tsp. dried basil
1-2 tsp. fresh oregano, *or*
  ½ tsp. dried oregano
1-2 tsp. fresh thyme, *or*
  ½ tsp. dried thyme
2 cups fresh tomatoes,
  crushed

1. Combine beans, water, and ham in saucepan. Bring to boil. Turn off heat and let stand 1 hour.

2. Combine onions, celery, and carrots in 2-3 cups water in another saucepan. Cook until soft. Mash slightly.

3. Combine all ingredients in slow cooker.

4. Cover. Cook on high 2 hours, and then on low 2 hours.

Exchange List Values
- Starch 2.0
- Meat, very lean 1.0
- Vegetable 1.0

Basic Nutritional Values
- Calories 222
  (Calories from Fat 13)
- Total Fat 1 gm
  (Saturated Fat 0.3 gm,
  Polyunsat Fat 0.5 gm,
  Monounsat Fat 0.3 gm)
- Cholesterol 13 mg
- Sodium 465 mg
- Total Carb 38 gm
- Dietary Fiber 10 gm
- Sugars 8 gm
- Protein 16 gm

Northern Bean Soup

Patricia Howard
Albuquerque, NM

Makes 8 servings

Prep. Time: 30 minutes
Soaking Time: 12 hours or
  overnight
Cooking Time: 12-14 hours
Ideal slow cooker size: 4-qt.

1 lb. dry Northern beans
1 lb. extra-lean, lower-
  sodium ham
2 medium onions, chopped
half a green bell pepper,
  chopped
1 cup chopped celery
16-oz. can diced tomatoes
4 carrots, peeled and
  chopped
4-oz. can green chili
  peppers
1 tsp. garlic powder
1-2 qts. water

1. Wash beans. Cover with water and soak overnight. Drain. Pour into slow cooker.

2. Dice ham into 1-inch pieces. Add to beans.

3. Stir in remaining ingredients.

4. Cover. Cook on high 2 hours, then on low 10-12 hours, or until beans are tender.

Exchange List Values
- Starch 2.0
- Meat, very lean 2.0
- Vegetable 2.0

Basic Nutritional Values
- Calories 272
  (Calories from Fat 17)
- Total Fat 2 gm
  (Saturated Fat 0.6 gm,
  Polyunsat Fat 0.6 gm,
  Monounsat Fat 0.4 gm)
- Cholesterol 26 mg
- Sodium 674 mg
- Total Carb 42 gm
- Dietary Fiber 13 gm
- Sugars 11 gm
- Protein 23 gm

Easy Lima Bean Soup

Barbara Tenney
Delta, PA

Makes 10 servings

Prep. Time: 30 minutes
Soaking Time: 12 hours or
  overnight
Cooking Time: 8-10 hours
Ideal slow cooker size: 5- or 6-qt.

1 lb. bag large dry lima
  beans
1 large onion, chopped
6 ribs celery, chopped
3 large potatoes, cut in
  ½-inch cubes
2 large carrots, cut in
  ¼-inch rounds
2 cups extra-lean, lower-
  sodium ham
1 tsp. salt
1 tsp. pepper
2 bay leaves
3 quarts water, *or*
  combination water and
  beef broth

1. Sort beans. Soak overnight. Drain.

2. Combine all ingredients in slow cooker.

3. Cover. Cook on low 8-10 hours.

Exchange List Values

- Starch 2.5
- Meat, very lean 1.0
- Vegetable 1.0

Basic Nutritional Values

- Calories 258
  (Calories from Fat 12)
- Total Fat 1 gm
  (Saturated Fat 0.4 gm,
  Polyunsat Fat 0.5 gm,
  Monounsat Fat 0.4 gm)
- Cholesterol 21 mg
- Sodium 648 mg
- Total Carb 43 gm
- Dietary Fiber 11 gm
- Sugars 9 gm
- Protein 19 gm

Variation:

For extra flavor, add 1 tsp. dried oregano before cooking.

Navy Bean Soup

Joyce Bowman
Lady Lake, FL

Makes 8 servings

Prep. Time: 15 minutes
Soaking Time: 12 hours or
overnight
Cooking Time: 8-10 hours
Ideal slow cooker size: 4-qt.

1 lb. dry navy beans,
stones picked out
8 cups water
1 onion, finely chopped
2 bay leaves
½ tsp. ground thyme
½ tsp. ground nutmeg
½ tsp. salt
½ tsp. lemon pepper
3 garlic cloves, minced
1-lb. extra-lean, lower-
sodium ham pieces

1. Soak beans in water overnight. Reserve liquid.

2. Combine all ingredients in slow cooker.
3. Cover. Cook on low 8-10 hours. Debone meat and cut into bite-sized pieces. Set ham aside.
4. Purée three-fourths of soup in blender in small batches. When finished blending, stir in meat.

Exchange List Values

- Starch 2.5
- Meat, very lean 2.0

Basic Nutritional Values

- Calories 264
  (Calories from Fat 17)
- Total Fat 2 gm
  (Saturated Fat 0.6 gm,
  Polyunsat Fat 0.5 gm,
  Monounsat Fat 0.5 gm)
- Cholesterol 26 mg
- Sodium 631 mg
- Total Carb 40 gm
- Dietary Fiber 9 gm
- Sugars 7 gm
- Protein 22 gm

Variation:

Add small chunks of cooked potatoes when stirring in ham pieces after blending

Slow Cooked Navy Beans with Ham

Julia Lapp
New Holland, PA

Makes 10 servings

Prep. Time: 20 minutes
Soaking Time: 4 hours
Cooking Time: 4-8 hours
Ideal slow cooker size: 4-qt.

1 lb. dry navy beans (2½
cups)
5 cups water
1 garlic clove, minced

1 ham hock, skin and all
visible fat removed
1 tsp. salt

1. Soak beans in water at least 4 hours in slow cooker.
2. Add garlic and ham hock.
3. Cover. Cook on low 7-8 hours, or high 4 hours. Add salt during last hour of cooking time.
4. Remove ham hock from cooker. Allow to cool. Cut ham from hock and stir back into bean mixture. Correct seasonings and serve in soup bowls with hot corn bread.

Exchange List Values

- Starch 2.0
- Meat, very lean 1.0
- Fat 0.5

Basic Nutritional Values

- Calories 199
  (Calories from Fat 34)
- Total Fat 4 gm
  (Saturated Fat 1.3 gm,
  Polyunsat Fat 0.6 gm,
  Monounsat Fat 1.4 gm)
- Cholesterol 9 mg
- Sodium 418 mg
- Total Carb 30 gm
- Dietary Fiber 7 gm
- Sugars 3 gm
- Protein 12 gm

Variation:

For added flavor, stir 1 chopped onion, 2-3 chopped celery stalks, 2-3 sliced carrots, and 3-4 cups canned tomatoes into cooker with garlic and ham hock.

White Bean with Fennel Soup

Karen Ceneviva
Seymour, CT

Makes 6 servings

Prep Time: 15 minutes
Cooking Time: 6-7 hours
Ideal slow-cooker size: 5½- or 6-qt.

4 cups fat-free, low-sodium
  vegetable broth
⅛ tsp. black pepper
1 small fennel bulb, sliced
  to yield about 2 cups
1 medium onion, chopped
2 cloves garlic, minced
10-oz. pkg. frozen spinach
14½-oz. can diced tomatoes
16-oz. can white kidney
  (cannellini) beans,
  undrained

1. Stir broth, black pepper,
fennel, onion, and garlic into
slow-cooker.
2. Cover and cook on low
for 6 to 7 hours.
3. Add spinach, tomato,
and undrained beans. Turn
to high. Cover and cook for 1
more hour or until vegetables
are tender.

Exchange List Values

• Starch 0.5   • Vegetable 2.0

Basic Nutritional Values

• Calories 115   Cholesterol 0 mg),
  (Calories from Fat 5)   Sodium 400 mg
• Total Fat 0.5 gm   • Total Carb 22 gm
  (Saturated Fat 0 gm, • Dietary Fiber 7 gm
  Polyunsat Fat 0 gm   • Sugars 5 gm
  Monounsat Fat 0 gm   • Protein 6 gm

Old-Fashioned Bean Soup

Gladys M. High
Ephrata, PA

Makes 7 servings

Prep. Time: 15 minutes
Soaking Time: 12 hours or
  overnight
Cooking Time: 8-9 hours
Ideal slow cooker size: 4-qt.

1 lb. dry navy beans, *or*
  dry green split peas
1 lb. extra-lean, lower-
  sodium ham pieces
⅛ tsp. salt
¼ tsp. ground pepper
½ cup chopped celery
  leaves
2 qts. water
1 medium onion, chopped
1 bay leaf, *optional*

1. Soak beans or peas
overnight. Drain, discarding
soaking water.
2. Combine all ingredients
in slow cooker.
3. Cover. Cook on high 8-9
hours.

Exchange List Values

• Starch 3.0   • Meat, very lean 2.0

Basic Nutritional Values

• Calories 300   • Cholesterol 30 mg
  (Calories from Fat 19) • Sodium 576 mg
• Total Fat 2 gm   • Total Carb 46 gm
  (Saturated Fat 0.7 gm, • Dietary Fiber 11 gm
  Polyunsat Fat 0.6 gm, • Sugars 7 gm
  Monounsat Fat 0.5 gm) • Protein 25 gm

Red and Green Bean Soup

Carol Duree, Salina, KS

Makes 8 servings

Prep. Time: 15 minutes
Cooking Time: 6½ hours
Ideal slow cooker size: 4-qt.

1 lb. dry navy beans
6 cups boiling water
1 cup sliced carrots
½ cup chopped onion
1½ lbs. ham hocks
salt and pepper to taste
1 cup chopped kale,
  spinach, *or* chard
½ cup roasted red peppers,
  chopped
Parmesan cheese, grated,
  optional

1. Rinse beans and place in
slow cooker.
2. Add all other ingredients
except kale and red peppers.
3. Cover. Cook on low
6-8 hours, or until beans are
tender but not mushy.
4. Ten minutes before serving, add kale and peppers.
Cover and continue to cook
10 more minutes.
5. Sprinkle Parmesan
cheese on top of individual
servings.

Exchange List Values

• Starch 2.0   • Lean Meat 2.0

Basic Nutritional Values

• Calories 260   • Cholesterol 15 mg
  (Calories from Fat 40) • Sodium 85 mg
• Total Fat 4.5 gm   • Total Carb 40 gm
  (Saturated Fat 1.5 gm, • Dietary Fiber 15 gm
  Polyunsat Fat 1.0 gm, • Sugars 3 gm
  Monounsat Fat 2.0 gm) • Protein 16 gm

Black Bean Chili Con Carne

Janie Steele
Moore, OK

Makes 18 1-cup servings

Soaking Time: 12 hours or overnight
Prep. Time: 20 minutes
Cooking Time: 8 hours
Ideal slow cooker size: 6-qt.

1 lb. black beans
3 lbs. lean ground beef
2 large onions, chopped
1 green pepper, chopped
3 cloves garlic, minced
2 tsp. salt
1 tsp. pepper
6-oz. can tomato paste
3 cups tomato juice
1 tsp. celery salt
1 Tbsp. Worcestershire sauce
1 tsp. dry mustard
cayenne pepper, to taste
cumin, to taste
3 Tbsp. chili powder

1. Soak beans 8 hours or overnight. Rinse and drain.
2. Brown ground beef in batches in large skillet. Drain.
3. Combine all ingredients in 6-qt. or larger slow cooker, or divide between 2 smaller cookers.
4. Cover. Cook on low 8 hours.

Exchange List Values
- Starch 1.0
- Vegetable 1.0
- Meat, lean 2.0
- Fat 0.5

Basic Nutritional Values
- Calories 237 (Calories from Fat 76)
- Total Fat 8 gm (Saturated Fat 3.1 gm, Polyunsat Fat 0.5 gm, Monounsat Fat 3.4 gm)
- Cholesterol 45 mg
- Sodium 510 mg
- Total Carb 21 gm
- Dietary Fiber 7 gm
- Sugars 5 gm
- Protein 20 gm

Tip:
Serve over salad greens or wrapped in tortillas, topped with lettuce and grated cheese.

Caribbean-Style Black Bean Soup

Sheryl Shenk
Harrisonburg, VA

Makes 10 servings

Prep. Time: 20 minutes
Soaking Time: overnight or 12 hours
Cooking Time: 4-10 hours
Ideal slow cooker size: 4-qt.

1 lb. dried black beans, washed and stones removed
3 medium onions, chopped
1 medium green bell pepper, chopped
4 cloves garlic, minced
¾ cup cubed ham
1 Tbsp. canola oil
1 Tbsp. ground cumin
2 tsp. dried oregano
1 tsp. dried thyme
2 tsp. salt
½ tsp. pepper
3 cups water
2 Tbsp. vinegar
fresh chopped cilantro

1. Soak beans overnight in 4 quarts water. Drain.
2. Combine beans, onions, green pepper, garlic, ham, oil, cumin, oregano, thyme, salt, pepper, and 3 cups fresh water. Stir well.
3. Cover. Cook on low 8-10 hours, or on high 4-5 hours.
4. For a thick soup, remove half of cooked bean mixture and purée until smooth in blender or mash with potato masher. Return to cooker. If you like a soup-ier soup, leave as is.
5. Add vinegar and stir well.
6. Serve in soup bowls with a dollop of sour cream in the middle of each individual serving, topped with fresh cilantro.

Exchange List Values
- Starch 1.5
- Vegetable 1.0
- Meat, very lean 1.0

Basic Nutritional Values
- Calories 188 (Calories from Fat 24)
- Total Fat 3 gm (Saturated Fat 0.4 gm, Polyunsat Fat 0.8 gm, Monounsat Fat 1.2 gm)
- Cholesterol 5 mg
- Sodium 582 mg
- Total Carb 30 gm
- Dietary Fiber 10 gm
- Sugars 6 gm
- Protein 12 gm

Nutrient-rich sweet potatoes and winter squashes are healthy starch choices.

Vegetable Bean Soup

Kathi Rogge
Alexandria, IN

Makes 8 servings

Prep. Time: 30 minutes
Cooking Time: 5-8 hours
Ideal slow cooker size: 4-qt.

6 cups cooked navy, pinto,
  or Great Northern beans
1 meaty ham bone (about
  6 oz. ham), visible fat
  and skin removed
1 cup cooked ham, diced
¼ tsp. garlic powder
1 bay leaf
1 cup cubed potatoes
1 cup chopped onions
1 cup chopped celery
1 cup chopped carrots
water

1. Combine all ingredients
except water in 4-quart slow
cooker. Add water to about 1
inch from top.
2. Cover. Cook on low 5-8
hours.
3. Remove bay leaf before
serving.

Exchange List Values
- Starch 2.0
- Vegetable 1.0
- Meat, very lean 2.0

Basic Nutritional Values
- Calories 261
  (Calories from Fat 25)
- Total Fat 3 gm
  (Saturated Fat 0.8 gm,
  Polyunsat Fat 0.6 gm,
  Monounsat Fat 1.0 gm)
- Cholesterol 20 mg
- Sodium 499 mg
- Total Carb 39 gm
- Dietary Fiber 11 gm
- Sugars 5 gm
- Protein 21 gm

Slow-Cooker Black Bean Chili

Mary Seielstad
Sparks, NV

Makes 8 servings

Prep. Time: 20 minutes
Cooking Time: 6-8 hours
Ideal slow cooker size: 4-qt.

1 lb. pork tenderloin, cut
  into 1-inch chunks
16-oz. jar thick chunky
  salsa
3 15-oz. cans black beans,
  rinsed and drained
½ cup chicken broth
1 medium red bell pepper,
  chopped
1 medium onion, chopped
1 tsp. ground cumin
2 tsp. chili powder
1-1½ tsp. dried oregano
¼ cup sour cream

1. Combine all ingredients
except sour cream in slow
cooker.
2. Cover. Cook on low 6-8
hours, or until pork is tender.
3. Garnish individual
servings with sour cream.

Exchange List Values
- Starch 1.5
- Vegetable 1.0
- Meat, very lean 2.0
- Fat 0.5

Basic Nutritional Values
- Calories 231
  (Calories from Fat 38)
- Total Fat 4 gm
  (Saturated Fat 1.6 gm,
  Polyunsat Fat 0.6 gm,
  Monounsat Fat 1.4 gm)
- Cholesterol 36 mg
- Sodium 389 mg
- Total Carb 28 gm
- Dietary Fiber 9 gm
- Sugars 6 gm
- Protein 21 gm

Katelyn's Black Bean Soup

Katelyn Bailey
Mechanicsburg, PA

Makes 6 servings

Prep. Time: 25 minutes
Cooking Time: 6-8 hours
Ideal slow cooker size: 4-qt.

⅓ cup chopped onions
1 garlic clove, minced
1-2 Tbsp. oil
2 15½-oz. cans black
  beans, undrained
1 cup water
1 tsp. sodium-free chicken
  bouillon powder
½ cup diced, cooked,
  smoked ham
½ cup diced carrots
1 dash cayenne pepper, *or*
  more to taste
1-2 drops Tabasco sauce, *or*
  more to taste
sour cream

1. Sauté onion and garlic in
oil in saucepan.
2. Purée or mash contents
of one can of black beans.
Add to sautéed ingredients.
3. Combine all ingredients
except sour cream in slow
cooker.
4. Cover. Cook on low 6-8
hours.
5. Add dollop of sour
cream to each individual bowl
before serving.

Exchange List Values
- Starch 1.5
- Meat, very lean 1.0

Basic Nutritional Values

- Calories 161
  (Calories from Fat 29)
- Total Fat 3 gm
  (Saturated Fat 0.4 gm,
  Polyunsat Fat 0.9 gm,
  Monounsat Fat 1.6 gm)
- Cholesterol 5 mg
- Sodium 540 mg
- Total Carb 22 gm
- Dietary Fiber 6 gm
- Sugars 3 gm
- Protein 11 gm

Mjeddrah or Esau's Lentil Soup

Dianna Milhizer
Springfield, VA

Makes 12 servings

Prep. Time: 20 minutes
Cooking Time: 6-8 hours
Ideal slow cooker size: 4-qt.

1 cup chopped carrots
1 cup diced celery
2 cups chopped onions
2 Tbsp. olive oil, *or butter, divided*
2 cups brown rice
6 cups water
1 lb. lentils, washed and drained
garden salad
vinaigrette

1. Sauté carrots, celery, and onions in 1 Tbsp. oil in skillet. When soft and translucent place in slow cooker.

2. Separately, brown rice in 1 Tbsp. oil until dry. Add to slow cooker.

3. Stir in water and lentils.

4. Cover. Cook on high 6-8 hours.

5. When thoroughly cooked, serve in individual soup bowls. Cover each with a serving of fresh garden salad (lettuce,

spinach leaves, chopped tomatoes, minced onions, chopped bell peppers, sliced olives, sliced radishes). Pour favorite vinaigrette over all.

Exchange List Values

- Starch 3.0
- Meat, very lean 1.0

Basic Nutritional Values

- Calories 269
  (Calories from Fat 33)
- Total Fat 4 gm
  (Saturated Fat 0.5 gm,
  Polyunsat Fat 0.7 gm,
  Monounsat Fat 2.1 gm)
- Cholesterol 0 mg
- Sodium 21 mg
- Total Carb 48 gm
- Dietary Fiber 10 gm
- Sugars 4 gm
- Protein 12 gm

French Onion Soup

Jenny R. Unternahrer
Wayland, IA

Janice Yoskovich
Carmichaels, PA

Makes 10 servings

Prep. Time: 30 minutes
Cooking Time: 5-7 hours
Ideal slow cooker size: 4-qt.

8-10 large onions, sliced
½ cup light, soft tub margarine
3 14 oz. cans 98% fat-free, lower-sodium beef broth
2½ cups water
3 tsp. sodium-free chicken bouillon powder
1½ tsp. Worcestershire sauce
3 bay leaves
10 (1 oz.) slices French bread, toasted

1. Sauté onions in butter until crisp-tender. Transfer to slow cooker.

2. Add beef broth, water and bouillon powder. Mix well. Add Worcestershire sauce and bay leaves.

3. Cover. Cook on low 5-7 hours, or until onions are tender. Discard bay leaves.

4. Ladle into bowls. Top each with a slice of bread and some cheese.

Exchange List Values

- Starch 1.0
- Vegetable 3.0
- Fat 0.5

Basic Nutritional Values

- Calories 178
  (Calories from Fat 35)
- Total Fat 4 gm
  (Saturated Fat 0.3 gm,
  Polyunsat Fat 0.9 gm,
  Monounsat Fat 2.0 gm)
- Cholesterol 0 mg
- Sodium 476 mg
- Total Carb 31 gm
- Dietary Fiber 4 gm
- Sugars 12 gm
- Protein 6 gm

Note:

For a more intense beef flavor, add one beef bouillon cube, or use home-cooked beef broth instead of canned broth.

Potato Soup

Jeanne Hertzog, Bethlehem, PA
Marcia S. Myer, Manheim, PA
Rhonda Lee Schmidt, Scranton, PA
Mitzi McGlynchey, Downingtown, PA
Vera Schmucker, Goshen, IN
Kaye Schnell, Falmouth, MA
Elizabeth Yoder, Millersburg, OH

Makes 10 servings

Prep. Time: 25 minutes
Cooking Time: 3-12 hours
Ideal slow cooker size: 4-qt.

6 potatoes, peeled and cubed
2 leeks, chopped
2 onions, chopped
1 rib celery, sliced
4 chicken bouillon cubes
1 Tbsp. dried parsley flakes
5 cups water
pepper to taste
3 Tbsp. light, soft tub
   margarine
12-oz. can fat-free
   evaporated milk
chopped chives

1. Combine all ingredients except milk and chives in slow cooker.
2. Cover. Cook on low 10-12 hours, or high 3-4 hours. Stir in milk during last hour.
3. If desired, mash potatoes before serving.
4. Garnish with chives.

Exchange List Values

• Carbohydrate 1.5

Basic Nutritional Values

• Calories 123
   (Calories from Fat 14)
• Total Fat 2 gm
   (Saturated Fat 0.1 gm,
   Polyunsat Fat 0.4 gm,
   Monounsat Fat 0.8 gm)
• Cholesterol 0 mg
• Sodium 447 mg
• Total Carb 23 gm
• Dietary Fiber 2 gm
• Sugars 7 gm
• Protein 5 gm

Variations:

1. Add one carrot, sliced, to vegetables before cooking.
2. Instead of water and bouillon cubes, use 4-5 cups chicken stock.

No-Fuss Potato Soup

Lucille Amos
Greensboro, NC

Lavina Hochstedler
Grand Blanc, MI

Betty Moore
Plano, IL

Makes 10 servings

Prep. Time: 35 minutes
Cooking Time: 7-8 hours
Ideal slow cooker size: 5- or 6-qt.

6 cups diced, peeled
   potatoes
5 cups water
2 cups diced onions
½ cup diced celery
½ cup chopped carrots
¼ cup light, soft tub
   margarine
4 tsp. sodium-free chicken
   bouillon powder
1 tsp. salt
¼ tsp. pepper
12-oz. can fat-free
   evaporated milk
3 Tbsp. chopped fresh
   parsley
8 oz. fat-free cheddar,
   shredded

1. Combine all ingredients except milk, parsley, and cheese in slow cooker.
2. Cover. Cook on high 7-8 hours, or until vegetables are tender.
3. Stir in milk and parsley. Stir in cheese until it melts. Heat thoroughly.

Exchange List Values

• Starch 1.5
• Vegetable 1.0
• Meat, very lean 1.0

Basic Nutritional Values

• Calories 173
   (Calories from Fat 19)
• Total Fat 2 gm
   (Saturated Fat 0.2 gm,
   Polyunsat Fat 0.5 gm,
   Monounsat Fat 1.0 gm)
• Cholesterol 2 mg
• Sodium 493 mg
• Total Carb 27 gm
• Dietary Fiber 2 gm
• Sugars 8 gm
• Protein 12 gm

Variations:

1. For added flavor, stir in 3 slices bacon, browned until crisp, and crumbled.
2. Top individual servings with chopped chives.

Limiting your egg yolk consumption to three per week can help you control cholesterol.

Creamy Potato Soup

Janeen Troyer
Fairview, MI

Makes 8 servings

Prep. Time: 30 minutes
Cooking Time: 3½ hours
Ideal slow cooker size: 4-qt.

3 cups chopped potatoes, peeled *or* unpeeled
1 cup water
½ cup chopped celery
½ cup chopped carrots
¼ cup chopped onion
2 cubes chicken, *or* vegetable, bouillon
1 tsp. parsley
½ tsp. salt
¼ tsp. pepper
1½ cups 1% milk
2 Tbsp. flour
5 oz. shredded 50% reduced-fat cheddar cheese

1. Combine potatoes, water, celery, carrots, onion, bouillon, parsley, salt, and pepper in slow cooker.

2. Cover. Cook on high 3 hours, or until vegetables are tender.

3. In a jar with a tight-fitting lid, add milk to flour. Cover tightly and shake until flour dissolves in milk. When smooth, add mixture to vegetables in cooker. Stir well.

4. Cover. Cook on high another 15-30 minutes, or until soup is thickened and smooth. Stir occasionally to prevent lumps from forming.

5. Add cheese. Stir until melted.

Exchange List Values
- Starch 1.0
- Lean Meat 1.0

Basic Nutritional Values
- Calories 130
- l(Calories from Fat 30)
- Total Fat 4 gm
  (Saturated Fat 2.0 gm,
  Polyunsat Fat 0 gm,
  Monounsat Fat 1.0 gm)
- Cholesterol 10 mg
- Sodium 510 mg
- Total Carb 18 gm
- Dietary Fiber 2 gm
- Sugars 4 gm
- Protein 8 gm

German Potato Soup

Lee Ann Hazlett
Freeport, IL

Makes 8 servings

Prep. Time: 35 minutes
Cooking Time: 4-10 hours
Ideal slow cooker size: 4-qt.

1 onion, chopped
1 leek, trimmed and diced
2 carrots, diced
1 cup chopped cabbage
¼ cup chopped fresh parsley
4 cups 99% fat-free, lower sodium beef broth
1 lb. potatoes, diced
1 bay leaf
1-2 tsp. black pepper
1 tsp. salt, *optional*
½ tsp. caraway seeds, *optional*
¼ tsp. nutmeg
½ lb. bacon, cooked and crumbled
½ cup fat-free sour cream

1. Combine all ingredients except bacon and sour cream.

2. Cover. Cook on low 8-10 hours, or high 4-5 hours.

3. Remove bay leaf. Use a slotted spoon to remove potatoes. Mash potatoes and mix with sour cream. Return to slow cooker. Stir in. Add bacon and mix together thoroughly.

Exchange List Values
- Starch 1.0
- Vegetable 1.0
- Fat 0.5

Basic Nutritional Values
- Calories 130
  (Calories from Fat 37)
- Total Fat 4 gm
  (Saturated Fat 1.3 gm,
  Polyunsat Fat 0.5 gm,
  Monounsat Fat 1.9 gm)
- Cholesterol 8 mg
- Sodium 384 mg
- Total Carb 17 gm
- Dietary Fiber 2 gm
- Sugars 4 gm
- Protein 6 gm

Black-Eyed Pea and Vegetable Chili

Julie Weaver
Reinholds, PA

Makes 6 servings

Prep. Time: 20 minutes
Cooking Time: 4-8 hours
Ideal slow cooker size: 4-qt.

1 cup minced onions
1 cup finely chopped carrots
1 cup finely chopped red *or* green pepper
1 garlic clove, minced
4 tsp. chili powder
1 tsp. ground cumin
2 Tbsp. chopped cilantro
14½-oz. can diced tomatoes
3 cups cooked black-eyed peas
4-oz. can chopped green chilies
¾ cup orange juice
¾ cup water *or* broth
1 Tbsp. cornstarch
2 Tbsp. water
½ cup shredded cheddar cheese
2 Tbsp. chopped cilantro

1. Combine all ingredients except cornstarch, 2 Tbsp. water, cheese, and cilantro.

2. Cover. Cook on low 6-8 hours, or high 4 hours.

3. Dissolve cornstarch in 2 Tbsp. water. Stir into soup mixture 30 minutes before serving.

4. Garnish individual servings with cheese and cilantro.

Exchange List Values
- Starch 1.5
- Fat 0.5
- Vegetable 2.0

Basic Nutritional Values
- Calories 205
  (Calories from Fat 38)
- Total Fat 4 gm
  (Saturated Fat 2.1 gm,
  Polyunsat Fat 0.6 gm,
  Monounsat Fat 1.1 gm)
- Cholesterol 10 mg
- Sodium 317 mg
- Total Carb 33 gm
- Dietary Fiber 9 gm
- Sugars 12 gm
- Protein 11 gm

Note:
Black-eyed peas are also known as crowder peas.

Veggie Chili

Wanda Roth
Napoleon, OH

Makes 6 servings

Prep. Time: 25 minutes
Cooking Time: 3-8 hours
Ideal slow cooker size: 4-qt.

2 qts. no-added-salt diced tomatoes, undrained
6-oz. can tomato paste
½ cup chopped onions
½ cup chopped celery
½ cup chopped green peppers
2 garlic cloves, minced
½ tsp. salt
1½ tsp. ground cumin
1 tsp. dried oregano
¼ tsp. cayenne pepper
3 Tbsp. brown sugar
15-oz. can garbanzo beans

1. Combine all ingredients except beans in slow cooker.

2. Cook on low 6-8 hours, or high 3-4 hours. Add beans one hour before serving.

Exchange List Values
- Starch 1.0
- Vegetable 4.0
- Carbohydrate 0.5

Basic Nutritional Values
- Calories 214
  (Calories from Fat 16)
- Total Fat 2 gm
  (Saturated Fat 0.1 gm,
  Polyunsat Fat 0.8 gm,
  Monounsat Fat 0.4 gm)
- Cholesterol 0 mg
- Sodium 571 mg
- Total Carb 47 gm
- Dietary Fiber 11 gm
- Sugars 22 gm
- Protein 8 gm

Variation:
If you prefer a less tomato-y taste, substitute 2 vegetable bouillon cubes and 1 cup water for tomato paste.

Vegetarian Chili

Connie Johnson
Loudon, NH

Makes 6 servings

Prep. Time: 25 minutes
Cooking Time: 6-8 hours
Ideal slow cooker size: 4-qt.

3 garlic cloves, minced
2 onions, chopped
1 cup textured vegetable protein (T.V.P.)
1-lb. can beans of your choice, drained
1 green bell pepper, chopped
1 jalapeño pepper, seeds removed, chopped
28-oz. can diced Italian tomatoes
1 bay leaf
1 Tbsp. dried oregano
½ tsp. salt
¼ tsp. pepper

1. Combine all ingredients in slow cooker.

2. Cover. Cook on low 6-8 hours.

Exchange List Values
- Starch 1.0
- Meat, very lean 1.0
- Vegetable 2.0

Basic Nutritional Values
- Calories 157
- Cholesterol 0 mg
- (Calories from Fat 6)
- Sodium 518 mg
- Total Fat 1 gm
- Total Carb 28 gm
- (Saturated Fat 0.1 gm,
- Dietary Fiber 9 gm
- Polyunsat Fat 0.3 gm,
- Sugars 11 gm
- Monounsat Fat 0.1 gm)
- Protein 14 gm

Hearty Black Bean Soup

Della Yoder
Kalona, IA

Makes 8 servings

Prep. Time: 30 minutes
Cooking Time: 9-10 hours
Ideal slow cooker size: 4-qt.

3 medium carrots, halved and thinly sliced
2 celery ribs, thinly sliced
1 medium onion, chopped
4 cloves garlic, minced
20-oz. can black beans, drained and rinsed
2 14½-oz. cans 98% fat-free, lower-sodium chicken broth
15-oz. can crushed tomatoes

1½ tsp. dried basil
½ tsp. dried oregano
½ tsp. ground cumin
½ tsp. chili powder
½ tsp. hot pepper sauce

1. Combine all ingredients in slow cooker.

2. Cover. Cook on low 9-10 hours.

Exchange List Values
- Starch 0.5
- Vegetable 2.0

Basic Nutritional Values
- Calories 104
- Cholesterol 0 mg
- (Calories from Fat 4)
- Sodium 481 mg
- Total Fat 0 gm
- Total Carb 19 gm
- (Saturated Fat 0.1 gm,
- Dietary Fiber 6 gm
- Polyunsat Fat 0.2 gm,
- Sugars 7 gm
- Monounsat Fat 0.1 gm)
- Protein 6 gm

Note:
   May be served over cooked rice.

Variation:
   If you prefer a thicker soup, use only 1 can chicken broth.

Black Bean and Corn Soup

Joy Sutter
Iowa City, IA

Makes 8 servings

Prep. Time: 15 minutes
Cooking Time: 5-6 hours
Ideal slow cooker size: 4-qt.

2 15-oz. cans black beans, drained and rinsed
14½-oz. can Mexican stewed tomatoes, undrained
14½-oz. can diced tomatoes, undrained
11-oz. can whole kernel corn, drained
4 green onions, sliced
2 Tbsp. chili powder
1 tsp. ground cumin
½ tsp. dried minced garlic

1. Combine all ingredients in slow cooker.

2. Cover. Cook on high 5-6 hours.

Exchange List Values
- Starch 1.5
- Vegetable 1.0

Basic Nutritional Values
- Calories 134
- Cholesterol 0 mg
- (Calories from Fat 10)
- Sodium 366 mg
- Total Fat 1 gm
- Total Carb 26 gm
- (Saturated Fat 0.1 gm,
- Dietary Fiber 8 gm
- Polyunsat Fat 0.5 gm,
- Sugars 7 gm
- Monounsat Fat 0.2 gm)
- Protein 7 gm

Variations:
   1. Use 2 cloves fresh garlic, minced, instead of dried garlic.
   2. Add 1 large rib celery, sliced thinly, and 1 small green pepper, chopped.

Try going meatless at least one day per week.
Use vegetables and legumes as meat substitutes.

Tuscan Garlicky Bean Soup

Sara Harter Fredette
Williamsburg, MA

Makes 10 servings

Prep. Time: 25 minutes
Standing Time: 1 hour
Cooking Time: 8-10 hours
Ideal slow cooker size: 4-qt.

1 lb. dry Great Northern beans
1 qt. water
1 qt. 99% fat-free, lower-sodium beef broth
3 Tbsp. olive oil
2 garlic cloves, minced
4 Tbsp. chopped parsley olive oil
1¼ tsp. salt
½ tsp. pepper

1. Place beans in large soup pot. Cover with water and bring to boil. Cook 2 minutes. Remove from heat. Cover pot and allow to stand for 1 hour. Drain, discarding water.
2. Combine beans, 1 quart fresh water, and beef broth in slow cooker.
3. Sauté garlic and parsley in olive oil in skillet. Stir into slow cooker. Add salt and pepper.
4. Cover. Cook on low 8-10 hours, or until beans are tender.

Exchange List Values
• Starch 1.5 • Fat 0.5
• Meat, very lean 1.0

Basic Nutritional Values
• Calories 174 • Cholesterol 0 mg
  (Calories from Fat 41) • Sodium 470 mg
• Total Fat 5 gm • Total Carb 24 gm
  (Saturated Fat 0.7 gm, • Dietary Fiber 8 gm
  Polyunsat Fat 0.5 gm, • Sugars 3 gm
  Monounsat Fat 3.0 gm) • Protein 10 gm

Bean Soup

Joyce Cox
Port Angeles, WA

Makes 12 servings

Prep. Time: 15 minutes
Soaking Time: 12 hours or overnight
Cooking Time: 5½-13 hours
Ideal slow cooker size: 4-qt.

1 cup dry Great Northern beans
1 cup dry red beans, *or* pinto beans
4 cups water
28-oz. can diced tomatoes
1 medium onion, chopped
2 Tbsp. vegetable bouillon granules, *or* 4 bouillon cubes
2 garlic cloves, minced
2 tsp. Italian seasoning
9-oz. pkg. frozen green beans, thawed

1. Soak beans in 5 cups water overnight or 12 hours. Drain and rinse soaked beans.
2. Combine all ingredients except green beans in slow cooker.
3. Cover. Cook on high 5½-6½ hours, or on low 11-13 hours.

4. Stir green beans into soup during last 2 hours.

Exchange List Values
• Starch 1.0 • Vegetable 1.0

Basic Nutritional Values
• Calories 114 • Cholesterol 0 mg
  (Calories from Fat 5) • Sodium 435 mg
• Total Fat 1 gm • Total Carb 22 gm
  (Saturated Fat 0.1 gm, • Dietary Fiber 7 gm
  Polyunsat Fat 0.2 gm, • Sugars 5 gm
  Monounsat Fat 0.0 gm) • Protein 7 gm

Green Beans and Sausage Soup

Bernita Boyts
Shawnee Mission, KS

Makes 6 servings

Prep. Time: 20-25 minutes
Cooking Time: 7-10 hours
Ideal slow cooker size: 4- to 5-qt.

⅓ lb. link sausage, sliced, *or* bulk sausage
1 medium onion, chopped
2 carrots, sliced
2 ribs celery, sliced
1 Tbsp. olive oil
5 medium potatoes, cubed
10-oz. pkg. frozen green beans
2 14½-oz. cans fat-free, lower-sodium chicken broth
2 broth cans water
2 Tbsp. chopped fresh parsley, *or* 2 tsp. dried parsley
1-2 Tbsp. chopped fresh oregano, *or* 1-2 tbsp. dried oregano
1 tsp. Italian seasoning
pepper to taste

1. Brown sausage in skillet. Stir frequently for even browning.

2. Remove meat from skillet and place in slow cooker. Reserve drippings.

3. Sauté onion, carrots, and celery in skillet drippings until tender.

4. Place sautéed vegetables in slow cooker, along with all remaining ingredients. Mix together well.

5. Cover. Cook on high 1-2 hours and then on low 6-8 hours.

Variation:

If you like it hot, add ground red pepper or hot sauce just before serving, or offer to individual eaters to add to their own bowls.

Exchange List Values
- Starch 1.5
- Fat 2.0
- Vegetable 2.0

Basic Nutritional Values
- Calories 255
  (Calories from Fat 80)
- Total Fat 9 gm
  (Saturated Fat 2.5 gm,
  Polyunsat Fat 1.5 gm,
  Monounsat Fat 4.5 gm)
- Cholesterol 20 mg
- Sodium 550 mg
- Total Carb 34 gm
- Dietary Fiber 5 gm
- Sugars 6 gm
- Protein 10 gm

Green Bean Soup

Loretta Krahn
Mountain Lake, MN

Makes 6 servings

Prep. Time: 20 minutes
Cooking Time: 4-6 hours
Ideal slow cooker size: 4-qt.

2 cups cubed, extra-lean, lower-sodium ham
1½ qts. water
1 large onion, chopped
2-3 cups chopped green beans
3 large carrots, sliced
2 large potatoes, peeled and cubed
1 Tbsp. parsley
1 Tbsp. summer savory
¼ tsp. pepper
1 cup fat-free half-and-half

1. Combine all ingredients except half-and-half in slow cooker.

2. Cover. Cook on high 4-6 hours.

3. Remove ham bone. Cut off meat and return to slow cooker.

4. Turn to low. Stir in cream or milk. Heat through and serve.

Exchange List Values
- Starch 1.0
- Meat, lean 1.0
- Vegetable 2.0

Basic Nutritional Values
- Calories 170
  (Calories from Fat 15)
- Total Fat 2 gm
  (Saturated Fat 0.6 gm,
  Polyunsat Fat 0.3 gm,
  Monounsat Fat 0.4 gm)
- Cholesterol 24 mg
- Sodium 468 mg
- Total Carb 27 gm
- Dietary Fiber 4 gm
- Sugars 10 gm
- Protein 12 gm

Vegetarian Minestrone Soup

Connie Johnson
Loudon, NH

Makes 8 servings

Prep. Time: 35 minutes
Cooking Time: 6-8 hours
Ideal slow cooker size: 4-qt.

6 cups fat-free, 60%-less sodium, vegetable broth
2 carrots, chopped
2 large onions, chopped
3 ribs celery, chopped
2 garlic cloves, minced
1 small zucchini, cubed
1 handful fresh kale, chopped
½ cup dry barley
15-oz. can chickpeas, *or* white kidney beans, rinsed and drained
1 Tbsp. parsley
½ tsp. dried thyme
1 tsp. dried oregano
28-oz. can crushed Italian tomatoes
¼ tsp. pepper

1. Combine all ingredients except cheese in slow cooker.

2. Cover. Cook on low 6-8 hours, or until vegetables are tender.

Exchange List Values
- Starch 1.5
- Vegetable 4.0

Basic Nutritional Values
- Calories 200
  (Calories from Fat 13)
- Total Fat 1 gm
  (Saturated Fat 0.1 gm,
  Polyunsat Fat 0.6 gm,
  Monounsat Fat 0.3 gm)
- Cholesterol 0 mg
- Sodium 641 mg
- Total Carb 41 gm
- Dietary Fiber 9 gm
- Sugars 12 gm
- Protein 7 gm

Joyce's Minestrone

Joyce Shackelford
Green Bay, Wisconsin

Makes 6 servings

Prep. Time: 30 minutes
Cooking Time: 4-16 hours
Ideal slow cooker size: 4- or 5-qt.

3½ cups 99% fat-free,
  lower-sodium beef broth
28-oz. can crushed
  tomatoes
2 medium carrots, thinly
  sliced
½ cup chopped onion
½ cup chopped celery
2 medium potatoes, thinly
  sliced
1-2 garlic cloves, minced
15-oz. can no-added-
  salt red kidney beans,
  drained
2 oz. thin spaghetti,
  broken into 2-inch pieces
2 Tbsp. parsley flakes
2-3 tsp. dried basil
1-2 tsp. dried oregano
1 bay leaf

1. Combine all ingredients
in slow cooker.
2. Cover. Cook on low
10-16 hours, or on high 4-6
hours.
3. Remove bay leaf. Serve.

Exchange List Values
• Starch 2.0   • Vegetable 2.0

Basic Nutritional Values
• Calories 213   • Cholesterol 0 mg
  (Calories from Fat 7)   • Sodium 655 mg
• Total Fat 1 gm   • Total Carb 42 gm
  (Saturated Fat 0.0 gm, • Dietary Fiber 9 gm
  Polyunsat Fat 0.4 gm,   • Sugars 11 gm
  Monounsat Fat 0.1 gm)   • Protein 10 gm

Grace's Minestrone Soup

Grace Ketcham
Marietta, GA

Makes 8 servings

Prep. Time: 20 minutes
Cooking Time: 8½ hours
Ideal slow cooker size: 4- or 5-qt.

¾ cup raw elbow macaroni
2 qts. 98% fat-free, lower-
  sodium chicken stock
2 large onions, diced
2 carrots, sliced
half a head of cabbage,
  shredded
½ cup celery, diced
1-lb. can no-salt-added
  tomatoes
½ tsp. dried oregano
1 Tbsp. minced parsley
¼ cup each frozen corn,
  peas, and lima beans
¼ tsp. pepper

1. Cook macaroni accord-
ing to package directions. Set
aside.
2. Combine all ingredients
except macaroni in large slow
cooker.
3. Cover. Cook on low 8
hours. Add macaroni during
last 30 minutes of cooking time.

Exchange List Values
• Starch 1.0   • Vegetable 2.0

Basic Nutritional Values
• Calories 112   • Cholesterol 0 mg
  (Calories from Fat 5)   • Sodium 559 mg
• Total Fat 1 gm   • Total Carb 22 gm
  (Saturated Fat 0.0 gm, • Dietary Fiber 4 gm
  Polyunsat Fat 0.3 gm,   • Sugars 8 gm
  Monounsat Fat 0.1 gm)   • Protein 6 gm

Cabbage Soup

Margaret Jarrett
Anderson, IN

Makes 8 servings

Prep. Time: 25 minutes
Cooking Time: 3½-4 hours
Ideal slow cooker size: 4-qt.

---

half a head of cabbage,
  sliced thin
2 ribs celery, sliced thin
2-3 carrots, sliced thin
1 onion, chopped
2 tsp. sodium-free chicken
  bouillon powder
2 garlic cloves, minced
1 qt. tomato juice
¼ tsp. pepper
water

1. Combine all ingredients
except water in slow cooker.
Add water to within 3 inches
of top of slow cooker.
2. Cover. Cook on high
3½-4 hours, or until veg-
etables are tender.

Exchange List Values
• Vegetable 2.0

Basic Nutritional Values
• Calories 55   • Cholesterol 0 mg
  (Calories from Fat 3)   • Sodium 474 mg
• Total Fat 0 gm   • Total Carb 13 gm
  (Saturated Fat 0.0 gm, • Dietary Fiber 3 gm
  Polyunsat Fat 0.1 gm,   • Sugars 8 gm
  Monounsat Fat 0.0 gm)   • Protein 2 gm

Winter Squash and White Bean Stew

Mary E. Herr
Three Rivers, MI

Makes 6 servings

Prep. Time: 30 minutes
Cooking Time: 3-4 hours
Ideal slow cooker size: 4-qt.

1 cup chopped onions
1 Tbsp. olive oil
½ tsp. ground cumin
¼ tsp. cinnamon
1 garlic clove, minced
3 cups peeled, butternut
 squash, cut into ¾-inch
 cubes
1½ cups chicken broth
19-oz. can cannellini
 beans, drained
14½-oz. can diced
 tomatoes, undrained
1 Tbsp. chopped fresh
cilantro

1. Combine all ingredients
in slow cooker.
2. Cover. Cook on high
1 hour. Reduce heat
to low and cook 2-3
hours.

Exchange List Values
- Starch 1.5   • Fat 0.5
- Vegetable 1.0

Basic Nutritional Values
- Calories 164   • Cholesterol 1 mg
 (Calories from Fat 30)   • Sodium 586 mg
- Total Fat 3 gm   • Total Carb 28 gm
 (Saturated Fat 0.5 gm,   • Dietary Fiber 7 gm
 Polyunsat Fat 0.6 gm,   • Sugars 6 gm
 Monounsat Fat 1.9 gm)   • Protein 8 gm

Variations:
 1. Beans can be puréed in
blender and added during the
last hour.
 2. Eight ounces dried beans
can be soaked overnight,
cooked until soft, and used in
place of canned beans.

Broccoli-Cheese Soup

Darla Sathre
Baxter, MN

Makes 8 servings

Prep. Time: 20 minutes
Cooking Time: 8-10 hours
Ideal slow cooker size: 4-qt.

2 16-oz. pkgs. frozen
 chopped broccoli
10¾-oz. can cheddar
 cheese soup
12-oz. can fat-free
 evaporated milk
2½ cups fat-free half-and-
 half
¼ cup finely chopped
 onion
1 Tbsp. Italian seasoning
 (see recipe on page 260)
¼ tsp. pepper
2 oz. fat-free cheddar cheese
sunflower seeds, *optional*
crumbled bacon, *optional*

1. Combine all ingredients
except sunflower seeds and
bacon in slow cooker.
2. Cover. Cook on low 8-10
hours.
3. Garnish with sunflower
seeds and bacon.

Exchange List Values
- Milk, fat-free 1.0   • Fat 0.5
- Vegetable 2.0

Basic Nutritional Values
- Calories 171   • Cholesterol 12 mg
 (Calories from Fat 36)   • Sodium 581 mg
- Total Fat 4 gm   • Total Carb 22 gm
 (Saturated Fat 1.6 gm,   • Dietary Fiber 4 gm
 Polyunsat Fat 0.9 gm,   • Sugars 12 gm
 Monounsat Fat 0.9 gm)   • Protein 12 gm

Cheese and Corn Chowder

Loretta Krahn
Mt. Lake, MN

Makes 8 servings

Prep. Time: 25 minutes
Cooking Time: 5-7 hours
Ideal slow cooker size: 4-qt.

¾ cup water
½ cup chopped onions
1½ cups sliced carrots
1½ cups chopped celery
¼ tsp. salt
½ tsp. pepper
15¼-oz. can whole kernel corn, drained
15-oz. can no-added-salt cream-style corn
1½ cups fat-free milk
1½ cups fat-free half-and-half
1 cup grated fat-free cheddar cheese

1. Combine water, onions, carrots, celery, salt, and pepper in slow cooker.
2. Cover. Cook on high 4-6 hours.
3. Add corn, milk, and cheese. Heat on high 1 hour, and then turn to low until you are ready to eat.

Exchange List Values
• Starch 1.0   • Milk, fat-free 1.0

Basic Nutritional Values
• Calories 168   • Cholesterol 12 mg
  (Calories from Fat 29) • Sodium 391 mg
• Total Fat 3 gm   • Total Carb 26 gm
  (Saturated Fat 1.3 gm, • Dietary Fiber 3 gm
  Polyunsat Fat 0.4 gm,   • Sugars 13 gm
  Monounsat Fat 0.9 gm)   • Protein 11 gm

Corn Chowder

Mary Rogers
Waseca, MN

Makes 12 servings

Prep. Time: 25 minutes
Cooking Time: 5-7 hours
Ideal slow cooker size: 6-qt.

6 oz. bacon
4 cups diced potatoes
2 cups chopped onions
2 cups fat-free sour cream
1½ cups 2% reduced fat milk
1 cup fat-free half-and-half
2 10¾-oz. cans 98% fat-free, lower-sodium cream of chicken soup
2 15¼-oz. cans corn, undrained

1. Cut bacon into 1″ pieces. Cook for 5 minutes in large skillet.
2. Add potatoes and onions and a bit of water. Cook 15-20 minutes, until tender, stirring occasionally. Drain. Transfer to slow cooker.
3. Combine sour cream, milk, chicken soup, and corn. Place in slow cooker.
4. Cover. Cook on low for 2 hours.

Exchange List Values
• Starch 1.0   • Fat 1.0
• Carbohydrate 1.0

Basic Nutritional Values
• Calories 202   • Cholesterol 14 mg
  (Calories from Fat 41) • Sodium 568 mg
• Total Fat 5 gm   • Total Carb 32 gm
  (Saturated Fat 1.5 gm, • Dietary Fiber 3 gm
  Polyunsat Fat 0.9 gm,   • Sugars 13 gm
  Monounsat Fat 1.5 gm)   • Protein 8 gm

Tip:
  Serve with homemade biscuits or a pan of steaming cornbread fresh from the oven.

Vegetables

Very Special Spinach

Jeanette Oberholtzer
Manheim, PA

Makes 8 servings

Prep. Time: 10 minutes
Cooking Time: 5 hours
Ideal slow cooker size: 4-qt.

3 10-oz. boxes frozen
  spinach, thawed and
  drained
2 cups 1% cottage cheese
1½ cups grated fat-free
  cheddar cheese
3 eggs
¼ cup flour
4 Tbsp. (¼ cup) light, soft
  tub margarine, melted

1. Mix together all ingredients.
2. Pour into slow cooker.
3. Cook on high 1 hour. Reduce heat to low and cook 4 more hours.

Exchange List Values
- Starch 0.5
- Vegetable 1.0
- Meat, lean 2.0

Basic Nutritional Values
- Calories 160
  (Calories from Fat 44)
- Total Fat 5 gm
  (Saturated Fat 1.3 gm,
  Polyunsat Fat 0.9 gm,
  Monounsat Fat 2.1 gm)
- Cholesterol 84 mg
- Sodium 520 mg
- Total Carb 11 gm
- Dietary Fiber 3 gm
- Sugars 3 gm
- Protein 19 gm

Eat 3 vegetables and 2 fruits today—fresh or frozen is best.

Caramelized Onions

Mrs. J.E. Barthold
Bethlehem, PA

Makes 8 servings

Prep. Time: 25 minutes
Cooking Time: 12 hours
Ideal slow cooker size: 4-qt.

**6 large Vidalia *or* other
  sweet onions
4 Tbsp. margarine
10-oz. can chicken, *or*
  vegetable, broth**

1. Peel onions. Remove stems and root ends. Place in slow cooker.
2. Pour butter and broth over.
3. Cook on low 12 hours.

Exchange List Values
- Vegetable 3.0   • Fat 1.0

Basic Nutritional Values
- Calories 123   • Cholesterol 1 mg
  (Calories from Fat 57)   • Sodium 325 mg
- Total Fat 6 gm   • Total Carb 15 gm
  (Saturated Fat 1.1 gm,   • Dietary Fiber 3 gm
  Polyunsat Fat 2.0 gm,   • Sugars 11 gm
  Monounsat Fat 2.7 gm)   • Protein 2 gm

Note:
  Serve as a side dish, or use onions and liquid to flavor soups or stews, or as topping for pizza.

Orange Glazed Carrots

Cyndie Marrara
Port Matilda, PA

Makes 8 servings

Prep. Time: 10 minutes
Cooking Time: 3-4 hours
Ideal slow cooker size: 4-qt.

**32-oz. (2 lbs.) pkg. baby
  carrots
3 Tbsp. brown sugar
brown sugar substitute to
  equal 2 Tbsp. sugar
½ cup orange juice
2 Tbsp. margarine
¾ tsp. cinnamon
¼ tsp. nutmeg
2 Tbsp. cornstarch
¼ cup water**

1. Combine all ingredients except cornstarch and water in slow cooker.
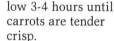
2. Cover. Cook on low 3-4 hours until carrots are tender crisp.
3. Put carrots in serving dish and keep warm, reserving cooking juices. Put reserved juices in small saucepan. Bring to boil.
4. Mix cornstarch and water in small bowl until blended. Add to juices. Boil one minute or until thickened, stirring constantly.
5. Pour over carrots and serve.

Exchange List Values
- Carbohydrate 0.5   • Fat 0.5
- Vegetable 2.0

Basic Nutritional Values
- Calories 108   • Cholesterol 0 mg
  (Calories from Fat 29)   • Sodium 115 mg
- Total Fat 3 gm   • Total Carb 20 gm
  (Saturated Fat 0.6 gm,   • Dietary Fiber 4 gm
  Polyunsat Fat 1.0 gm,   • Sugars 12 gm
  Monounsat Fat 1.3 gm)   • Protein 1 gm

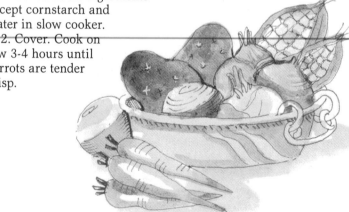

Eat plenty of green leafy vegetables; red, orange, and yellow fruits and vegetables; citrus fruits; nuts and seeds; and meat and fish. They are good for your heart and help prevent cancer.

Barbecued Green Beans

Arlene Wengerd
Millersburg, OH

Makes 6 servings

Prep. Time: 20 minutes
Cooking Time: 3-8 hours
Ideal slow cooker size: 3- or 4-qt.

4 slices bacon
¼ cup chopped onions
cooking spray
½ cup ketchup
2 Tbsp. brown sugar
brown sugar substitute to equal 2 Tbsp. sugar
3 tsp. Worcestershire sauce
⅛ tsp. salt
4 cups green beans

1. Brown bacon in skillet until crisp and then break into pieces.
2. Sauté onions in non-fat cooking spray.
3. Combine ketchup, brown sugar, Worcestershire sauce, and salt. Stir into bacon and onions.
4. Pour mixture over green beans and mix lightly.
5. Pour into slow cooker and cook on high 3-4 hours, or on low 6-8 hours.

Exchange List Values
• Carbohydrate 0.5   • Fat 0.5
• Vegetable 2.0

Basic Nutritional Values
• Calories 98
(Calories from Fat 22)
• Total Fat 2 gm
(Saturated Fat 0.7 gm,
Polyunsat Fat 0.3 gm,
Monounsat Fat 0.9 gm)
• Cholesterol 3 mg
• Sodium 386 mg
• Total Carb 18 gm
• Dietary Fiber 3 gm
• Sugars 9 gm
• Protein 3 gm

Dutch Green Beans

Edwina Stoltzfus
Narvon, PA

Makes 12 servings

Prep. Time: 20 minutes
Cooking Time: 4½ hours
Ideal slow cooker size: 4- or 5-qt.

6 slices bacon
4 medium onions, sliced
2 Tbsp. canola oil
2 qts. fresh, frozen, *or* canned, green beans
4 cups diced, fresh tomatoes
½ tsp. salt
¼ tsp. pepper

1. Brown bacon until crisp in skillet. Drain. Crumble bacon into small pieces.
2. Sauté onions in canola oil.
3. Combine all ingredients in slow cooker.
4. Cover. Cook on low 4½ hours.

Exchange List Values
• Vegetable 3.0   • Fat 0.5

Basic Nutritional Values
• Calories 99
(Calories from Fat 39)
• Total Fat 4 gm
(Saturated Fat 0.7 gm,
Polyunsat Fat 1.1 gm,
Monounsat Fat 2.1 gm)
• Cholesterol 3 mg
• Sodium 154 mg
• Total Carb 14 gm
• Dietary Fiber 4 gm
• Sugars 6 gm
• Protein 4 gm

Easy Flavor-Filled Green Beans

Paula Showalter
Weyers Cave, VA

Makes 10 servings

Prep. Time: 15 minutes
Cooking Time: 3-4 hours
Ideal slow cooker size: 4- or 5-qt.

2 qts. canned green beans, drained
⅓ cup chopped onions
4-oz. can mushrooms, drained
1 Tbsp. brown sugar
brown sugar substitute to equal 1½ tsp. sugar
3 Tbsp. light, soft tub margarine
pepper to taste

1. Combine beans, onions, and mushrooms in slow cooker.
2. Sprinkle with brown sugar.
3. Dot with margarine.
4. Sprinkle with pepper.
5. Cover. Cook on high 3-4 hours. Stir just before serving.

Exchange List Values
• Vegetable 2.0

Basic Nutritional Values
• Calories 47
(Calories from Fat 14)
• Total Fat 2 gm
(Saturated Fat 0.0 gm,
Polyunsat Fat 0.4 gm,
Monounsat Fat 0.8 gm)
• Cholesterol 0 mg
• Sodium 339 mg
• Total Carb 7 gm
• Dietary Fiber 3 gm
• Sugars 4 gm
• Protein 2 gm

Green Bean Casserole

Vicki Dinkel
Sharon Springs, KS

Makes 11 servings

Prep. Time: 15 minutes
Cooking Time: 3-10 hours
Ideal slow cooker size: 3- or 4-qt.

3 10-oz. pkgs. frozen, cut
　green beans
1½ 10½-oz. cans cheddar
　cheese soup
½ cup water
¼ cup chopped green
　onions
4-oz. can sliced
　mushrooms, drained
8-oz. can water chestnuts,
　drained and sliced,
　optional
½ cup slivered almonds
¼ tsp. pepper

1. Combine all ingredients
in lightly greased slow cooker.
Mix well.
2. Cover. Cook on low 8-10
hours or on high 3-4 hours.

Exchange List Values
• Carbohydrate 0.5 　• Fat 1.0
• Vegetable 1.0

Basic Nutritional Values
• Calories 102
　(Calories from Fat 51)
• Total Fat 6 gm
　(Saturated Fat 1.4 gm,
　Polyunsat Fat 1.6 gm,
　Monounsat Fat 2.6 gm)
• Cholesterol 7 mg
• Sodium 407 mg
• Total Carb 10 gm
• Dietary Fiber 3 gm
• Sugars 3 gm
• Protein 4 gm

Stewed Tomatoes

Michelle Showalter
Bridgewater, VA

Makes 12 servings

Prep. Time: 10 minutes
Cooking Time: 3-4 hours
Ideal slow cooker size: 4-qt.

2 qts. canned tomatoes
2½ Tbsp. sugar
sugar substitute to equal
　1½ Tbsp. sugar
½ tsp. salt
dash of pepper
1½ Tbsp. light, soft tub
　margarine
2 cups bread cubes

1. Place tomatoes in slow
cooker.
2. Sprinkle with sugar, salt,
and pepper.
3. Lightly toast bread cubes
in melted butter. Spread over
tomatoes.
4. Cover. Cook on high 3-4
hours.

Exchange List Values
• Vegetable 2.0

Basic Nutritional Values
• Calories 62
　(Calories from Fat 9)
• Total Fat 1 gm
　(Saturated Fat 0.0 gm,
　Polyunsat Fat 0.4 gm,
　Monounsat Fat 0.4 gm)
• Cholesterol 0 mg
• Sodium 377 mg
• Total Carb 13 gm
• Dietary Fiber 2 gm
• Sugars 7 gm
• Protein 2 gm

Variation:
If you prefer bread that is
less moist and soft, add bread
cubes 15 minutes before
serving and continue cooking
without lid.

Glazed Tzimmes

Elaine Vigoda
Rochester, NY

Makes 8 servings

Prep. Time: 40 minutes
Cooking Time: 10 hours
Ideal slow cooker size: 6-qt.

1 sweet potato
6 carrots, sliced
1 potato, peeled and diced
1 onion, chopped
2 apples, peeled and sliced
1 medium (about 1½ lbs.)
　butternut squash, peeled
　and sliced
¼ cup dry white wine *or*
　apple juice
½ lb. dried apricots
1 Tbsp. ground cinnamon
1 Tbsp. apple pie spice
1 Tbsp. maple syrup *or*
　honey
1 tsp. salt
1 tsp. ground ginger

1. Combine all ingredients
in large slow cooker, or mix
all ingredients in large bowl
and place in slow cooker.
2. Cover. Cook on low 10
hours.

Exchange List Values
• Starch 1.0 　　• Vegetable 1.0
• Fruit 1.5

Basic Nutritional Values
• Calories 179
　(Calories from Fat 5)
• Total Fat 1 gm
　(Saturated Fat 0.1 gm,
　Polyunsat Fat 0.2 gm,
　Monounsat Fat 0.1 gm)
• Cholesterol 0 mg
• Sodium 332 mg
• Total Carb 45 gm
• Dietary Fiber 6 gm
• Sugars 27 gm
• Protein 3 gm

Note:

This is a special dish served primarily on Jewish holidays, such as Rosh Hashana and Passover. The sweetness of the vegetables and fruit signifies wishes for a sweet year.

Vegetable Medley

Teena Wagner
Waterloo, ON

Makes 8 servings

Prep. Time: 20 minutes
Cooking Time: 2-3 hours
Ideal slow cooker size: 4-qt.

2 medium parsnips
4 medium carrots
1 turnip, about 4½ inches diameter
½ cup water
1 tsp. salt
3 Tbsp. sugar
2 Tbsp. canola *or* olive oil
½ tsp. salt

1. Clean and peel vegetables. Cut in 1-inch pieces.
2. Dissolve salt in water in saucepan. Add vegetables and boil for 10 minutes. Drain, reserving ½ cup liquid.
3. Place vegetables in slow cooker. Add liquid.
4. Stir in sugar, oil, and salt.
5. Cover. Cook on low 2-3 hours.
6. Remove vegetables from juice in pot to serve.

Janie's Vegetable Medley

Janie Steele, Moore, OK

Makes 8 servings

Prep Time: 25-30 minutes
Cooking Time: 1-1¼ hours
Ideal slow-cooker size: 4 qt.

large potato, peeled and cut into small cubes
2 onions, chopped
2 carrots, sliced thin
¾ cup uncooked long-grain rice
2 Tbsp. lemon juice
¼ cup olive oil
2 1-lb. cans diced tomatoes, *divided*
1 cup water, *divided*
large green pepper, chopped
2 zucchini, chopped
2 Tbsp. parsley, chopped
half a 1-lb. pkg. frozen green peas
¾ tsp. salt
1 cup cheese, grated
hot sauce, *optional*

Exchange List Values
• Starch 1.0

Basic Nutritional Values
• Calories 63 (Calories from Fat 17)
• Total Fat 2 gm (Saturated Fat 0.1 gm, Polyunsat 0.6 gm, Monounsat Fat 1.0 gm)
• Cholesterol 0 mg
• Sodium 327 mg
• Total Carb 12 gm
• Dietary Fiber 2 gm
• Sugars 6 gm
• Protein 1 gm

1. Combine cubed potato, chopped onions, sliced carrots, uncooked rice, lemon juice, olive oil, 1 can of tomatoes, and ½ cup water in slow-cooker.
2. Cover and cook on high 1 hour.
3. Stir in remaining ingredients—except grated cheese and hot sauce. Cover and cook 30-60 minutes, or until vegetables are tender but not mushy.
4. Serve in bowls, topped with grated cheese. Pass hot sauce to be added individually.

Exchange List Values
• Starch 1.5
• Vegetable 2.0
• Fat 2.0

Basic Nutritional Values
• Calories 260 (Calories from Fat 90)
• Total Fat 10 gm (Saturated Fat 2.5 gm, Polyunsat 1.0 gm, Monounsat Fat 6.0 gm)
• Cholesterol 5 mg
• Sodium 580 mg
• Total Carb 36 gm
• Dietary Fiber 5 gm
• Sugars 9 gm
• Protein 9 gm

If you tend to eat quickly, try using chopsticks to slow down and avoid overeating.

Easy Olive Bake

Jean Robinson
Cinnaminson, NJ

Makes 8 servings

Prep. Time: 20 minutes
Cooking Time: 3 hours
Ideal slow cooker size: 4-qt.

1 cup uncooked rice
2 medium onions, chopped
2 Tbsp. light soft tub
  margarine, melted
2 cups stewed tomatoes
2 cups water
1 cup black olives,
  quartered
½ tsp. chili powder
1 Tbsp. Worcestershire
  sauce
4-oz. can mushrooms
  with juice
½ cup grated fat-free
  cheese

1. Wash and drain rice.
Place in slow cooker.
2. Add remaining ingredi-
ents except cheese. Mix well.
3. Cover. Cook on high 1
hour, then on low 2 hours,
or until rice is tender but not
mushy.
4. Add cheese before
serving.

Exchange List Values
• Starch 1.0   • Fat 0.5
• Vegetable 2.0

Basic Nutritional Values
• Calories 163   • Cholesterol 1 mg
  (Calories from Fat 28) • Sodium 492 mg
• Total Fat 3 gm   • Total Carb 29 gm
  (Saturated Fat 0.2 gm, • Dietary Fiber 2 gm
  Polyunsat Fat 0.5 gm, • Sugars 5 gm
  Monounsat Fat 1.9 gm) • Protein 6 gm

Tip:
This is a good accompani-
ment to baked ham.

Zucchini Special

Louise Stackhouse
Benten, PA

Makes 8 servings

Prep. Time: 25 minutes
Cooking Time: 6-8 hours
Ideal slow cooker size: 4-qt.

1 medium to large zucchini,
  peeled and sliced
1 medium onion, sliced
1 qt. stewed, no-added-salt
  tomatoes with juice, *or*
  2 14-oz. cans stewed,
  no-added-salt tomatoes
  with juice
½ tsp. salt
1 tsp. dried basil
4 oz. (1 cup) reduced-fat
  mozzarella cheese,
  shredded

1. Layer zucchini, onion,
and tomatoes in slow cooker.
2. Sprinkle with salt, basil,
and cheese.
3. Cover. Cook on low 6-8
hours.

Exchange List Values
• Vegetable 2.0   • Fat 0.5

Basic Nutritional Values
• Calories 79   • Cholesterol 8 mg
  (Calories from Fat 21) • Sodium 273 mg
• Total Fat 2 gm   • Total Carb 11 gm
  (Saturated Fat 1.3 gm, • Dietary Fiber 2 gm
  Polyunsat Fat 0.3 gm, • Sugars 5 gm
  Monounsat Fat 0.4 gm) • Protein 6 gm

Squash Casserole

Sharon Anders
Alburtis, PA

Makes 9 servings

Prep. Time: 25 minutes
Cooking Time: 7-9 hours
Ideal slow cooker size: 4-qt.

2 lbs. yellow summer
  squash *or* zucchini,
  thinly sliced (about 6
  cups)
half a medium onion,
  chopped
1 cup peeled, shredded
  carrot
10¾-oz. can 98% fat-
  free, lower-sodium,
  condensed cream of
  chicken soup
½ cup fat-free sour cream
2 Tbsp. flour
4-oz. (½ of 8 oz. pkg.)
  seasoned stuffing
  crumbs
2 Tbsp. canola oil

1. Combine squash, onion,
carrots, and soup.
2. Mix together sour cream
and flour. Stir into vegetables.
3. Toss stuffing mix with
butter. Spread half in bottom
of slow cooker. Add vegetable
mixture. Top with remaining
crumbs.
4. Cover. Cook on low 7-9
hours.

Exchange List Values
• Starch 1.0   • Fat 1.0
• Vegetable 1.0

Basic Nutritional Values

- Calories 140
  (Calories from Fat 38)
- Total Fat 4 gm
  (Saturated Fat 0.5 gm,
  Polyunsat Fat 1.4 gm,
  Monounsat Fat 2.1 gm)
- Cholesterol 4 mg
- Sodium 486 mg
- Total Carb 21 gm
- Dietary Fiber 3 gm
- Sugars 5 gm
- Protein 4 gm

Squash Medley

Evelyn Page
Riverton, WY

Makes 8 servings

Prep. Time: 25 minutes
Cooking Time: 4-6 hours
Ideal slow cooker size: 4-qt.

8 (up to 8 oz. total)
  summer squash, each
  about 4" long, thinly
  sliced
½ tsp. salt
2 tomatoes, peeled and
  chopped
¼ cup sliced green onions
half a small green bell
  pepper, chopped
1 chicken bouillon cube
¼ cup hot water
4 slices bacon, fried and
  crumbled
¼ cup fine dry bread
  crumbs

1. Sprinkle squash with
salt.

2. In slow cooker, layer
half the squash, tomatoes,
onions, and pepper. Repeat
layers.

3. Dissolve bouillon in hot
water. Pour into slow cooker.

4. Top with bacon. Sprinkle
bread crumbs over top.

5. Cover. Cook on low 4-6
hours.

Exchange List Values

- Vegetable 1.0
- Fat 0.5

Basic Nutritional Values

- Calories 47
  (Calories from Fat 17)
- Total Fat 2 gm
  (Saturated Fat 0.5 gm,
  Polyunsat Fat 0.3 gm,
  Monounsat Fat 0.8 gm)
- Cholesterol 3 mg
- Sodium 339 mg
- Total Carb 6 gm
- Dietary Fiber 1 gm
- Sugars 2 gm
- Protein 2 gm

Select a mix of colorful vegetables each day.
Different colored vegetables provide different
nutrients.

Baked Acorn Squash

Dale Peterson
Rapid City, SD

Makes 4 servings

Prep. Time: 25 minutes
Cooking Time: 5-6 hours
Ideal slow cooker size: 3- or 4-qt.

2 small (1¼ lb. each) acorn
  squash
½ cup cracker crumbs
¼ cup coarsely chopped
  pecans
2 Tbsp. light, soft tub
  margarine, melted
2 Tbsp. brown sugar
brown sugar substitute to
  equal 1 Tbsp. sugar
¼ tsp. salt
¼ tsp. ground nutmeg
2 Tbsp. orange juice

1. Cut squash in half.
Remove seeds.

2. Combine remaining
ingredients. Spoon into
squash halves. Place squash
in slow cooker.

3. Cover. Cook on low
5-6 hours, or until squash is
tender.

Exchange List Values

- Starch 2.0
- Carbohydrate 0.5
- Fat 1.0

Basic Nutritional Values

- Calories 229
  (Calories from Fat 82)
- Total Fat 9 gm
  (Saturated Fat 0.8 gm,
  Polyunsat Fat 2.3 gm,
  Monounsat Fat 5.1 gm)
- Cholesterol 0 mg
- Sodium 314 mg
- Total Carb 38 gm
- Dietary Fiber 8 gm
- Sugars 15 gm
- Protein 3 gm

Apple Walnut Squash

Michele Ruvola
Selden, NY

Makes 4 servings

Prep. Time: 25 minutes
Cooking Time: 3-4 hours
Ideal slow cooker size: 3- or 4-qt.

¼ cup water
2 small (1¼ lb. each) acorn
    squash
2 Tbsp. brown sugar
brown sugar substitute to
    equal 1 Tbsp. sugar
2 Tbsp. light, soft tub
    margarine
3 Tbsp. apple juice
1½ tsp. ground cinnamon
¼ tsp. salt
1 cup toasted walnuts halves
1 medium apple, unpeeled,
    chopped

1. Pour water into slow cooker.
2. Cut squash crosswise in half. Remove seeds. Place in slow cooker, cut sides up.
3. Combine brown sugar, butter, apple juice, cinnamon, and salt. Spoon into squash.
4. Cover. Cook on high 3-4 hours, or until squash is tender.
5. Combine walnuts and chopped apple. Add to center of squash and mix with sauce to serve.

Exchange List Values
• Starch 1.5   • Fat 1.5
• Fruit 1.0

Basic Nutritional Values
• Calories 244   • Cholesterol 0 mg
  (Calories from Fat 96)   • Sodium 202 mg
• Total Fat 11 gm   • Total Carb 39 gm
  (Saturated Fat 0.8 gm,   • Dietary Fiber 9 gm
  Polyunsat Fat 6.5 gm,   • Sugars 19 gm
  Monounsat Fat 2.4 gm)   • Protein 4 gm

Tip:
Goes well with a pork dish.

Stuffed Acorn Squash

Jean Butzer
Batavia, NY

Makes 6 servings

Prep. Time: 25 minutes
Cooking Time: 2½ hours
Ideal slow cooker size: 4-qt.

3 small (1¼ lb. each) acorn
    squash
5 Tbsp. instant brown rice
3 Tbsp. dried cranberries
3 Tbsp. diced celery
3 Tbsp. minced onion
pinch of ground sage
1 tsp. butter, *divided*
3 Tbsp. orange juice
½ cup water

1. Slice off points on the bottoms of squash so they will stand in slow cooker. Slice off tops and discard. Scoop out seeds. Place squash in slow cooker.
2. Combine rice, cranberries, celery, onion, and sage. Stuff into squash.
3. Dot with butter.
4. Pour 1 Tbsp. orange juice into each squash.
5. Pour water into bottom of slow cooker.
6. Cover. Cook on low 2½ hours.

Tip:
Serve with cooked turkey breast.

Exchange List Values
• Starch 2.0

Basic Nutritional Values
• Calories 131   • Cholesterol 2 mg
  (Calories from Fat 10)   • Sodium 18 mg
• Total Fat 1 gm   • Total Carb 31 gm
  (Saturated Fat 0.4 gm,   • Dietary Fiber 7 gm
  Polyunsat Fat 0.2 gm,   • Sugars 11 gm
  Monounsat Fat 0.3 gm)   • Protein 2 gm

Note:
To make squash easier to slice, microwave whole squash on high for 5 minutes to soften skin.

Caponata

Katrine Rose
Woodbridge, VA

Makes 10 servings

Prep. Time: 20 minutes
Cooking Time: 7-8 hours
Ideal slow cooker size: 4-qt.

1 medium (1 lb.) eggplant,
    peeled and cut into ½"
    cubes
14-oz. can diced tomatoes
1 medium onion, chopped
1 red bell pepper, cut into
    ½" pieces
¾ cup salsa

¼ cup olive oil
2 Tbsp. capers, drained
3 Tbsp. balsamic vinegar
3 garlic cloves, minced
1¼ tsp. dried oregano
⅓ cup, packed, chopped
  fresh basil

1. Combine all ingredients except basil and bread in slow cooker.
2. Cover. Cook on low 7-8 hours, or until vegetables are tender.
3. Stir in basil. Serve on toasted French bread.

Exchange List Values
• Vegetable 2.0   • Fat 1.0

Basic Nutritional Values
• Calories 84   • Cholesterol 0 mg
  (Calories from Fat 51) • Sodium 182 mg
• Total Fat 6 gm   • Total Carb 9 gm
  (Saturated Fat 0.7 gm,   • Dietary Fiber 2 gm
  Polyunsat Fat 0.6 gm,   • Sugars 5 gm
  Monounsat Fat 4.0 gm) • Protein 1 gm

Julia's Broccoli and Cauliflower with Cheese
Julia Lapp
New Holland, PA

Makes 6 servings

Prep. Time: 25 minutes
Cooking Time: 1½ hours
Ideal slow cooker size: 4-qt.

5 cups chopped broccoli
  and cauliflower
¼ cup water

2 Tbsp. margarine
2 Tbsp. flour
½ tsp. salt
1 cup fat-free milk
1 cup fat-free shredded
  cheddar cheese

1. Cook broccoli and cauliflower in saucepan in water, until just crisp-tender. Set aside.
2. Make white sauce by melting the margarine in another pan over low heat. Blend in flour and salt. Add milk all at once. Cook quickly, stirring constantly until mixture thickens and bubbles. Add cheese. Stir until melted and smooth.
3. Combine vegetables and sauce in slow cooker. Mix well.
4. Cook on low 1½ hours.

Exchange List Values
• Carbohydrate 0.5   • Meat, lean 1.0
• Vegetable 1.0

Basic Nutritional Values
• Calories 108   • Cholesterol 3 mg
  (Calories from Fat 37) • Sodium 412 mg
• Total Fat 4 gm   • Total Carb 9 gm
  (Saturated Fat 0.8 gm,   • Dietary Fiber 2 gm
  Polyunsat Fat 1.3 gm,   • Sugars 5 gm
  Monounsat Fat 1.7 gm) • Protein 10 gm

Variation:
Substitute green beans and carrots or other vegetables for broccoli and cauliflower.

Golden Cauliflower
Carol Peachey
Lancaster, PA

Makes 6 servings

Prep. Time: 15 minutes
Cooking Time: 4-5 hours
Ideal slow cooker size: 4-qt.

2 10-oz. pkgs. frozen
  cauliflower, thawed
2 Tbsp. light soft tub
  margarine, melted
1 Tbsp. flour
1 cup evaporated fat-free
  milk
1 oz. (¼ cup) fat-free
  cheddar cheese
2 Tbsp. 1% fat cottage
  cheese
2 tsp. Parmesan cheese
4 slices bacon, crisply
  browned and crumbled

1. Place cauliflower in slow cooker
2. Melt margarine on stove. Add flour and evaporated milk. Heat till thickened. Add cheeses.
3. Pour sauce over cauliflower. Top with bacon.
3. Cover. Cook on high 1½ hours and then reduce to low for an additional 2 hours. Or cook only on low 4-5 hours.

Exchange List Values
• Carbohydrate 0.5   • Meat, lean 1.0

Basic Nutritional Values
• Calories 106   • Cholesterol 5 mg
  (Calories from Fat 37) • Sodium 228 mg
• Total Fat 4 gm   • Total Carb 10 gm
  (Saturated Fat 0.8 gm,   • Dietary Fiber 2 gm
  Polyunsat Fat 0.6 gm,   • Sugars 6 gm
  Monounsat Fat 1.9 gm) • Protein 8 gm

Quick Broccoli Fix

Willard E. Roth
Elkhart, IN

Makes 6 servings

Prep. Time: 20 minutes
Cooking Time: 5-6 hours
Ideal slow cooker size: 4-qt.

1 lb. fresh *or* frozen
   broccoli, cut up
10¾-oz. can 98% fat-free,
   reduced-sodium cream
   of mushroom soup
¼ cup fat-free mayonnaise
½ cup fat-free plain yogurt
½ lb. sliced fresh
   mushrooms
1 cup shredded fat-free
   cheddar cheese, *divided*
1 cup crushed saltine
   crackers with unsalted
   tops
sliced almonds, *optional*

1. Microwave broccoli for
3 minutes. Place in greased
slow cooker.

2. Combine soup, mayon-
naise, yogurt, mushrooms,
and ½ cup cheese. Pour over
broccoli.

3. Cover. Cook on low 5-6
hours.

4. Top with remaining
cheese and crackers for last
half hour of cooking time.

5. Top with sliced almonds,
for a special touch, before
serving.

Exchange List Values
• Carbohydrate 1.0 • Meat, lean 1.0
• Vegetable 1.0

Basic Nutritional Values
• Calories 158   • Cholesterol 3 mg
  (Calories from Fat 28) • Sodium 523 mg
• Total Fat 3 gm   • Total Carb 22 gm
  (Saturated Fat 0.4 gm, • Dietary Fiber 3 gm
  Polyunsat 0.8 gm,   • Sugars 5 gm
  Monounsat Fat 1.0 gm) • Protein 12 gm

Broccoli and Rice Casserole

Deborah Swartz
Grottoes, VA

Makes 6 servings

Prep. Time: 20 minutes
Cooking Time: 3-4 hours
Ideal slow cooker size: 4-qt.

1 lb. chopped broccoli,
   fresh *or* frozen, thawed
1 medium onion, chopped
1 Tbsp. canola oil
1 cup minute rice, *or* 1½
   cups cooked rice
10¾-oz. can 98% fat-
   free, reduced-sodium
   cream of chicken *or*
   mushroom soup
¼ cup fat-free milk
1⅓ cups fat-free
   cheddar cheese,
   shredded

1. Cook broccoli
for 5 minutes in
saucepan in boiling
water. Drain and set
aside.

2. Sauté onion in butter in
saucepan until tender. Add to
broccoli.

3. Combine remaining
ingredients. Add to broccoli
mixture. Pour into greased
slow cooker.

4. Cover. Cook on low 3-4
hours.

Exchange List Values
• Starch 1.5   • Meat, lean 1.0
• Vegetable 1.0

Basic Nutritional Values
• Calories 188   • Cholesterol 7 mg
  (Calories from Fat 33) • Sodium 404 mg
• Total Fat 4 gm   • Total Carb 26 gm
  (Saturated Fat 0.5 gm, • Dietary Fiber 3 gm
  Polyunsat Fat 1.2 gm, • Sugars 5 gm
  Monounsat Fat 1.6 gm) • Protein 13 gm

*Low-sodium, low-fat vegetable soups can be
cooked down until thickened and used as a sauce.*

Sweet-Sour Cabbage

Irma H. Schoen
Windsor, CT

Makes 6 servings

Prep. Time: 35 minutes
Cooking Time: 3-5 hours
Ideal slow cooker size: 4-qt.

1 medium-sized head
   red *or* green cabbage,
   shredded
2 medium onions, chopped
4 medium tart apples,
   pared, quartered
½ cup raisins
¼ cup lemon juice
¼ cup cider, *or* apple juice
1 Tbsp. honey
1 Tbsp. caraway seeds
⅛ tsp. allspice
½ tsp. salt

1. Combine all ingredients
in slow cooker.
2. Cook on high 3-5 hours,
depending upon how crunchy
or soft you want the cabbage
and onions.

Exchange List Values
• Fruit 1.0   • Vegetable 2.0

Basic Nutritional Values
• Calories 112   • Cholesterol 0 mg
(Calories from Fat 6)   • Sodium 154 mg
• Total Fat 1 gm   • Total Carb 27 gm
(Saturated Fat 0.0 gm,   • Dietary Fiber 5 gm
Polyunsat Fat 0.3 gm,   • Sugars 21 gm
Monounsat Fat 0.1 gm)   • Protein 3 gm

Bavarian Cabbage

Joyce Shackelford
Green Bay, WI

Makes 8 servings

Prep. Time: 30 minutes
Cooking Time: 3-8 hours
Ideal slow cooker size: 4-qt.

1 small (1½ lb.) head red
   cabbage, sliced
1 medium onion, chopped
3 medium tart apples,
   unpeeled, cored and
   quartered
1 tsp. salt
1 cup hot water
1 Tbsp. sugar
sugar substitute to equal
   ½ Tbsp. sugar
⅓ cup vinegar
1½ Tbsp. bacon drippings

1. Place all ingredients in
slow cooker in order listed.
2. Cover. Cook on low 8
hours, or high 3 hours. Stir
well before serving.

Exchange List Values
• Fruit 0.5   • Fat 0.5
• Vegetable 1.0

Basic Nutritional Values
• Calories 85   • Cholesterol 2 mg
(Calories from Fat 24)   • Sodium 313 mg
• Total Fat 3 gm   • Total Carb 16 gm
(Saturated Fat 1.1 gm,   • Dietary Fiber 3 gm
Polyunsat Fat 0.3 gm,   • Sugars 12 gm
Monounsat Fat 1.0 gm)   • Protein 1 gm

Variation:
Add 6 slices bacon, browned
until crisp and crumbled.

Jean M. Butzer
Batavia, NY

Cabbage Casserole

Edwina Stoltzfus
Narvon, PA

Makes 6 servings

Prep. Time: 40 minutes
Cooking Time: 4-5 hours
Ideal slow cooker size: 4-qt.

1 large head cabbage,
   chopped
2 cups water
3 Tbsp. margarine
¼ cup flour
¼ tsp. salt
¼ tsp. pepper
1⅓ cups fat-free milk
1⅓ cups fat-free shredded
   cheddar

1. Cook cabbage in saucepan
in boiling water for 5 minutes.
Drain. Place in slow cooker.
2. In saucepan, melt margarine. Stir in flour, salt, and
pepper. Add milk, stirring
constantly on low heat for 5
minutes. Remove from heat. Stir
in cheese. Pour over cabbage.
3. Cover. Cook on low 4-5
hours.

Exchange List Values
• Carbohydrate 0.5   • Meat, lean 1.0
• Vegetable 2.0   • Fat 0.5

Basic Nutritional Values
• Calories 179   • Cholesterol 4 mg
(Calories from Fat 57)   • Sodium 400 mg
• Total Fat 6 gm   • Total Carb 19 gm
(Saturated Fat 1.1 gm,   • Dietary Fiber 5 gm
Polyunsat Fat 2.1 gm,   • Sugars 10 gm
Monounsat Fat 2.6 gm)   • Protein 13 gm

Variation:
Replace cabbage with
cauliflower.

199

Vegetable Curry

Sheryl Shenk
Harrisonburg, VA

Makes 10 servings

Prep. Time: 25 minutes
Cooking Time: 3-10 hours
Ideal slow cooker size: 4- or 5-qt.

16-oz. pkg. baby carrots
3 medium potatoes,
   unpeeled, cubed
1 lb. fresh *or* frozen green
   beans, cut in 2-inch
   pieces
1 medium green pepper,
   chopped
1 medium onion, chopped
1-2 cloves garlic, minced
15-oz. can garbanzo beans,
   drained
28-oz. can crushed
   tomatoes
3 Tbsp. minute tapioca
3 tsp. curry powder
1¾ cups boiling water
1½ tsp. chicken bouillon
   granules

1. Combine carrots, potatoes, green beans, pepper, onion, garlic, garbanzo beans, and crushed tomatoes in large bowl.
2. Stir in tapioca and curry powder.
3. Dissolve bouillon in boiling water. Pour over vegetables. Mix well. Spoon into large cooker, or two medium-sized ones.
4. Cover. Cook on low 8-10 hours, or high 3-4 hours. Serve with cooked rice.

Exchange List Values
• Starch 1.0   • Vegetable 3.0

Basic Nutritional Values
• Calories 166   • Cholesterol 0 mg
  (Calories from Fat 10) • Sodium 436 mg
• Total Fat 1 gm   • Total Carb 35 gm
  (Saturated Fat 0.1 gm, • Dietary Fiber 8 gm
  Polyunsat Fat 0.5 gm, • Sugars 10 gm
  Monounsat Fat 0.2 gm) • Protein 6 gm

Wild Mushrooms Italian

Connie Johnson
Loudon, NH

Makes 10 servings

Prep. Time: 45 minutes
Cooking Time: 6-8 hours
Ideal slow cooker size: 4-qt.

2 large onions, chopped
3 large red bell peppers,
   chopped
3 large green bell peppers,
   chopped
2 Tbsp. canola oil
12-oz. pkg. oyster
   mushrooms, cleaned and
   chopped
4 garlic cloves, minced
3 fresh bay leaves
10 fresh basil leaves,
   chopped
1 tsp. salt
1½ tsp. pepper
28-oz. can Italian plum
   tomatoes, crushed *or*
   chopped

1. Sauté onions and peppers in oil in skillet until soft. Stir in mushrooms and garlic. Sauté just until mushrooms begin to turn brown. Pour into slow cooker.
2. Add remaining ingredients. Stir well.
3. Cover. Cook on low 6-8 hours.

Exchange List Values
• Vegetable 3.0   • Fat 0.5

Basic Nutritional Values
• Calories 82   • Cholesterol 0 mg
  (Calories from Fat 29) • Sodium 356 mg
• Total Fat 3 gm   • Total Carb 13 gm
  (Saturated Fat 0.2 gm, • Dietary Fiber 4 gm
  Polyunsat Fat 1.0 gm, • Sugars 8 gm
  Monounsat Fat 1.7 gm) • Protein 3 gm

Note:
   Good as an appetizer or on pita bread, or serve over rice or pasta for main dish.

To reduce your sodium intake, avoid salting the water when cooking pasta or rice.

Stuffed Mushrooms

Melanie L. Thrower
McPherson, KS

Makes 6 servings

Prep. Time: 25 minutes
Cooking Time: 2-4 hours
Ideal slow cooker size: 3- or 4-qt.

12 large mushrooms
¼ tsp. minced garlic
1 Tbsp. canola oil
dash of salt
dash of pepper
dash of cayenne pepper
¼ cup grated reduced-fat Monterey Jack cheese

1. Remove stems from mushrooms and dice.
2. Heat oil in skillet. Sauté diced stems with garlic until softened. Remove skillet from heat.
3. Stir in seasonings and cheese. Stuff into mushroom shells. Place in slow cooker.
4. Cover. Heat on low 2-4 hours.

Exchange List Values
• Vegetable 1.0   • Fat 0.5

Basic Nutritional Values
• Calories 46   • Cholesterol 3 mg
(Calories from Fat 30)   • Sodium 39 mg
• Total Fat 3 gm   • Total Carb 2 gm
(Saturated Fat 0.8 gm,   • Dietary Fiber 1 gm
Polyunsat Fat 0.8 gm,   • Sugars 1 gm
Monounsat Fat 1.6 gm)   • Protein 3 gm

Variations:
1. Add 1 Tbsp. minced onion to Step 2.
2. Use Monterey Jack cheese with jalapeños.

Corn Pudding

Barbara A. Yoder
Goshen, IN

Makes 15 servings

Prep. Time: 10 minutes
Cooking Time: 2-3 hours
Ideal slow cooker size: 4- or 5-qt.

2 10-oz. cans whole kernel corn with juice
2 1-lb. cans no-added-salt creamed corn
2 6.5 oz. boxes corn muffin mix, only requiring water
2 Tbsp. margarine
8 oz. fat-free sour cream

1. Combine all ingredients in slow cooker.
2. Cover. Cook on low 2-3 hours until thickened and set.

Exchange List Values
• Starch 2.0   • Fat 0.5

Basic Nutritional Values
• Calories 166   • Cholesterol 1 mg
(Calories from Fat 39)   • Sodium 456 mg
• Total Fat 4 gm   • Total Carb 30 gm
(Saturated Fat 0.7 gm,   • Dietary Fiber 2 gm
Polyunsat Fat 0.9 gm,   • Sugars 8 gm
Monounsat Fat 1.6 gm)   • Protein 4 gm

Corn on the Cob

Donna Conto
Saylorsburg, PA

Makes 6 servings

Prep. Time: 10 minutes
Cooking Time: 2-3 hours
Ideal slow cooker size: 5- or 6-qt.

6 small (5½-6½" long) ears of corn (in husk)
½ cup water

1. Remove silk from corn, as much as possible, but leave husks on.
2. Cut off ends of corn. Lay in slow cooker, or stand on end.
3. Add water.
4. Cover. Cook on low 2-3 hours.

Exchange List Values
• Starch 1.0

Basic Nutritional Values
• Calories 68   • Cholesterol 0 mg
(Calories from Fat 5)   • Sodium 3 mg
• Total Fat 1 gm   • Total Carb 16 gm
(Saturated Fat 0.1 gm,   • Dietary Fiber 2 gm
Polyunsat Fat 0.3 gm,   • Sugars 2 gm
Monounsat Fat 0.2 gm)   • Protein 2 gm

Cheesy Corn

Tina Snyder
Manheim, PA
Jeannine Janzen
Elbing, KS
Nadine Martinitz
Salina, KS

Makes 10 servings

Prep. Time: 10 minutes
Cooking Time: 4 hours
Ideal slow cooker size: 4-qt.

3 16-oz. pkgs. frozen corn
8-oz. pkg. fat-free cream
  cheese, cubed
2 Tbsp. light soft tub
  margarine
3 Tbsp. water
3 Tbsp. fat-free milk
2 Tbsp. sugar
6 slices reduced-fat
  American cheese, cut
  into squares

  1. Combine all ingredients in slow cooker. Mix well.
  2. Cover. Cook on low 4 hours, or until heated through and the cheese is melted.

Exchange List Values
• Starch 2.0   • Fat 0.5

Basic Nutritional Values
• Calories 176   • Cholesterol 8 mg
(Calories from Fat 29) • Sodium 220 mg
• Total Fat 3 gm   • Total Carb 33 gm
(Saturated Fat 1.3 gm, • Dietary Fiber 3 gm
Polyunsat Fat 0.5 gm, • Sugars 7 gm
Monounsat Fat 1.2 gm) • Protein 7 gm

Creamy Corn

Lauren M. Eberhard
Seneca, IL

Makes 8 servings

Prep. Time: 10 minutes
Cooking Time: 6 hours
Ideal slow cooker size: 5-qt.

12 oz. fat-free cottage cheese
1 cup reduced-fat Colby
  cheese, shredded
1 egg
pepper to taste
2 lbs. frozen corn

  1. Cream cottage cheese, Colby cheese, and egg in food processor until well-mixed.
  2. Stir in pepper and corn.
  3. Pour mixture into slow cooker.
  4. Cover. Cook on low 6 hours.

Exchange List Values
• Starch 2.0   • Lean Meat 1.0

Basic Nutritional Values
• Calories 180   • Cholesterol 30 mg
(Calories from Fat 35) • Sodium 265 mg
• Total Fat 4 gm   • Total Carb 27 gm
(Saturated Fat 2.0 gm, • Dietary Fiber 2 gm
Polyunsat Fat 0.5 gm, • Sugars 4 gm
Monounsat Fat 1.0 gm) • Protein 12 gm

Super Creamed Corn

Ruth Ann Penner
Hillsboro, KS
Alix Nancy Botsford
Seminole, OK

Makes 12 servings

Prep. Time: 10 minutes
Cooking Time: 4 hours
Ideal slow cooker size: 4-qt.

2 lbs. frozen corn
8-oz. pkg. fat-free cream
  cheese, cubed
2 Tbsp. margarine, melted
1 Tbsp. sugar
sugar substitute to equal
  ½ Tbsp. sugar
2-3 Tbsp. water, *optional*

  1. Combine ingredients in slow cooker.
  2. Cover. Cook on low 4 hours.

Exchange List Values
• Starch 1.0   • Fat 0.5

Basic Nutritional Values
• Calories 99   • Cholesterol 2 mg
(Calories from Fat 20) • Sodium 129 mg
• Total Fat 2 gm   • Total Carb 17 gm
(Saturated Fat 0.4 gm, • Dietary Fiber 2 gm
Polyunsat Fat 0.8 gm, • Sugars 3 gm
Monounsat Fat 0.9 gm) • Protein 5 gm

Tip:
  Serve with meat loaf, turkey, or hamburgers. It's a great addition to a holiday because it is easy and requires no last-minute preparation. It also frees the stove and oven for other food preparation.

Use low-fat ingredients, such as low-fat yogurt or milk, in recipes whenever possible.

Baked Corn

Velma Stauffer
Akron, PA

Makes 8 servings

Prep. Time: 15 minutes
Cooking Time: 3¾ hours
Ideal slow cooker size: 3-qt.

1 qt. corn, frozen *or* fresh
2 eggs, beaten
1 tsp. salt
1 cup fat-free milk
⅛ tsp. pepper
2 tsp. oil
1½ Tbsp. sugar
sugar substitute to equal
   2 tsp. sugar
3 Tbsp. flour

1. Combine all ingredients well. Pour into greased slow cooker.
2. Cover. Cook on high 3 hours and then on low 45 minutes.

Exchange List Values
• Starch 1.5   • Fat 0.5

Basic Nutritional Values
• Calories 125   • Cholesterol 54 mg
 (Calories from Fat 25)   • Sodium 324 mg
• Total Fat 3 gm   • Total Carb 22 gm
 (Saturated Fat 0.7 gm,   • Dietary Fiber 2 gm
 Polyunsat Fat 0.7 gm,   • Sugars 6 gm
 Monounsat Fat 1.3 gm)   • Protein 5 gm

Note:
  If you use home-grown sweet corn, you could reduce the amount of sugar.

Scalloped Corn

Rebecca Plank Leichty
Harrisonburg, VA

Makes 8 servings

Prep. Time: 15 minutes
Cooking Time: 3-6 hours
Ideal slow cooker size: 4-qt.

2 eggs
10¾-oz. can cream of
  celery soup
⅔ cup unseasoned bread
  crumbs
2 cups whole-kernel corn,
  drained, *or* cream-style
  corn
1 tsp. minced onion
⅛ tsp. pepper
1 Tbsp. sugar
1 Tbsp. light, soft tub
  margarine, melted

1. Beat eggs with fork. Add soup and bread crumbs. Mix well.
2. Add remaining ingredients and mix thoroughly. Pour into greased slow cooker.
3. Cover. Cook on high 3 hours or on low 6 hours.

Exchange List Values
• Starch 1.0   • Fat 1.0

Basic Nutritional Values
• Calories 132   • Cholesterol 55 mg
 (Calories from Fat 44)   • Sodium 473 mg
• Total Fat 5 gm   • Total Carb 19 gm
 (Saturated Fat 1.4 gm,   • Dietary Fiber 1 gm
 Polyunsat Fat 1.5 gm,   • Sugars 3 gm
 Monounsat Fat 1.5 gm)   • Protein 4 gm

Baked Corn and Noodles

Ruth Hershey
Paradise, PA

Makes 6 servings

Prep. Time: 20 minutes
Cooking Time: 3-8 hours
Ideal slow cooker size: 4-qt.

3 cups noodles, cooked al
  dente
2 cups fresh *or* frozen corn,
  thawed
¾ cup grated fat-free
  cheddar cheese
1 egg, beaten
2 Tbsp. light, soft tub
  margarine, melted
½ tsp. salt

1. Combine all ingredients in slow cooker.
2. Cover. Cook on low 6-8 hours or on high 3-4 hours.

Exchange List Values
• Starch 2.0   • Fat 0.5

Basic Nutritional Values
• Calories 198   • Cholesterol 63 mg
 (Calories from Fat 34)   • Sodium 343 mg
• Total Fat 4 gm   • Total Carb 32 gm
 (Saturated Fat 0.6 gm,   • Dietary Fiber 2 gm
 Polyunsat Fat 0.9 gm,   • Sugars 3 gm
 Monounsat Fat 1.6 gm)   • Protein 11 gm

Mexican Corn

Betty K. Drescher
Quakertown, PA

Makes 8 servings

Prep. Time: 10 minutes
Cooking Time: 2¾-4¾ hours
Ideal slow cooker size: 3- or 4-qt.

2 10-oz. pkgs. frozen corn,
  partially thawed
4-oz. jar chopped pimentos
⅓ cup chopped green
  peppers
⅓ cup water
1 tsp. salt
¼ tsp. pepper
½ tsp. paprika
½ tsp. chili powder

1. Combine all ingredients
in slow cooker.
2. Cover. Cook on high
45 minutes, then on low 2-4
hours. Stir occasionally.

Exchange List Values
• Starch 1.0

Basic Nutritional Values
• Calories 63   • Cholesterol 0 mg
  (Calories from Fat 3)   • Sodium 298 mg
• Total Fat 0 gm   • Total Carb 15 gm
  (Saturated Fat 0.1 gm, • Dietary Fiber 2 gm
  Polyunsat Fat 0.2 gm,   • Sugars 2 gm
  Monounsat Fat 0.1 gm)   • Protein 2 gm

Variations:

For more fire, add ⅓ cup
salsa to the ingredients, and
increase the amounts of pepper, paprika, and chili powder
to match your taste.

Confetti Scalloped Corn

Rhoda Atzeff
Harrisburg, PA

Makes 12 servings

Prep. Time: 20 minutes
Cooking Time: 2-2½ hours
Ideal slow cooker size: 4-qt.

2 eggs, beaten
1 cup fat-free sour cream
2 Tbsp. light, soft tub
  margarine, melted
1 small onion, finely
  chopped
11-oz. can Mexicorn, drained
14-oz. can cream-style corn
2-3 Tbsp. green jalapeño
  salsa, regular salsa, *or*
  chopped green chilies
8½-oz. pkg. cornbread mix

1. Combine all ingredients.
Pour into lightly greased slow
cooker.
2. Cover. Bake on high
2-2½ hours, or until corn is
fully cooked.

Exchange List Values
• Starch 2.0

Basic Nutritional Values
• Calories 147   • Cholesterol 37 mg
  (Calories from Fat 32) • Sodium 408 mg
• Total Fat 4 gm   • Total Carb 29 gm
  (Saturated Fat 1.1 gm, • Dietary Fiber 1 gm
  Polyunsat Fat 0.6 gm,   • Sugars 10 gm
  Monounsat Fat 1.2 gm)   • Protein 4 gm

Cornbread Casserole

Arlene Groff
Lewistown, PA

Makes 16 servings

Prep. Time: 15 minutes
Cooking Time: 3½-4 hours
Ideal slow cooker size: 4-qt.

1 qt. frozen whole-kernel
  corn, thawed
1 qt. creamed corn
8.5-oz. pkg. corn muffin mix
1 egg
2 Tbsp. light, soft tub
  margarine
¼ tsp. garlic powder
2 Tbsp. sugar
¼ cup fat-free milk
½ tsp. salt
¼ tsp. pepper

1. Combine ingredients in
greased slow cooker.
2. Cover. Cook on low
3½-4 hours, stirring once
halfway through.

Exchange List Values
• Starch 2.0

Basic Nutritional Values
• Calories 141   • Cholesterol 13 mg
  (Calories from Fat 23) • Sodium 412 mg
• Total Fat 3 gm   • Total Carb 31 gm
  (Saturated Fat 0.7 gm, • Dietary Fiber 2 gm
  Polyunsat Fat 0.5 gm,   • Sugars 10 gm
  Monounsat Fat 0.8 gm)   • Protein 3 gm

Almonds, pecans, peanuts, and cashews are sources of healthy fats. Enjoy them as a snack or on a salad.

Slow-Cooker Rice

Dorothy Horst
Tiskilwa, IL

Makes 20 servings

Prep. Time: 5 minutes
Cooking Time: 2-3 hours
Ideal slow cooker size: 5- or 6-qt.

1 Tbsp. margarine
4 cups converted long-
    grain rice, uncooked
4 cups water
2 tsp. salt

1. Pour rice, water, and salt into greased slow cooker.
2. Cover. Cook on high 2-3 hours, or until rice is tender, but not overcooked. Stir occasionally.

Exchange List Values
• Starch 2.0

Basic Nutritional Values
• Calories 140
  (Calories from Fat 7)
• Total Fat 1 gm
  (Saturated Fat 0.1 gm,
Polyunsat Fat 0.2 gm,
Monounsat Fat 0.3 gm)
• Cholesterol 0 mg
• Sodium 241 mg
• Total Carb 30 gm
• Dietary Fiber 0 gm
• Sugars 0 gm
• Protein 3 gm

Fruited Wild Rice with Pecans

Dottie Schmidt
Kansas City, MO

Makes 8 servings

Prep. Time: 15 minutes
Cooking Time: 1½-2 hours
Ideal slow cooker size: 4-qt.

½ cup chopped onions
1 Tbsp. canola oil
6-oz. pkg. long-grain and
    wild rice
seasoning packet from
    wild rice pkg.
1½ cups hot water
⅔ cup apple juice
1 large tart apple, chopped
¼ cup raisins
¼ cup coarsely chopped
    pecans

1. Combine all ingredients except pecans in slow cooker sprayed with non-fat cooking spray.
2. Cover. Cook on high 2-2½ hours.
3. Stir in pecans. Serve.

Exchange List Values
• Starch 1.0
• Fruit 1.0
• Fat 0.5

Basic Nutritional Values
• Calories 154
  (Calories from Fat 43)
• Total Fat 5 gm
  (Saturated Fat 0.4 gm,
Polyunsat Fat 1.3 gm,
Monounsat Fat 2.7 gm)
• Cholesterol 0 mg
• Sodium 237 mg
• Total Carb 27 gm
• Dietary Fiber 2 gm
• Sugars 9 gm
• Protein 3 gm

Wild Rice

Ruth S. Weaver
Reinholds, PA

Makes 5 servings

Prep. Time: 20 minutes
Cooking Time: 2½-3 hours
Ideal slow cooker size: 3- or 4-qt.

1 cup wild rice, uncooked
½ cup sliced mushrooms
½ cup diced onions
½ cup diced green, *or* red,
    bell peppers
1 Tbsp. oil
¼ tsp. salt
¼ tsp. pepper
2½ cups 98% fat-free,
    reduced-sodium chicken
    broth

1. Layer rice and vegetables in slow cooker. Pour oil, salt, and pepper over vegetables. Stir.
2. Heat chicken broth. Pour over ingredients in slow cooker.
3. Cover. Cook on high 2½-3 hours, or until rice is soft and liquid is absorbed.

Exchange List Values
• Starch 2.0

Basic Nutritional Values
• Calories 157
  (Calories from Fat 28)
• Total Fat 3 gm
  (Saturated Fat 0.2 gm,
Polyunsat Fat 1.0 gm,
Monounsat Fat 1.7 gm)
• Cholesterol 0 mg
• Sodium 370 mg
• Total Carb 27 gm
• Dietary Fiber 3 gm
• Sugars 3 gm
• Protein 6 gm

Wild Rice Casserole

Carolyn Baer
Coranth, WI

Makes 8 servings

*Soaking Time for rice:
  overnight, or 8 hours*
Prep Time: 35-40 minutes
Cooking Time: 3-4 hours
Ideal slow-cooker size: 3- or 4-qt.

1 cup uncooked wild rice
¼ lb. loose pork sausage
¾ lb. 95% lean ground beef
1 medium onion, chopped
1 cup chopped celery
1 green pepper, chopped
2 medium carrots, grated
2 tsp. light soy sauce
1 tsp. Worcestershire sauce
10¾-oz. can low-fat,
  low-sodium cream of
  mushroom soup
10¾-oz. can low-fat, low-
  sodium cream of chicken
  soup
1 cup sliced mushrooms,
  optional
½ cup water, *or more*

1. Wash and soak rice overnight.
2. Brown sausage and beef together in large skillet.
3. Drain off drippings. Place meat in slow cooker.
4. Drain rice.
5. Add rice, chopped onion, celery, green pepper, and carrots to slow cooker.
6. Stir in soy sauce, Worcestershire sauce, soups, and mushrooms if you wish.
7. Mix in water.

8. Cover. Cook on high 1 hour. Stir. If dish seems somewhat dry, add another ½ cup water.
9. Cover. Cook on low 2 hours. Or cook on low a total of 4 hours.

Exchange List Values
• Carbohydrate 1.5   • Fat 0.5
• Lean Meat 2.0

Basic Nutritional Values
• Calories 210   • Cholesterol 35 mg
  (Calories from Fat 65) • Sodium 455 mg
• Total Fat 7 gm   • Total Carb 23 gm
  (Saturated Fat 2.5 gm, • Dietary Fiber 3 gm
  Polyunsat Fat 1.5 gm,   • Sugars 6 gm
  Monounsat Fat 2.5 gm)   • Protein 14 gm

Risi Bisi (Peas and Rice)

Cyndie Marrara
Port Matilda, PA

Makes 8 servings

Prep. Time: 15 minutes
Cooking Time: 2½-3½ hours
Ideal slow cooker size: 4-qt.

1½ cups converted long-
  grain white rice,
  uncooked
¾ cup chopped onion
2 garlic cloves, minced
2 14½-oz. cans reduced-
  sodium chicken broth
⅓ cup water
¾ tsp. Italian herb
  seasoning
½ tsp. dried basil
½ cup frozen baby peas,
  thawed
¼ cup freshly grated

Parmesan cheese

1. Combine rice, onions, and garlic in slow cooker.
2. In saucepan, mix together chicken broth and water. Bring to boil. Add Italian seasoning and basil leaves. Stir into rice mixture.
3. Cover. Cook on low 2-3 hours, or until liquid is absorbed.
4. Stir in peas. Cover. Cook 30 minutes. Stir in cheese.

Exchange List Values
• Starch 2.0

Basic Nutritional Values
• Calories 165   • Cholesterol 3 mg
  (Calories from Fat 11) • Sodium 409 mg
• Total Fat 1 gm   • Total Carb 32 gm
  (Saturated Fat 0.5 gm, • Dietary Fiber 1 gm
  Polyunsat Fat 0.1 gm,   • Sugars 2 gm
  Monounsat Fat 0.4 gm)   • Protein 6 gm

Green Rice Casserole

Ruth Hofstetter
Versailles, Missouri

Makes 6 servings

Prep. Time: 20 minutes
Cooking Time: 5-7 hours
Ideal slow cooker size: 4-qt.

1⅓ cups fat-free evaporated
  milk
2 Tbsp. vegetable oil
3 eggs
2 Tbsp. minced fresh onion
half a carrot, minced
2 cups minced fresh
  parsley, *or* 10-oz. pkg.

frozen chopped spinach,
thawed and drained
¼ tsp. salt
¼ tsp. pepper
1 cup shredded fat-free
    sharp cheddar cheese
3 cups cooked long grain
    rice

1. Beat together milk, oil,
and eggs until well combined.
2. Stir in remaining
ingredients. Mix well. Pour
into greased slow cooker.
3. Cover. Cook on high 1
hour. Stir. Reduce heat to low
and cook 4-6 hours.

Exchange List Values

- Starch 1.5
- Milk, fat-free 0.5
- Meat, medium fat 1.0
- Fat 1.0

Basic Nutritional Values

- Calories 264
  (Calories from Fat 67)
- Total Fat 7 gm
  (Saturated Fat 1.4 gm,
  Polyunsat Fat 1.8 gm,
  Monounsat Fat 3.8 gm)
- Cholesterol 109 mg
- Sodium 345 mg
- Total Carb 32 gm
- Dietary Fiber 1 gm
- Sugars 7 gm
- Protein 16 gm

Baked Potatoes

Lucille Metzler
Wellsboro, PA
Elizabeth Yutzy
Wauseon, OH
Glenda S. Weaver
Manheim, PA
Mary Jane Musser
Manheim, PA
Esther Becker
Gordonville, PA

Makes 6 servings

Prep. Time: 5 minutes
Cooking Time: 3-10 hours
Ideal slow cooker size: 4-qt.

6 medium (5¾ oz.) baking
    potatoes
1 Tbsp. margarine

1. Prick potatoes with fork.
Rub each with margarine.
Place in slow cooker.
2. Cover. Cook on high 3-5
hours, or low 6-10 hours.

Exchange List Values

- Starch 2.0

Basic Nutritional Values

- Calories 147
  (Calories from Fat 17)
- Total Fat 2 gm
  (Saturated Fat 0.3 gm,
  Polyunsat Fat 0.7 gm,
  Monounsat Fat 0.8 gm)
- Cholesterol 0 mg
- Sodium 34 mg
- Total Carb 29 gm
- Dietary Fiber 3 gm
- Sugars 3 gm
- Protein 4 gm

Pizza Potatoes

Margaret Wenger Johnson
Keezletown, VA

Makes 8 servings

Prep. Time: 20 minutes
Cooking Time: 6-10 hours
Ideal slow cooker size: 4-qt.

6 (5¾ oz.) medium
    potatoes, sliced
1 large onion, thinly sliced
2 Tbsp. olive oil
6 oz. (1½ cups) grated
    mozzarella fat-free
    cheese
2 oz. sliced turkey
    pepperoni
8-oz. can pizza sauce

1. Sauté potato and onion
slices in oil in skillet until
onions appear transparent.
Drain well.
2. In slow cooker, combine
potatoes, onions, cheese, and
pepperoni.
3. Pour pizza sauce over
top.
4. Cover. Cook on low 6-10
hours, or until potatoes are
soft.

Exchange List Values

- Starch 2.0
- Meat, lean 1.0

Basic Nutritional Values

- Calories 205
  (Calories from Fat 43)
- Total Fat 5 gm
  (Saturated Fat 0.9 gm,
  Polyunsat Fat 0.8 gm,
  Monounsat Fat 2.9 gm)
- Cholesterol 12 mg
- Sodium 417 mg
- Total Carb 27 gm
- Dietary Fiber 3 gm
- Sugars 6 gm
- Protein 13 gm

Did you know that one trip to the salad bar can add up to more than 1,000 calories? Watch out for side dishes like potato salad, pasta salad, and creamy soups; choose low-fat or fat-free dressing.

Garlic Mashed Potatoes

Katrine Rose
Woodbridge, VA

Makes 6 servings

Prep. Time: 40 minutes
cooking Time: 4-7 hours
Ideal slow cooker size: 4-qt.

2 lbs. baking potatoes, unpeeled and cut into ½" cubes
¼ cup water
3 Tbsp. light, soft tub margarine
¾ tsp. salt
¾ tsp. garlic powder
¼ tsp. black pepper
1 cup 2% milk

1. Combine all ingredients, except milk, in slow cooker. Toss to combine.
2. Cover. Cook on low 7 hours, or on high 4 hours.
3. Add milk to potatoes during last 30 minutes of cooking time.
4. Mash potatoes with potato masher or electric mixer until fairly smooth.

Exchange List Values
- Starch 2.0   • Fat 0.5

Basic Nutritional Values
- Calories 167 • Cholesterol 3 mg
  (Calories from Fat 29) • Sodium 361 mg
- Total Fat 3 gm • Total Carb 31 gm
  (Saturated Fat 0.4 gm, • Dietary Fiber 3 gm
  Polyunsat Fat 0.6 gm, • Sugars 4 gm
  Monounsat Fat 1.6 gm) • Protein 4 gm

Company Mashed Potatoes

Eileen Eash
Carlsbad, NM

Makes 12 servings

Prep. Time: 40 minutes
Cooking Time: 12-15 hours
Ideal slow cooker size: 6-qt.

15 (5 lb. total) medium-sized potatoes
1 cup reduced-fat sour cream
1 small onion, diced fine
1 tsp. salt
¼ tsp. pepper
1 cup buttermilk
1 cup fresh, chopped spinach
1 cup grated Colby *or* cheddar cheese, *optional*

1. Peel and quarter potatoes. Place in slow cooker. Barely cover with water.
2. Cover. Cook on low 8-10 hours. Drain water.
3. Mash potatoes. Add remaining ingredients except cheese.
4. Cover. Heat on low 4-6 hours.
5. Sprinkle with cheese 5 minutes before serving.

Exchange List Values
- Starch 2.0

Basic Nutritional Values
- Calories 160 • Cholesterol 7 mg
  (Calories from Fat 18) • Sodium 236 mg
- Total Fat 2 gm • Total Carb 32 gm
  (Saturated Fat 1.1 gm, • Dietary Fiber 3 gm
  Polyunsat Fat 0.1 gm, • Sugars 5 gm
  Monounsat Fat 0.5 gm) • Protein 5 gm

Tip:
Buttermilk gives mashed potatoes a unique flavor that most people enjoy. I often serve variations of this recipe for guests and they always ask what I put in the potatoes.

Notes:
1. I save the water drained from cooking the potatoes and use it to make gravy or a soup base.
2. Small amounts of leftovers from this recipe add a special flavor to vegetable or noodle soup for another meal.

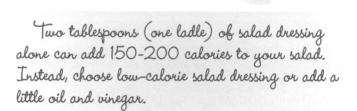

Two tablespoons (one ladle) of salad dressing alone can add 150-200 calories to your salad. Instead, choose low-calorie salad dressing or add a little oil and vinegar.

Creamy Mashed Potatoes

Brenda S. Burkholder
Port Republic, VA

Makes 12 servings

Prep. Time: 25 minutes
Cooking Time: 3-5 hours
Ideal slow cooker size: 5-qt.

1 tsp. salt
4 Tbsp. margarine, melted
2¼ cups fat-free milk
6⅞ cups potato flakes
6 cups water
1 cup fat-free sour cream
4 oz. fat-free cream cheese, softened

1. Combine first five ingredients as directed on potato box.
2. Whip cream cheese with electric mixer until creamy. Blend in sour cream.
3. Fold potatoes into cheese and sour cream. Beat well. Place in slow cooker.
4. Cover. Cook on low 3-5 hours.

Exchange List Values
- Starch 2.0   • Fat 0.5

Basic Nutritional Values
- Calories 173   • Cholesterol 3 mg
  (Calories from Fat 36)   • Sodium 361 mg
- Total Fat 4 gm   • Total Carb 29 gm
  (Saturated Fat 0.8 gm,   • Dietary Fiber 2 gm
  Polyunsat Fat 1.2 gm,   • Sugars 4 gm
  Monounsat Fat 1.7 gm)   • Protein 6 gm

Herbed Potatoes

Jo Haberkamp
Fairbank, IA

Makes 6 servings

Prep. Time: 20 minutes
Cooking Time: 2½-3 hours
Ideal slow cooker size: 4-qt.

1½ lbs. small new potatoes
¼ cup water
¼ cup light, soft tub margarine, melted
3 Tbsp. chopped fresh parsley
1 Tbsp. lemon juice
1 Tbsp. chopped fresh chives
1 Tbsp. dill weed
¼ tsp. salt
¼ tsp. pepper

1. Wash potatoes. Peel a strip around the center of each potato. Place in slow cooker.
2. Add water.
3. Cover. Cook on high 2½-3 hours. Drain well.
4. In saucepan, heat margarine, parsley, lemon juice, chives, dill, salt, and pepper. Pour over potatoes.

Exchange List Values
- Starch 1.5   • Fat 0.5

Basic Nutritional Values
- Calories 122   • Cholesterol 0 mg
  (Calories from Fat 28)   • Sodium 163 mg
- Total Fat 3 gm   • Total Carb 22 gm
  (Saturated Fat 0.0 gm,   • Dietary Fiber 2 gm
  Polyunsat Fat 0.7 gm,   • Sugars 2 gm
  Monounsat Fat 1.7 gm)   • Protein 2 gm

Tip:
Serve with ham or any meat dish that does not make gravy.

Potatoes Perfect

Naomi Ressler
Harrisonburg, VA

Makes 6 servings

Prep. Time: 35 minutes
Cooking Time: 3-10 hours
Ideal slow cooker size: 4-qt.

¼ lb. bacon, diced and browned until crisp
2 medium-sized onions, thinly sliced
6-8 medium-sized potatoes, thinly sliced
4 oz. fat-free cheddar cheese, thinly sliced
pepper to taste
2 Tbsp. light, soft tub margarine

1. Layer half of bacon, onions, potatoes, and cheese in greased slow cooker. Season to taste.
2. Dot with butter. Repeat layers.
3. Cover. Cook on low 8-10 hours or on high 3-4 hours, or until potatoes are soft.

Exchange List Values
- Starch 2.0   • Fat 1.0
- Vegetable 1.0

Basic Nutritional Values
- Calories 224   • Cholesterol 6 mg
  (Calories from Fat 38)   • Sodium 262 mg
- Total Fat 4 gm   • Total Carb 35 gm
  (Saturated Fat 0.9 gm,   • Dietary Fiber 4 gm
  Polyunsat Fat 0.7 gm,   • Sugars 7 gm
  Monounsat Fat 2.1 gm)   • Protein 12 gm

Lotsa Scalloped Potatoes

Fannie Miller
Hutchinson, KS

Makes 25 servings

Prep. Time: 40 minutes
Cooking Time: 2-3 hours
Ideal slow cooker size: 6-qt.

5 lbs. potatoes, cooked and sliced
2 lbs. extra-lean, lower sodium cooked ham, cubed
¼ lb. light, soft tub margarine
½ cup flour
2 cups fat-free half-and-half
¼ lb. reduced-fat mild cheese, shredded
¼-½ tsp. pepper

1. Place layers of sliced potatoes and ham in slow cooker.
2. Melt margarine in saucepan on stove. Whisk in flour. Gradually add half and half to make a white sauce, stirring constantly until smooth and thickened.
3. Stir in cheese, salt, and pepper. Stir until cheese is melted. Pour over potatoes and ham.
4. Cover. Cook on low 2-3 hours.

Exchange List Values
- Starch 1.0
- Meat, lean 1.0

Basic Nutritional Values
- Calories 136 (Calories from Fat 24)
- Total Fat 3 gm (Saturated Fat 1.0 gm, Polyunsat Fat 0.4 gm, Monounsat Fat 0.9 gm)
- Cholesterol 21 mg
- Sodium 379 mg
- Total Carb 19 gm
- Dietary Fiber 1 gm
- Sugars 4 gm
- Protein 10 gm

Note:
A great way to free up oven space.

Cheese Potatoes

Joyce Shackelford
Green Bay, WI

Makes 10 servings

Prep. Time: 30 minutes
Cooking Time: 8¼ hours
Ideal slow cooker size: 5-qt.

6 potatoes, peeled and cut into ¼" strips
3 oz. reduced-fat sharp cheddar cheese, shredded
10¾-oz. can 98% fat-free, lower-sodium cream of chicken soup
1 small onion, chopped
4 Tbsp. margarine, melted
1 tsp. salt
1 tsp. pepper
1 cup sour cream
2 cups seasoned stuffing cubes
3 Tbsp. margarine, melted

1. Toss together potatoes and cheese. Place in slow cooker.
2. Combine soup, onion, 4 Tbsp. margarine, salt, and pepper. Pour over potatoes.
3. Cover. Cook on low 8 hours.
4. Stir in sour cream. Cover and heat for 10 more minutes.
5. Meanwhile, toss together stuffing cubes and 3 Tbsp. margarine. Sprinkle over potatoes just before serving.

Exchange List Values
- Starch 2.0
- Fat 1.0

Basic Nutritional Values
- Calories 190 (Calories from Fat 54)
- Total Fat 6 gm (Saturated Fat 1.5 gm, Polyunsat Fat 1.2 gm, Monounsat Fat 2.5 gm)
- Cholesterol 10 mg
- Sodium 390 mg
- Total Carb 29 gm
- Dietary Fiber 2 gm
- Sugars 5 gm
- Protein 7 gm

Hot German Potato Salad

Judi Manos
West Islip, NY

Makes 7 servings

Prep. Time: 30 minutes
Cooking Time: 8-10 hours
Ideal slow cooker size: 4- or 5-qt.

5 medium-sized potatoes, cut ¼" thick
1 large onion, chopped
⅓ cup water
⅓ cup vinegar
2 Tbsp. flour
2 Tbsp. sugar
1 tsp. salt

Use plain yogurt mixed with herbs and spices instead of sour cream on baked potatoes.

½ tsp. celery seed
¼ tsp. pepper
4 slices bacon, cooked
  crisp and crumbled
chopped fresh parsley

1. Combine potatoes and onions in slow cooker.
2. Combine remaining ingredients, except bacon and parsley. Pour over potatoes.
3. Cover. Cook on low 8-10 hours.
4. Stir in bacon and parsley.

Exchange List Values
• Starch 2.0

Basic Nutritional Values
• Calories 149
  (Calories from Fat 17)
• Total Fat 2 gm
  (Saturated Fat 0.6 gm,
  Polyunsat Fat 0.3 gm,
  Monounsat Fat 0.8 gm)
• Cholesterol 3 mg
• Sodium 397 mg
• Total Carb 30 gm
• Dietary Fiber 3 gm
• Sugars 8 gm
• Protein 4 gm

Tip:
  Serve warm or at room temperature with grilled bratwurst or Polish sausage, dilled pickles, pickled beets, and apples.

Creamy Hash Browns
Judy Buller, Bluffton, OH
Elaine Patton, West Middletown, PA
Melissa Raber, Millersburg, OH

Makes 14 servings

Prep. Time: 25 minutes
Cooking Time: 4-5 hours
Ideal slow cooker size: 4- or 5-qt.

2-lb. pkg. frozen, cubed hash brown potatoes
2 cups cubed *or* shredded fat-free American cheese
12 oz. fat-free sour cream
10¾-oz. can cream of celery soup
10¾-oz. can 98% fat-free, lower-sodium cream of chicken soup
¼ lb. sliced bacon, cooked and crumbled
1 medium onion, chopped
2 Tbsp. margarine, melted
¼ tsp. pepper

1. Place potatoes in slow cooker. Combine remaining ingredients and pour over potatoes. Mix well.
2. Cover. Cook on low 4-5 hours, or until potatoes are tender.

Exchange List Values
• Starch 1.0   • Fat 1.0
• Carbohydrate 0.5

Basic Nutritional Values
• Calories 167
  (Calories from Fat 44)
• Total Fat 5 gm
  (Saturated Fat 1.4 gm,
  Polyunsat Fat 1.5 gm,
  Monounsat Fat 1.6 gm)
• Cholesterol 9 mg
• Sodium 578 mg
• Total Carb 23 gm
• Dietary Fiber 2 gm
• Sugars 4 gm
• Protein 8 gm

Candied Sweet Potatoes
Julie Weaver
Reinholds, PA

Makes 8 servings

Prep. Time: 30 minutes
Cooking Time: 4½ hours
Ideal slow cooker size: 4-qt.

6 medium (6½ oz. each) sweet potatoes
½ tsp. salt
2 Tbsp. margarine, melted
20-oz. can crushed pineapples, undrained
2 Tbsp. brown sugar
brown sugar substitute to equal 1 Tbsp. sugar
1 tsp. nutmeg
1 tsp. cinnamon

1. Cook sweet potatoes until soft. Peel. Slice and place in slow cooker.
2. Combine remaining ingredients. Pour over sweet potatoes.
3. Cover. Cook on high 4 hours.

Exchange List Values
• Starch 1.5   • Fat 0.5
• Fruit 1.0

Basic Nutritional Values
• Calories 186
  (Calories from Fat 30)
• Total Fat 3 gm
  (Saturated Fat 0.7 gm,
  Polyunsat Fat 1.1 gm,
  Monounsat Fat 1.3 gm)
• Cholesterol 0 mg
• Sodium 193 mg
• Total Carb 39 gm
• Dietary Fiber 3 gm
• Sugars 19 gm
• Protein 2 gm

Sweet Potato Casserole

Jean Butzer
Batavia, NY

Makes 10 servings

Prep. Time: 25 minutes
Cooking Time: 3-4 hours
Ideal slow cooker size: 4- or 5-qt.

2 29-oz. cans no-sugar-added sweet potatoes, drained and mashed
2½ Tbsp. light, soft tub margarine
1 Tbsp. sugar
1 Tbsp. brown sugar
brown sugar substitute to equal ½ tsp. sugar
1 Tbsp. orange juice
2 eggs, beaten
½ cup fat-free milk
⅓ cup chopped pecans
2 Tbsp. brown sugar
brown sugar substitute to equal 1½ Tbsp. sugar
2 Tbsp. flour
2 tsp. light, soft tub margarine, melted

1. Combine sweet potatoes, ⅓ cup magarine, 2 Tbsp. sugar, and 2 Tbsp. brown sugar.
2. Beat in orange juice, eggs, and milk. Transfer to greased slow cooker.
3. Combine pecans, ⅓ cup brown sugar, flour, and 2 tsp. margarine. Spread over sweet potatoes.
4. Cover. Cook on high 3-4 hours.

Exchange List Values
• Starch 2.0   • Fat 0.5
• Carbohydrate 0.5

Basic Nutritional Values
• Calories 218   • Cholesterol 43 mg
  (Calories from Fat 51) • Sodium 64 mg
• Total Fat 6 gm   • Total Carb 40 gm
  (Saturated Fat 0.7 gm, • Dietary Fiber 5 gm
  Polyunsat Fat 1.4 gm,   • Sugars 24 gm
  Monounsat Fat 2.9 gm)   • Protein 5 gm

Orange Yams

Gladys Longacre
Susquehanna, PA

Makes 8 servings

Prep. Time: 30 minutes
Cooking Time: 3 hours
Ideal slow cooker size: 4- or 5-qt.

40-oz. can no-sugar-added yams, drained
2 apples, cored, peeled, thinly sliced
1½ Tbsp. light, soft tub margarine, melted
2 tsp. orange zest
1 cup orange juice
2 Tbsp. cornstarch
¼ cup brown sugar
brown sugar substitute to equal 2 Tbsp. sugar
1 tsp. salt
dash of ground cinnamon *and/or* nutmeg

1. Place yams and apples in slow cooker.
2. Add butter and orange zest.
3. Combine remaining ingredients and pour over yams.

4. Cover. Cook on high 1 hour and on low 2 hours, or until apples are tender.

Exchange List Values
• Starch 2.0   • Carbohydrate 1.0

Basic Nutritional Values
• Calories 199   • Cholesterol 0 mg
  (Calories from Fat 11) • Sodium 324 mg
• Total Fat 1 gm   • Total Carb 48 gm
  (Saturated Fat 0.1 gm, • Dietary Fiber 4 gm
  Polyunsat Fat 0.4 gm,   • Sugars 32 gm
  Monounsat Fat 0.5 gm)   • Protein 3 gm

Variation:
  Substitute 6-8 medium-sized cooked sweet potatoes, or approximately 4 cups cubed butternut squash, for yams.

Sweet Potatoes and Apples

Bernita Boyts
Shawnee Mission, KS

Makes 8 servings

Prep. Time: 25 minutes
Cooking Time: 6-8 hours
Ideal slow cooker size: 4-qt.

3 large sweet potatoes, peeled and cubed
3 large tart and firm apples, peeled and sliced
½ tsp. salt
⅛-¼ tsp. pepper
1 tsp. dried sage
1 tsp. ground cinnamon
4 Tbsp. light, soft tub margarine, melted
2 Tbsp. maple syrup
brown sugar substitute to equal 1 Tbsp. sugar

toasted sliced almonds *or* chopped pecans, *optional*

1. Place half the sweet potatoes in slow cooker. Layer in half the apple slices.
2. Mix together seasonings. Sprinkle half over apples.
3. Mix together margarine, maple syrup, and brown sugar. Spoon half over seasonings.
4. Repeat layers.
5. Cover. Cook on low 6-8 hours or until potatoes are soft, stirring occasionally.
6. To add a bit of crunch, sprinkle with toasted almonds or pecans when serving. Serve with pork or poultry.

Exchange List Values
- Starch 1.0
- Fat 0.5
- Fruit 1.0

Basic Nutritional Values
- Calories 152
  (Calories from Fat 24)
- Total Fat 3 gm
  (Saturated Fat 0.1 gm,
  Polyunsat Fat 0.7 gm,
  Monounsat Fat 1.3 gm)
- Cholesterol 0 mg
- Sodium 201 mg
- Total Carb 32 gm
- Dietary Fiber 3 gm
- Sugars 17 gm
- Protein 1 gm

Sweet Potatoes with Applesauce

Judi Manos
West Islip, NY

Makes 8 servings

Prep. Time: 30 minutes
Cooking Time: 6-7 hours
Ideal slow cooker size: 4-qt.

6 medium-sized sweet potatoes *or* yams
1½ cups unsweetened applesauce
¼ cup packed brown sugar
brown sugar substitute to equal 2 Tbsp. sugar
2 Tbsp. light, soft tub margarine, melted
1 tsp. ground cinnamon
½ cup chopped pecans

1. Peel sweet potatoes and cut into ½" cubes. Place in slow cooker.
2. Combine remaining ingredients, except nuts. Spoon over potatoes.
3. Cover. Cook on low 6-7 hours or until potatoes are very tender.
4. Sprinkle with nuts.

Exchange List Values
- Starch 1.5
- Fat 1.0
- Fruit 1.0

Basic Nutritional Values
- Calories 213
  (Calories from Fat 63)
- Total Fat 7 gm
  (Saturated Fat 0.5 gm,
  Polyunsat Fat 1.9 gm,
  Monounsat Fat 3.9 gm)
- Cholesterol 0 mg
- Sodium 40 mg
- Total Carb 37 gm
- Dietary Fiber 3 gm
- Sugars 17 gm
- Protein 2 gm

Barbecued Black Beans with Sweet Potatoes

Barbara Jean Fabel
Wausau, WI

Makes 8 servings

Prep. Time: 15 minutes
Cooking Time: 2-4 hours
Ideal slow cooker size: 4-qt.

4 large (10 oz. each) sweet potatoes, peeled and cut into 8 chunks each
15-oz. can black beans, rinsed and drained
1 medium onion, diced
2 ribs celery, sliced
9 ozs. Sweet Baby Ray's Barbecue Sauce

1. Place sweet potatoes in slow cooker.
2. Combine remaining ingredients. Pour over sweet potatoes.
3. Cover. Cook on high 2-3 hours, or on low 4 hours.

Exchange List Values
- Starch 2.5

Basic Nutritional Values
- Calories 180
  (Calories from Fat 10)
- Total Fat 1 gm
  (Saturated Fat 0.2 gm,
  Polyunsat Fat 0.4 gm,
  Monounsat Fat 0.3 gm)
- Cholesterol 0 mg
- Sodium 321 mg
- Total Carb 38 gm
- Dietary Fiber 5 gm
- Sugars 11 gm
- Protein 5 gm

Potato Filling

Miriam Nolt
New Holland, PA

Makes 32 servings

Prep. Time: 25 minutes
Cooking Time: 3 hours
Ideal slow cooker size: 5- or 6-qt.

1 cup minced celery
1 medium onion, minced
2 Tbsp. light soft tub
  margarine
2 Tbsp. canola oil
2 15-oz. pkgs. unseasoned
  bread cubes, toasted
3 eggs, beaten
4 egg whites
1 qt. fat-free milk
1 qt. mashed potatoes
2 pinches saffron
1 cup boiling water
1 tsp. pepper

1. Sauté celery and onion in margarine and canola oil in skillet for about 15 minutes.
2. Combine sautéed mixture with bread cubes. Stir in remaining ingredients. Add more milk if mixture isn't very moist.
3. Pour into large, or several medium-sized, slow cookers.
4. Cook on high 3 hours, stirring up from bottom every hour or so to make sure the filling isn't sticking.

Exchange List Values
• Starch 1.5   • Fat 0.5

Basic Nutritional Values
• Calories 147   • Cholesterol 22 mg
  (Calories from Fat 36) • Sodium 280 mg
• Total Fat 4 gm   • Total Carb 22 gm
  (Saturated Fat 1.5 gm, • Dietary Fiber 1 gm
  Polyunsat Fat 1.1 gm,   • Sugars 4 gm
  Monounsat Fat 1.2 gm)   • Protein 5 gm

Mild Dressing

Jane Steiner
Orrville, OH

Makes 8 servings

Prep. Time: 20 minutes
Drying Time: 12-24 hours
Cooking Time: 3½ hours
Ideal slow cooker size: 4-qt.

16-oz. loaf white bread
2 eggs, beaten
½ cup celery
¼ cup diced onions
¼ tsp. salt
½ tsp. pepper
1 cup chopped, cooked
  giblets
1 cup fat-free milk

1. Set bread slices out to dry the day before using. Cut into small cubes.
2. Combine all ingredients except milk.
3. Moisten mixture with enough milk to make bread cubes soft but not soggy.
4. Pour into greased slow cooker. Cook on low 3½ hours, stirring every hour. When stirring, add a small amount of milk to sides of cooker—if needed—to keep dressing moist and to prevent sticking.

Exchange List Values
• Starch 2.0   • Meat, lean 1.0

Basic Nutritional Values
• Calories 213   • Cholesterol 135 mg
  (Calories from Fat 37) • Sodium 427 mg
• Total Fat 4 gm   • Total Carb 31 gm
  (Saturated Fat 1.1 gm, • Dietary Fiber 2 gm
  Polyunsat Fat 1.4 gm,   • Sugars 4 gm
  Monounsat Fat 1.1 gm)   • Protein 12 gm

Moist Poultry Dressing

Virginia Bender
Dover, DE

Josie Boilman
Maumee, OH

Sharon Brubaker
Myerstown, PA

Joette Droz
Kalona, IA

Jacqueline Stefl
E. Bethany, NY

Makes 14 servings

Prep. Time: 30 minutes
Cooking Time: 5½ hours
Ideal slow cooker size: 5-qt.

2 4½-oz. cans sliced
  mushrooms, drained
4 celery ribs, chopped
  (about 2 cups)
2 medium onions, chopped
¼ cup minced fresh
  parsley
¼ cup margarine
13 cups cubed day-old
  bread
¼ tsp. salt
1½ tsp. sage
1 tsp. poultry seasoning
1 tsp. dried thyme
½ tsp. pepper

2 eggs
14½-oz. cans fat-free, reduced sodium chicken broth

1. In large skillet, sauté mushrooms, celery, onions, and parsley in margarine until vegetables are tender.
2. Toss together bread cubes, salt, sage, poultry seasoning, thyme, and pepper. Add mushroom mixture.
3. Combine eggs and broth and add to bread mixture. Mix well.
4. Pour into greased slow cooker. Cook on low 5 hours, or until meat thermometer reaches 160°.

Exchange List Values
- Starch 1.0
- Fat 1.0
- Vegetable 1.0

Basic Nutritional Values
- Calories 151
- (Calories from Fat 48)
- Total Fat 5 gm
- (Saturated Fat 1.1 gm, Polyunsat Fat 1.8 gm, Monounsat Fat 2.0 gm)
- Cholesterol 31 mg
- Sodium 409 mg
- Total Carb 20 gm
- Dietary Fiber 2 gm
- Sugars 3 gm
- Protein 5 gm

Note:
This is a good way to free up the oven when you're making a turkey.

Variations:
1. Use 2 bags bread cubes for stuffing. Make one mixed bread (white and wheat) and the other corn bread cubes.
2. Add ½ tsp. dried marjoram to Step 2.

Arlene Miller
Hutchinson, KS

Slow Cooker Stuffing

Dede Peterson
Rapid City, SD

Makes 12 servings

Prep. Time: 30 minutes
Cooking Time: 4½ hours
Ideal slow cooker size: 6-qt.

12 cups toasted bread crumbs, *or* dressing mix
4 oz. 50% less fat bulk sausage, browned and drained
2 Tbsp. canola oil
1 cup *or* more finely chopped onions
1 cup *or* more finely chopped celery
8-oz. can sliced mushrooms, with liquid
¼ cup chopped fresh parsley
2 tsp. poultry seasoning (omit if using dressing mix)
dash of pepper
2 eggs, beaten
4 tsp. salt-free bouillon powder
4 cups water

1. Combine bread crumbs and sausage.
2. Melt butter in skillet. Add onions and celery and sauté until tender. Stir in mushrooms and parsley. Add seasonings. Pour over bread crumbs and mix well.
3. Stir in eggs and bouillon mixed with water.
4. Pour into slow cooker and bake on high 1 hour, and on low an additional 3 hours.

Exchange List Values
- Starch 2.0
- Fat 1.0

Basic Nutritional Values
- Calories 209
- (Calories from Fat 68)
- Total Fat 8 gm
- (Saturated Fat 1.5 gm, Polyunsat Fat 1.9 gm, Monounsat Fat 2.4 gm)
- Cholesterol 44 mg
- Sodium 423 mg
- Total Carb 28 gm
- Dietary Fiber 2 gm
- Sugars 4 gm
- Protein 8 gm

Variations:
1. For a less spicy stuffing, reduce the poultry seasoning to ½ tsp.

Dolores Metzler
Mechanicsburg, PA

2. Substitute 3½-4½ cups cooked and diced giblets in place of sausage. Add another can mushrooms and 2 tsp. sage in Step 2.

Mrs. Don Martins
Fairbank, IA

Instead of basting meats with drippings, try a little wine, vegetable juice, or fat-free broth.

Slow Cooker Cornbread Dressing

Marie Shank
Harrisonburg, VA

Makes 20 servings

Prep. Time: 45 minutes
Cooling Time: 2 hours
Cooking Time: 3-9 hours
Ideal slow cooker size: 6-qt.

2 (8.5 oz.) boxes Jiffy
   Cornbread mix
8 slices day-old bread
3 eggs
1 onion, chopped
½ cup chopped celery
2 10¾-oz. cans 98% fat-
   free, lower-sodium
   cream of chicken soup
2 tsp. salt-free chicken
   bouillon powder
2 cups water
½ tsp. pepper
1½ Tbsp. sage *or* poultry
   seasoning

1. Prepare and bake
cornbread according to
package instructions. Cool.
2. Crumble cornbread and
bread together.
3. In large bowl combine
all ingredients and spoon into
6-qt. greased slow cooker, or
2 smaller cookers.
4. Cover. Cook on high 2-4
hours or on low 3-8 hours

Exchange List Values
• Starch 1.5   • Fat 0.5

Basic Nutritional Values
• Calories 133   • Cholesterol 35 mg
  (Calories from Fat 34) • Sodium 387 mg
• Total Fat 4 gm   • Total Carb 26 gm
  (Saturated Fat 1.5 gm, • Dietary Fiber 1 gm
  Polyunsat Fat 0.9 gm,   • Sugars 6 gm
  Monounsat Fat 1.1 gm)   • Protein 4 gm

Variations:
1. Prepare your favorite
cornbread recipe in an
8"-square baking pan instead
of using the cornbread mix.
2. Serve with roast chicken
or turkey drumsticks.
Helen Kenagy
Carlsbad, NM

Mashed Potato Filling

Betty K. Drescher
Quakertown, PA

Makes 10 servings

Prep. Time: 20 minutes
Cooking Time: 4½ hours
Ideal slow cooker size: 6-qt.

½ cup diced onions
1 cup diced celery
2 Tbsp. canola oil
2½ cups fat-free milk
4 large eggs, beaten
8 oz. unseasoned bread
   cubes, toasted
4 cups mashed potatoes

¾ tsp. salt
¼ tsp. pepper

1. Sauté onions and celery in
oil in skillet for 5-10 minutes,
or until vegetables are tender.
2. Combine onions and
celery, milk, and eggs. Pour
over bread cubes. Mix lightly
to absorb liquid.
3. Stir in potatoes and
seasonings. Pour into greased
slow cooker.
4. Cover. Cook on low 4
hours.

Exchange List Values
• Starch 2.0   • Fat 1.0

Basic Nutritional Values
• Calories 214   • Cholesterol 88 mg
  (Calories from Fat 54) • Sodium 382 mg
• Total Fat 6 gm   • Total Carb 32 gm
  (Saturated Fat 1.4 gm, • Dietary Fiber 2 gm
  Polyunsat Fat 1.6 gm,   • Sugars 8 gm
  Monounsat Fat 2.7 gm)   • Protein 8 gm

Variation:
For more flavor, add the
packet of seasoning from the
bread cube package in Step 3.

*Make sure your bread really is "whole wheat"—if
it doesn't have "whole wheat flour" listed as the first
ingredient, it's white bread in disguise.*

Desserts

Bread Pudding

Winifred Ewy, Newton, KS
Helen King, Fairbank, IA
Elaine Patton, West Middletown, PA

Makes 9 servings

Prep. Time: 35 minutes
Cooking Time: 4-5 hours
Ideal slow cooker size: 4-qt.

8 slices bread (raisin bread
  is especially good), cubed
3 eggs
2 egg whites
2 cups fat-free half-and-half
2 Tbps. Sugar
sugar substitute to equal
  1 Tbsp. sugar
½ cup raisins (use only ¼
  cup if using raisin bread)
½ tsp. cinnamon

Sauce:
  2 Tbsp. light, soft tub
    margarine
  2 Tbsp. flour

1 cup water
6 Tbsp. sugar
sugar substitute to equal
  3 Tbsp. sugar
1 tsp. vanilla

1. Place bread cubes in greased slow cooker.
2. Beat together eggs and milk. Stir in sugar, raisins, and cinnamon. Pour over bread and stir.
3. Cover and cook on high 1 hour. Reduce heat to low and cook 3-4 hours, or until thermometer reaches 160°.
4. Make sauce just before pudding is done baking. Begin by melting margarine in saucepan. Stir in flour until smooth. Gradually add water, sugar, and vanilla. Bring to boil. Cook, stirring constantly for 2 minutes, or until thickened.
5. Serve sauce over warm bread pudding.

Exchange List Values
• Carbohydrate 2.0 • Fat 1.0

Basic Nutritional Values
• Calories 200   • Cholesterol 75 mg
  (Calories from Fat 40)   • Sodium 221 mg
• Total Fat 4 gm   • Total Carb 34 gm
  (Saturated Fat 1.4 gm,   • Dietary Fiber 1 gm
  Polyunsat Fat 0.6 gm,   • Sugars 21 gm
  Monounsat Fat 1.7 gm)   • Protein 6 gm

Variations:
1. Use dried cherries instead of raisins. Use cherry flavoring in sauce instead of vanilla.
    Char Hagnes
    Montague, MI

2. Use ¼ tsp. ground cinnamon and ¼ tsp. ground nutmeg, instead of ½ tsp. ground cinnamon in pudding.
3. Use 8 cups day-old unfrosted cinnamon rolls instead of the bread.
    Beatrice Orgist
    Richardson, TX

4. Use ½ tsp. vanilla and ¼ tsp. ground nutmeg instead of ½ tsp. cinnamon.
    Nanci Keatley
    Salem, OR

Simple Bread Pudding

Melanie L. Thrower
McPherson, KS

Makes 8 servings

Prep. Time: 25 minutes
Cooking Time: 3 hours
Ideal slow cooker size: 4-qt.

6-8 slices bread, cubed
2 cups fat-free milk
2 eggs
¼ cup sugar
1 tsp. ground cinnamon
1 tsp. vanilla

Sauce:
   6-oz. can concentrated
      grape juice
   1 Tbsp. cornstarch

1. Place bread in slow cooker.
2. Whisk together milk, eggs, sugar, cinnamon, and vanilla. Pour over bread.
3. Cover. Cook on high 2-2½ hours, or until mixture is set.
4. Combine cornstarch and concentrated juice in saucepan. Heat until boiling, stirring constantly, until sauce is thickened. Serve drizzled over bread pudding.

Tip:
   This is a fine dessert with a cold salad main dish.

Exchange List Values
• Carbohydrate 2.5

Basic Nutritional Values
• Calories 179   • Cholesterol 55 mg
   (Calories from Fat 19)   • Sodium 153 mg
• Total Fat 2 gm   • Total Carb 35 gm
   (Saturated Fat 0.7 gm,   • Dietary Fiber 1 gm
   Polyunsat Fat 0.6 gm,   • Sugars 24 gm
   Monounsat Fat 0.6 gm)   • Protein 5 gm

Apple-Nut Bread Pudding

Ruth Ann Hoover
New Holland, PA

Makes 10 servings

Prep. Time: 20 minutes
Cooking Time: 3-4 hours
Ideal slow cooker size: 4-qt.

8 slices raisin bread, cubed
2 medium-sized tart
   apples, peeled and sliced
1 cup chopped pecans,
   toasted
½ cup sugar
sugar substitute to equal
   ¼ cup sugar
1 tsp. ground cinnamon
½ tsp. ground nutmeg
1 egg, lightly beaten
3 egg whites, lightly beaten
2 cups fat-free half-and-
   half
¼ cup apple juice
2 Tbsp. light, soft tub
   margarine, melted

1. Place bread cubes, apples, and pecans in greased slow cooker and mix together gently.
2. Combine sugar, cinnamon, and nutmeg. Add remaining ingredients. Mix well. Pour over bread mixture.

3. Cover. Cook on low 3-4 hours, or until knife inserted in center comes out clean.

Exchange List Values
• Carbohydrate 2.0   • Fat 2.0

Basic Nutritional Values
• Calories 231   • Cholesterol 25 mg
   (Calories from Fat 87)   • Sodium 191 mg
• Total Fat 10 gm   • Total Carb 32 gm
   (Saturated Fat 1.4 gm,   • Dietary Fiber 2 gm
   Polyunsat Fat 2.3 gm,   • Sugars 20 gm
   Monounsat Fat 5.1 gm)   • Protein 6 gm

Mama's Rice Pudding

Donna Barnitz
Jenks, OK

Shari Jensen
Fountain, CO

Makes 8 servings

Prep. Time: 10 minutes
Cooking Time: 6-7 hours
Chilling Time: minimum 4 hours
Ideal slow cooker size: 4-qt.

½ cup white rice,
   uncooked
¼ cup sugar
sugar substitute to equal
   2 Tbsp. sugar
1 tsp. vanilla
1 tsp. lemon extract
1 cup plus 2 Tbsp. fat-free
   milk
1 tsp. butter
2 eggs, beaten
1 tsp. cinnamon
½ cup raisins
1 cup fat-free whipped
   topping
nutmeg for garnish

1. Combine all ingredients except whipped cream and nutmeg in slow cooker. Stir well.

2. Cover crock. Cook on low 6-7 hours, until rice is tender and milk absorbed. Be sure to stir once every 2 hours during cooking.

3. Pour into serving bowl. Cover and chill.

4. Before serving, fold in whipped topping and sprinkle with nutmeg.

Exchange List Values
- Carbohydrate 2.0

Basic Nutritional Values

• Calories 148	• Cholesterol 55 mg
(Calories from Fat 17)	• Sodium 43 mg
• Total Fat 2 gm	• Total Carb 28 gm
(Saturated Fat 0.8 gm,	• Dietary Fiber 1 gm
Polyunsat Fat 0.2 gm,	• Sugars 15 gm
Monounsat Fat 0.7 gm)	• Protein 4 gm

Deluxe Tapioca Pudding
Michelle Showalter
Bridgewater, VA

Makes 16 servings

Prep. Time: 10 minutes
Cooking Time: 3½ hours
Chilling Time: minimum 4 hours
Ideal slow cooker size: 5-qt.

2 qts. fat-free milk
¾ cup dry small pearl
**   tapioca**
¾ cup sugar
sugar substitute to equal
**   6 Tbsp. sugar**
4 eggs, beaten

2 tsp. vanilla
3 cups fat-free frozen
**   whipped topping,**
**   thawed**

1. Combine milk, tapioca, and sugar in slow cooker.

2. Cook on high 3 hours.

3. Add a little of the hot milk to the eggs. Stir. Whisk eggs into milk mixture. Add vanilla.

4. Cover. Cook on high 20-30 minutes.

5. Cool. Chill in refrigerator at least 4 hours. When fully chilled, beat with hand mixer to fluff the pudding.

6. Stir in whipped topping.

Exchange List Values
- Carbohydrate 2.0

Basic Nutritional Values

• Calories 147	• Cholesterol 56 mg
(Calories from Fat 12)	• Sodium 77 mg
• Total Fat 1 gm	• Total Carb 27 gm
(Saturated Fat 0.6 gm,	• Dietary Fiber 0 gm
Polyunsat Fat 0.2 gm,	• Sugars 17 gm
Monounsat Fat 0.5 gm)	• Protein 6 gm

Slow-Cooker Tapioca
Nancy W. Huber
Green Park, PA

Makes 12 servings

Prep. Time: 10 minutes
Cooking Time: 3½ hours
Chilling Time: minimum 4 hours
Ideal slow cooker size: 4-qt.

2 quarts fat-free milk
1 cup small pearl tapioca
½ cups sugar
sugar substitute to equal
**   ¼ cup sugar**
4 eggs, beaten
1 tsp. vanilla
fruit of choice, *optional*

1. Combine milk, tapioca, and sugar in slow cooker. Cook on high 3 hours.

2. Mix together eggs, vanilla, and a little hot milk from slow cooker. Add to slow cooker. Mix. Cook on high 20 more minutes.

3. Chill thoroughly, at least 4 hours. Serve with fruit.

Exchange List Values
- Carbohydrate 2.0

Basic Nutritional Values

• Calories 160	• Cholesterol 74 mg
(Calories from Fat 16)	• Sodium 93 mg
• Total Fat 2 gm	• Total Carb 28 gm
(Saturated Fat 0.9 gm,	• Dietary Fiber 0 gm
Polyunsat Fat 0.2 gm,	• Sugars 17 gm
Monounsat Fat 0.7 gm)	• Protein 8 gm

Blushing Apple Tapioca

Julie Weaver
Reinholds, PA

Makes 10 servings

Prep. Time: 35 minutes
Cooking Time: 3-4 hours
Ideal slow cooker size: 4-qt.

8-10 medium tart apples
¼ cup sugar
sugar substitute to equal
  2 Tbsp. sugar
4 Tbsp. minute tapioca
4 Tbsp. red cinnamon
  candy
½ cup water
whipped topping, *optional*

1. Pare and core apples.
Cut into eighths lengthwise
and place in slow cooker.
2. Mix together sugar,
tapioca, candy, and water.
Pour over apples.
3. Cook on high 3-4 hours.
4. Serve hot or cold. Top
with whipped cream.

Exchange List Values
• Carbohydrate 2.0

Basic Nutritional Values
• Calories 117
  (Calories from Fat 3)
• Total Fat 0 gm
  (Saturated Fat 0.0 gm,
  Polyunsat Fat 0.1 gm,
  Monounsat Fat 0.0 gm)
• Cholesterol 0 mg
• Sodium 0 mg
• Total Carb 30 gm
• Dietary Fiber 2 gm
• Sugars 23 gm
• Protein 0 gm

Raisin Nut-Stuffed Apples

Margaret Rich
North Newton, KS

Makes 6 servings

Prep. Time: 20 minutes
Cooking Time: 6-8 hours
Ideal slow cooker size: 4-qt.

6 medium baking apples,
  cored
1½ Tbsp. light, soft tub
  margarine, melted
2 Tbsp. packed brown
  sugar
brown sugar substitute to
  equal 1 Tbsp. sugar
¾ cup raisins
3 Tbsp. chopped walnuts
½ cup water

1. Peel a strip around apple
about one-third of the way
below the stem end to prevent
splitting.
2. Mix together butter and
brown sugar. Stir in raisins
and walnuts. Stuff into apple
cavities.
3. Place apples in slow
cooker. Add water.
4. Cover and cook on low
6-8 hours.

Exchange List Values
• Fruit 2.0   • Fat 0.5
• Carbohydrate 0.5

Basic Nutritional Values
• Calories 187
  (Calories from Fat 35)
• Total Fat 4 gm
  (Saturated Fat 0.4 gm,
  Polyunsat Fat 2.1 gm,
  Monounsat Fat 1.0 gm)
• Cholesterol 0 mg
• Sodium 29 mg
• Total Carb 41 gm
• Dietary Fiber 5 gm
• Sugars 32 gm
• Protein 2 gm

Caramel Apples

Elaine Patton
West Middletown, PA
Rhonda Lee Schmidt
Scranton, PA
Renee Shirk
Mount Joy, PA

Makes 8 servings

Prep. Time: 30 minutes
Cooking Time: 4-6 hours
Ideal slow cooker size: 4-qt.

4 very large tart apples,
  cored
½ cup apple juice
4 Tbsp. brown sugar
brown sugar substitute to
  equal 2 Tbsp. sugar
12 hot cinnamon candies
4 Tbsp. light, soft tub
  margarine
8 caramel candies
¼ tsp. ground cinnamon
whipped cream, *optional*

1. Remove ½-inch-wide
strip of peel off the top of
each apple and place apples in
slow cooker.
2. Pour apple juice over
apples.
3. Fill the center of each
apple with 2 Tbsp. brown
sugar, 3 hot cinnamon
candies, 1 Tbsp. margarine,
and 2 caramel candies.
Sprinkle with cinnamon.
4. Cover and cook on low
4-6 hours, or until tender.
5. Serve hot with juice
from bottom of slow cooker
and optional whipped cream.

Exchange List Values
• Carbohydrate 2.0

Cranberry Baked Apples

Judi Manos
West Islip, NY

Makes 8 servings

Prep. Time: 30 minutes
Cooking Time: 4-6 hours
Ideal slow cooker size: 3- or 4-qt.

4 large cooking apples
⅓ cup packed brown sugar
¼ cup dried cranberries
½ cup cran-apple juice
  cocktail
2 Tbsp. light, soft tub
  margarine, melted
½ tsp. ground cinnamon
¼ tsp. ground nutmeg
chopped nuts, *optional*

1. Core apples. Fill centers with brown sugar and cranberries. Place in slow cooker.
2. Combine cran-apple juice and margarine. Pour over apples.
3. Sprinkle with cinnamon and nutmeg.

4. Cover. Cook on low 4-6 hours.
5. To serve, spoon sauce over apples and sprinkle with nuts.

Exchange List Values

- Carbohydrate 2.0

Note:
This was one of our favorite recipes while growing up. When it's cooking, the house smells delicious. I'm suddenly full of memories of days gone by and a much more relaxing time. My mother passed away in October and I re-found this recipe among her collection of favorites. We love these apples with vanilla ice cream.

Wagon Master Apple-Cherry Sauce

Sharon Timpe
Mequon, WI

Makes 15 servings

Prep. Time: 10 minutes
Cooking Time: 3-4 hours
Ideal slow cooker size: 4-qt.

2 21-oz. cans apple pie
  filling
2-3 cups frozen tart red
  cherries
1 Tbsp. margarine
½ tsp. ground cinnamon
½ tsp. ground nutmeg
⅛ tsp. ground ginger
⅛ tsp. ground cloves

1. Combine all ingredients in slow cooker.
2. Cover. Heat on low 3-4 hours, until hot and bubbly. Stir occasionally.

Exchange List Values

- Carbohydrate 1.5

Tip:
Serve warm over vanilla ice cream, pudding, pound cake, or shortcake biscuits. Top with whipped cream.

You can often reduce the amount of sugar in a recipe by ¼ to ⅓ without changing the taste.

Apple Crisp

Michelle Strite
Goshen, IN

Makes 12 servings

Prep. Time: 15 minutes
Cooking Time: 2-3 hours
Ideal slow cooker size: 4-qt.

⅔ cup sugar
1¼ cups water
3 Tbsp. cornstarch
4 cups sliced, peeled apples
½ tsp. ground cinnamon
¼ tsp. ground allspice
¾ cup quick oatmeal
¼ cup brown sugar
brown sugar substitute to
    equal 2 Tbsp. sugar
½ cup flour
¼ cup light, soft tub
    margarine, at room
    temperature

1. Combine ⅔ cup sugar, water, cornstarch, apples, cinnamon, and allspice. Place in cooker.
2. Combine remaining ingredients until crumbly. Sprinkle over apple filling.
3. Cover. Cook on low 2-3 hours.

Exchange List Values
• Carbohydrate 2.0

Basic Nutritional Values
• Calories 134
  (Calories from Fat 18)
• Total Fat 2 gm
  (Saturated Fat 0.2 gm,
  Polyunsat Fat 0.5 gm,
  Monounsat Fat 0.9 gm)
• Cholesterol 0 mg
• Sodium 34 mg
• Total Carb 29 gm
• Dietary Fiber 2 gm
• Sugars 15 gm
• Protein 1 gm

Hot Fruit Salad

Sharon Miller
Holmesville, OH

Makes 16 servings

Prep. Time: 10 minutes
Cooking Time: 3-4 hours
Ideal slow cooker size: 5-qt.

25-oz. jar chunky
    unsweetened applesauce
21-oz. can light cherry pie
    filling
20-oz. can pineapple
    chunks, packed in juice
15½-oz. can sliced peaches,
    packed in juice
15½-oz. can apricot halves,
    packed in juice
11-oz. can mandarin
    oranges, packed in juice
1 tsp. ground cinnamon

1. Combine fruit in slow cooker, stirring gently.
2. Sprinkle cinnamon over mixture.
3. Cover. Bake on low 3-4 hours.

Exchange List Values
• Fruit 2.0

Basic Nutritional Values
• Calories 105
  (Calories from Fat 1)
• Total Fat 0 gm
  (Saturated Fat 0.0 gm,
  Polyunsat Fat 0.1 gm,
  Monounsat Fat 0.1 gm)
• Cholesterol 0 mg
• Sodium 12 mg
• Total Carb 27 gm
• Dietary Fiber 2 gm
• Sugars 24 gm
• Protein 1 gm

Curried Fruit

Jane Meiser
Harrisonburg, VA

Makes 10 servings

Prep. Time: 15 minutes
Standing Time: 2-8 hours
Cooking Time: 8-10 hours
Ideal slow cooker size: 4- or 5-qt.

16-oz. can peaches,
    undrained
16-oz. can apricots,
    undrained
16-oz. can pears, undrained
20-oz. can pineapple
    chunks, undrained
16-oz. can black cherries,
    undrained
2 Tbsp. brown sugar
brown sugar substitute to
    equal 1 Tbsp. sugar
1 tsp. curry powder
3-4 Tbsp. quick-cooking
    tapioca, depending upon
    how thickened you'd like
    the finished dish to be
margarine, *optional*

1. Combine fruit. Let stand for at least 2 hours, or up to 8, to allow flavors to blend. Drain. Place in slow cooker.
2. Add remaining ingredients. Mix well. Top with margarine, if you want.
3. Cover. Cook on low 8-10 hours.
4. Serve warm or at room temperature.

Exchange List Values
• Fruit 2.0

Basic Nutritional Values

- Calories 107
  (Calories from Fat 1)
- Total Fat 0 gm
  (Saturated Fat 0.0 gm,
  Polyunsat Fat 0.0 gm,
  Monounsat Fat 0.0 gm)
- Cholesterol 0 mg
- Sodium 7 mg
- Total Carb 27 gm
- Dietary Fiber 2 gm
- Sugars 21 gm
- Protein 1 gm

Fruit Dessert Topping

Lavina Hochstedler
Grand Blanc, MI

Makes 40 (2 Tbsp.) servings

Prep. Time: 15 minutes
Cooking Time: 3½-4½ hours
Ideal slow cooker size: 4-qt.

3 tart apples, peeled and sliced
3 pears, peeled and sliced
1 Tbsp. lemon juice
2 Tbsp. brown sugar
brown sugar substitute to equal 1 Tbsp. sugar
2 Tbsp. maple syrup
2 Tbsp. light, soft tub margarine, melted
½ cup chopped pecans
¼ cup raisins
2 cinnamon sticks
1 Tbsp. cornstarch
2 Tbsp. cold water

1. Toss apples and pears in lemon juice in slow cooker.
2. Combine brown sugar, maple syrup, and butter. Pour over fruit.

3. Stir in pecans, raisins, and cinnamon sticks.
4. Cover. Cook on low 3-4 hours.
5. Combine cornstarch and water until smooth. Gradually stir into slow cooker.
6. Cover. Cook on high 30-40 minutes, or until thickened.
7. Discard cinnamon sticks.

Exchange List Values
- Carbohydrate 0.5

Basic Nutritional Values

- Calories 33
  (Calories from Fat 13)
- Total Fat 1 gm
  (Saturated Fat 0.1 gm,
  Polyunsat Fat 0.4 gm,
  Monounsat Fat 0.8 gm)
- Cholesterol 0 mg
- Sodium 5 mg
- Total Carb 6 gm
- Dietary Fiber 1 gm
- Sugars 5 gm
- Protein 0 gm

Tip:
1. Serve over pound cake or ice cream.
2. We also like this served along with pancakes or an egg casserole. We always use Fruit Topping for our breakfasts at church camp.

Puréed fruits can often be used to replace part of the oil in baked goods.

Zesty Pears

Barbara Walker
Sturgis, SD

Makes 8 servings

Prep. Time: 35 minutes
Cooking Time: 4-6 hours
Ideal slow cooker size: 3- or 4-qt.

6 fresh pears
½ cup raisins
¼ cup brown sugar
1 tsp. grated lemon peel
¼ cup brandy
½ cup sauterne wine
½ cup crumbled macaroons
fat-free sour cream, *optional*

1. Peel and core pears. Cut into thin slices.
2. Combine raisins, sugar, and lemon peel. Layer alternately with pear slices in slow cooker.
3. Pour brandy and wine over top.
4. Cover. Cook on low 4-6 hours.
5. Spoon into serving dishes. Cool. Sprinkle with macaroons. Serve plain or topped with sour cream.

Exchange List Values
- Carbohydrate 2.0

Basic Nutritional Values

- Calories 140
  (Calories from Fat 13)
- Total Fat 1 gm
  (Saturated Fat 0.9 gm,
  Polyunsat Fat 0.1 gm,
  Monounsat Fat 0.1 gm)
- Cholesterol 0 mg
- Sodium 11 mg
- Total Carb 33 gm
- Dietary Fiber 3 gm
- Sugars 28 gm
- Protein 1 gm

Fruit Compote Dessert

Beatrice Orgish
Richardson, TX

Makes 8 servings

Prep. Time: 25 minutes
Cooking Time: 3-4 hours
Ideal slow cooker size: 4-qt.

2 medium tart apples,
  peeled
2 medium fresh peaches,
  peeled and cubed
2 cups unsweetened
  pineapple chunks
1¼ cups unsweetened
  pineapple juice
¼ cup honey
2 ¼-inch thick lemon slices
3½-inch cinnamon stick
1 medium firm banana,
  thinly sliced
whipped cream, *optional*
sliced almonds, *optional*
maraschino cherries,
  optional

1. Cut apples into ¼-inch
slices and then in half
horizontally. Place in slow
cooker.
2. Add peaches, pineapple,
pineapple juice, honey, lemon,
and cinnamon. Cover and
cook on low 3-4 hours.
3. Stir in banana slices
just before serving. Garnish
with whipped cream, sliced
almonds, and cherries, if you
wish.

Exchange List Values
• Fruit 2.0

Basic Nutritional Values
• Calories 117   • Cholesterol 0 mg
 (Calories from Fat 4) • Sodium 2 mg
• Total Fat 0 gm   • Total Carb 31 gm
 (Saturated Fat 0.0 gm, • Dietary Fiber 2 gm
 Polyunsat Fat 0.1 gm, • Sugars 27 gm
 Monounsat Fat 0.1 gm) • Protein 1 gm

Scandinavian Fruit Soup

Willard E. Roth
Elkhart, IN

Makes 14 servings

Prep. Time: 15 minutes
Cooking Time: 8 hours
Ideal slow cooker size: 4-qt.

1 cup dried apricots
1 cup dried sliced apples
1 cup dried pitted, dried
  plums
1 cup canned pitted red
  cherries
½ cup quick-cooking
  tapioca
1 cup grape juice *or* re
  wine
3 cups water, *or* more
½ cup orange juice
¼ cup lemon juice
1 Tbsp. grated orange peel
2 Tbsp. brown sugar
brown sugar substitute to
  equal 1 Tbsp. sugar

1. Combine apricots,
apples, prunes, cherries, tapioca, and grape juice in slow
cooker. Cover with water.
2. Cook on low for at least
8 hours.
3. Before serving, stir in
orange juice, lemon juice,
orange peel, brown sugar, and
brown sugar substitute.
4. Serve warm or cold, as
a soup or dessert. Delicious
served chilled over vanilla ice
cream or frozen yogurt.

Exchange List Values
• Fruit 2.0

Basic Nutritional Values
• Calories 120   • Cholesterol 0 mg
 (Calories from Fat 1) • Sodium 10 mg
• Total Fat 0 gm   • Total Carb 31 gm
 (Saturated Fat 0.0 gm, • Dietary Fiber 2 gm
 Polyunsat Fat 0.0 gm, • Sugars 21 gm
 Monounsat Fat 0.1 gm) • Protein 1 gm

Using extracts, such as vanilla or peppermint, enhances the sweetness of a dish without adding too much sugar.

Rhubarb Sauce

Esther Porter
Minneapolis, MN

Makes 6 servings

Prep. Time: 20 minutes
Cooking Time: 4-5 hours
Chilling Time: 4 hours
* minimum*
Ideal slow cooker size: 3- or 4-qt.

1½ lbs. rhubarb
⅛ tsp. salt
½ cup water
½ cup sugar

1. Cut rhubarb into ½-inch slices.
2. Combine all ingredients in slow cooker. Cook on low 4-5 hours.
3. Serve chilled.

Exchange List Values
• Carbohydrate 1.0

Basic Nutritional Values
• Calories 80   • Cholesterol 0 mg
  (Calories from Fat 1) • Sodium 54 mg
• Total Fat 0 gm   • Total Carb 20 gm
  (Saturated Fat 0.0 gm, • Dietary Fiber 2 gm
  Polyunsat Fat 0.0 gm,   • Sugars 17 gm
  Monounsat Fat 0.0 gm)   • Protein 1 gm

Variation:
Add 1 pint sliced strawberries about 30 minutes before removing from heat.

Strawberry Rhubarb Sauce

Tina Snyder
Manheim, PA

Makes 8 servings

Prep. Time: 15 minutes
Cooking Time: 6-7 hours
Chilling Time: 4 hours or more
Ideal slow cooker size: 4-qt.

6 cups chopped rhubarb
1 cup sugar
1 cinnamon stick
½ cup white grape juice
2 cups sliced strawberries

1. Place rhubarb in slow cooker. Pour sugar over rhubarb. Add cinnamon stick and grape juice. Stir well.
2. Cover and cook on low 5-6 hours, or until rhubarb is tender.
3. Stir in strawberries. Cook 1 hour longer.
4. Remove cinnamon stick. Chill at least 4 hours.

Exchange List Values
• Carbohydrate 2.0

Basic Nutritional Values
• Calories 132   • Cholesterol 0 mg
  (Calories from Fat 3) • Sodium 5 mg
• Total Fat 0 gm   • Total Carb 33 gm
  (Saturated Fat 0.0 gm, • Dietary Fiber 3 gm
  Polyunsat Fat 0.1 gm,   • Sugars 29 gm
  Monounsat Fat 0.0 gm)   • Protein 1 gm

Tip:
Serve over cake or ice cream.

Spiced Applesauce

Judi Manos
West Islip, NY

Makes 12 servings

Prep. Time: 20 minutes
Cooking Time: 2½-7 hours
Ideal slow cooker size: 4-qt.

12 cups pared, cored, thinly sliced, medium cooking apples
¼ cup sugar
sugar substitute to equal 2 Tbsp. sugar
½ tsp. cinnamon
1 cup water
1 Tbsp. lemon juice
freshly grated nutmeg, *optional*

1. Place apples in slow cooker.
2. Combine sugar and cinnamon. Mix with apples. Stir in water and lemon juice, and nutmeg, if desired.
3. Cover. Cook on low 5-7 hours, or high 2½-3½ hours. Serve hot or cold.

Exchange List Values
• Carbohydrate 1.0

Basic Nutritional Values
• Calories 75   • Cholesterol 0 mg
  (Calories from Fat 3) • Sodium 0 mg
• Total Fat 0 gm   • Total Carb 20 gm
  (Saturated Fat 0.0 gm, • Dietary Fiber 2 gm
  Polyunsat Fat 0.1 gm,   • Sugars 18 gm
  Monounsat Fat 0.0 gm)   • Protein 0 gm

Homemade Applesauce

Renita Denlinger
Denver, PA

Makes 8 servings

Prep. Time: 10-20 minutes
Cooking Time: 3½ hours
Ideal slow cooker size: 5- or 6-qt.

10 large apples, halved, cored and peeled
½ tsp. cinnamon
dash nutmeg
dash ground cloves
1 Tbsp. water

1. Spray slow cooker with non-stick spray.
2. Put apples in slow cooker.
3. Sprinkle cinnamon, nutmeg, cloves, and water over apples. Stir.
4. Cover. Cook on low 3½ hours, or until apples are soft. If you're home and available, stir the apples after they've cooked for 2 hours. It's okay to mash them up a bit as you stir.
5. Serve warm or chilled.

Note:
This makes the whole house smell wonderful.

Exchange List Values
• Fruit 2.0

Basic Nutritional Values
• Calories 115   Cholesterol 0 mg)
(Calories from Fat 0)   Sodium 0 mg
• Total Fat 0 gm   • Total Carb 31 gm
(Saturated Fat 0 gm, • Dietary Fiber 3 gm
Polyunsat Fat 0 gm,   • Sugars 24 gm
Monounsat Fat 0 gm   • Protein 1 gm

Quick Yummy Peaches

Willard E. Roth
Elkhart, IN

Makes 8 servings

Prep. Time: 20 minutes
Cooking Time: 5 hours
Ideal slow cooker size: 4-qt.

⅓ cup buttermilk baking mix
⅔ cup dry quick oats
¼ cup brown sugar
brown sugar substitute to equal 2 Tbsp. sugar
1 tsp. cinnamon
4 cups sliced peaches, canned *or* fresh
½ cup peach juice *or* water

1. Mix together baking mix, oats, brown sugar, and cinnamon in greased slow cooker.
2. Stir in peaches and peach juice.
3. Cook on low for at least 5 hours. If you like a drier cobbler, remove lid for last 15-30 minutes of cooking.

Exchange List Values
• Carbohydrate 2.0

Basic Nutritional Values
• Calories 131   • Cholesterol 0 mg
(Calories from Fat 11) • Sodium 76 mg
• Total Fat 1 gm   • Total Carb 29 gm
(Saturated Fat 0.1 gm, • Dietary Fiber 3 gm
Polyunsat Fat 0.5 gm, • Sugars 20 gm
Monounsat Fat 0.4 gm) • Protein 2 gm

Scalloped Pineapples

Shirley Hinh
Wayland, IA

Makes 8 servings

Prep. Time: 15 minutes
Cooking Time: 3 hours
Ideal slow cooker size: 4-qt.

½ cup sugar
sugar substitute to equal ¼ cup sugar
3 eggs
¼ cup light, soft margarine, melted
¾ cup milk
20 oz. can crushed pineapple, drained
8 slices bread (crusts removed), cubed

1. Mix together all ingredients in slow cooker.
2. Cook on high 2 hours. Reduce heat to low and cook 1 more hour.

Exchange List Values
• Carbohydrate 2.0   • Fat 0.5

Basic Nutritional Values
• Calories 181   • Cholesterol 81 mg
(Calories from Fat 44) • Sodium 176 mg
• Total Fat 5 gm   • Total Carb 30 gm
(Saturated Fat 1.1 gm, • Dietary Fiber 1 gm
Polyunsat Fat 1.1 gm, • Sugars 21 gm
Monounsat Fat 2.1 gm) • Protein 5 gm

Tip:
Delicious served as a side dish to ham or poultry, or as a dessert served warm or cold.

Black and Blue Cobbler

Renee Shirk
Mount Joy, PA

Makes 12 servings

Prep. Time: 30 minutes
Cooking Time: 2½-3 hours
Ideal slow cooker size: 5-qt.

1 cup flour
6 Tbsp. sugar
sugar substitute to equal
   3 Tbsp. sugar
1 tsp. baking powder
¼ tsp. salt
¼ tsp. ground cinnamon
¼ tsp. ground nutmeg
2 eggs, beaten
2 Tbsp. milk
2 Tbsp. vegetable oil
2 cups fresh, *or* frozen,
   blueberries
2 cups fresh, *or* frozen,
   blackberries
¾ cup water
1 tsp. grated orange peel
6 Tbsp. sugar
sugar substitute to equal
   3 Tbsp. sugar
whipped topping *or* ice
   cream, *optional*

1. Combine flour, ¾ cup sugar, baking powder, salt, cinnamon, and nutmeg.
2. Combine eggs, milk, and oil. Stir into dry ingredients until moistened.
3. Spread the batter evenly over bottom of greased 5-quart slow cooker.
4. In saucepan, combine berries, water, orange peel, and ¾ cup sugar. Bring to boil. Remove from heat and pour over batter. Cover.
5. Cook on high 2-2½ hours, or until toothpick inserted into batter comes out clean. Turn off cooker.
6. Uncover and let stand 30 minutes before serving. Spoon from cooker and serve with whipped topping or ice cream, if desired.

Exchange List Values
• Carbohydrate 2.0 • Fat 0.5

Basic Nutritional Values
• Calories 170
(Calories from Fat 31)
• Total Fat 3 gm
(Saturated Fat 0.5 gm,
Polyunsat Fat 0.9 gm,
Monounsat Fat 1.7 gm)
• Cholesterol 36 mg
• Sodium 92 mg
• Total Carb 34 gm
• Dietary Fiber 2 gm
• Sugars 23 gm
• Protein 3 gm

Cranberry Pudding

Margaret Wheeler
North Bend, OR

Makes 12 servings

Prep. Time: 35 minutes
Cooking Time: 3½-4½ hours
Ideal slow cooker size: 4- or 5-qt.

Pudding:
  1⅓ cups flour
  ½ tsp. salt
  2 tsp. baking soda
  ⅓ cup boiling water
  6 Tbsp. dark molasses
  2 cups whole cranberries
  ½ cup chopped walnuts
  ½ cup water

Butter Sauce:
  1 cup confectioners sugar
  ½ cup fat-free half-and-half
  4 Tbsp. light, soft tub margarine
  1 tsp. vanilla

1. Mix together flour and salt.
2. Dissolve soda in boiling water. Add to flour and salt.
3. Stir in molasses. Blend well.
4. Fold in cranberries and nuts.
5. Pour into well-greased and floured bread or cake pan that will sit in your cooker. Cover with greased tin foil.
6. Pour ½ cup water into cooker. Place foil-covered pan in cooker. Cover with cooker-lid and steam on high 3 to 4 hours, or until pudding tests done with a wooden pick.
7. Remove pan and uncover. Let stand 5 minutes, then unmold.
8. To make butter sauce, mix together all ingredients in saucepan. Cook, stirring over medium heat until sugar dissolves.
9. Serve warm butter sauce over warm cranberry pudding.

Exchange List Values
• Carbohydrate 2.0 • Fat 0.5

Basic Nutritional Values
• Calories 177
(Calories from Fat 46)
• Total Fat 5 gm
(Saturated Fat 0.5 gm,
Polyunsat Fat 2.7 gm,
Monounsat Fat 1.3 gm)
• Cholesterol 1 mg
• Sodium 355 mg
• Total Carb 31 gm
• Dietary Fiber 1 gm
• Sugars 18 gm
• Protein 3 gm

Slow-Cooker Pumpkin Pie

Colleen Heatwole
Burton, MI
Joette Droz
Kalona, IA

Makes 8 servings

Prep. Time: 10 minutes
Cooking Time: 3-4 hours
Cooling Time: 2-4 hours
Ideal slow cooker size: 3-qt.

15-oz. can solid-pack
  pumpkin
12-oz. can fat-free
  evaporated milk
¾ cup sugar
½ cup low-fat buttermilk
  baking mix
2 eggs, beaten
2 Tbsp. tub-type
  margarine, melted
1½ tsp. cinnamon
¾ tsp. ground ginger
¼ tsp. ground nutmeg
whipped topping

1. Spray slow cooker with cooking spray.
2. Mix all ingredients together in slow cooker, except whipped topping.
3. Cover. Cook on low 3-4 hours, or until a toothpick inserted in center comes out clean.
4. Allow to cool to warm, or chill, before serving with whipped topping.

Variation:
   You can substitute 2½ Tbsp. pumpkin pie spice in place of cinnamon, ginger, and nutmeg.

Exchange List Values
• Carbohydrate 2.0   • Fat 1.0

Basic Nutritional Values
• Calories 200   • Cholesterol 50 mg
  (Calories from Fat 45) • Sodium 175 mg
• Total Fat 5 gm   • Total Carb 34 gm
  (Saturated Fat 1.5 gm, • Dietary Fiber 2 gm
  Polyunsat Fat 1.0 gm,   • Sugars 26 gm
  Monounsat Fat 1.5 gm)   • Protein 6 gm

Low-Fat Apple Cake

Sue Hamilton
Minooka, IL

Makes 10 servings

Prep. Time: 25 minutes
Cooking Time: 2½-3 hours
Ideal slow cooker size: 4-qt.

1 cup flour
¾ cup sugar
sugar substitute to equal
  2 Tbsp. sugar
2 tsp. baking powder
1 tsp. ground cinnamon
¼ tsp. salt
4 medium-sized cooking
  apples, chopped
2 eggs, beaten
2 tsp. vanilla

1. Combine flour, sugar, baking powder, cinnamon, and salt.
2. Add apples, stirring lightly to coat.
3. Combine eggs and vanilla. Add to apple mixture. Stir until just moistened. Spoon into lightly greased slow cooker.
4. Cover. Bake on high 2½-3 hours. Serve warm.

Exchange List Values
• Carbohydrate 2.0

Basic Nutritional Values
• Calories 152   • Cholesterol 43 mg
  (Calories from Fat 11) • Sodium 144 mg
• Total Fat 1 gm   • Total Carb 33 gm
  (Saturated Fat 0.4 gm, • Dietary Fiber 2 gm
  Polyunsat Fat 0.2 gm,   • Sugars 22 gm
  Monounsat Fat 0.4 gm)   • Protein 3 gm

Variation:
   Stir ½ cup broken English or black walnuts, or ½ cup raisins, into Step 2.

Note:
   The slow cooker is great for baking desserts. Your guests will be pleasantly surprised to see a cake coming from your slow cooker.

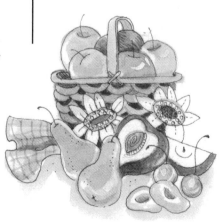

Creamy Orange Cheesecake

Jeanette Oberholtzer
Manheim, PA

Makes 10 servings

Prep. Time: 35 minutes
Cooking Time: 2½-3 hours
Cooling Time: 4 or more hours
Chilling Time: 4 or more hours
Ideal slow cooker size: 5- or 6-qt.

Crust:
- ¾ cup graham cracker crumbs
- 2 Tbsp. sugar
- 3 Tbsp. melted, light, soft tub margarine

Filling:
- 2 8-oz. pkgs. fat-free cream cheese, at room temperature
- ⅔ cup sugar
- 2 eggs
- 1 egg yolk
- ¼ cup frozen orange juice concentrate
- 1 tsp. orange zest
- 1 Tbsp. flour
- ½ tsp. vanilla

1. Combine crust ingredients. Pat into 7" or 9" springform pan, whichever size fits into your slow cooker.
2. Cream together cream cheese and sugar. Add eggs and yolk. Beat for 3 minutes.
3. Beat in juice, zest, flour, and vanilla. Beat 2 minutes.
4. Pour batter into crust. Place on rack in slow cooker.
5. Cover. Cook on high 2½-3 hours. Turn off and leave stand for 1-2 hours, or until cool enough to remove from cooker.
6. Cool completely before removing sides of pan. Chill at least 4 hours before serving.

Exchange List Values
- Carbohydrate 1.5
- Meat, lean 1.0

Basic Nutritional Values
- Calories 159 (Calories from Fat 23)
- Total Fat 3 gm (Saturated Fat 0.7 gm, Polyunsat Fat 0.6 gm, Monounsat Fat 1.1 gm)
- Cholesterol 69 mg
- Sodium 300 mg
- Total Carb 25 gm
- Dietary Fiber 0 gm
- Sugars 19 gm
- Protein 9 gm

Tip:
Serve with thawed frozen whipped topping and fresh or mandarin orange slices.

Lemon Pudding Cake

Jean Butzer
Batavia, NY

Makes 6 servings

Prep. Time: 30 minutes
Cooking Time: 2-3 hours
Ideal slow cooker size: 3- or 4-qt.

- 3 eggs, separated
- 1 tsp. grated lemon peel
- ¼ cup lemon juice
- 1 Tbsp. melted light, soft tub margarine
- 1½ cups fat-free half-and-half
- ½ cup sugar
- sugar substitute to equal 2 Tbsp. sugar
- ¼ cup flour
- ⅛ tsp. salt

1. Beat eggs whites until stiff peaks form. Set aside.
2. Beat eggs yolks. Blend in lemon peel, lemon juice, margarine, and half-and-half.
3. In separate bowl, combine sugar, flour, and salt. Add to egg-lemon mixture, beating until smooth.
4. Fold into beaten egg whites.
5. Spoon into slow cooker.
6. Cover and cook on high 2-3 hours.
7. Serve with spoon from cooker.

Exchange List Values
- Carbohydrate 2.0
- Fat 0.5

Basic Nutritional Values
- Calories 169 (Calories from Fat 37)
- Total Fat 4 gm (Saturated Fat 1.5 gm, Polyunsat Fat 0.5 gm, Monounsat Fat 1.4 gm)
- Cholesterol 111 mg
- Sodium 185 mg
- Total Carb 27 gm
- Dietary Fiber 0 gm
- Sugars 20 gm
- Protein 5 gm

Roasting fruits and vegetables is a healthy way to enhance their natural flavors.

Carrot Cake

Colleen Heatwole
Burton, MI

Makes 10 servings

Prep. Time: 35 minutes
Cooking Time: 3-4 hours
Cooling Time: 10 minutes
Ideal slow cooker size: 4- or 5-qt.

⅓ cup canola oil
2 eggs
1 Tbsp. hot water
½ cup grated raw carrots
¾ cup flour
¾ cup sugar
½ tsp. baking powder
⅛ tsp. salt
¼ tsp. ground allspice
½ tsp. ground cinnamon
⅛ tsp. ground cloves
½ cup chopped nuts
½ cup raisins *or* chopped
  dates
2 Tbsp. flour

1. In large bowl, beat oil, eggs, and water for 1 minute.
2. Add carrots. Mix well.
3. Stir together flour, sugar, baking powder, salt, allspice, cinnamon, and cloves. Add to creamed mixture.
4. Toss nuts and raisins in bowl with 2 Tbsp. flour. Add to creamed mixture. Mix well.
5. Pour into greased and floured 3-lb. coffee can, 9×5 bread pan, or slow cooker baking insert. Place can, pan, or baking insert in slow cooker.
6. Cover insert with its lid, or cover can/pan with 8 paper towels, folded down over edge of slow cooker to absorb moisture. Cover paper towels with cooker lid. Cook on high 3-4 hours.
7. Remove can, pan or insert from cooker and allow to cool on rack for 10 minutes. Run knife around edge of cake. Invert onto serving plate.

Exchange List Values
• Carbohydrate 2.0 • Fat 3.0

Basic Nutritional Values
• Calories 274
(Calories from Fat 147)
• Total Fat 16 gm
(Saturated Fat 1.5 gm,
Polyunsat Fat 6.4 gm,
Monounsat Fat 7.6 gm)
• Cholesterol 43 mg
• Sodium 66 mg
• Total Carb 30 gm
• Dietary Fiber 1 gm
• Sugars 20 gm
• Protein 4 gm

Dump Cake

Janice Muller
Derwood, MD

Makes 15 servings

Prep. Time: 20 minutes
Cooking Time: 2-3 hours
Ideal slow cooker size: 4- or 5-qt.

20-oz. can crushed
  pineapple
21-oz. can light blueberry
  or cherry pie filling
18½-oz. pkg. yellow cake
  mix
cinnamon
⅓ cup light, soft tub
  margarine
⅓ cup chopped walnuts

1. Grease bottom and sides of slow cooker.
2. Spread layers of pineapple, blueberry pie filling, and dry cake mix. Be careful not to mix the layers.
3. Sprinkle with cinnamon.
4. Top with thin layers of butter chunks and nuts.
5. Cover. Cook on high 2-3 hours.

Exchange List Values
• Carbohydrate 2.5 • Fat 1.0

Basic Nutritional Values
• Calories 219
(Calories from Fat 57)
• Total Fat 6 gm
(Saturated Fat 1.5 gm,
Polyunsat Fat 2.4 gm,
Monounsat Fat 2.2 gm)
• Cholesterol 0 mg
• Sodium 250 mg
• Total Carb 41 gm
• Dietary Fiber 1 gm
• Sugars 28 gm
• Protein 2 gm

Variation:
Use a pkg. of spice cake mix and apple pie filling.

Chocolate Peanut Butter Cake

Ruth Ann Gingerich
New Holland, PA

Makes 11 servings

Prep. Time: 20 minutes
Cooking Time: 2-3 hours
Cooling Time: 2 hours minutes
Ideal slow cooker size: 4-qt.

2 cups (half a package)
  milk chocolate cake mix
½ cup water
¼ cup peanut butter
1 egg
2 egg whites
6 Tbsp. chopped walnuts

1. Combine all ingredients. Beat 2 minutes in electric mixer.
2. Pour into greased and floured 3-lb. coffee can or 9×5 bread pan. Place can/pan in slow cooker.
3. Cover top of can/pan with 8 paper towels.
4. Cover cooker. Bake on high 2-3 hours.
5. Allow to cool for 10 minutes. Run knife around edge and invert cake onto serving plate. Cool completely before slicing and serving.

Exchange List Values
• Carbohydrate 1.5 • Fat 1.5

Basic Nutritional Values
• Calories 165   • Cholesterol 19 mg
  (Calories from Fat 75) • Sodium 255 mg
• Total Fat 8 gm   • Total Carb 20 gm
  (Saturated Fat 1.5 gm, • Dietary Fiber 1 gm
  Polyunsat Fat 3.6 gm,   • Sugars 11 gm
  Monounsat Fat 2.8 gm) • Protein 4 gm

Graham Cracker Cookies

Cassandra Ly
Carlisle, PA

Makes 96 (1 cookie) servings

Prep. Time: 45 minutes
Cooking Time: 1½ hours
Baking Time: 7-9 minutes per
  cookie sheet
Ideal slow cooker size: 4-qt.

12-oz. pkg. (2 cups) semi-
  sweet chocolate chips
2 1-oz. squares unsweetened
  baking chocolate, shaved
2 14-oz. cans fat-free
  sweetened condensed
  milk
3¾ cups crushed graham
  cracker crumbs, *divided*
1 cup finely chopped
  walnuts

1. Place chocolate in slow cooker.
2. Cover. Cook on high 1 hour, stirring every 15 minutes. Continue to cook on low heat, stirring every 15 minutes, or until chocolate is melted (about 30 minutes).
3. Stir milk into melted chocolate.
4. Add 3 cups graham cracker crumbs, 1 cup at a time, stirring after each addition.
5. Stir in nuts. Mixture should be thick but not stiff.
6. Stir in remaining graham cracker crumbs to reach consistency of cookie dough.
7. Drop by heaping teaspoonfuls onto lightly

greased cookie sheets. Keep remaining mixture warm by covering and turning the slow cooker to warm.
8. Bake at 325° for 7-9 minutes, or until tops of cookies begin to crack. Remove from oven. Cool 1-2 minutes before transferring to waxed paper.

Exchange List Values
• Carbohydrate 0.5 • Fat 0.5

Basic Nutritional Values
• Calories 65   • Cholesterol 0 mg
  (Calories from Fat 23) • Sodium 29 mg
• Total Fat 3 gm   • Total Carb 10 gm
  (Saturated Fat 0.9 gm, • Dietary Fiber 0 gm
  Polyunsat Fat 0.8 gm,   • Sugars 8 gm
  Monounsat Fat 0.9 gm) • Protein 1 gm

Note:
1. These cookies freeze well.
2. This delectable fudge-like cookie is a family favorite. The original recipe (from my maternal grandmother) was so involved and yielded so few cookies that my mom and I would get together to make a couple of batches only at Christmas-time. Adapting the recipe for using a slow cooker, rather than a double boiler, allows me to prepare a double batch without help.

Cherry Delight

Anna Musser
Manheim, PA
Marianne J. Troyer
Millersburg, OH

Makes 12 servings

Prep. Time: 20 minutes
Cooking Time: 2-4 hours
Cooling Time: 1-2 hours
Ideal slow cooker size: 4-qt.

20-oz. can cherry pie
　fillng, light
½ pkg. yellow cake mix
¼ cup light, soft tub
　margarine, melted
⅓ cup walnuts, *optional*

1. Place pie filling in greased slow cooker.
2. Combine dry cake mix and butter (mixture will be crumbly). Sprinkle over filling. Sprinkle with walnuts.
3. Cover and cook on low 4 hours, or on high 2 hours.
4. Allow to cool, then serve in bowls with dips of ice cream.

Exchange List Values
• Carbohydrate 2.0

Basic Nutritional Values
• Calories 137	• Cholesterol 0 mg
(Calories from Fat 33)	• Sodium 174 mg
• Total Fat 4 gm	• Total Carb 26 gm
(Saturated Fat 0.9 gm,	• Dietary Fiber 1 gm
Polyunsat Fat 0.9 gm,	• Sugars 19 gm
Monounsat Fat 1.6 gm)	• Protein 1 gm

Apple Peanut Crumble

Phyllis Attig
Reynolds, IL
Joan Becker
Dodge City, KS
Pam Hochstedler
Kalona, IA

Makes 8 servings

Prep. Time: 25 minutes
Cooking Time: 5-6 hours
Ideal slow cooker size: 4-qt.

4 medium cooking apples,
　peeled and sliced
⅓ cup packed brown sugar
brown sugar substitute to
　equal 3 Tbsp. sugar
½ cup flour
½ cup quick oats
½ tsp. cinnamon
¼-½ tsp. nutmeg
¼ cup light, soft tub
　margarine, softened
2 Tbsp. peanut butter
ice cream *or* whipped
　cream

1. Place apple slices in slow cooker.
2. Combine brown sugar, flour, oats, cinnamon, and nutmeg.
3. Cut in butter and peanut butter. Sprinkle over apples.
4. Cover cooker and cook on low 5-6 hours.
5. Serve warm or cold, plain or with ice cream or whipped cream.

Exchange List Values
• Carbohydrate 2.0　• Fat 0.5

Basic Nutritional Values
• Calories 164	• Cholesterol 0 mg
(Calories from Fat 45)	• Sodium 71 mg
• Total Fat 5 gm	• Total Carb 29 gm
(Saturated Fat 0.7 gm,	• Dietary Fiber 2 gm
Polyunsat Fat 1.3 gm,	• Sugars 18 gm
Monounsat Fat 2.4 gm)	• Protein 3 gm

Hot Fudge Cake

Maricarol Magil
Freehold, NJ

Makes 10 servings

Prep. Time: 25 minutes
Cooking Time: 2-3 hours
Ideal slow cooker size: 4-qt.

¾ cup packed brown sugar,
　divided
brown sugar substitute
　to equal ½ cup sugar,
　divided
1 cup flour
¼ cup plus 3 Tbsp.
　unsweetened cocoa
　powder, *divided*
2 tsp. baking powder
½ tsp. salt
½ cup fat-free half-and-half
2 Tbsp. melted butter
½ tsp. vanilla
1¾ cups boiling water
vanilla ice cream, *optional*

1. Mix together ½ cup brown sugar, ¼ cup brown sugar substitute, flour, 3 Tbsp. cocoa, baking powder, and salt.
2. Stir in milk, butter, and vanilla. Spread over the bottom of slow cooker.

Control the diabetes so it doesn't control you.

3. Mix together ¼ cup brown sugar, ¼ cup brown sugar substitute, and ¼ cup cocoa. Sprinkle over mixture in slow cooker.

4. Pour in boiling water. Do not stir.

5. Cover and cook on high 2-3 hours, or until a toothpick inserted comes out clean.

6. Serve warm with vanilla ice cream.

Exchange List Values
• Carbohydrate 2.0

Basic Nutritional Values
• Calories 143
  (Calories from Fat 11)
• Total Fat 1 gm
  (Saturated Fat 0.4 gm,
  Polyunsat Fat 0.2 gm,
  Monounsat Fat 0.4 gm)
• Cholesterol 1 mg
• Sodium 226 mg
• Total Carb 32 gm
• Dietary Fiber 2 gm
• Sugars 21 gm
• Protein 2 gm

Peanut Butter and Hot Fudge Pudding Cake

Sara Wilson
Blairstown, MO

Makes 6 servings

Prep. Time: 25 minutes
Cooking Time: 2-3 hours
Ideal slow cooker size: 4-qt.

½ cup flour
½ cup sugar, *divided*
sugar substitute to equal
   2 Tbsp. sugar
¾ tsp. baking powder
⅓ cup fat-free milk
1 Tbsp. canola oil
½ tsp. vanilla
¼ cup peanut butter

3 Tbsp. unsweetened cocoa
   powder
1 cup boiling water
vanilla ice cream, *optional*

1. Combine flour, ¼ cup sugar, sugar substitute and baking powder. Add milk, oil, and vanilla. Mix until smooth. Stir in peanut butter. Pour into slow cooker.

2. Mix together remaining ¼ cup sugar and cocoa powder. Gradually stir in boiling water. Pour mixture over batter in slow cooker. Do not stir.

3. Cover and cook on high 2-3 hours, or until toothpick inserted comes out clean.

4. Serve warm with ice cream.

Exchange List Values
• Carbohydrate 2.0 • Fat 1.0

Basic Nutritional Values
• Calories 197
  (Calories from Fat 73)
• Total Fat 8 gm
  (Saturated Fat 1.1 gm,
  Polyunsat Fat 2.1 gm,
  Monounsat Fat 4.2 gm)
• Cholesterol 0 mg
• Sodium 92 mg
• Total Carb 29 gm
• Dietary Fiber 2 gm
• Sugars 18 gm
• Protein 5 gm

Chocolate Rice Pudding

Michele Ruvola, Selden, NY

Makes 12 servings

Prep. Time: 20 minutes
Cooking Time: 2½-3½ hours
Ideal slow cooker size: 3- or 4-qt.

4 cups cooked white rice
½ cup sugar
sugar substitute to equal
   2 Tbsp. sugar
¼ cup baking cocoa powder
2 Tbsp. light, soft tub
   margarine, melted
1 tsp. vanilla
2 12-oz. cans fat-free
   evaporated milk
whipped cream, *optional*
sliced toasted almonds,
   optional
maraschino cherries,
   optional

1. Combine first 6 ingredients in greased slow cooker.

2. Cover. Cook on low 2½-3½ hours, or until liquid is absorbed.

3. Serve warm or chilled. Top individual servings with a dollop of whipped cream, sliced toasted almonds, and a maraschino cherry.

Exchange List Values
• Carbohydrate 2.5

Basic Nutritional Values
• Calories 180
  (Calories from Fat 15)
• Total Fat 2 gm
  (Saturated Fat 0.3 gm,
  Polyunsat Fat 0.3 gm,
  Monounsat Fat 0.8 gm)
• Cholesterol 0 mg
• Sodium 104 mg
• Total Carb 35 gm
• Dietary Fiber 1 gm
• Sugars 18 gm
• Protein 7 gm

Appetizers

Levi's Sesame Chicken Wings

Shirley Unternahrer Hinh
Wayland, IA

Makes 16 appetizer servings

Prep. Time: 40 minutes
Cooking Time: 2½-5 hours
Ideal slow cooker size: 4-qt.

3 lbs. chicken wings
salt, to taste
pepper, to taste
1 cup honey
sugar substitute to equal
  6 Tbsp. sugar
¾ cup light soy sauce
½ cup no-salt-added ketchup
2 Tbsp. canola oil
2 Tbsp. sesame oil
2 garlic cloves, minced
toasted sesame seeds

1. Rinse wings. Cut at joint.
Sprinkle with salt and pepper.
Place on broiler pan.
   2. Broil 5 inches from top,
10 minutes on each side.
Place chicken in slow cooker.
   3. Combine remaining
ingredients except sesame
seeds. Pour over chicken.
   4. Cover. Cook on low 5
hours or high 2½ hours.
   5. Sprinkle sesame seeds
over top just before serving.
   6. Serve as appetizer, or
with brown rice and shredded
lettuce for a meal.

Exchange List Values
• Carbohydrate 1.5 • Meat, high fat 1.0

Basic Nutritional Values
• Calories 192   • Cholesterol 22 mg
  (Calories from Fat 77) • Sodium 453 mg
• Total Fat 9 gm   • Total Carb 21 gm
  (Saturated Fat 1.8 gm, • Dietary Fiber 0 gm
  Polyunsat Fat 2.3 gm,   • Sugars 21 gm
  Monounsat Fat 3.7 gm)   • Protein 9 gm

Note:
   My husband and his co-
workers have a potluck lunch
at work. I think this is a nice
way to break the monotony
of the week or month. And it
gives them a chance to share.
What better way to keep it
ready than a slow cooker!

Keep healthy snacks handy! A delayed meal or change in your schedule can happen anytime, so keep snacks in your desk, briefcase, pocketbook, or glove compartment.

Quick and Easy Nacho Dip

Kristina Shull
Timberville, VA

Makes 20 servings

Prep. Time: 15 minutes
Cooking Time: 2 hours
Ideal slow cooker size: 3-qt.

½ lb. 85%-lean ground beef
pepper, *optional*
onion powder, *optional*
2 garlic cloves, minced,
   optional
2 16-oz. jars salsa (as hot *or*
   mild as you like)
15-oz. can fat-free refried
   beans
1½ cups fat-free sour cream
1½ cups shredded reduced-
   fat sharp cheddar
   cheese, *divided*

1. Brown ground beef.
Drain. Add pepper, onion
powder, and minced garlic.
2. Combine beef, salsa,
beans, sour cream, and 1 cup
cheese in slow cooker.
3. Cover. Heat on low 2
hours. Just before serving
sprinkle with ½ cup cheese.
4. Serve with tortilla chips.

Exchange List Values
• Carbohydrate 0.5 • Meat, lean 1.0

Basic Nutritional Values
• Calories 80   • Cholesterol 14 mg
  (Calories from Fat 27) • Sodium 298 mg
• Total Fat 3 gm   • Total Carb 8 gm
  (Saturated Fat 1.5 gm, • Dietary Fiber 2 gm
  Polyunsat Fat 0.2 gm,   • Sugars 3 gm
  Monounsat Fat 1.0 gm)   • Protein 6 gm

Red Pepper Cheese Dip

Ann Bender
Ft. Defiance, VA

Makes 12-15 servings

Prep. Time: 10 minutes
Cooking Time: 2 hours
Ideal slow cooker size: 3- or 4-qt.

2 Tbsp. olive oil
4 large red peppers, cut
   into 1" squares
4 oz. feta cheese

1. Pour oil into slow cooker.
Stir in peppers.
2. Cover. Cook on low 2
hours.
3. Serve with feta cheese
on crackers.

Exchange List Values
• Vegetable 1.0   • Fat 0.5

Basic Nutritional Values
• Calories 49   • Cholesterol 7 mg
  (Calories from Fat 32) • Sodium 86 mg
• Total Fat 4 gm   • Total Carb 3 gm
  (Saturated Fat 1.4 gm, • Dietary Fiber 1 gm
  Polyunsat Fat 0.3 gm,   • Sugars 2 gm
  Monounsat Fat 1.7 gm)   • Protein 2 gm

Pizza Fondue

Lisa Warren
Parkesburg, PA

Makes 18 servings

Prep. Time: 15 minutes
Cooking Time: 2-3 hours
Ideal slow cooker size: 3-qt.

½ lb. 85%-lean ground beef
2 15 oz. cans pizza sauce
   with cheese
4 oz. grated fat-free
   cheddar cheese
4 oz. grated reduced-fat
   mozzarella cheese
1 tsp. dried oregano
½ tsp. fennel seed, *optional*
1 Tbsp. cornstarch

1. Brown beef, crumble
fine, and drain.
2. Combine all ingredients
except tortilla chips in slow
cooker.
3. Cover. Heat on low 2-3
hours.
4. Serve with tortilla chips.

Exchange List Values
• Meat, medium fat 1.0

Basic Nutritional Values
• Calories 76   • Cholesterol 13 mg
  (Calories from Fat 34) • Sodium 392 mg
• Total Fat 4 gm   • Total Carb 4 gm
  (Saturated Fat 1.4 gm, • Dietary Fiber 0 gm
  Polyunsat Fat 0.9 gm,   • Sugars 3 gm
  Monounsat Fat 0.9 gm)   • Protein 6 gm

Hot Cheese and Bacon Dip

Lee Ann Hazlett
Freeport, IL

Makes 25 servings

Prep. Time: 15 minutes
Cooking Time: 1 hour
Ideal slow cooker size: 1-qt.

9 slices bacon, diced
2 8-oz. pkgs. fat-free cream
  cheese, cubed and
  softened
8 oz. shredded reduced-fat
  mild cheddar cheese
1 cup fat-free half-and-half
2 tsp. Worcestershire sauce
1 tsp. dried minced onion
½ tsp. dry mustard
½ tsp. salt
2-3 drops Tabasco

1. Brown and drain bacon.
Set aside.
2. Mix remaining ingredients in slow cooker.
3. Cover. Cook on low 1
hour, stirring occasionally
until cheese melts.
4. Stir in bacon.
5. Serve with fruit slices
or French bread slices. (Dip
fruit in lemon juice to prevent
browning.)

Exchange List Values
• Meat, lean 1.0

Basic Nutritional Values
• Calories 54
  (Calories from Fat 28)
• Total Fat 3 gm
  (Saturated Fat 1.5 gm,
  Polyunsat Fat 0.2 gm,
  Monounsat Fat 1.1 gm)
• Cholesterol 11 mg
• Sodium 273 mg
• Total Carb 2 gm
• Dietary Fiber 0 gm
• Sugars 1 gm
• Protein 6 gm

Cheesy Hot Bean Dip

John D. Allen
Rye, CO

Makes 20 servings

Prep. Time: 10 minutes
Cooking Time: 2 hours
Ideal slow cooker size: 3-qt.

16-oz. can refried beans
1 cup salsa
2 cups (8 ozs.) shredded
  reduced-fat Monterey
  Jack and reduced fat
  cheddar cheeses, mixed
1 cup fat-free sour cream
3-oz. pkg. fat-free cream
  cheese, cubed
1 Tbsp. chili powder
¼ tsp. ground cumin

1. Combine all ingredients
except chips in slow cooker.
2. Cover. Cook on high 2
hours. Stir 2-3 times during
cooking.
3. Serve warm from the
cooker with chips.

Exchange List Values
• Carbohydrate 0.5 • Fat 0.5

Basic Nutritional Values
• Calories 65
  (Calories from Fat 22)
• Total Fat 2 gm
  (Saturated Fat 1.5 gm,
  Polyunsat Fat 0.1 gm,
  Monounsat Fat 0.7 gm)
• Cholesterol 11 mg
• Sodium 275 mg
• Total Carb 6 gm
• Dietary Fiber 1 gm
• Sugars 2 gm
• Protein 6 gm

Note:
  This bean dip is a favorite.
Once you start on it, it's hard
to leave it alone. We have
been known to dip into it
even when it's cold.

Refried Bean Dip

Maryann Markano
Wilmington, DE

Makes 12 servings

Prep. Time: 10 minutes
Cooking Time: 1-2½ hours
Ideal slow cooker size: 3-qt.

20-oz. can fat-free refried
  beans
1 cup shredded fat-free
  cheddar cheese
½ cup chopped green
  onions
2-4 Tbsp. bottled taco
  sauce (depending upon
  how spicy a dip you like)
tortilla chips

1. Combine beans, cheese,
onions, salt, and taco sauce in
slow cooker.
2. Cover. Cook on low 2-2½
hours, or cook on high 30
minutes and then on low 30
minutes.
3. Serve with tortilla chips.

Exchange List Values
• Starch 0.5 • Meat, very lean 1.0

Basic Nutritional Values
• Calories 56
  (Calories from Fat 0)
• Total Fat 0 gm
  (Saturated Fat 0.0 gm,
  Polyunsat Fat 0.0 gm,
  Monounsat Fat 0.0 gm)
• Cholesterol 1 mg
• Sodium 270 mg
• Total Carb 8 gm
• Dietary Fiber 2 gm
• Sugars 1 gm
• Protein 5 gm

Slow-Cooked Salsa

Joleen Albrecht
Gladstone, MI

Makes 34 ¼-cup servings

Prep Time: 15-20 minutes
Cooking Time: 3 hours
Ideal slow-cooker size: 3-qt.

10 fresh Roma, *or* plum, tomatoes, chopped coarsely
2 garlic cloves, minced
1 onion, chopped
2 jalapeño peppers
¼ cup cilantro leaves
½ tsp. salt

1. Place tomatoes, garlic, and onion in slow cooker.

2. Remove stems from jalapeños. Remove seeds, too, if you prefer a milder flavor. Chop jalapeños. Stir into slow cooker.

3. Cover. Cook on high 2½ to 3 hours, or until vegetables are softened.

4. Allow to cool.

5. When cooled, combine cooked mixture with cilantro and salt in a blender or food processor. Blend or process to the consistency that you like.

Exchange List Values
• Free food

Basic Nutritional Values
• Calories 10   Cholesterol 0 mg),
  (Calories from Fat 0)   Sodium 35 mg
• Total Fat 0 gm   • Total Carb 2 gm
  (Saturated Fat 0 gm,   • Dietary Fiber 0 gm
  Polyunsat Fat 0 gm   • Sugars 1 gm
  Monounsat Fat 0 gm   • Protein 0 gm

Reuben Spread

Clarice Williams
Fairbank, IA
Julie McKenzie
Punxsutawney, PA

Makes 52 servings

Prep. Time: 15 minutes
Cooking Time: 1-2 hours
Ideal slow cooker size: 3-qt.

½ lb. corned beef, shredded *or* chopped, all visible fat removed
16-oz. can sauerkraut, well drained
1 cups shredded Swiss cheese
1 cups shredded cheddar cheese
1 cup mayonnaise
Thousand Island dressing, *optional*

1. Combine all ingredients except bread and Thousand Island dressing in slow cooker. Mix well.

2. Cover. Cook on high 1-2 hours until heated through, stirring occasionally.

3. Turn to low and keep warm in cooker while serving. Put spread on bread slices. Top individual servings with Thousand Island dressing, if desired.

Exchange List Values
• Fat 1.0

Basic Nutritional Values
• Calories 58   • Cholesterol 10 mg
  (Calories from Fat 49)   • Sodium 113 mg
• Total Fat 5 gm   • Total Carb 1 gm
  (Saturated Fat 1.5 gm,   • Dietary Fiber 0 gm
  Polyunsat Fat 1.9 gm,   • Sugars 0 gm
  Monounsat Fat 1.6 gm)   • Protein 2 gm

Note:
  Low-fat cheese and mayonnaise are not recommended for this spread.

Variation:
  Use dried beef instead of corned beef.

Good snack choices include grains, fruits, and vegetables.

237

Hearty Beef Dip Fondue

Ann Bender
Ft. Defiance, VA
Charlotte Shaffer
East Earl, PA

Makes 10 (¼ cup) servings

Prep. Time: 25 minutes
Cooking Time: 6 hours
Ideal slow cooker size: 3-qt.

1 cup fat-free milk
¾ cup fat-free half-and-half
2 8-oz. pkgs. fat-free cream
   cheese, cubed
2 tsp. dry mustard
¼ cup chopped green onions
2½ oz. sliced dried beef,
   shredded

1. Heat milk and half-and-half in slow cooker on high until steaming.
2. Add cheese. Stir until melted.
3. Add mustard, green onions, and dried beef. Stir well.
4. Cover. Cook on low for up to 6 hours.
5. Serve by dipping toasted bread pieces on long forks into mixture.

Exchange List Values
• Carbohydrate 0.5   • Meat, very lean 1.0

Basic Nutritional Values
• Calories 72   • Cholesterol 10 mg
(Calories from Fat 6) • Sodium 508 mg
• Total Fat 1 gm   • Total Carb 6 gm
(Saturated Fat 0.1 gm, • Dietary Fiber 0 gm
Polyunsat Fat 0.0 gm, • Sugars 4 gm
Monounsat Fat 0.1 gm) • Protein 10 gm

Variations:
Add ½ cup chopped pecans, 2 Tbsp. chopped olives, or 1 tsp. minced onion in Step 3.

Note:
I make this on cold winter evenings as we sit around the table playing games.

Hot Crab Dip

Cassandra Ly
Carlisle, PA
Miriam Nolt
New Holland, PA

Makes 20 servings

Prep. Time: 15 minutes
Cooking Time: 3-4 hours
Ideal slow cooker size: 3- or 4-qt.

½ cup milk
⅓ cup salsa
3 8-oz. pkgs. fat-free cream
   cheese, cubed
2 8-oz. pkgs. imitation
   crabmeat, flaked
1 cup thinly sliced green
   onions
4-oz. can chopped green
   chilies
assorted crackers *or* bread
   cubes

1. Combine milk and salsa. Transfer to greased slow cooker.
2. Stir in cream cheese, crabmeat, onions, and chilies.
3. Cover. Cook on low 3-4 hours, stirring every 30 minutes.

4. Serve with crackers or bread.

Exchange List Values
• Carbohydrate 0.5   • Meat, very lean 1.0

Basic Nutritional Values
• Calories 60   • Cholesterol 9 mg
(Calories from Fat 4) • Sodium 410 mg
• Total Fat 0 gm   • Total Carb 5 gm
(Saturated Fat 0.1 gm, • Dietary Fiber 0 gm
Polyunsat Fat 0.2 gm, • Sugars 4 gm
Monounsat Fat 0.1 gm) • Protein 8 gm

Liver Paté

Barbara Walker
Sturgis, SD

Makes 12 (2 Tbsp.) servings

Prep. Time: 20 minutes
Cooking Time: 4-5 hours
Ideal slow cooker size: 3-qt.

1 lb. chicken livers
½ cup dry wine
1 tsp. instant chicken
   bouillon
1 tsp. minced parsley
1 Tbsp. instant minced
   onion
¼ tsp. ground ginger
½ tsp. seasoning salt
1 Tbsp. light soy sauce
¼ tsp. dry mustard
¼ cup light, soft tub
   margarine
1 Tbsp. brandy

1. In slow cooker, combine all ingredients except butter and brandy.
2. Cover. Cook on low 4-5 hours. Let stand in liquid until cool.

3. Drain. Place in blender or food grinder. Add margarine and brandy. Process until smooth.

4. Serve with crackers or toast.

Exchange List Values
• Meat, lean 1.0

Basic Nutritional Values
• Calories 61
(Calories from Fat 28)
• Total Fat 3 gm
(Saturated Fat 0.6 gm,
Polyunsat Fat 0.6 gm,
Monounsat Fat 1.2 gm)
• Cholesterol 137 mg
• Sodium 235 mg
• Total Carb 1 gm
• Dietary Fiber 0 gm
• Sugars 0 gm
• Protein 6 gm

Cheesy New Orleans Shrimp Dip

Kelly Amos
Pittsboro, NC

Makes 20 servings

Prep. Time: 25 minutes
Cooking Time: 1 hour
Ideal slow cooker size: 1-qt.

1 slice bacon
3 medium onions, chopped
1 garlic clove, minced
4 jumbo shrimp, peeled and deveined
1 medium tomato, peeled and chopped
7 oz. (1¾ cups) reduced-fat Monterey Jack cheese, shredded
4 drops Tabasco sauce
⅛ tsp. cayenne pepper dash of black pepper
milk to thin dip, *optional*
chips

---

1. Cook bacon until crisp. Drain on paper towel. Crumble.

2. Sauté onion and garlic in skillet sprayed with non-fat cooking spray. Drain on paper towel.

3. Coarsely chop shrimp.

4. Combine all ingredients except chips in slow cooker.

5. Cover. Cook on low 1 hour, or until cheese is melted. Thin with milk if too thick. Serve with chips.

Exchange List Values
• Meat, lean 1.0

Basic Nutritional Values
• Calories 43
(Calories from Fat 18)
• Total Fat 2 gm
(Saturated Fat 1.5 gm,
Polyunsat Fat 0.1 gm,
Monounsat Fat 0.6 gm)
• Cholesterol 13 mg
• Sodium 90 mg
• Total Carb 2 gm
• Dietary Fiber 0 gm
• Sugars 2 gm
• Protein 4 gm

Roasted Pepper and Artichoke Spread

Sherril Bieberly
Sauna, KS

Makes 24 servings

Prep. Time: 20 minutes
Cooking Time: 1 hour
Ideal slow cooker size: 1-qt.

1 cup grated Parmesan cheese
½ cup reduced-fat mayonnaise
8-oz. pkg. fat-free cream cheese, softened
1 garlic clove, minced

14-oz. can artichoke hearts, drained and chopped finely
⅓ cup finely chopped roasted red bell peppers
crackers, cut-up fresh vegetables, *or* snack-bread slices

1. Combine Parmesan cheese, mayonnaise, cream cheese, and garlic in food processor. Process until smooth. Place mixture in slow cooker.

2. Add artichoke hearts and red bell pepper. Stir well.

3. Cover. Cook on low 1 hour. Stir again.

4. Use as spread for crackers, cut-up fresh vegetables, or snack-bread slices.

Exchange List Values
• Fat 1.0

Basic Nutritional Values
• Calories 49
(Calories from Fat 29)
• Total Fat 3 gm
(Saturated Fat 1.3 gm,
Polyunsat Fat 0.7 gm,
Monounsat Fat 0.9 gm)
• Cholesterol 8 mg
• Sodium 209 mg
• Total Carb 2 gm
• Dietary Fiber 0 gm
• Sugars 1 gm
• Protein 4 gm

Baked Brie with Cranberry Chutney

Amymarlene Jensen
Fountain, CO

Makes 25 servings

Prep. Time: 25 minutes
Cooking Time: 4½ hours
Ideal slow cooker size: 1-qt.

1 cup fresh, *or dried,*
    cranberries
½ cup brown sugar
⅓ cup cider vinegar
2 Tbsp. water, *or orange*
    juice
2 tsp. minced crystallized
    ginger
¼ tsp. cinnamon
⅛ tsp. ground cloves
oil
8-oz. round of Brie cheese
1 Tbsp. sliced almonds,
    toasted
crackers

1. Mix together cranberries, brown sugar, vinegar, water or juice, ginger, cinnamon, and cloves in slow cooker.

2. Cover. Cook on low 4 hours. Stir once near the end to see if it is thickening. If not, remove top, turn heat to high and cook 30 minutes without lid.

3. Put cranberry chutney in covered container and chill for up to 2 weeks. When ready to serve, bring to room temperature.

4. Brush shallow baking dish or ovenproof plate with vegetable oil, place Brie, still in rind, on plate.

5. Bake uncovered at 350° for 9 minutes, until cheese is soft and partially melted. Remove from oven.

6. Top with half the chutney and garnish with almonds. Serve with crackers.

Exchange List Values
• Fat 1.0

Basic Nutritional Values
• Calories 38   • Cholesterol 8 mg
  (Calories from Fat 23)   • Sodium 67 mg
• Total Fat 3 gm   • Total Carb 3 gm
  (Saturated Fat 1.5 gm,   • Dietary Fiber 0 gm
  Polyunsat Fat 0.1 gm,   • Sugars 3 gm
  Monounsat Fat 0.8 gm)   • Protein 1 gm

Hot Artichoke Dip

Mary E. Wheatley
Mashpee, MA

Makes 30 (¼ cup) servings

Prep. Time: 20 minutes
Cooking Time: 1-4 hours
Ideal slow cooker size: 4-qt.

2 14¾ oz. jars marinated
    artichoke hearts, drained
1 cup fat-free mayonnaise
1 cup fat-free sour cream
1 cup water chestnuts,
    chopped
2 cups freshly grated
    Parmesan cheese
¼ cup finely chopped
    scallions

1. Cut artichoke hearts into small pieces. Add mayonnaise, sour cream, water chestnuts, cheese, and scallions. Pour into slow cooker.

2. Cover. Cook on high 1-2 hours or on low 3-4 hours.

3. Serve with crackers or crusty French bread.

Exchange List Values
• Carbohydrate 0.5   • Fat 0.5

Basic Nutritional Values
• Calories 57   • Cholesterol 6 mg
  (Calories from Fat 26)   • Sodium 170 mg
• Total Fat 3 gm   • Total Carb 5 gm
  (Saturated Fat 1.2 gm,   • Dietary Fiber 0 gm
  Polyunsat Fat 0.7 gm,   • Sugars 2 gm
  Monounsat Fat 0.9 gm)   • Protein 3 gm

Artichokes

Susan Yoder Graber
Eureka, IL

Makes 4 servings

Prep. Time: 20 minutes
Cooking Time: 2-10 hours
Ideal slow cooker size: 3-qt.

4 artichokes
1 tsp. salt
2 Tbsp. lemon juice

1. Wash and trim artichokes by cutting off the stems flush with the bottoms of the artichokes and by cutting ¾-1-inch off the tops. Stand upright in slow cooker.
2. Mix together salt and lemon juice and pour over artichokes.
3. Pour in water to cover ¾ of artichokes.
4. Cover. Cook on low 8-10 hours, or high 2-4 hours.
5. Serve with melted butter. Pull off individual leaves and dip bottom of each into butter. Using your teeth, strip the individual leaf of the meaty portion at the bottom of each leaf.

Exchange List Values
• Vegetable 3.0

Basic Nutritional Values
• Calories 60
(Calories from Fat 2)
• Total Fat 0 gm
(Saturated Fat 0.0 gm,
Polyunsat Fat 0.1 gm,
Monounsat Fat 0.0 gm)
• Cholesterol 0 mg
• Sodium 397 mg
• Total Carb 13 gm
• Dietary Fiber 6 gm
• Sugars 1 gm
• Protein 4 gm

Note:
3 vegetable exchanges = 1 carbohydrate exchange

Chili Nuts

Barbara Aston
Ashdown, AR

Makes 80 (1 Tbsp.) servings

Prep. Time: 10 minutes
Cooking Time: 2½-3 hours
Ideal slow cooker size: 3-qt.

half stick (¼ cup) melted butter
2 12-oz. cans cocktail peanuts
1⅝-oz. pkg. chili seasoning mix

1. Pour butter over nuts in slow cooker. Sprinkle in dry chili mix. Toss together.
2. Cover. Heat on low 2-2½ hours. Turn to high. Remove lid and cook 10-15 minutes.
3. Serve warm or cool.

Exchange List Values
• Fat 1.0

Basic Nutritional Values
• Calories 56
(Calories from Fat 43)
• Total Fat 5 gm
(Saturated Fat 1.0 gm,
Polyunsat Fat 1.4 gm,
Monounsat Fat 2.3 gm)
• Cholesterol 2 mg
• Sodium 104 mg
• Total Carb 2 gm
• Dietary Fiber 1 gm
• Sugars 0 gm
• Protein 2 gm

Curried Almonds

Barbara Aston
Ashdown, AR

Makes 64 (1 Tbsp.) servings

Prep. Time: 5 minutes
Cooking Time: 3½-4½ hours
Ideal slow cooker size: 3-qt.

2 Tbsp. melted butter
1 Tbsp. curry powder
½ tsp. seasoned salt
1 lb. blanched almonds

1. Combine butter with curry powder and seasoned salt.
2. Pour over almonds in slow cooker. Mix to coat well.
3. Cover. Cook on low 2-3 hours. Turn to high. Uncover cooker and cook 1-1½ hours.
4. Serve warm or room temperature.

Exchange List Values
• Fat 1.0

Basic Nutritional Values
• Calories 45
(Calories from Fat 36)
• Total Fat 4 gm
(Saturated Fat 0.5 gm,
Polyunsat Fat 0.9 gm,
Monounsat Fat 2.4 gm)
• Cholesterol 1 mg
• Sodium 18 mg
• Total Carb 1 gm
• Dietary Fiber 1 gm
• Sugars 0 gm
• Protein 2 gm

Eat some avocado, olives, almonds, or sesame seeds today. Small amounts give your body the good fat that it needs.

All-American Snack

Doris M. Coyle-Zipp
South Ozone Park, NY

Melissa Raber
Millersburg, OH

Ada Miller
Sugarcreek, OH

Nanci Keatley
Salem, OR

Makes 48 (¼ cup) servings

Prep. Time: 15 minutes
Cooking Time: 2½ hours
Ideal slow cooker size: 4-qt.

3 cups thin pretzel sticks
4 cups Wheat Chex
4 cups Cheerios
12-oz. can salted peanuts
¼ cup melted butter, *or* **margarine**
1 tsp. garlic powder
1 tsp. celery salt
½ tsp. seasoned salt
2 Tbsp. grated Parmesan cheese

1. Combine pretzels, cereal, and peanuts in large bowl.
2. Melt butter. Stir in garlic powder, celery salt, seasoned salt, and Parmesan cheese. Pour over pretzels and cereal. Toss until well mixed.
3. Pour into large slow cooker. Cover. Cook on low 2½ hours, stirring every 30 minutes.
4. Remove lid and cook another 30 minutes on low.
5. Serve warm or at room temperature. Store in tightly covered container.

Exchange List Values
- Starch 0.5 • Fat 1.0

Basic Nutritional Values
- Calories 77   • Cholesterol 3 mg
  (Calories from Fat 44) • Sodium 174 mg
- Total Fat 5 gm   • Total Carb 7 gm
  (Saturated Fat 1.2 gm,   • Dietary Fiber 1 gm
  Polyunsat Fat 1.2 gm,   • Sugars 1 gm
  Monounsat Fat 2.1 gm) • Protein 3 gm

Variations:

1. Use 3 cups Wheat Chex (instead of 4 cups) and 3 cups Cheerios (instead of 4 cups). Add 3 cups Corn Chex.

Marcia S. Myer
Manheim, PA

Apple Butter from Scratch

Joanna Harrison
Lafayette, CO

Makes 6 cups, 2 Tbsp. per serving

Prep. Time: 20 minutes
Cooking Time: 26 hours (yes, that's right!)
Ideal slow cooker size: 2-qt.

12 tart cooking apples (enough to make about 16 cups)
1 cup apple juice
1 cup sugar
1-1½ tsp. cinnamon
½-¾ tsp. allspice
⅛ tsp. ground cloves, *optional*

1. Lightly grease inside of slow cooker. Wash, core, and quarter apples. No need to peel them.
2. Place apples and apple juice in cooker. Cover. Cook on low 10-18 hours.
3. When apples are tender, blend in food processor or blender.
4. Return apples to slow cooker. Stir in sugar, cinnamon, allspice, and cloves, blending well.
5. Cover. Cook on high 6-8 hours, stirring every 2 hours.
6. Remove lid after 3 hours to allow fruit and juice to cook down.
7. Spoon into hot sterilized jars and can, or store in the refrigerator.

Exchange List Values
- Carbohydrate 0.5

Basic Nutritional Values
- Calories 40   Cholesterol 0 mg),
  (Calories from Fat 0)   Sodium 0 mg
- Total Fat 0 gm   • Total Carb 11 gm
  (Saturated Fat 0 gm,   • Dietary Fiber 1 gm
  Polyunsat Fat 0 gm   • Sugars 9 gm
  Monounsat Fat 0 gm   • Protein 0 gm

Note:
This smells good while cooking and makes a great gift.

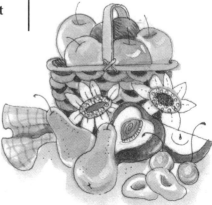

Rhonda's Apple Butter

Rhonda Burgoon
Collingswood, NJ

Makes 24 (2 Tbsp.)servings

Prep. Time: 20 minutes
Cooking Time: 12-14 hours
Ideal slow cooker size: 3-qt.

4 lbs. apples
2 tsp. cinnamon
½ tsp. ground cloves

1. Peel, core, and slice apples. Place in slow cooker.
2. Cover. Cook on high 2-3 hours. Reduce to low and cook 8 hours. Apples should be a rich brown and be cooked down by half.
3. Stir in spices. Cook on high 2-3 hours with lid off. Stir until smooth.
4. Pour into freezer containers and freeze, or into sterilized jars and seal.

Exchange List Values
• Fruit 0.5

Basic Nutritional Values
• Calories 37	• Cholesterol 0 mg
(Calories from Fat 2)	• Sodium 0 mg
• Total Fat 0 gm	• Total Carb 10 gm
(Saturated Fat 0.0 gm,	• Dietary Fiber 1 gm
Polyunsat Fat 0.1 gm,	• Sugars 8 gm
Monounsat Fat 0.0 gm)	• Protein 0 gm

Ann's Apple Butter

Ann Bender
Ft. Defiance, VA

Makes 32 (2 Tbsp.) servings

Prep. Time: 5 minutes
Cooking Time: 8-10 hours
Ideal slow cooker size: 3-qt.

7 cups unsweetened
applesauce
1 cup sugar
sugar substitute to equal
½ cup sugar
2 tsp. cinnamon
1 tsp. ground nutmeg
¼ tsp. allspice

1. Combine all ingredients in slow cooker.
2. Put a layer of paper towels under lid to prevent condensation from dripping into apple butter.
3. Cook on high 8-10 hours. Remove lid during last hour. Stir occasionally.

Exchange List Values
• Carbohydrate 1.0

Basic Nutritional Values
• Calories 48	• Cholesterol 0 mg
(Calories from Fat 1)	• Sodium 1 mg
• Total Fat 0 gm	• Total Carb 13 gm
(Saturated Fat 0.0 gm,	• Dietary Fiber 1 gm
Polyunsat Fat 0.0 gm,	• Sugars 11 gm
Monounsat Fat 0.0 gm)	• Protein 0 gm

Variation:
Use canned peaches, pears, or apricots in place of applesauce.

Pear Butter

Betty Moore
Plano, IL

Makes 40 (2 Tbsp.) servings

Prep. Time: 30 minutes
Cooking Time: 11-13 hours
Ideal slow cooker size: 4-qt.

10 large pears (about 4 lbs.)
1 cup orange juice
1 cup sugar
sugar substitute to equal
½ cup sugar
1 tsp. ground cinnamon
1 tsp. ground cloves
½ tsp. ground allspice

1. Peel and quarter pears. Place in slow cooker.
2. Cover. Cook on low 10-12 hours. Drain and then discard liquid.
3. Mash or purée pears. Add remaining ingredients. Mix well and return to slow cooker.
4. Cover. Cook on high 1 hour.
5. Place in hot sterile jars and seal. Process in hot water bath for 10 minutes. Allow to cool undisturbed for 24 hours.

Exchange List Values
• Carbohydrate 1.0

Basic Nutritional Values
• Calories 56	• Cholesterol 0 mg
(Calories from Fat 2)	• Sodium 0 mg
• Total Fat 0 gm	• Total Carb 14 gm
(Saturated Fat 0.0 gm,	• Dietary Fiber 1 gm
Polyunsat Fat 0.0 gm,	• Sugars 13 gm
Monounsat Fat 0.0 gm)	• Protein 0 gm

Peach or Apricot Butter

Charlotte Shaffer
East Earl, PA

Makes 48 (2 Tbsp.) servings

Prep. Time: 15 minutes
Cooking Time: 8-10 hours
Ideal slow cooker size: 4-qt.

4 1-lb. 13-oz. cans peaches,
   or apricots
1½ cups sugar
sugar substitute to equal
   ¾ cup sugar
2 tsp. cinnamon
1 tsp. ground cloves

1. Drain fruit. Remove pits.
Purée in blender. Pour into
slow cooker.
2. Stir in remaining
ingredients.
3. Cover. Cook on high 8-10
hours. Remove cover during
last half of cooking. Stir
occasionally.

Exchange List Values
• Carbohydrate 0.5

Basic Nutritional Values
• Calories 39   • Cholesterol 0 mg
  (Calories from Fat 0)   • Sodium 2 mg
• Total Fat 0 gm   • Total Carb 10 gm
  (Saturated Fat 0.0 gm,   • Dietary Fiber 1 gm
  Polyunsat Fat 0.0 gm,   • Sugars 10 gm
  Monounsat Fat 0.0 gm)   • Protein 0 gm

Note:
  Spread on bread, or use
as a topping for ice cream or
toasted pound cake.

Pumpkin Butter

Emily Fox
Bethel, PA

Makes approximately 6½ cups

Prep. Time: 5-10 minutes
Cooking Time: 11-12 hours
Ideal slow cooker size: 3-qt.

6 cups pumpkin purée
2¾ cups light brown sugar,
   packed
2½ tsp. pumpkin pie spice

1. Mix pumpkin purée,
brown sugar, and pumpkin
pie spice together in slow
cooker.
2. Cook, uncovered, on low
for 11-12 hours, depending
on how thick you'd like the
butter to be. Cool.
3. Serve on bread or rolls
for seasonal flair.

Note:
  Refrigerate or freeze until
ready to use.

Exchange List Values
• Carbohydrate 0.5

Basic Nutritional Values
• Calories 25   Cholesterol 0 mg),
  (Calories from Fat 0)   Sodium 0 mg
• Total Fat 0 gm   • Total Carb 7 gm
  (Saturated Fat 0 gm,   • Dietary Fiber 0 gm
  Polyunsat Fat 0 gm   • Sugars 6 gm
  Monounsat Fat 0 gm   • Protein 0 gm

Beverages

Hot Mulled Cider

Phyffis Attig, Reynolds, IL
Jean Butzer, Batavia, NY
Doris G. Herr, Manheim, PA
Mary E. Martin, Goshen, IN
Leona Miller, Millersburg, OH
Marjora Miller, Archbold, OH
Janet L. Roggie, Lowville, NY
Shirley Sears, Tiskilwa, IL
Charlotte Shaffer, East Earl, PA
Berenice M. Wagner, Dodge City, KS
Connie B. Weaver, Bethlehem, PA
Maryann Westerberg, Rosamond, CA
Carole Whaling, New Tripoli, PA

Makes 16 (½-cup) servings

Prep. Time: 15 minutes
Cooking Time: 2-8 hours
Ideal slow cooker size: 4-qt.

¼ cup brown sugar
2 quarts apple cider
1 tsp. whole allspice
1½ tsp. whole cloves
2 cinnamon sticks

2 oranges sliced, with
  peels on

1. Combine brown sugar and cider in slow cooker.
2. Put spices in tea strainer or tie in cheesecloth. Add to slow cooker. Stir in orange slices.
3. Cover and simmer on low 2-8 hours.

Exchange List Values

• Fruit 1.0

Basic Nutritional Values

• Calories 76
  (Calories from Fat 1)
• Total Fat 0 gm
  (Saturated Fat 0.0 gm,
  Polyunsat Fat 0.0 gm,
  Monounsat Fat 0.0 gm)
• Cholesterol 0 mg
• Sodium 5 mg
• Total Carb 19 gm
• Dietary Fiber 0 gm
• Sugars 18 gm
• Protein 0 gm

Variation:
  Add a dash of ground nutmeg and salt.
                    Marsha Sabus
                    Fallbrook, CA

Dried fruits make a great snack, but watch your serving size: they are concentrated carbohydrates.

Cider Snap

Cathy Boshart
Lebanon, PA

Makes 16 servings

Prep. Time: 15 minutes
Cooking Time: 2 hours
Ideal slow cooker size: 4-qt.

2 qts. apple cider *or* apple juice
4 Tbsp. red cinnamon candies
at least 16 apple slices
at least 16 cinnamon sticks

1. Combine cider and cinnamon candies in slow cooker.
2. Cover. Cook on high for 2 hours until candies dissolve and cider is hot.
3. Ladle into mugs and serve with apple slice floaters and cinnamon stick stirrers.

Exchange List Values
• Fruit 1.5

Basic Nutritional Values
• Calories 81   • Cholesterol 0 mg
(Calories from Fat 1) • Sodium 4 mg
• Total Fat 0 gm   • Total Carb 20 gm
(Saturated Fat 0.0 gm, • Dietary Fiber 0 gm
Polyunsat Fat 0.0 gm, • Sugars 18 gm
Monounsat Fat 0.0 gm) • Protein 0 gm

Note:
   This is a cold-winter-night luxury. Make it in the morning and keep it on low throughout the day so its good fragrance can fill the house.

Maple Mulled Cider

Leesa Lesenski
Wheately, MA

Makes 10 servings

Prep. Time: 10 minutes
Cooking Time: 2 hours
Ideal slow cooker size: 4-qt.

½ gallon apple cider
3-4 cinnamon sticks
2 tsp. whole cloves
2 tsp. whole allspice
1-2 Tbsp. orange juice concentrate, *optional*
1 Tbsp. maple syrup, *optional*

1. Combine ingredients in slow cooker.
2. Cover. Heat on low for 2 hours. Serve warm.

Exchange List Values
• Fruit 1.5

Basic Nutritional Values
• Calories 98   • Cholesterol 0 mg
(Calories from Fat 1) • Sodium 7 mg
• Total Fat 0 gm   • Total Carb 25 gm
(Saturated Fat 0.0 gm, • Dietary Fiber 0 gm
Polyunsat Fat 0.1 gm, • Sugars 23 gm
Monounsat Fat 0.0 gm) • Protein 0 gm

Note:
   Serve at Halloween, Christmas caroling, or sledding parties.

Deep Red Apple Cider

Judi Manos
West Islip, NY

Makes 16 (½ cup) servings

Prep. Time: 10 minutes
Cooking Time: 3-4 hours
Ideal slow cooker size: 4-qt.

5 cups apple cider
3 cups dry red wine
¼ cup brown sugar
½ tsp. whole cloves
¼ tsp. whole allspice
1 stick cinnamon

1. Combine all ingredients in slow cooker.
2. Cover. Cook on low 3-4 hours.
3. Remove cloves, allspice, and cinnamon before serving.

Exchange List Values
• Fruit 1.0

Basic Nutritional Values
• Calories 58   • Cholesterol 0 mg
(Calories from Fat 1) • Sodium 7 mg
• Total Fat 0 gm   • Total Carb 14 gm
(Saturated Fat 0.0 gm, • Dietary Fiber 0 gm
Polyunsat Fat 0.0 gm, • Sugars 14 gm
Monounsat Fat 0.0 gm) • Protein 0 gm

Variation:
   You can use 8 cups apple cider and no red wine.

Use slices of avocado on a sandwich instead of mayonnaise.

Hot Mulled Apple Tea

Barbara Tenney
Delta, PA

Makes 16 1-cup servings

Prep. Time: 10 minutes
Cooking Time: 2 hours
Ideal slow cooker size: 5-qt.

½ gallon apple cider
½ gallon strong tea
1 sliced lemon
1 sliced orange
3 3-inch cinnamon sticks
1 Tbsp. whole cloves
1 Tbsp. allspice

1. Combine all in slow cooker.
2. Heat on low 2 hours.

Exchange List Values
• Fruit 1.0

Basic Nutritional Values
• Calories 59
(Calories from Fat 1)
• Total Fat 0 gm
(Saturated Fat 0.0 gm,
Polyunsat Fat 0.0 gm,
Monounsat Fat 0.0 gm)
• Cholesterol 0 mg
• Sodium 7 mg
• Total Carb 15 gm
• Dietary Fiber 0 gm
• Sugars 13 gm
• Protein 0 gm

Spiced Apple Cider

Janice Muller
Derwood, MD

Makes 40 servings

Prep. Time: 20 minutes
Cooking Time: 4-6 hours
Ideal slow cooker size: 5- or 6-qt.

2 sticks cinnamon
1 cup orange juice
1 tsp. cinnamon
1 tsp. ground cloves
¼ cup lemon juice
2 tsp. whole cloves
1 gallon apple cider
2 tsp. ground nutmeg
½ cup pineapple juice
1 tsp. ginger
1 tsp. lemon peel
¼ cup sugar
sugar substitute to equal
¼ cup sugar

1. Mix all ingredients in slow cooker.
2. Simmer on low 4-6 hours.

Exchange List Values
• Fruit 1.0

Basic Nutritional Values
• Calories 58
(Calories from Fat 1)
• Total Fat 0 gm
(Saturated Fat 0.0 gm,
Polyunsat Fat 0.0 gm,
Monounsat Fat 0.0 gm)
• Cholesterol 0 mg
• Sodium 4 mg
• Total Carb 14 gm
• Dietary Fiber 0 gm
• Sugars 13 gm
• Protein 0 gm

Hot Wassail Drink

Dale Peterson
Rapid City, SC

Makes 54 (½-cup) servings

Prep. Time: 15 minutes
Cooking Time: 1-2 hours
Ideal slow cooker size: 6-qt.

12-oz. can frozen orange juice
12-oz. can frozen lemonade
2 qts. apple juice
1 cup sugar
sugar substitute to equal
½ cup sugar
3 Tbsp. whole cloves
2 Tbsp. ground ginger
4 tsp. ground cinnamon
10 cups hot water
6 cups strong tea

1. Mix juices, sugar, and spices in slow cooker.
2. Add hot water and tea.
3. Heat on high 1-2 hours or until hot, then on low while serving.

Exchange List Values
• Fruit 1.0

Basic Nutritional Values
• Calories 61
(Calories from Fat 1)
• Total Fat 0 gm
(Saturated Fat 0.0 gm,
Polyunsat Fat 0.0 gm,
Monounsat Fat 0.0 gm)
• Cholesterol 0 mg
• Sodium 3 mg
• Total Carb 16 gm
• Dietary Fiber 0 gm
• Sugars 15 gm
• Protein 0 gm

Almond Tea

Frances Schrag
Newton, KS

Makes 12 1-cup servings

Prep. Time: 10 minutes
Cooking Time: 1 hour
Ideal slow cooker size: 4-qt.

10 cups boiling water
1 Tbsp. instant tea
⅔ cup lemon juice
½ cup sugar
½ cup Splenda
1 tsp. vanilla
1 tsp. almond extract

1. Mix together all ingredients in slow cooker.
2. Turn to high and heat thoroughly, about 1 hour. Turn to low while serving.

Exchange List Values
• Carbohydrate 0.5

Basic Nutritional Values
• Calories 40
  (Calories from Fat 0)
• Total Fat 0 gm
  (Saturated Fat 0.0 gm,
  Polyunsat Fat 0.0 gm,
  Monounsat Fat 0.0 gm)
• Cholesterol 0 mg
• Sodium 3 mg
• Total Carb 10 gm
• Dietary Fiber 0 gm
• Sugars 9 gm
• Protein 0 gm

Hot Cranberry Cider

Kristi See
Weskan, KS

Makes 20 (½ cup) servings

Prep. Time: 15 minutes
Cooking Tome: 5-9 hours
Ideal slow cooker size: 4-qt.

2 qts. apple cider *or* apple juice
1 pt. cranberry juice cocktail
¼ cup sugar
2 cinnamon sticks
1 tsp. whole allspice
1 orange, studded with whole cloves
sweetener substitute to equal 2 Tbsp. sugar

1. Put all ingredients in slow cooker.
2. Cover. Cook on high 1 hour, then on low 4-8 hours. Serve warm.

Exchange List Values
• Fruit 1.0

Basic Nutritional Values
• Calories 71
  (Calories from Fat 1)
• Total Fat 0 gm
  (Saturated Fat 0.0 gm,
  Polyunsat Fat 0.0 gm,
  Monounsat Fat 0.0 gm)
• Cholesterol 0 mg
• Sodium 4 mg
• Total Carb 18 gm
• Dietary Fiber 0 gm
• Sugars 17 gm
• Protein 0 gm

Note:
  To garnish wassail with an orange, insert 10-12½"-long whole cloves halfway into orange. Place studded orange in flat baking pan with ¼ cup water. Bake at 325° for 30 minutes. Just before serving, float orange on top of wassail.

Johnny Appleseed Tea

Sheila Plock
Boalsburg, PA

Makes 9 cups

Prep. Time: 15 minutes
Cooking Time: 2 hours
Ideal slow cooker size: 4-qt.

2 qts. water, *divided*
6 tea bags of your favorite flavor
6 ozs. frozen apple juice, thawed
3 Tbsp. packed brown sugar
brown sugar substitute to equal 2 Tbsp. sugar

1. Bring 1 quart water to boil. Add tea bags. Remove from heat. Cover and let steep 5 minutes. Pour into slow cooker.
2. Add remaining ingredients and mix well.
3. Cover. Heat on low until hot, 2-3 hours. Continue on low while serving from slow cooker.

Exchange List Values
• Fruit 1.0

Basic Nutritional Values
• Calories 60
  (Calories from Fat 1)
• Total Fat 0 gm
  (Saturated Fat 0.0 gm,
  Polyunsat Fat 0.0 gm,
  Monounsat Fat 0.0 gm)
• Cholesterol 0 mg
• Sodium 12 mg
• Total Carb 15 gm
• Dietary Fiber 0 gm
• Sugars 14 gm
• Protein 0 gm

Note:
  I serve this wonderful hot beverage with cookies at our

Open House Tea and Cookies afternoon, which I host at Christmas-time for friends and neighbors.

Orange Cider Punch

Naomi Ressler
Harrisonburg, VA

Makes 16 (½ cup) servings

Prep. Time: 10 minutes
Cooking Time: 2-10 hours
Ideal slow cooker size: 4-qt.

½ cup sugar
sugar substitute to equal
¼ cup sugar
2 cinnamon sticks
1 tsp. whole nutmeg
2 cups apple cider *or* apple juice
6 cups orange juice
1 orange, sliced thinly

1. Combine ingredients in slow cooker.
2. Cover. Cook on low 4-10 hours or high 2-3 hours.
3. Float orange slices in cooker before serving.

Exchange List Values
• Fruit 1.5

Basic Nutritional Values
• Calories 81
(Calories from Fat 2)
• Total Fat 0 gm
(Saturated Fat 0.0 gm,
Polyunsat Fat 0.1 gm,
Monounsat Fat 0.0 gm)
• Cholesterol 0 mg
• Sodium 2 mg
• Total Carb 20 gm
• Dietary Fiber 0 gm
• Sugars 19 gm
• Protein 1 gm

Spicy Autumn Punch

Marlene Bogard
Newton, KS

Makes 16 servings

Prep. Time: 20 minutes
Cooking Time: 3½-4½ hours
Ideal slow cooker size: 4-qt.

2 oranges
8 whole cloves
6 cups apple juice
1 cinnamon stick
¼ tsp. ground nutmeg
3 Tbsp. lemon juice
¼ cup honey
2¼ cups pineapple juice

1. Press cloves into oranges. Place on baking tray. Bake at 350° for 30 minutes.
2. Meanwhile, combine apple juice and cinnamon stick in slow cooker.
3. Cover. Cook on high 1 hour.
4. Add remaining ingredients except oranges.
5. Cover. Cook on low 2-3 hours. Add oranges at end, either whole or in quarters.

Exchange List Values
• Fruit 1.5

Basic Nutritional Values
• Calories 80
(Calories from Fat 1)
• Total Fat 0 gm
(Saturated Fat 0.0 gm,
Polyunsat Fat 0.0 gm,
Monounsat Fat 0.0 gm)
• Cholesterol 0 mg
• Sodium 4 mg
• Total Carb 20 gm
• Dietary Fiber 0 gm
• Sugars 19 gm
• Protein 0 gm

Hot Cranberry Tea

Sherrill Bieberly
Salina, KS

Makes 21 (⅔-cup) servings

Prep. Time: 10 minutes
Cooking Time: 1½ hours
Ideal slow cooker size: 4- or 5-qt.

½ cup sugar
sugar substitute to equal
¼ cup sugar
2 qts. water
3 cinnamon sticks
1 qt. cranberry juice
6-oz. can frozen orange juice
1¼ cups water
3 Tbsp. lemon juice
fresh lemon *and/or* orange slices

1. In saucepan, mix together sugar, 2 quarts water, and cinnamon sticks. Bring to boil.
2. Pour into slow cooker along with remaining ingredients.
3. Cover and cook on high 1 hour. Turn to low. Serve warm.

Exchange List Values
• Carbohydrate 1.0

Basic Nutritional Values
• Calories 58
(Calories from Fat 1)
• Total Fat 0 gm
(Saturated Fat 0.0 gm,
Polyunsat Fat 0.0 gm,
Monounsat Fat 0.0 gm)
• Cholesterol 0 mg
• Sodium 1 mg
• Total Carb 15 gm
• Dietary Fiber 0 gm
• Sugars 15 gm
• Protein 0 gm

Christmas Wassail

Dottie Schmidt
Kansas City, MO

Makes 10 servings

Prep. Time: 10 minutes
Cooking Time: 1 hour
Ideal slow cooker size: 4-qt.

2 cups cranberry juice
  cocktail
3¼ cups hot water
3 Tbsp. sugar
sugar substitute to equal
  1½ Tbsp. sugar
6-oz. can lemonade
  concentrate
1 stick cinnamon
5 whole cloves
2 oranges, cut in thin slices

1. Combine all ingredients except oranges in slow cooker. Stir until sugar is dissolved.
2. Cover. Cook on high 1 hour. Strain out spices.
3. Serve hot with an orange slice floating in each cup.

Exchange List Values
• Carbohydrate 1.5

Basic Nutritional Values
• Calories 90
  (Calories from Fat 3)
• Total Fat 0 gm
  (Saturated Fat 0.1 gm,
  Polyunsat Fat 0.1 gm,
  Monounsat Fat 0.0 gm)
• Cholesterol 0 mg
• Sodium 5 mg
• Total Carb 24 gm
• Dietary Fiber 0 gm
• Sugars 22 gm
• Protein 0 gm

Mulled Wine

Julie McKenzie
Punxsutawney, PA

Makes 8 1-cup servings

Prep. Time: 10 minutes
Cooking Time: 1 hour
Ideal slow cooker size: 3- or 4-qt.

½ cup sugar
1½ cups boiling water
half a lemon, sliced thin
3 cinnamon sticks
3 whole cloves
1 bottle red wine, a table
  wine such as burgundy
  or claret

1. Dissolve sugar in boiling water in saucepan. Pour into slow cooker.
2. Add remaining ingredients.
3. Heat on low for at least 1 hour, until wine is hot. Do not boil.
4. Serve from cooker into mugs.

Exchange List Values
• Carbohydrate 1.0

Basic Nutritional Values
• Calories 91
  (Calories from Fat 1)
• Total Fat 0 gm
  (Saturated Fat 0.0 gm,
  Polyunsat Fat 0.1 gm,
  Monounsat Fat 0.0 gm)
• Cholesterol 0 mg
• Sodium 6 mg
• Total Carb 14 gm
• Dietary Fiber 0 gm
• Sugars 13 gm
• Protein 0 gm

Hot (Buttered) Lemonade

Janie Steele
Moore, OK

Makes 6 servings

Prep. Time: 10 minutes
Cooking Time: 2½ hours
Ideal slow cooker size: 4-qt.

4½ cups water
6 Tbsp. sugar
sugar substitute to equal
  3 Tbsp. sugar
1½ tsp. grated lemon peel
¾ cup lemon juice
2 Tbsp. light, soft tub
  margarine
6 cinnamon sticks

1. Combine water, sugar, lemon peel, lemon juice, and butter in slow cooker.
2. Cover. Cook on high for 2½ hours, or until well heated through.
3. Serve very hot with a cinnamon stick in each mug.

Exchange List Values
• Carbohydrate 1.0

Basic Nutritional Values
• Calories 69
  (Calories from Fat 13)
• Total Fat 1 gm
  (Saturated Fat 0.1 gm,
  Polyunsat Fat 0.3 gm,
  Monounsat Fat 0.8 gm)
• Cholesterol 0 mg
• Sodium 36 mg
• Total Carb 15 gm
• Dietary Fiber 0 gm
• Sugars 14 gm
• Protein 0 gm

Hot Chocolate with Stir-Ins

Stacy Schmucker Stoltzfus
Enola, PA

Makes 12 6-oz. servings

Prep. Time: 15 minutes
Cooking Time: 2 hours
Ideal slow cooker size: 4- or 5-qt.

9½ cups water
1½ cups hot chocolate mix
Stir-ins:
    smooth peanut butter
    chocolate-mint candies,
      chopped
    candy canes, broken
    assorted flavored syrups:
      hazelnut, almond,
      raspberry, Irish creme
    instant coffee granules
    cinnamon
    nutmeg
whipped topping
candy sprinkles

1. Pour water into slow cooker. Heat on high 1-2 hours. (Or heat water in tea kettle and pour into slow cooker.) Turn cooker to low to keep hot for hours.
2. Stir in hot chocolate mix until blended.
3. Arrange stir-ins in small bowls.
4. Instruct guests to place approximately 1 Tbsp. of desired stir-in in mug before ladling hot chocolate in. Stir well.
5. Top with whipped topping and candy sprinkles.

Note:
1 serving of each stir-in used in analysis.

Exchange List Values
• Carbohydrate 1.0

Basic Nutritional Values
• Calories 63
(Calories from Fat 14)
• Total Fat 2 gm
(Saturated Fat 0.3 gm,
Polyunsat Fat 0.4 gm,
Monounsat Fat 0.7 gm)
• Cholesterol 0 mg
• Sodium 32 mg
• Total Carb 12 gm
• Dietary Fiber 0 gm
• Sugars 3 gm
• Protein 1 gm

Crockery Cocoa

Betty Hostetler
Allensville, PA

Makes 12 servings

Prep. Time: 10 minutes
Cooking Time: 1-1½ hours
Ideal slow cooker size: 4- or 5-qt.

½ cup sugar
½ cup unsweetened cocoa powder
2 cups boiling water
3½ cups nonfat dry milk powder
6 cups water
1 tsp. vanilla
1 tsp. ground cinnamon

1. Combine sugar and cocoa powder in slow cooker. Add 2 cups boiling water. Stir well to dissolve.
2. Add dry milk powder, 6 cups water, and vanilla. Stir well to dissolve.
3. Cover. Cook on low 4 hours or high 1-1½ hours.
4. Before serving, beat with rotary beater to make frothy.

Ladle into mugs. Top with marshmallows and sprinkle with cinnamon.

Exchange List Values
• Milk, fat-free 1.0   • Carbohydrate 0.5

Basic Nutritional Values
• Calories 111
(Calories from Fat 6)
• Total Fat 1 gm
(Saturated Fat 0.3 gm,
Polyunsat Fat 0.0 gm,
Monounsat Fat 0.2 gm)
• Cholesterol 4 mg
• Sodium 110 mg
• Total Carb 21 gm
• Dietary Fiber 1 gm
• Sugars 19 gm
• Protein 8 gm

Variations:
1. Add⅛ tsp. ground nutmeg, along with ground cinnamon in Step 4.
2. Mocha-style—Stir ¾ tsp. coffee crystals into each serving in Step 4.
3. Coffee-Cocoa—Pour half-cups of freshly brewed, high quality coffee; top with half-cups of Crockery Cocoa.

Breakfast Dishes

Cheese Soufflé Casserole

Iva Schmidt
Fergus Falls, MN

Makes 6 servings

Prep. Time: 20 minutes
Cooking Time: 3-4 hours
Ideal slow cooker size: 3- or 4-qt.

---

8 slices bread (crusts removed), cubed *or* torn into squares
2 cups (8 oz.) grated fat-free cheddar cheese
1 cup cooked, chopped extra-lean, lower sodium ham
4 eggs
1 cup fat-free half-and-half
1 cup fat-free evaporated milk
1 Tbsp. parsley
paprika

1. Lightly grease slow cooker. Alternate layers of bread and cheese and ham.

2. Beat together eggs, milk, salt, and parsley. Pour over bread in slow cooker.

3. Sprinkle with paprika.

4. Cover and cook on low 3-4 hours. The longer cooking time yields a firmer, dryer dish.

5. About 30 minutes before finish, increase temperature to high and remove lid.

Exchange List Values
- Starch 1.0
- Milk, fat-free 0.5
- Meat, lean 2.0

Basic Nutritional Values
- Calories 233
  (Calories from Fat 46)
- Total Fat 5 gm
  (Saturated Fat 1.9 gm,
  Polyunsat Fat 0.9 gm,
  Monounsat Fat 1.6 gm)
- Cholesterol 159 mg
- Sodium 650 mg
- Total Carb 22 gm
- Dietary Fiber 0 gm
- Sugars 9 gm
- Protein 23 gm

Egg and Broccoli Casserole

Joette Droz
Kalona, IA

Makes 8 servings

Prep. Time: 20 minutes
Cooking Time: 3½-4 hours
Ideal slow cooker size: 4-qt.

24-oz. carton small-curd 1% milkfat cottage cheese
10-oz. pkg. frozen chopped broccoli, thawed and drained
1½ cups shredded cheddar cheese
6 eggs, beaten
⅓ cup flour
2 Tbsp. canola oil
3 Tbsp. finely chopped onion
shredded cheese, *optional*

1. Combine first 7 ingredients. Pour into greased slow cooker.

2. Cover and cook on high 1 hour. Stir. Reduce heat to low. Cover and cook 2½-3 hours, or until temperature reaches 160° and eggs are set.

3. Sprinkle with cheese and serve.

Exchange List Values
• Carbohydrate 0.5 • Meat, lean 3.0

Basic Nutritional Values
• Calories 211   • Cholesterol 165 mg
  (Calories from Fat 74) • Sodium 550 mg
• Total Fat 8 gm   • Total Carb 10 gm
  (Saturated Fat 2.3 gm, • Dietary Fiber 1 gm
  Polyunsat Fat 1.6 gm,   • Sugars 5 gm
  Monounsat Fat 3.7 gm)   • Protein 23 gm

Mexican-Style Grits

Mary Sommerfeld
Lancaster, PA

Makes 12 servings

Prep. Time: 25 minutes
Cooking Time: 2-6 hours
Ideal slow cooker size: 4-qt.

1½ cups instant grits
4 oz. fat-free cheddar cheese, cubed
½ tsp. garlic powder
2 4-oz. cans diced chilies
2 Tbsp. light, soft tub margarine

1. Prepare grits according to package directions.
2. Stir in cheese, garlic powder, and chilies, until cheese is melted.
3. Stir in margarine. Pour into greased slow cooker.
4. Cover. Cook on high 2-3 hours or on low 4-6 hours.

Exchange List Values
• Starch 1.0

Basic Nutritional Values
• Calories 91   • Cholesterol 1 mg
  (Calories from Fat 9) • Sodium 167 mg
• Total Fat 1 gm   • Total Carb 16 gm
  (Saturated Fat 0.1 gm,• Dietary Fiber 2 gm
  Polyunsat Fat 0.3 gm, • Sugars 0 gm
  Monounsat Fat 0.5 gm) • Protein 5 gm

Creamy Old-Fashioned Oatmeal

Mary Wheatley
Mashpee, MA

Makes 5 servings

Prep. Time: 5 minutes
Cooking Time: 6 hours
Ideal slow cooker size: 3-qt.

1⅓ cups dry rolled oats
2½ cups, plus 1 Tbsp., water
dash of salt

1. Mix together cereal, water, and salt in slow cooker.
2. Cook on low 6 hours.

Exchange List Values
• Starch 1.0

Basic Nutritional Values
• Calories 83   • Cholesterol 0 mg
  (Calories from Fat 12) • Sodium 1 mg
• Total Fat 1 gm   • Total Carb 14 gm
  (Saturated Fat 0.3 gm, • Dietary Fiber 2 gm
  Polyunsat Fat 0.5 gm, • Sugars 0 gm
  Monounsat Fat 0.4 gm) • Protein 3 gm

Note:
The formula is this: for one serving, use ⅓ cup dry oats and ⅔ cup water, plus a few grains salt. Multiply by the number of servings you need.

Variation:
Before cooking, stir in a few chopped dates or raisins for each serving, if you wish.
Cathy Boshart
Lebanon, PA

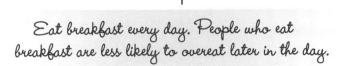

Eat breakfast every day. People who eat breakfast are less likely to overeat later in the day.

Apple Oatmeal

Frances B. Musser
Newmanstown, PA

Makes 5 servings

Prep. Time: 20 minutes
Cooking Time: 5-6 hours
Ideal slow cooker size: 3-qt.

2 cups fat-free milk
1 Tbsp. honey
1 Tbsp. light, soft tub margarine
¼ tsp. salt
½ tsp. cinnamon
1 cup dry rolled oats
1 cup chopped apples
½ cup chopped walnuts
1 Tbsp. brown sugar
brown sugar substitute to equal ½ Tbsp. sugar

1. Mix together all ingredients in greased slow cooker.
2. Cover. Cook on low 5-6 hours.
3. Serve with milk or ice cream.

Exchange List Values
• Carbohydrate 2.0 • Fat 1.5

Basic Nutritional Values
• Calories 220
(Calories from Fat 89)
• Total Fat 10 gm
(Saturated Fat 1.1 gm,
Polyunsat Fat 6.3 gm,
Monounsat Fat 1.9 gm)
• Cholesterol 2 mg
• Sodium 180 mg
• Total Carb 28 gm
• Dietary Fiber 3 gm
• Sugars 15 gm
• Protein 8 gm

Variation:
Add ½ cup light or dark raisins to mixture.
Jeanette Oberholtzer
Manheim, PA

Oatmeal Morning

Barbara Forrester Landis
Lititz, PA

Makes 6 servings

Prep. Time: 10 minutes
Cooking Time: 2½-6 hours
Ideal slow cooker size: 3-qt.

1 cup uncooked steel cut oats
1 cup dried cranberries
1 cup walnuts
½ tsp. salt
1 Tbsp. cinnamon
2 cups water
2 cups fat-free milk

1. Combine all dry ingredients in slow cooker. Stir well.
2. Pour in milk and water. Mix together well.
3. Cover. Cook on high 2½ hours, or on low 5-6 hours.

Exchange List Values
• Carbohydrate 2.0 • Fat 3.0

Basic Nutritional Values
• Calories 275
(Calories from Fat 125)
• Total Fat 14 gm
(Saturated Fat 1.5 gm,
Polyunsat Fat 10.0 gm,
Monounsat Fat 2.0 gm)
• Cholesterol 0 mg
• Sodium 235 mg
• Total Carb 34 gm
• Dietary Fiber 4 gm
• Sugars 18 gm
• Protein 8 gm

Peanut Butter Granola

Dawn Ranck, Harrisonburg, VA

Makes 26 servings

Prep. Time: 20 minutes
Cooking Time: 1½ hours
Ideal slow cooker size: 5-qt.

6 cups dry oatmeal
½ cup wheat germ
¼ cup toasted coconut
½ cup sunflower seeds
½ cup raisins
8 Tbsp. light, soft tub margarine
¾ cup peanut butter
½ cup brown sugar
brown sugar substitute to equal 4 Tbsp. sugar

1. Combine oatmeal, wheat germ, coconut, sunflower seeds, and raisins in large slow cooker.
2. Melt together butter, peanut butter, and brown sugar. Pour over oatmeal in cooker. Mix well.
3. Cover. Cook on low 1½ hours, stirring every 15 minutes.
4. Allow to cool in cooker, stirring every 30 minutes or so, or spread onto cookie sheet. When thoroughly cooled, break into chunks and store in airtight container.

Exchange List Values
• Starch 0.5 • Fat 1.5
• Carbohydrate 1.0

Basic Nutritional Values
• Calories 179
(Calories from Fat 73)
• Total Fat 8 gm
(Saturated Fat 1.5 gm,
Polyunsat Fat 2.8 gm,
Monounsat Fat 3.3 gm)
• Cholesterol 0 mg
• Sodium 70 mg
• Total Carb 22 gm
• Dietary Fiber 3 gm
• Sugars 7 gm
• Protein 6 gm

Breakfast Apple Cobbler

Anona M. Teel
Bangor, PA

Makes 8 servings

Prep. Time: 25 minutes
Cooking Time: 2-9 hours
Ideal slow cooker size: 4- or 5-qt.

8 medium apples, cored, peeled, sliced
2 Tbsp. sugar
sugar substitute to equal 1 Tbsp. sugar
dash of cinnamon
juice of 1 lemon
2 Tbsp. light, soft tub margarine, melted
2 cups granola

1. Combine ingredients in slow cooker.
2. Cover. Cook on low 7-9 hours (while you sleep!), or on high 2-3 hours (after you're up in the morning).

Exchange List Values
• Starch 1.5   • Fat 1.0
• Fruit 1.5

Basic Nutritional Values
• Calories 221   • Cholesterol 0 mg
(Calories from Fat 57)   • Sodium 102 mg
• Total Fat 6 gm   • Total Carb 42 gm
(Saturated Fat 2.1 gm,   • Dietary Fiber 4 gm
Polyunsat Fat 1.9 gm,   • Sugars 29 gm
Monounsat Fat 1.7 gm)   • Protein 2 gm

Dulce de Leche (Sweet Milk)

Dorothy Horst
Tiskilwa, IL

Makes 38 (1 Tbsp.) servings

Prep. Time: 5 minutes
Cooking Time: 2 hours
Ideal slow cooker size: 3- or 4-qt.

2 14-oz. cans fat-free sweetened condensed milk

1. Place unopened cans of milk in slow cooker. Fill cooker with warm water so that it comes above the cans by 1½-2 inches.
2. Cover cooker. Cook on high 2 hours.
3. Cool unopened cans. Do not open until thoroughly cool!
4. When opened, the contents should be thick and spreadable. Use as a filling between 2 cookies or crackers.

Exchange List Values
• Carbohydrate 1.0

Basic Nutritional Values
• Calories 58   • Cholesterol 0 mg
(Calories from Fat 0)   • Sodium 21 mg
• Total Fat 0 gm   • Total Carb 13 gm
(Saturated Fat 0.0 gm,   • Dietary Fiber 0 gm
Polyunsat Fat 0.1 gm,   • Sugars 13 gm
Monounsat Fat 0.5 gm)   • Protein 2 gm

Note:
When on a tour in Argentina, we were served this at breakfast time as a spread on toast or thick slices of bread. We were also presented with a container of prepared Dulce Leche as a parting gift to take home. This dish also sometimes appears on Mexican menus.

Skim the solidified fat off the top of refrigerated, leftover soups and stews before reheating.

Breads

Healthy Whole Wheat Bread

Esther Becker
Gordonville, PA

Makes 16 servings

Prep. Time: 20 minutes
Cooking Time: 2½-3 hours
Ideal slow cooker size: 5- or 6-qt.

2 cups warm reconstituted
fat-free powdered milk
(⅔ cups powder to 1⅓
cup water)
2 Tbsp. canola oil
¼ cup honey, *or* brown
sugar
¾ tsp. salt
1 pkg. active dry yeast
2½ cups whole wheat flour
1¼ cups white flour

1. Mix together milk, oil,
honey or brown sugar, salt,

yeast, and half the flour in
electric mixer bowl. Beat with
mixer for 2 minutes. Add
remaining flour. Mix well.

2. Place dough in well-
greased bread or cake pan
that will fit into your cooker.
Cover with greased tin foil.
Let stand for 5 minutes. Place
in slow cooker.

3. Cover cooker and bake
on high 2½-3 hours. Remove
pan and uncover. Let stand
for 5 minutes. Serve warm.

Exchange List Values:
• Starch 2.0

Basic Nutritional Values
• Calories 140   • Cholesterol 0 mg
 (Calories from Fat 20) • Sodium 125 mg
• Total Fat 2 gm   • Total Carb 27 gm
 (Saturated Fat 0.2 gm, • Dietary Fiber 3 gm
 Polyunsat Fat 0.7 gm,   • Sugars 6 gm
 Monounsat Fat 1.1 gm)   • Protein 5 gm

Boston Brown Bread

Jean Butzer
Batavia, NY

Makes 3 loaves, 7 servings per loaf

Prep. Time: 45 minutes
Cooking Time: 4 hours
Ideal slow cooker size: 6-qt.

3 16-oz. vegetable cans,
emptied and cleaned,
lid discarded

½ cup rye flour
½ cup yellow cornmeal
½ cup whole wheat flour
3 Tbsp. sugar
1 tsp. baking soda
¾ tsp. salt

½ cup chopped walnuts
½ cup raisins
1 cup low-fat buttermilk
⅓ cup molasses

1. Spray insides of vegetable cans with nonstick cooking spray. Spray three 6"-square pieces of foil also with the cooking spray. Set aside.

2. Combine rye flour, cornmeal, whole wheat flour, sugar, baking soda and salt in a large bowl.

3. Stir in walnuts and raisins.

4. Whisk together buttermilk and molasses. Add to dry ingredients. Stir until well mixed. Spoon into prepared cans.

5. Place one piece of foil, greased side down, on top of each can. Secure foil with rubberbands or cotton string. Place upright in slow cooker.

6. Pour boiling water into slow cooker to come halfway up sides of cans. Make sure foil tops do not touch boiling water.

7. Cover cooker. Cook on low 4 hours, or until skewer inserted in center of bread comes out clean.

8. To remove bread, lay cans on their sides. Roll and tap gently on all sides until bread releases. Cool completely on wire racks.

9. Serve with butter or cream cheese and bowls of soup.

Exchange List Values:
• Carbohydrate 1.0 • Fat 0.5

Basic Nutritional Values
• Calories 85
  (Calories from Fat 20)
• Total Fat 2 gm
  (Saturated Fat 0.2 gm,
  Polyunsat Fat 1.4 gm,
  Monounsat Fat 0.3 gm)
• Cholesterol 0 mg
• Sodium 158 mg
• Total Carb 16 gm
• Dietary Fiber 2 gm
• Sugars 8 gm
• Protein 2 gm

Corn Bread From Scratch

Dorothy M. Van Deest
Memphis, TN

Makes 9 servings

Prep. Time: 15 minutes
Cooking Time: 2-3 hours
Ideal slow cooker size: 6-qt.

1¼ cups flour
¾ cup yellow cornmeal
¼ cup sugar
4½ tsp. baking powder
½ tsp. salt
1 egg, slightly beaten
1 cup fat-free milk
¼ cup melted canola oil

1. In mixing bowl sift together flour, cornmeal, sugar, baking powder, and salt. Make a well in the center.

2. Pour egg, milk, and oil into well. Mix into the dry mixture until just moistened.

3. Pour mixture into a greased 2-quart mold or casserole dish. Cover with a plate or lid. Place on a trivet or rack in the bottom of slow cooker.

4. Cover. Cook on high 2-3 hours.

Exchange List Values
• Starch 2.0 • Fat 1.0

Basic Nutritional Values
• Calories 200
  (Calories from Fat 64)
• Total Fat 7 gm
  (Saturated Fat 0.7 gm,
  Polyunsat Fat 2.1 gm,
  Monounsat Fat 4.0 gm)
• Cholesterol 24 mg
• Sodium 330 mg
• Total Carb 29 gm
• Dietary Fiber 1 gm
• Sugars 7 gm
• Protein 4 gm

Broccoli Corn Bread

Winifred Ewy
Newton, KS

Makes 10 servings

Prep. Time: 25 minutes
Cooking Time: 5-6 hours
Ideal slow cooker size: 3- or 4-qt.

3 Tbsp. light, tub-style margarine, melted
10-oz. pkg. chopped broccoli, cooked and drained
1 medium onion, chopped
8.5-oz. box corn bread mix
1 egg, well beaten
3 egg whites
8 oz. 1% fat cottage cheese
⅛ tsp. salt

1. Combine all ingredients. Mix well.

2. Pour into greased slow cooker. Cook on low 6 hours, or until toothpick inserted in center comes out clean.

3. Serve from the crock with a spoon, or invert the pot, remove bread, and cut into wedges.

Exchange List Values
• Starch 1.0   • Fat 0.5
• Vegetable 1.0

Basic Nutritional Values
• Calories 119
  (Calories from Fat 34)
• Total Fat 4 gm
  (Saturated Fat 1.4 gm,
  Polyunsat Fat 0.6 gm,
  Monounsat Fat 1.4 gm)
• Cholesterol 22 mg
• Sodium 370 mg
• Total Carb 20 gm
• Dietary Fiber 2 gm
• Sugars 7 gm
• Protein 7 gm

Lemon Bread

Ruth Ann Gingrich
New Holland, PA

Makes 12 servings

Prep. Time: *20 minutes*
Cooking Time: *2¼ hours*
Ideal slow cooker size: *4-qt.*

¼ cup canola oil
6 Tbsp. sugar
sugar substitute to equal
   3 Tbsp. sugar
2 eggs, beaten
1⅔ cups flour
1⅔ tsp. baking powder
½ tsp. salt
½ cup fat-free milk
4 oz. chopped walnuts
grated peel from 1 lemon

Glaze:
  ¼ cup powdered sugar
  juice of 1 lemon

1. Cream together oil and sugar. Add eggs. Mix well.
2. Sift together flour, baking powder, and salt. Add flour mixture and milk alternately to shortening mixture.
3. Stir in nuts and lemon peel.
4. Spoon batter into well-greased 2-pound coffee can or 9×5 loaf pan and cover with well-greased tin foil. Place in cooker set on high for 2-2¼ hours, or until done. Remove bread from coffee can or pan.
5. Mix together powdered sugar and lemon juice. Pour over loaf.

Exchange List Values
- Starch 1.5
- Fat 1.0

Basic Nutritional Values
- Calories 176
  (Calories from Fat 66)
- Total Fat 7 gm
  (Saturated Fat 0.9 gm,
  Polyunsat Fat 2.7 gm,
  Monounsat Fat 3.3 gm)
- Cholesterol 37 mg
- Sodium 168 mg
- Total Carb 24 gm
- Dietary Fiber 1 gm
- Sugars 10 gm
- Protein 4 gm

Date and Nut Loaf

Jean Butzer
Batavia, NY

Makes 20 servings

Prep. Time: *25 minutes*
Cooking Time: *3½-4 hours*
Ideal slow cooker size: *6-qt.*

1½ cups boiling water
1½ cups chopped dates
¾ cup sugar
sugar substitute to equal
   ¼ cup sugar
1 egg
2 tsp. baking soda
½ tsp. salt
1 tsp. vanilla
1 Tbsp. light, soft tub
   margarine, melted
2½ cups flour
1 cup walnuts, chopped
2 cups hot water

1. Pour 1½ cups boiling water over dates. Let stand 5-10 minutes.
2. Stir in sugar, egg, baking soda, salt, vanilla, and butter.
3. In separate bowl, combine flour and nuts. Stir into date mixture.
4. Pour into 2 greased 11.5-oz. coffee cans or one 8-cup baking insert. If using coffee cans, cover with foil and tie. If using baking insert, cover with its lid. Place cans or insert on rack in slow cooker. (If you don't have a rack, use rubber jar rings instead.)
5. Pour hot water around cans, up to half their height.
6. Cover slow cooker tightly. Cook on high 3½-4 hours.
7. Remove cans or insert from cooker. Let bread stand in coffee cans or baking insert 10 minutes. Turn out onto cooling rack. Slice. Spread with butter, cream cheese, or peanut butter.

Exchange List Values
- Carbohydrate 2.0
- Fat 0.5

Basic Nutritional Values
- Calories 168
  (Calories from Fat 41)
- Total Fat 5 gm
  (Saturated Fat 0.5 gm,
  Polyunsat Fat 3.0 gm,
  Monounsat Fat 0.8 gm)
- Cholesterol 11 mg
- Sodium 193 mg
- Total Carb 30 gm
- Dietary Fiber 2 gm
- Sugars 17 gm
- Protein 3 gm

When cooking with less fat, use spices and herbs to add more flavor to the dish.

Old-Fashioned Gingerbread

Mary Ann Westerberg
Rosamond, CA

Makes 16 servings

Prep. Time: 25 minutes
Cooking Time: 2½-3 hours
Ideal slow cooker size: 4-qt.

4 Tbsp. margarine, softened
4 Tbsp. sugar
sugar substitute to equal
   2 Tbsp. sugar
1 egg
1 cup light molasses
2½ cups flour
1½ tsp. baking soda
1 tsp. ground cinnamon
2 tsp. ground ginger
½ tsp. ground cloves
½ tsp. salt
1 cup hot water
warm applesauce, *optional*
whipped cream, *optional*
nutmeg, *optional*

1. Cream together butter and sugar. Add egg and molasses. Mix well.

2. Stir in flour, baking soda, cinnamon, ginger, cloves, and salt. Mix well.

3. Add hot water. Beat well.

4. Pour batter into greased and floured 2-pound coffee can.

5. Place can in cooker. Cover top of can with 8 paper towels. Cover cooker and bake on high 2½-3 hours.

6. Serve with optional applesauce. Top with optional whipped cream and sprinkle with nutmeg.

Exchange List Values
• Carbohydrate 2.0 • Fat 0.5

Basic Nutritional Values
• Calories 168
(Calories from Fat 30)
• Total Fat 3 gm
(Saturated Fat 0.7 gm,
Polyunsat Fat 1.0 gm,
Monounsat Fat 1.4 gm)
• Cholesterol 13 mg
• Sodium 235 mg
• Total Carb 32 gm
• Dietary Fiber 1 gm
• Sugars 16 gm
• Protein 2 gm

Banana Loaf

Sue Hamilton
Minooka, IL

Makes 10 servings

Prep. Time: 20 minutes
Cooking Time: 2-2½ hours
Ideal slow cooker size: 4- or 5-qt.

3 very ripe, medium
   bananas
¼ cup margarine, softened
2 eggs
1 tsp. vanilla
½ cup sugar
sugar substitute to equal
   ¼ cup sugar
1 cup flour
1 tsp. baking soda

1. Combine all ingredients in an electric mixing bowl. Beat 2 minutes or until well blended. Pour into well-greased 2-lb. coffee can or 9×5 loaf pan.

2. Place can/pan in slow cooker. Cover can/pan with 6 layers of paper towels between cooker lid and bread.

3. Cover cooker. Bake on high 2-2½ hours, or until

toothpick inserted in center comes out clean. Cool 15 minutes before removing from pan.

Exchange List Values
• Carbohydrate 2.0 • Fat 1.0

Basic Nutritional Values
• Calories 177
(Calories from Fat 53)
• Total Fat 6 gm
(Saturated Fat 1.3 gm,
Polyunsat Fat 1.7 gm,
Monounsat Fat 2.5 gm)
• Cholesterol 43 mg
• Sodium 192 mg
• Total Carb 29 gm
• Dietary Fiber 1 gm
• Sugars 16 gm
• Protein 3 gm

From-Scratch Replacement Recipes

Italian Seasoning Mix

Madelyn Wheeler
Zionsville, IN

Makes 13 (1 Tbsp.) servings

6 tsp. marjoram, dried
6 tsp. thyme leaves, dried
6 tsp. rosemary, dried
6 tsp. savory, ground
3 tsp. sage, dry, ground
6 tsp. oregano leaves, dried
6 tsp. basil leaves, dried

1. Combine all ingredients.
2. Store leftover mix for future use.

Exchange List Values
• Free food

Basic Nutritional Values
• Calories 8
  (Calories from Fat 2)
• Total Fat 0 gm
  (Saturated Fat 0.1 gm,
  Polyunsat Fat 0.1 gm,
  Monounsat Fat 0.0 gm)
• Cholesterol 0 mg
• Sodium 1 mg
• Total Carb 2 gm
• Dietary Fiber 1 gm
• Sugars 0 gm
• Protein 0 gm

Tip:
   This recipe should be made with dried leaves if available, rather than ground.

Onion Soup Mix, Dry, Salt-Free

Madelyn Wheeler
Zionsville, IN

Makes 1 serving (equivalent to Lipton's dry onion soup mix)

2⅔ Tbsp. dried onion, minced, flaked, *or* chopped
4 tsp. beef instant bouillon powder, sodium free
1 tsp. onion powder
¼ tsp. celery seed

1. Combine all ingredients.

Exchange List Values
• Carbohydrate 1.5

Basic Nutritional Values
• Calories 106
 (Calories from Fat 2)
• Total Fat 0 gm
 (Saturated Fat 0.0 gm,
 Polyunsat Fat 0.1 gm,
 Monounsat Fat 0.1 gm)
• Cholesterol 0 mg
• Sodium 5 mg
• Total Carb 23 gm
• Dietary Fiber 2 gm
• Sugars 11 gm
• Protein 2 gm

Taco Seasoning Mix, Low Sodium

Madelyn Wheeler
Zionsville, IN

Makes 3 servings

Serving size is ⅓ recipe (about 7 tsp.)

6 tsp. chili powder
5 tsp. paprika
4½ tsp. cumin seed
3 tsp. Spices, onion powder
1 tsp. garlic powder
⅔ Tbsp. cornstarch, raw

1. Combine all ingredients in a bowl.
2. ⅓ of mix (about 7 tsp.) is equivalent to 1 pkg. (1.25 oz.) purchased taco seasoning mix.

Exchange List Values
• Carbohydrate 0.5

Basic Nutritional Values
• Calories 56
 (Calories from Fat 19)
• Total Fat 2 gm
 (Saturated Fat 0.0 gm,
 Polyunsat Fat 0.9 gm,
 Monounsat Fat 0.7 gm)
• Cholesterol 0 mg
• Sodium 61 mg
• Total Carb 10 gm
• Dietary Fiber 3 gm
• Sugars 3 gm
• Protein 2 gm

Phyllis' Homemade Barbecue Sauce

Phyllis Barrier
Little Rock, AR

Makes 16 (2 Tbsp.) servings

2 8-oz. cans tomato sauce, no-added-salt
¼ cup cider vinegar
brown sugar substitute to equal 2 Tbsp. sugar
½ cup fresh onions, minced
1 tsp. garlic powder
½ tsp. dry mustard powder
6 tsp. chili powder
⅛ tsp. Tabasco sauce
½ tsp. Spices, black pepper
6 tsp. Worcestershire sauce
1 tsp. paprika
1 tsp. liquid smoke
¼ tsp. salt

1. Mix all ingredients together and cook in microwave until minced onion is tender and sauce has thickened.

Exchange List Values
• Carbohydrate 0.5

Basic Nutritional Values
• Calories 24
 (Calories from Fat 2)
• Total Fat 0 gm
 (Saturated Fat 0.0 gm,
 Polyunsat Fat 0.1 gm,
 Monounsat Fat 0.0 gm)
• Cholesterol 0 mg
• Sodium 81 mg
• Total Carb 5 gm
• Dietary Fiber 1 gm
• Sugars 5 gm
• Protein 0 gm

Try growing your own food — the closer to the ground it is, the better your food is going to be.

Equivalent Measurements

dash = little less than ⅛ tsp.

3 teaspoons = 1 Tablespoon

2 Tablespoons = 1 oz.

4 Tablespoons = ¼ cup

5 Tablespoons plus 1 tsp. = ⅓ cup

8 Tablespoons = ½ cup

12 Tablespoons = ¾ cup

16 Tablespoons = 1 cup

1 cup = 8 ozs. liquid

2 cups = 1 pint

4 cups = 1 quart

4 quarts = 1 gallon

1 stick butter = ¼ lb.

1 stick butter = ½ cup

1 stick butter = 8 Tbsp.

Beans, 1 lb. dried = 2-2½ cups (depending upon the size of the beans)

Bell peppers, 1 large = 1 cup chopped

Cheese, hard (for example, cheddar, Swiss, Monterey Jack, mozzarella), 1 lb. grated = 4 cups

Cheese, cottage, 1 lb. = 2 cups

Chocolate chips, 6-oz. pkg. = 1 scant cup

Crackers (butter, saltines, snack), 20 single crackers = 1 cup crumbs

Herbs, 1 Tbsp. fresh = 1 tsp. dried

Lemon, 1 medium-sized = 2-3 Tbsp. juice

Lemon, 1 medium-sized = 2-3 tsp. grated rind

Mustard, 1 Tbsp. prepared = 1 tsp. dry or ground mustard

Oatmeal, 1 lb. dry = about 5 cups dry

Onion, 1 medium-sized = ½ cup chopped

Pasta

Macaronis, penne, and other small or tubular shapes, 1 lb. dry = 4 cups uncooked

Noodles, 1 lb. dry = 6 cups uncooked

Spaghetti, linguine, fettucine, 1 lb. dry = 4 cups uncooked

Potatoes, white, 1 lb. = 3 medium-sized potatoes = 2 cups mashed

Potatoes, sweet, 1 lb. = 3 medium-sized potatoes = 2 cups mashed

Rice, 1 lb. dry = 2 cups uncooked

Sugar, confectioners, 1 lb. = 3½ cups sifted

Whipping cream, 1 cup unwhipped = 2 cups whipped

Whipped topping, 8-oz. container = 3 cups

Yeast, dry, 1 envelope (¼ oz.) = 1 Tbsp.

Kitchen Tools and Equipment You Really Ought to Have

1 Make sure you have a little electric vegetable chopper, the size that will handle 1 cup of ingredients at a time.

2 Don't try to cook without a good paring knife that's sharp (and holds its edge) and fits in your hand.

3 Almost as important—a good chef's knife (we always called it a "butcher" knife) with a wide, sharp blade that's about 8 inches long, good for making strong cuts through meats.

4 You really ought to have a good serrated knife with a long blade, perfect for slicing bread.

5 Invest in at least one broad, flexible, heat-resistant spatula. And also a narrow one.

6 You ought to have a minimum of 2 wooden spoons, each with a 10-12 inch-long handle. They're perfect for stirring without scratching.

7 Get a washable cutting board. You'll still need it, even though you have an electric vegetable chopper (#1 above).

8 A medium-sized whisk takes care of persistent lumps in batters, gravies, and sauces when there aren't supposed to be any.

9 Get yourself a salad spinner.

Tips for Using Your Slow Cooker: A Friendly Year-Round Appliance

1. What to buy

• A good standard size for a household of four is a 4-quart slow cooker. If you often cook for more, or you like to prepare sizable roasts, turkey breasts, or chicken legs and thighs, you'll want a 6-quart cooker.

For parties or buffets, a 1½- to 2-quart size works well for dips and snacks.

• Cookers which allow you to program "On," the length of the cooking time, and "Off," are convenient. If your model doesn't include that feature, you might want to get a digital appliance timer, which gives you that option. Make sure the timer is adequate for the electrical flow that your cooker demands.

• A baking insert, a cooking rack, a temperature probe, and an insulated carrying tote are all useful additions offered with some models. Or you can buy some of them separately by going to the manufacturers' websites.

2. Learn to know your slow cooker

• Some newer slow cookers cook at a very high temperature. You can check the temperature of your slow cooker this way:

1. Place 2 quarts of water in your slow cooker.
2. Cover. Heat on Low 8 hours.
3. Lift the lid. Immediately check the water temp with an accurate thermometer.
4. The temperature of the water should be 185°F. If the temperature is higher, foods may overcook and you should reduce the overall cooking time. If the temperature is lower, your foods will probably not reach a safe temperature quickly enough, and the cooker should be discarded.

3. Maximizing what a slow cooker does best

- Slow cookers tend to work best when they're ⅔ full. You many need to increase the cooking time if you've exceeded that amount, or reduce it if you've put in less than that.

- Cut the hard veggies going into your cooker into chunks of about equal size. In other words, make your potato and carrot pieces about the same size. Then they'll be done cooking at nearly the same time. Softer veggies, like bell peppers and zucchini, cook faster, so they don't need to be cut as small. But again, keep them similar in size to each other so they finish together.

- Because raw vegetables are notoriously tough customers in a slow cooker, layer them over the bottom and around the sides of the cooker, as much as possible. That puts them in more direct contact with the heat.

- There are consequences to lifting the lid on your slow cooker while it's cooking. To compensate for the lost heat, you should plan to add 15-20 minutes of cooking time for each time the lid was lifted off.

On the other hand, moisture gathers in a slow cooker as it works. To allow that to cook off, or to thicken the cooking juices, take the lid off during the last half hour of cooking time.

- Use only the amount of liquid called for in a recipe. In contrast to an oven or a stovetop, a slow cooker tends to draw juices out of food and then harbor it.

Of course, if you sense that the food in your cooker is drying out, or browning excessively before it finishes cooking, you may want to add ½ cup of *warm* liquid to the cooker.

- Important variables to remember that don't show up in recipes:
  - The fuller your slow cooker, the longer it will take its contents to cook.
  - The more densely packed the cooker's contents are, the longer they will take to cook.
  - The larger the chunks of meat or vegetables, the more time they will need to cook.

4. Debunking the myths

• Slow cookers are *a handy year-round appliance.* They don't heat up a kitchen in warm weather. They allow you to escape to the pool or lake or lawn or gardens – so why not let them work for you when it's hot outdoors. A slow cooker fixes your dinner while you're at your child's soccer game, too.

So don't limit its usefulness. Remember the dozens of recipes-beyond-beef-stew in this collection!

One more thing – a slow cooker provides a wonderful alternative if your oven is full – no matter the season.

• You can overdo food in a slow cooker. If you're tempted to stretch a recipe's 6-hour stated cooking time to 8 or 10 hours, you may be disappointed in your dinner. Yes, these cookers work their magic using slow, moist heat. Yes, many dishes cook a long time. But these outfits have their limits.

For example, chicken can overcook in a slow cooker. Especially boneless, skinless breasts. But legs and thighs aren't immune either. Once they go past the falling-off-the-bone stage, they are prone to move on to deeply dry.

Cooked pasta and sour cream do best if added late in the cooking process, ideally 10 minutes before the end of the cooking time if the cooker is on high; 30 minutes before the end of the cooking time if it's on low.

5. Safety

• A working slow cooker gets hot on the outside – and I mean the outer electrical unit as well as the inner vessel. Make sure that curious and unsuspecting children or adults don't grab hold of either part. Use oven mitts when lifting any part of a hot cooker.

• To prevent a slow cooker from bubbling over, either when it's sitting still on a counter, or when it's traveling to a carry-in dinner, fill the cooker only ⅔ full.

If you're going to exceed that limit, pull out your second slow cooker (what – you have only one?!) and divide the contents between them.

6. Adapting stove-top or oven recipes for a slow cooker

• Many stove-top and oven recipes can be adapted for a slow cooker. If you want to experiment, use these conversion factors:

- Low (in a slow cooker) = 200°F approximately (in an oven).
- High (in a slow cooker) = 300°F approximately (in an oven).
- In a slow cooker, 2 hours on Low = 1 hour, approximately, on High.

7. More than one slow cooker?!

• If you run the food services for an active household, or if you often have guests, consider having more than one slow cooker. If you own two different sizes, you can do sides or appetizers or desserts in the smaller one. Or you may want two of similar, or the same, size so you can double the portions of your favorite dishes.

Index

Index

Index

Index

Index

Index

Index

About the Author

Phyllis Pellman Good is a *New York Times* bestselling author whose books have sold nearly 10 million copies.

Good is the author of the nationally acclaimed *Fix-It and Forget-It* slow-cooker cookbooks, several of which have appeared on *The New York Times* bestseller list, as well as the bestseller lists of *USA Today*, *Publishers Weekly*, and *Book Sense*.

In addition to this book, the series includes:

- **Fix-It and Forget-It Cookbook (Revised and Updated)**
  700 Great Slow-Cooker Recipes

- **Fix-It and Forget-It Lightly (Revised and Updated)**
  600 Healthy, Low-Fat Recipes for Your Slow Cooker

- **Fix-It and Forget-It Christmas Cookbook**
  600 Slow-Cooker Holiday Recipes

- **Fix-It and Forget-It 5-Ingredient Favorites**
  Comforting Slow-Cooker Recipes

- **Fix-It and Forget-It Vegetarian Cookbook**
  250 Delicious Slow Cooker Recipes with 250 Stove-Top and Oven Recipes, plus 50 Suggested Menus

- **Fix-It and Forget-It PINK Cookbook**
  More than 700 Great Slow-Cooker Recipes!

- **Fix-It and Forget-It Kids' Cookbook**
  50 Favorite Recipes to Make in a Slow Cooker

Good is also the author of the *Fix-It and Enjoy-It* series, a "cousin" series to the phenomenally successful *Fix-It and Forget-It* cookbooks.

- **Fix-It and Enjoy-It Cookbook**
  All-Purpose, Welcome-Home Recipes

- **Fix-It and Enjoy-It Potluck Heaven**
  543 Stove-Top and Oven Recipes That Everyone Loves

- **Fix-It and Enjoy-It 5-Ingredient Recipes**
  Quick and Easy—for Stove-Top and Oven!

- **Fix-It and Enjoy-It Diabetic Cookbook**
  Stove-Top and Oven Recipes—for Everyone!
  (with the American Diabetes Association)

- **Fix-It and Enjoy-It Healthy Cookbook**
  400 Great Stove-Top and Oven Recipes
  (with nutritional expertise from Mayo Clinic)

Phyllis Pellman Good is Executive Editor at Good Books. (Good Books has published hundreds of titles by more than 135 authors.) She received her B.A. and M.A. in English from New York University. She and her husband, Merle, live in Lancaster, Pennsylvania. They are the parents of two young-adult daughters.

For a complete listing of books by Phyllis Pellman Good, as well as excerpts and reviews, visit www.Fix-ItandForget-It.com or www.GoodBooks.com.

Good and her family are also proprietors of **The Good Cooking Store** in the small Lancaster County village of Intercourse. Located near the Good Books offices, the Store is the home of *Fix-It and Forget-It* cookbooks, as well as offering gadgets and wares for your kitchen, and cooking classes.